The Study
of Programming
Languages

The Study of Programming Languages

RYAN STANSIFER

University of North Texas

PRENTICE HALL, Englewood Cliffs, New Jersey 07632

Library of Congress Cataloging-in-Publication Data

Stansifer, Ryan D.
    The study of programming languages / Ryan Stansifer.
        p.   cm.
    Includes bibliographical references and index.
    ISBN 0-13-726936-6
    1. Programming languages (Electronic computers)   I. Title.
QA76.7.S72   1994
    005.13--dc20
                                                           94-14862
                                                              CIP

Acquisitions Editor: Bill Zobrist
Project Manager: Bayani Mendoza de Leon
Copy Editor: Brenda Melissaratos
Cover Designer: Jerry Votta
Production Coordinator: Linda Behrens
Editorial Assistant: Phyllis Morgan

©1995 by Prentice-Hall, Inc
A Paramount Communications Company
Englewood Cliffs, New Jersey   07632

Printed in the United States of America
10 9 8 7 6 5 4 3 2 1

ISBN 0-13-726936-6

Prentice-Hall International (UK) Limited, *London*
Prentice-Hall of Australia Pty. Limited, *Sydney*
Prentice-Hall Canada, Inc., *Toronto*
Prentice-Hall Hispanoamericana, S.A., *Mexico*
Prentice-Hall of India Private Limited, *New Delhi*
Prentice-Hall of Japan, Inc., *Tokyo*
Simon & Schuster Asia Pte. Ltd., *Singapore*
Editora Prentice-Hall do Brasil, Ltda., *Rio de Janeiro*

Contents

List of figures

Preface

The author is allowed to make all kinds of wild and reckless claims in the preface because so few read it. It is my opinion that the social sciences—sociology, economics, and philosophy, to name a few—have been harmed by the overformalization of their subjects. In these disciplines the underlying phenomena involve an inconsistent subject—mankind. I doubt that this will change in whatever time is left to the legacy of Aristotelian science. The fundamental fact about formalization was captured well by Albert Einstein:

> In so far as the theorems of mathematics relate to reality, they are not certain, and in so far as they are certain, they do not relate to reality.

Ignoring this distinction between Platonic ideals and reality causes a great deal of needless friction and much heated palaver.

On the one hand, computer science is a mathematical science, because it studies to a large extent creations of mind not bound to expectations born of past experience. For many reasons computer science, and especially programming, is not viewed this way. Programming is often viewed as more of a management problem, not a mathematical one. The result is that many people miss the opportunity to change the world through the power of conceptualization. Putting man on the moon is not just a triumph of computation (among many other things) but also a triumph in realizing physical theory. Likewise the study of programming yields results that are significant to society.

Yet the subject of computer science is engineering, not only in the sense of applying pure science to practical application, but also in a more fundamental and exhilarating sense. In computer science we build new creations that have powerful effects on the real world. The new artifacts are some of the most beautiful and complex of engineering accomplishments. Single programmers are able to create these superb artifacts out of the most malleable substance yet discovered. This was put well by Frederick Brooks, Jr:

> the programmer, like the poet, works only slightly removed from pure thought-stuff. He builds his castles in the air, from air, creating by exertion of the imagination. Few media of creation are so flexible, so easy

to polish and rework, so rapidly capable of realizing grand conceptual structures.

The subject of programming languages is at the exciting juncture of theory and practice—where the mind meets the computer.

Target audience. The intended audience for this book is a senior or graduate student in programming languages. We presuppose acquaintance with programming in some languages already, some basic knowledge of other areas in computer science (a compiler course would be helpful in some places, a course in discrete mathematics in other places), and some degree of mathematical sophistication. As with all subjects, the more students bring to the subject, the more they can take away. The purpose of the book is to address some of the interesting and conceptually more challenging topics and show what the field of programming languages is like. Too often programming language courses and texts, although covering many interesting aspects of languages, fail to convey a sense of the study of programming languages.

This book does not try to teach any one programming language. However, it uses many examples from Ada, Modula-3, and ML, and so it is helpful to know these languages or spend some time learning these languages and programming in them. There are numerous sources concerning Ada. For Modula-3 and ML we mention a couple:

Harbison, Samuel P. *Modula-3*. Prentice Hall, Englewood Cliffs, New Jersey, 1992.

Stansifer, Ryan. *ML Primer*. Prentice Hall, Englewood Cliffs, New Jersey, 1992.

On the other hand, the book tries not to call for too much prerequisite knowledge. This has the advantage of making the book accessible to graduate students who may not have had an undergraduate course in programming languages. The important topics that are fundamental to the field of programming languages are:

1. BNF notation

2. some acquaintance with Ada

3. programming in a functional language

4. programming in PROLOG

5. modules and classes

6. exception handling

7. pointers

8. type equivalence

9. static versus dynamic type checking

10. parameter passing

The interesting and important topics not usually found in undergraduate textbooks but essential for graduate students in computer science are:

1. attribute grammars

2. type reconstruction

3. term rewriting

4. formal semantics

5. Hoare logic

6. lambda calculus

7. combinators

8. Post systems

This list is in agreement with the recommendations of the ACM Task Force on the Core of Computer Science.[1] This book does not cover all the topics mentioned in the task force's report in the area of programming languages. Topics that deal more with implementation are left to the traditional compiler construction course. More theoretical details are left to the traditional formal languages course and theory of computation course.

There is a most obvious omission in the coverage of this book and that is concurrency. This important topic deserves a course of its own, and already there is too much material in this book for a one-semester course.

Bibliography. Each chapter has its own bibliography, which serves to give some guidance to the literature by topic. It is not possible to be complete, but some worthwhile source can be found for nearly every topic. Two collections have reprinted many important papers:

Horowitz, Ellis, editor. *Programming Languages: A Grand Tour.* Third edition. Computer Science Press, Rockville, Maryland, 1987.

Wasserman, Anthony I., editor. *Tutorial, Programming Language Design.* IEEE Computer Society Press, Los Alamitos, California, 1980.

The references indicate if they can be found in these secondary sources.

---

[1] Peter J. Denning, Douglas E. Comer, David Gries, Michael C. Mulder, and Allen Tucker. "Computing as a discipline." *Communications of the ACM*, volume 32, number 1, January 1989.

Acknowledgments. This book would not be possible without the many people who taught me programming languages: Robert Cartwright, Alan Demers, James Donahue, and David Gries, who taught me that programming is hard. I am grateful to the reviewers Edgar Knapp and Brian Malloy who devoted considerable effort in making someone else's words more understandable. The many students I have taught also contributed greatly to this book. I would especially like to thank Edward Pershits for pointing out many weaknesses in the text.

Ryan Stansifer
University of North Texas

The Study
of Programming
Languages

Chapter 1

History of programming languages

The purpose of language is communication. Human beings use natural languages to communicate among themselves. Programming languages are used to communicate with literal-minded machines. We are most often struck by the differences in these kinds of communication, but in some respects they are alike. Writing programs is like writing an English essay; many can write in English, but few write well. It is in this spirit that Donald Knuth calls his multivolume magnum opus "The Art of Computer Programming."

To completely master the art of communication with computers we must understand the medium. In this first chapter we look at some selected landmarks in the intellectual development of formal languages, starting with ancient history.

1.1 The first formal languages

Speech is probably as old as man, that is, at least 300,000 years old. Spoken language is extremely complex, and currently no formal theory is capable of wholly describing its richness. Fortunately we can focus on written languages, which are more amenable to formal analysis. In particular, the evolution of writing systems to record language reveals the first steps toward formal notation and unambiguous communication.

1.1.1 Sumerian

The world's oldest extant written documents are in Sumerian, the language of the people living in the ancient city-states of southern Mesopotamia. A large number of texts written in clay dating between 4000 and 3000 B.C. have been discovered. For the most part these texts record agricultural transactions and astronomical

1

observations. It has been suggested that the Sumerian system of writing evolved from small, three-dimensional tokens used for counting things like grain, wine, and cattle [31]. Such a practice was apparently in use for many millenniums throughout western Asia. These tokens were initially sealed in little clay containers called bullae. The bullae were sometimes marked on the outside with impressions of the concealed tokens, so the contents could be known without breaking open the container. Eventually the tokens inside were eliminated in favor of just the markings on the outside, and the two-dimensional representation of information was born.

The Sumerian culture was not the only one to have invented written language. Egyptian hieroglyphics also emerged about 3000 B.C. Two other cultures discovered writing: the Harappan in the Indus Valley and the Mayan in the new world. Other cultures used "analog" devices for nonverbal communication, like the quipu of the Incan civilization in which knots were tied in strings. But apparently the four cultures mentioned were the only ones to come up with a system for writing that was largely independent of the media used to represent it. Of course, the utility of writing was quickly grasped and soon adopted by many.

The Sumerian language remains largely undeciphered, so it is not known with certainty how the language relates to others. However, it is not Indo-European, as English, Russian, Farsi, and Hindi are. Among the Indo-European languages, Sanskrit was the first to be written down. The Veda, the most ancient extant scriptures of Hinduism, is written in Sanskrit.

1.1.2   Evolution of the alphabet

The Sumerian system of writing persisted until the first century A.D. It evolved from a few crude drawings to many stylized pictures written with one particular marking device. This wedge-tipped stick was used to make slim triangular marks called cuneiform. The cuneiform system was adopted by the Akkadians, the Babylonians, and the Assyrians. However, cuneiform is not the system of writing that evolved into the present-day English alphabet used on this page.

The origin of most of the alphabets used in the world today can be traced to the Phoenicians, who flourished in the area of the Mediterranean around 1000 B.C. The evolution of the alphabet as a system of writing appears to have gone through several conceptual stages. At first, writing was composed of individual *pictographs*, pictures of concepts. There was a nonarbitrary relation between picture and meaning. The only way a pictograph communicates a concept is for the meaning to be evident in the drawing.

Gradually there was an evolution to *ideographs*, symbols for ideas. These symbols are not pictures but are stylized. Their meaning is understood by convention. Since the idea is no longer conveyed solely by the picture, education becomes important to transmit the conventions. For example, Roman numerals are ideographs: I, II, III, IV. The symbol IV stands for the idea of four, not the word "four." Of course, the distinction between an ideograph and a pictograph may sometimes be small: the numerals I, II, and III retain their pictographic character.

When the convention used to understand an ideograph depends on the sound of the spoken language, then the symbol is a *phonogram*. For example, consider the symbol ☼. As a pictograph we might consider ☼ to mean the sun. As an ideograph we might consider ☼ to mean the daytime. As a phonogram we might consider ☼ to mean a son, since the words "sun" and "son" are spoken identically in English.

This leads naturally to capturing the entire spoken language by a series of phonograms. For example, we might write the word "sunny" as ☼+E. This sort of *rebus writing* continues to be a popular sort of intellectual puzzle. But the approach of assigning conventional symbols for syllables of the spoken language is still used in the writing systems in several languages.

One further step in the development of the English alphabet—the development of a consonantal alphabet—is crucial, for it reduces the number of symbols required to a manageable number. This development appears to have taken place among Semitic people in the Sinai Peninsula about 1700 B.C. But it was the Phoenicians who spread the consonantal alphabet around the Mediterranean Sea and eventually to the Greeks, although when and how much are still disputed. In a consonantal alphabet several basic phonograms are selected to represent the sound of their initial consonants in all words containing the consonant. This works quite well in Semitic languages, where vowels are not essential to the meaning. The roots of Semitic words are given by the consonants alone. Other details are given by vowels. This is somewhat like the forms of the word "sing" in English: "sang," "song," and "sung."

The Greeks added the last innovation necessary to create the present-day alphabet. The Greek language, being Indo-European, needed signs for vowels. They adapted the signs for the Semitic consonants not present in Greek for use as vowels.

Figure 1.1 shows the development of the first four letters of the Roman alphabet. Their evolution reflects the intellectual stages mentioned above. The Greek names of the letters, *alpha, beta, gamma, delta*, and so on, have no meaning in Greek, but their Semitic equivalents, *aleph, beth, gimel, daleth*, and so on, are Semitic words. In the ancient Semitic *aleph* means ox, *beth* means house, *gimel* means camel, and *daleth* means tent door. The original pictographic symbols can still be visualized. The two horns of the ox are still apparent in the two legs of the letter "A" despite the enormous changes that separate us from the ancient Semitic people who mined turquoise in the Sinai over 2,600 years ago.

1.2 Algorithms and mathematical notation

The earliest known algorithms are due to the Babylonians of 3000 to 1500 B.C. They used a base 60 notation for arithmetic, including fractions. Base 60 is not a particularly convenient choice for doing arithmetic, but it has survived to this day

A	B	C	D	modern Roman majuscule
A	B	Γ	Δ	modern Greek majuscule
α	β	γ	δ	modern Greek minuscule
alpha	beta	gamma	delta	names of the Greek letters
א	ב	ג	ד	modern Hebrew
aleph	beth	gimel	daleth	names of Hebrew letters
(plosive laryngeal)	[b]	[g]	[d]	phonetic values
ox	house	camel	door	meaning

Figure 1.1: The development of the letters: a, b, c, and d

in the measurement of minutes and hours, and degrees of arc. (This is proof of the importance of picking the right constants!) The Babylonians had extensive tables of elementary mathematical functions. Their textbooks were mostly examples for learning calculations. These examples can be considered early forms of algorithms because they were clearly designed to be prescriptions of how to perform calculations. The algorithmic nature of these examples is evident because multiplication by 1 would explicitly appear even though it is pointless to perform that calculation.

The Greeks likewise presented their algorithms by example. One of the most famous algorithms, the Euclidean algorithm, is named after the famous Greek mathematician Euclid, who around 300 B.C. wrote down the algorithm for determining the greatest common divisor of two numbers. Euclid did not consider zero or one a number and so had special cases for these numbers.

Even earlier, the Greek mathematicians contributed the single most remarkable trait of abstract science: proof. The recognition that proof is required or desirable initiates a never-ending search for the foundations of our conclusions. Pythagoras, who lived before 500 B.C. in southern Italy, is responsible for one of the oldest mathematical demonstrations. He proved that the sum of the square of the sides of a right triangle equals the square of the hypotenuse. Ironically, this act may be more a rite of numerology than a demonstration of the reasonable effectiveness of mathematics. Or is the belief in the effectiveness of mathematics any different from Pythagoras' belief that the whole numbers control man's destiny?

1.2.1   Arabic mathematics

From the point of view of programming, one of the more noteworthy Arab mathematicians is Abu Jáfar Mohammed ibn Musa al-Khorezmi (780–850). As his Arabic name indicates, he was Mohammed from Khorezm, the father of Jáfar and the son of Moses. The ancient kingdom of Khorezm was located in central Asia along the border of the present states of Uzbekistan and Turkmenistan. He was active at Baghdad's "House of Wisdom," then the world's center of learning.

One of his books, *Kitâ al-jabr wa'l-muqâbala*, literally "The calculations of reduction and confrontation," gives rise to the word "algebra" (al-jabr) and, somewhat remotely, to the mathematical field of algebra. The book's Latin title is *Liber algebrai et almucbala*. This book was used as a mathematical text for eight centuries.

Another book, the original Arabic version of which is now lost, is one of the sources by which the positional number system was introduced to Latin-speaking Europe. This book was called the Hindu art of reckoning. The Latin title is *Algorthmi de numero Indorum*, giving rise to the word "algorithm." The following is a passage from the book. In it an algorithm for solving quadratic equations is given [36, page 56].

> Chapter I. Concerning squares equal to roots
>
> The following is an example of squares equal to roots: a square is equal to 5 roots $[x^2 = 5x]$. The root of the square then is 5, and 25 forms its square which, of course, equals five of its roots.
>
> Another example: the third part of a square equals four roots $[\frac{1}{3}x^2 = 4x]$. Then the root of the square is 12 and 144 designates its square. And similarly, five squares equal 10 roots $[5x^2 = 10x]$. Therefore one square equals two roots and the root of the square is 2. Four represents the square.
>
> In the same manner, then, that which involves more than one square, or is less than one, is reduced to one square. Likewise you perform the same operation upon the roots which accompany the squares.

One of the most important symbols in mathematics is the sign for zero. Any sort of arithmetic becomes clumsy without a sign for zero, so it was an important achievement. The clay tablets from Mesopotamia dating around 300 B.C. show that mathematicians of the Seleucid Kingdom used a symbol for zero [21]. But the origins of the positional system of arithmetic are unclear. The Arabic scientists gave credit for the technique to the Indians.

Four hundred years after the zenith of the House of Wisdom, the use of zero crept into European mathematics. A notable link in this development was Leonardo da Pisano also called Fibonacci (for *filius Bonaccia*, the son of Bonaccia), son of the head of one of Pisa's overseas custom houses in Bugia on the coast of North Africa (now Bejaïa, Algeria). His beginning of *Liber abaci* (Book of the Abacus) first published in 1202 opens with the sentence [36, page 2]:

> These are the nine figures of the Indians 9 8 7 6 5 4 3 2 1. With these nine figures, and with this sign 0 which in Arabic is called zephirum, any number can be written, as will below be demonstrated.

Notice the order of the digits: right to left, as in Arabic. It is as if Fibonacci feared that writing them left to right, as in Latin, would somehow diminish their magic. An air of mystery remained for centuries with those that knew algorism, the art of reckoning with decimal digits. This is responsible for the word "cipher," meaning to code a message into symbols to hide its meaning. Although less common today, the phrase "to cipher" means to do arithmetic.

Actually Fibonacci's book itself was not particularly influential. Other books, primarily *Carmen de Algorismo* (The Poem of Algorism) by Alexander de Villa Dei, were apparently more influential. The *Carmen de Algorismo* dates back to about the year 1220 and was entirely in hexameter verse.

1.2.2   Pre-19th-century mathematics

From the European continent during the six centuries before the "modern era" the field of mathematics slowly emerged into the "queen of science" as we recognize it today. The, to many laymen, mysterious notation of the contemporary scientist is now the lingua franca of scientific discourse from Beijing to London. The ideas and mathematical notation we now take for granted developed erratically. We now use the signs "+" and "−" first used by Johann Widman in 1489, the equals sign "=" used by Robert Recorde (1557), times "×" by William Oughtred (1631), exponentiation "x^2" by James Hume (1636), division "÷" by Johann Rahn (1659), and the ratio "π" by William Jones (1706), to mention but a few of the most frequent and elementary symbols [5]. The path toward a universal mathematical language and toward a common mathematical body of knowledge is uneven. Because of this mathematics before 1850 is not easily accessible to modern readers. We look at a couple of contributions from this era.

François Viète (1540–1603) a privy councilor under Henry IV, king of Navarre, was the first to use letters systematically for unknown quantities in an algebraic problem. He gave the clearest expression to that time of the generality of algebraic methods. Before that time mathematics was mostly concerned with geometry, and this greatly influenced the form of mathematical writing. The dimension, or unit of measurement, was an integral part of an unknown quantity. The *cossists* of the Renaissance used the words for thing (*cosa* in Italian means thing), square, cube for what today we would write x, x^2, x^3, etc. Scalars (from the Latin word for "ladder") are the coefficients, the dimensionless numbers that can multiply any quantity. As far back as the Babylonians the word "ladder" was used for powers [21].

An important contributor to the development of formal languages is Gottfried Wilhelm Leibniz (1646–1716). Leibniz searched for a general science of all sciences, to be carried on by a method that he called *characteristica generalis* or *lingua generalis*. This notion appears in a letter, written toward the end of his life. It mentions Leibniz's idea of a method more general than that which Viète had tried to embody in his algebra [36, page 123]:

> I would like to give a method ... in which all truths of the reason would be reduced to a kind of calculus. This could at the same time be a kind of language or universal script, but very different from all that have

been projected hitherto, because the characters and even the words would guide reason, and the errors (except those of fact) would only be errors of computation. It would be very difficult to form or invent this Language or Characteristic, but very easy to learn it without any Dictionaries.

Leibniz also built a multiplying machine (to be found today in the Landesbibliothek in Hannover [38]).

Mechanical computing devices have a substantial history of their own. One of the most sophisticated designs for a calculating machine in this period was accomplished by Charles Babbage (1792–1871). His is a pathetic story. He struggled for money and never got enough to finish his analytic engine. Ada Augusta, Countess of Lovelace and daughter of the famous poet Lord Byron, was a friend of Babbage and contributed to the theory of his machine. She is sometimes said to be the first computer programmer. In long letters to Babbage she described how to use the analytic engine to compute small mathematical tasks [15, 17, 26]. The machine forced them to think about communicating mathematical tasks to wooden gears.

Like Viète and Leibniz, Babbage sought to capture at least some of the precision in mathematics in new, artificial languages. In his paper "On the influence of signs in mathematical reasoning" [2] he expresses the value of language well:

Examples of the power of a well-contrived notation to condense into small space a meaning which would—in ordinary language—require several lines, or even pages, can hardly have escaped the notice of most of my readers: in the calculus of functions, this condensation is carried to a far greater extent than in any other branch of analysis, and yet, instead of creating any obscurity, the expressions are far more readily understood than if they were written at length.

1.3 Contributions from modern mathematics

After 1800, mathematics began to expand rapidly. Several mathematicians have contributed ideas that are important to formal language.

1.3.1 Gottlob Frege (1848–1925)

Friedrich Ludwig Gottlob Frege was born in 1848 in Wismar, Germany (on the Baltic Sea). Seventy years later he retired to nearby Bad Kleinen, where he died in 1925. He began his academic studies at the University of Jena, Germany, and after getting his doctorate in Göttingen, he returned to Jena, where he remained for his entire career. Frege's masterpiece, a booklet entitled *Begriffsschrift*, was first published in 1879. As the German title *Concept Writing* indicates, this work is in the tradition of Leibniz, as it is a proposal for a universal language of reasoning. Although this language was the most significant advance in logic since the time of ancient Greek civilization, the notation was clumsy; for example, the proposition that B implies A would be written:

Frege's innovative, two-dimensional notation did not catch on. Giuseppe Peano (1858–1932), a mathematician and amateur typesetter who set his own articles, invented more practical, linear notation including the horseshoe (actually a backward "C") for implication, and the backward "E" for "there exists." This notation was popularized by Bertrand Russell. But as Frege said, "The comfort of the typesetter is certainly not the *summum bonum.*"

Frege's contribution to mathematics is monumental. In that one short book alone he introduced the truth-functional propositional calculus as opposed to the Greek syllogistic approach, function and argument as opposed to subject and predicate, a systematic theory of quantification, and derivation according to form. All these contributions play a significant role in the study of programming languages. Propositional and quantified logic are key in understanding the programming language PROLOG. The application of functions to arguments is omnipresent in programming languages, especially functional languages. And derivation according to form is the primary means of reasoning about formal languages.

1.3.2   Bertrand Russell (1872–1970)

Bertrand Russell was a famous English philosopher, mathematician, and pacifist. His most influential mathematical work is the unreadable *Principia Mathematica*, a work in three volumes, published between 1910 and 1913, which he wrote with Alfred Whitehead (1861–1947). These volumes attempt to formalize all of mathematics by reducing arithmetic and geometry to logic and the theory of sets. For the amount of sheer notation few works are as dense. It took Russell and Whitehead over 300 pages to prove $1 + 1 = 2$. Figure 1.2 shows some examples of the notation they used. Page after page of the work is covered with these symbols.

The impetus for such a careful and tedious development of mathematics was to avoid the logical inconsistency Russell found in Frege's formalization of mathematics in the *Begriffsschrift.* This inconsistency, known as *Russell's paradox,* has been explained in several popular guises, such as this:

> In a remote village all the men shave themselves or they go to the village barber who shaves them. One day the municipal authorities issued the following directive: the village barber is required to shave all (and only) the men who do not shave themselves.

The village barber, if male, will find it impossible to comply. For if he shaves himself, then the barber must not shave him, yet he is the barber. And if he

$\phi\hat{x}$ functional abstraction

$\breve{R}$ the converse of the relation R

$R`y$ the term x which has the relation R to y

$R``\beta$ the terms which have the relation R to members of β

$\iota`x$ the class of terms identical to x

$\overrightarrow{R}`y$ is the same as $\hat{x}(xRy)$

$\overleftarrow{R}`x$ is the same as $\hat{y}(xRy)$

Figure 1.2: Some notation used in *Principia Mathematica*

does not shave himself, he, as barber, is required to shave himself. Either way the directive is violated.

In the summary to *Mathematical Logic as Based on the Theory of Types* published in 1908, Russell explains that the paradoxes arose

> from the fact that an expression referring to *all* of some collection may itself appear to denote one of the collection . . . . We explained a doctrine of *types* of variables, proceeding upon the principle that any expression which refers to *all* of some type must, if it denotes anything, denote something of a higher type than that to all of which it refers.

Types play a role in programming languages not merely as data structures, but by constraining computational expression to ways that are free from the problems that befell Frege and naive set theory.

1.3.3 Constructive mathematics

In 1888 the great German mathematician David Hilbert (1861–1943) published a proof that every field has a finite basis, solving a problem posed by Paul Gordon (1837–1912). While the solution showed that it was contradictory to hold that a field did not have a finite basis, it did not show how to construct a basis. When Gordon saw the proof he is reported to have said, "This is not mathematics, this is theology."

This subtle difference marks the divergence between mathematics and algorithms. Some mathematicians were concerned about the change and advocated the traditional "constructive" approach in which the existence of mathematical objects had to be proved by exhibiting a construction. This controversy has since died down, and the body of contemporary mathematics does not appear to be troubled by the use of nonconstructive methods.

On the other hand, programming languages are languages for the construction of objects representable by a computer. Consequently the methods of constructive mathematics may well be important to computer science. In fact, constructive logic can be viewed as a programming language, and several languages have been implemented [6]. Some other work on constructive mathematics can be found in [4, 9].

1.3.4   Formal semantics

The Polish-trained mathematician Alfred Tarski (1902–1983) formalized the distinction between symbols and their meaning by a semantic definition of the predicate calculus. Tarski defined a function $\mathcal{M}$ from the syntax of predicate logic to mathematical entities. We might write a case of this definition as follows:

$$\mathcal{M}[\![A \wedge B]\!] = \mathcal{M}[\![A]\!] \text{ and } \mathcal{M}[\![B]\!]$$

As usual in the study of programming language semantics we enclose pieces of syntax with double brackets. The definition above does not immediately look illuminating. It appears we have defined conjunction using itself, which is not a useful definition at all. With this definition Tarski was trying to communicate that the meaning of the syntactic phrase $A \wedge B$[1] is given by combining the meaning of A and B. Here for the first time the syntax of a language is stripped of any residual meaning. This makes it possible, indeed necessary, that a semantics be given to the language. The dichotomy between syntax and semantics, object language and meta-language, is important. Now language can be studied mathematically. Out of the study of the language of mathematics and logic, the study of programming languages begins.

1.4   Early programming formalisms

Due to Kurt Gödel's famous negative results about the nature of the mathematical concept of computation, it was necessary to understand more about the nature of computation. From this perspective emerged two early programming formalisms, Turing machines and the lambda calculus. At about the same time, the first primitive computers were being built. So computation was no longer abstract but realizable in the actions of gigantic machines.

1.4.1   Turing machines

During World War II a British mathematician, Alan M. Turing (1912–1954), was involved in the very secret Enigma project, which used computers to decode German messages. But several years before that he had written a paper introducing an abstract machine with which to study the nature of computing.

   The definition of a Turing machine is formal and familiar to students of computer science. Many variations on the definition are to be found in the literature.

---

[1]Tarski was the one who introduced the symbol $\wedge$ for conjunction.

Turing's original version is not particularly easy to follow, so we give a popular, modern one. The differences are all inconsequential. A Turing machine is a 7-tuple $\langle Q, T, I, \delta, b, q_0, q_f \rangle$ where

1. Q is the set of states,

2. T is the set of tape symbols,

3. I is the set of input symbols, $I \subseteq T$,

4. δ is the transition function,

5. $b \in T \setminus I$ is the designated symbol for a blank,

6. q_0 is the initial state, and

7. q_f is the final or accepting state.

The operation of a Turing machine is simple and is governed by the transition function. At every point in its operation a Turing machine examines an input symbol on the tape, then writes a symbol and moves the tape according to its current state and the transition function δ. The machine continues this process until (if ever) it reaches the final state. This simple machine is as powerful as any conceivable computing device. Many seemingly significant additions to the basic machine have been studied and none of them increases the power of the machine. Although the theory of computation has been profoundly influenced by the Turing machine, programming languages have not.

1.4.2 Lambda calculus

Another formalism developed with the purpose of studying the nature of computation mathematically and without reference to technological feasibility is the lambda calculus. The Greek letter lambda is used as part of the syntax and hence its name. The language of lambda expressions was created by Alonzo Church at the Princeton Institute of Advanced Studies. Unlike Turing machines, lambda expressions have had a profound impact on programming languages. So great is this impact that chapter 7 is devoted to the subject.

Lambda expressions form the underlying basis of functional programming. Essentially every lambda expression is a function or an application of a function to an argument. Every algorithm can be expressed as a lambda expression. This is remarkable in light of the simplicity of the language. Moreover the language does not exhibit any time-variant behavior, like Turing machines, making it more amenable to formal analysis.

1.4.3   Zuse's Plan Calculus

Konrad Zuse had been working on electromechanical computers in Germany since 1936. But World War II disrupted the work on the computer and freed him to consider how to program the computer whether or not a suitable machine could be constructed. Zuse developed a three-address notation he called the *Plankalkül*, or Plan Calculus. The notation spread across several lines. Subscripts, for instance, appeared below the variable names.

Particularly interesting about the Plan Calculus was that it had a rich collection of data structures. It started with data of a single bit whose value is either "−" or "+". Zuse denoted this "boolean" type by "S0" or "So." From n data types $\tau_0, \ldots, \tau_n$ the n-fold cartesian product type could be formed: $(\tau_0, \ldots, \tau_n)$. Arrays were denoted $n \times \tau$. The type of a variable-length homogeneous list was denoted $\Box \times \tau$.

Types for floating-point numbers could be created. For example, the type AΔ1 could be defined as follows:

$$(3 \times \text{S0}, 7 \times \text{S0}, 22 \times \text{S0})$$

The first three bits indicated whether the number was real or imaginary and whether the number was positive, zero, or negative. The rest of the structure held the exponent and mantissa. Such general and sophisticated data structuring would not appear again until ALGOL 68 and Pascal.

1.4.4   Flow diagrams

Around the year 1946, Herman H. Goldstine and John von Neumann developed a pictorial representation of programming called "flow diagrams" in which they formalized the description of an algorithm. This approach had great influence, although the original diagrams bear little resemblance to the typical flow charts that programmers sometimes use as a design tool today.

Recently graphical programming systems have attracted a lot of attention as input devices and display mediums become more sophisticated and less character-oriented [32]. Also special purpose systems like spreadsheets find it convenient to have a two-dimensional interface with users.

1.5   Early programming languages

During the 1950s machine hardware began to dominate the story of programming languages. In this era the goal was to implement what was possible on the available hardware. This was an exciting and challenging period given the paucity, primitiveness, and the newness of the computers of that time. Some of the more important machine-oriented languages from this time are the Algebraic Interpreter developed at MIT for the Whirlwind computer and A-2 developed at UNIVAC under the direction of Grace Murray Hopper. The English and the Russians also had implemented "automatic coders" at about this time.

We do not go into any details about these machine-oriented languages. The comprehensive survey by Knuth and Prado [22] contains many details of these early languages, and the book by Williams discusses the hardware technology and its origins [38]. As soon as it became apparent that hardware was going to be useful, it became apparent that the language in which to instruct the hardware was important. And so the field of programming languages was born.

1.5.1 FORTRAN

Work on FORTRAN began in 1953 by a group led by John Backus at the International Business Machines Corporation (IBM). The programming language FORTRAN is first in many ways. It led the way in languages with acronymic names. FORTRAN is short for "FORmula TRANslating." The name is important because it captures the early perspective with regard to programming languages. FORTRAN was a high-level language (higher than machine language) because it sought to express mathematical formulas—entities of the mind and not of the machine. Yet it was not conceived as a universal algorithmic language, but as a notation for mathematical formulas that could be translated by a machine for a machine.

> As far as we were aware, we simply made up the language as we went along. We did not regard language design as a difficult problem, merely a simple prelude to the real problem: designing a compiler which could produce efficient programs. [3, page 30]

The goal was to eliminate bookkeeping details and repetitive planning. In 1954 it was thought that FORTRAN would virtually eliminate coding and debugging. FORTRAN was closer to the thought process, required fewer keystrokes, and was easier to learn. Certainly this was true in comparison with the hardware languages. But rather than ending the technological development of programming languages, FORTRAN initiated the search for languages that communicate with the computer at a high level, a level closer to the way humans think.

Work on the FORTRAN compiler (or "translator" as it was called then) started in 1955. It was supposed to take six months—they finished in 1957. Variables in FORTRAN could be one or two characters in length. Spaces are ignored because the original designers thought that spaces would confuse the human typist. At the time, a coder would write code on paper and a typist would punch the codes into cards.

Here is example of an early FORTRAN program (from [22]).

```
      DIMENSION A(11)
      READ A
2     DO 3,8,11 J=1,11
```

```
3      I=11-J
       Y=SQRT(ABS(A(I+1)))+5*A(I+1)**3
       IF (400. >= Y) 8,4
4      PRINT I,999.
       GO TO 2
8      PRINT I,Y
11     STOP
```

This program, called TPK by Knuth and Pardo, is used by them to compare many early programming languages. The TPK program does not do anything particularly useful, but does illustrate a few aspects of programming.

Modern FORTRAN is much different, so the TPK program may require some explanation. The first line calls for the creation of an array A with 11 elements holding floating-point numbers. The next line fills the array with 11 numbers provided from the input device. The statement labeled 2 causes statements 3 through 8 to be executed 11 times. Starting from the end of the array the function $f(x) = \sqrt{|x|} + 5x^3$ is applied to each member. If the result is less than 400, then x and $f(x)$ are printed; otherwise 999 is printed. After this, control goes to the statement labeled 11. Notice the explicit GO TO 2 that initiates the next iteration of the loop.

The language has evolved and continues to evolve. The FORTRAN language has been standardized under the auspices of the American National Standards Institute (ANSI) and the International Standards Organization (ISO), once in 1966, again in 1978, and finally in 1992. The latest FORTRAN standard ANSI X3.198-1992 was adopted September 21, 1992, after a long period of discussion. FORTRAN 90, as it is called, includes a number of new features including dynamic storage allocation, modules, and recursion. Appropriate to this evolution is the following aphorism attributed to C. A. R. Hoare:

> I don't know what the language of the year 2000 will look like but I know it will be called FORTRAN.

This quotation and others (some less polite) were gathered for Pioneer Day at the 1982 National Computer Conference honoring the 25th anniversary of FORTRAN.

1.5.2   ALGOL

Although never popular in the United States, ALGOL has had a profound effect on programming language design. Many languages, like Pascal and Ada, are "ALGOL-like." This means they have the following characteristics:

- variables are changed

- block and procedures are the basic units

- procedures may call themselves recursively

- data are organized into different types

- identifiers have lexical scope

It is fair to say that the majority of programming languages have these features and can be said to have evolved from ALGOL (see figure 1.3 in section 1.6).

ALGOL (for ALGOrithmic Language) was designed by committee. In the late 1950s committees of the GAMM (Gesellschaft für angewandte Mathematik und Mechanik) and tha ACM (Association for Computing Machinery) were considering designing a universal programming language for communicating programs among users and to computers. In 1958 four members of each organization met at the Eidgenössische Technische Hochschule in Zürich. They hammered out the first draft of the new language. It was initially called IAL (the International Algebraic Language) by the Americans, but soon came to be known as ALGOL [28, 29]. In 1960 members of both organizations met again, this time in Paris. Proposals to include blocks, call-by-value and call-by-name, and recursion made it into the language. What emerged was a revolutionary new language. The process of designing and implementing the language has contributed heavily to the field of programming language. BNF notation was developed to describe the syntax of ALGOL, and compiler technology for block-structured languages was developed first for ALGOL.

Here is the TPK program written in ALGOL 60 from [22]:

```
TPK:    begin integer i; real array a[0 : 10];
            real procedure f(t); real t; value t;
            f := sqrt(abs(t)) + 5 × t ↑ 3;
            for i := 0 step 1 until 10 do read(a[i])
            for i := 10 step −1 until 0 do
            begin y := f(a[i]);
                if y > 400 then write(i, "TOO LARGE")
                            else write(i, y);
        end
    end.
```

The ALGOL committee advocated a syntax for the language suitable for publication and, hence suitable for communicating algorithms. This syntax was purposely unlinked from the syntax actually accepted by an implementation of the language. At the time, there was no widely accepted character set (and the committee could not agree on the syntax of the decimal point). In the publication language keywords were written in a bold font, as in the program above. Programs appearing in the computing literature often appear this way. Since that time, the ASCII character set has been accepted (ANSI standard X3.41-1974 was approved May 14, 1974—for earlier developments see [24]) as the standard for electronic information exchange. Practically all language descriptions now use the ASCII character set.

The decade of the 1960s saw substantial discussion and disagreement about revising the language. Eventually ALGOL 68 emerged from a committee of the International Federation of Information Processing. Even before this, Niklaus Wirth introduced a revision of ALGOL 60 known as ALGOL W [42]. This language had records, pointers, a `case` statement, and parameter passing using call-by-value, copy-out, and copy-in/copy-out. Records could only be accessed with pointers and arrays were all static.

ALGOL 68 had a long list of features. It had parallel computation and semaphores. It had implementation-dependent constants (e.g., the maximum integer) and coercions. It had a large collection of types: complex numbers, bit patterns, long and short numbers, strings, and flexible arrays. It had user-defined overloading and the case statement invented by Hoare. ALGOL 68 did simplify the baroque `for` construct introduced in ALGOL 60.

But the dream of a universal algorithmic language was petering out as the diversity of computer programming blossomed. ALGOL 68 did not see widespread use. The language was hard to implement: one compiler for the language needed six passes. Only the former Soviet Union had an official standard for ALGOL 68. Does ALGOL 68 have a future?

> The honest answer must now be 'No'. The world has moved on. To be accepted now, your language needs modules, exception handling, polymorphism, safe parallelism, and clean interfaces to everything else (not to mention a rich and powerful sponsor). [23, page 126]

1.5.3   LISP

Initially the only conceivable use for computers was numeric computation. Notation and code for exponentiation, transcendental functions, and even differential equations were considered the essence of programming language design. Today nonnumeric processing—from word processing to database transactions—is dominant. The innovation in the late 1950s of a language capable of doing symbolic processing cannot be underestimated.

John McCarthy and his colleagues at MIT developed a language whose primary data structure was a list of symbols. A list of symbols could represent words in a sentence, a list of attributes, a payroll record, or a symbolic differential equation. At first it may seem odd that a data structure as complex as a list would serve as the fundamental data structure of a language. But a list consists of only a "nil" element and a pair element—a pair of pointers, one to an element of the list and one to the rest of the list.

Indeed, programs themselves are also lists of symbols. LISP represents both data and programs as lists. A uniform representation of data and programs like this is found only in LISP. In LISP a program can create a program (a list), just as it might any value, and then execute it. A list is written in parentheses:

$$(element_1\ element_2\ \cdots\ element_n)$$

And a program is written with expressions of the form:

$$(operator\ argument_1\ \cdots\ argument_n)$$

representing the invocation of the operation *operator* applied to n arguments. Each argument could itself be another LISP expression, as in `(PLUS 3 (MINUS 6 2))`. Indeed, the operator itself could be another LISP expression. This syntax, sometimes called Cambridge Polish notation, is utterly simple. This makes it natural for use in describing the essence of any programming language without the distraction of learning idiosyncratic syntax [1, 13, 19]. Lists also give rise to the language's name, LISt Processing.

Literal lists have to be protected from evaluation by the LISP system by "quoting" them. Thus `(QUOTE (PLUS X Y))` must be given to a LISP system to result in the three-element list consisting of the atoms named `PLUS`, `X`, and `Y`. Without the `QUOTE` the values of `X` and `Y` would be added together.

In FORTRAN the programmer explicitly allocates the storage as in an array with 25 elements. But LISP uses lists as data structures, and these are created dynamically when the programmer adds elements to lists and appends list together. Since references to the structures may disappear when they are combined to form other structures, it is important to reclaim the storage occupied by lists that are no longer being used. LISP introduced automatic storage management to programming languages.

LISP has always been important to the artificial intelligence community. The original impetus for LISP came from general problem solving, something humans are good at, but computers clumsy. For the 1960s and 1970s LISP and artificial intelligence were closely related. But since then, progress in compiler technology and the clean semantics of purely functional programming have led to the emergence of a second major programming language family in contrast to the original imperative family.

Originally, despite the different syntax, LISP was fairly conventional in that programming required a sequence of side effects. But LISP had a conditional construct and functions. The importance of recursive functions as a programming paradigm came to be appreciated. Instead of iteration, as in the FORTRAN `DO` loop, recursive functions could be used. Functions without side effects are easy to develop and reason about. Languages that rely solely on functions and function application are said to be *functional languages*. Purely functional language are rare; most allow some side effects and sequencing.

So LISP was cleaned up, standardized, and consensus was reached on numerous extensions that had fractured LISP into many dialects. From 1975 to 1985 the languages Scheme and Common LISP were developed.

The strong-typing of Pascal influenced some parts of the functional language community and new, typed functional languages have been developed like ML and Haskell. These languages have recursive data type in addition to recursive functions.

The programming language ML was originally designed in the 1980s for use as the metalanguage in the Logic for Computable Functions verification system. Hence the source of the name for the language, ML, for MetaLanguage. Despite its origins as a language for a specific purpose, it is a general, strongly typed, functional language. Robin Milner was awarded the Turing Award in 1992, in part, because of his development of ML.

Haskell, designed by committee, is also strongly typed but representative of another variation in the functional programming field. Arguments to functions are not evaluated immediately as in ML, but only when needed. This permits infinite data structures to be built.

1.5.4   SIMULA

The development of SIMULA was carried out at the Norwegian Computing Center, a semigovernmental research institute supervised by the Royal Norwegian Council for Scientific and Industrial Research. SIMULA was closely related to ALGOL and, like ALGOL, has had significant influence on programming language development but is not widely used.

The impetus for the language was the need to simulate situations like queues at a supermarket, response times of emergency services, or chain reactions of nuclear reactors—thus the name SIMULA. Kristen Nygaard and Ole-Johan Dahl designed and implemented the language in the early 1960s.

At the outset SIMULA was a system description language for discrete event networks. After a period of use Nygaard and Dahl had the opportunity to revise the language.

> Much time was spent during the autumn of 1966 in trying to adapt Hoare's record class construct to meet our requirements, without success. The solution came suddenly, with the idea of "prefixing," in December 1966. We were thinking in terms of a toll booth on a bridge, with a queue of cards which were either trucks or buses. A "stripped" list structure, consisting of a "set head" and a variable number of "links," had been written down, when we saw that both our problems could be solved by a mechanism for "gluing" each of the various processes (trucks, buses) on to a "link" to make each link-process pair *one block instance.* [7, pages 460–461]

The language moved toward a general-purpose language and incorporated classes of objects. Simulating physical entities stimulated the idea of objects with independent existence as opposed to the hierarchical existence of data items popularized by the static nesting of blocks in ALGOL The new language came to be called SIMULA 67. After complex administrative and commercial problems were overcome the Norwegian Computing Center completed the implemented SIMULA 67 on the IBM System/360 and UNIVAC 1100 series computers in the spring of

1969. More than 20 years later a successor to SIMULA, called Beta, has been
designed [25].

1.5.5   COBOL

The United States Department of Defense sponsored a meeting in May 1959. The
goal of the meeting was to foster a common programming language for data-
processing applications—an application important to a large organization like the
Department of Defense. A result of the meeting was the formation of the CODASYL
(Committee on Data Systems Languages) Executive Committee to oversee the
work and two task groups to examine the problem in the short-term and the
intermediate-term future. In six months the short-term committee had fashioned
a new language called COBOL (COmmon Business Oriented Language) seen as a
"stopgap" solution to curtail the proliferation of languages by individual computer
manufacturers (IBM, Honeywell, RCA, and Sylvania, among others). Although
not on the committee, Grace Murray Hopper influenced the language through her
previous work in designing the first data-processing compiler: Flow-matic. In April
1960 the Department of Defense published the initial specifications for COBOL. By
December 1960, the first compilers had been implemented on RCA and Remington-
Rand UNIVAC computers. ANSI standards appeared in 1968, 1974, and 1985.
COBOL is still widely used in data-processing applications at least in part because
of the influence of the Department of Defense.

One major goal in the design of the language was to have a more English-like
programming language suitable for business data processing. Since FORTRAN was
designed for scientists and engineers, such a language was needed in 1960. COBOL,
since it was designed for processing large collections of data (like a payroll), had
special facilities for the machine-dependent environment, including files. COBOL
introduced a primitive form of structure to cope with the organization of files into
a collection of records.

COBOL has not made a major contribution to the development of programming languages. It developed largely independently of the enormous events
surrounding ALGOL. No other language has favored as verbose a syntax as that
of COBOL. Also, language implementations tend now to provide abstractions for
files, usually as a stream of characters, regardless of the underlying machine. This
provides a high-level, machine-independent interface that is easier for programmers.

1.5.6   APL

Kenneth E. Iverson began developing APL before 1960. At first the language was
not intended for implementation. It was designed to describe computer architecture
and was influenced by the field of linear algebra. In particular, arrays are the
principle data structure. For example, the expression $\lozenge A$ transposes the array
A. The language has many operators, from an unusual set of symbols, and the
operators apply to scalars, vectors, two-dimensional matrices, and so on. The

following sequence of APL expressions develops a test if N is prime. For purposes of illustration we take N to be seven. Seven is prime because none of the numbers two through six divide seven evenly.

APL expression	value
$N-2$	5
$\iota N-2$	1 2 3 4 5
$1+\iota N-2$	2 3 4 5 6
$(1+\iota N-2)\,|\,N$	1 1 3 2 1
$0\neq(1+\iota N-2)\,|\,N$	1 1 1 1 1
$\wedge/0\neq(1+\iota N-2)\,|\,N$	1

In this example, binary operators $x+y$ and $x|y$ (the remainder of y divided by x) are applied to arguments that are vectors. In this case the operation is applied component wise to each element of the vector. The binary operator $x\wedge y$ (conjunction) is inserted in between every element of a vector by the *reduction* / operator. In APL there is no precedence among operators and evaluation is performed strictly right to left. The number one is taken as a real number or the boolean value true as needed.

The guiding principles in the language design were said to be simplicity and practicality [10]:

> Simplicity enters in four guises: *uniformity* (rules are few and simple), *generality* (a small number of general functions provide as special cases a host of more specialized functions), *familiarity* (familiar symbols and usages are adopted whenever possible), and *brevity* (economy of expression is sought). Practicality is manifested in two respects: concern with actual application of the language, and concern with the practical limitations imposed by existing equipment.

APL is known for its compact notation and nonstandard character set. The well-nigh cryptic notation is loved by devotees for its power to express operations concisely. Iverson's thesis is that clear notation is important. The concrete syntax was carefully considered.

> As a practical matter it was clear that we would have to accept a linearization of the language (with no superscripts or subscripts) as well as a strict limit on the size of the primary character set. Although we expected these limitations to have a deleterious effect, and at first found unpleasant some of the linearity forced upon us, we now feel that the changes were beneficial, and that many led to important generalizations. For example:

. . .

The linearization of the inner and outer product notation (from $M \overset{+}{\times} N$ and $M \overset{\circ}{\times} N$ to $M+.\times N$ and $M\circ.\times N$) led eventually to the recognition of the operator (which was now represented by an explicit symbol, the period) as a separate and important component of the language. [11, page 665]

The notation first was described in 1962 in the book *A Programming Language* by Iverson. The first letters of the title, APL, give the language its name. Not long afterward, the first implementations were developed at IBM.

In early 1966 we began to consider an implementation on System/360, work that started in earnest in July and culminated in a running system in the fall. The fact that this interpretive and experimental implementation also proved to be remarkably practical and efficient is a tribute to the skill of the implementers, recognized in 1973 by the award to the principals (L. M. Breed, R. H. Lathwell, and R. D. Moore) of ACM's Grace Murray Hopper Award. The fact that many APL implementations continue to be largely interpretive may be attributed to the array character of the language which makes possible efficient interpretive execution. [11, page 666]

Iverson won the 1979 ACM Turing Award in large part due to design of the programming language APL. IBM continues to develop the language. There is now a commercially available version called APL2 and an interface between APL2 and the X Window System has been developed at the IBM Cambridge Scientific Center. A recent descendent of APL is the language J.

1.5.7 SNOBOL

The programming language SNOBOL (pronounced "snowball") was developed by David J. Farber, Ralph Griswold, and Ivan P. Polonsky while at Bell Telephone Laboratories in the mid 1960s. The language was designed primarily to process string data. The language was distributed free, which contributed to its dissemination and influence.

Griswold claims that it took them longer to find a name for the language than to implement it. At first SEXI (String EXpressions Interpreter) was proposed, and rejected. The commonly accepted interpretation of the acronym SNOBOL is StriNg Oriented symBOlic Language, but this was actually not proposed seriously. There are a number of spin-offs from the original SNOBOL language. Some of them have catchy names of their own: SPITBOL (speedy implementation), FASBOL, SLOBOL, and SNOBAT. The most familiar version is SNOBOL4.

Now there is an ALGOL-like successor of SNOBOL called Icon developed by Griswold at the University of Arizona. The name Icon was chosen merely because Griswold liked the word and not because it is an acronym or because of any relation to icons in user interfaces. We give an Icon program for the TPK algorithm.

```
procedure f (x)
    return (sqrt(abs(x)) + 5.0*x*x*x)
end

procedure main (args)
    A := table (0);          # let A be a table with default value 0
    every A[0 to 10] := read()
    every i := 10-(0 to 10) do
        write (i, " ",   400.0 > f(A[i]) | "TOO LARGE", "\n")
end
```

An unusual feature of Icon is that of generators. Two generators appear in the TPK program: x to y and x | y. The latter generates x and, if necessary, y. The former generates x, $x + 1$, and so on up to y. Thus the expression 10-(0 to 10) produces 10, 9, ..., 0. The expression 400.0 > x | "TOO LARGE" generates x, if it is less than 400; otherwise it generates the string "TOO LARGE". The Icon translator does not determine the types of expressions. Numbers are converted to strings during program execution whenever the context demands it.

1.6 More recent events

In the previous section we have briefly introduced the salient programming languages of the 1960s: FORTRAN, ALGOL, LISP, SIMULA, COBOL, APL, and SNOBOL. In this section we review some more recent events. Figure 1.3 gives a rough overview of the evolution of imperative programming languages. LISP and the functional languages are omitted, as they form another path of development. After the development of FORTRAN, most of the growth in the language "tree" occurs in the ALGOL branch with various directions explored: systems programming, modules, objects, and others. In the next few sections we will look at several of these languages in more detail.

The programming language SETL [19, 1] sits by itself in figure 1.3 because it has a significantly different character. SETL was developed at New York University in the 1970s with sets as data type. Sets in SETL can sometimes be manipulated in the abstract manner that mathematicians are accustomed to. This makes it possible to prototype complex projects easily. The first validated Ada translator was written in SETL.

1.6.1 PL/I, BASIC, C

PL/I

In the mid-1960s IBM launched a major effort to replace FORTRAN and COBOL with a new and better language. The effort failed in part because FORTRAN and COBOL were too entrenched and in part because PL/I was too big and complex,

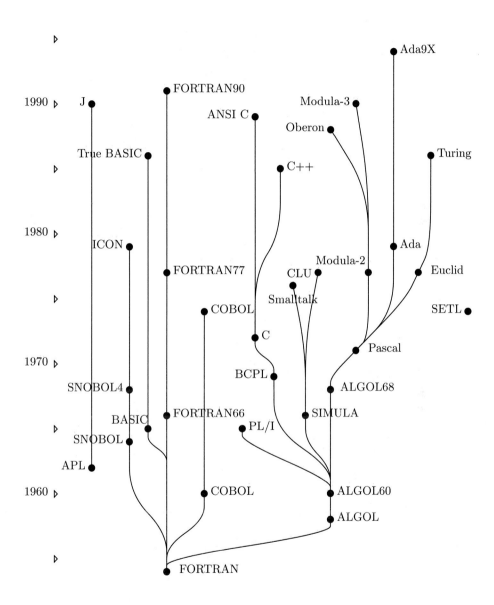

Figure 1.3: Evolution of imperative programming languages

and maybe a little premature. PL/I borrowed block structure and recursive procedures from ALGOL, making it more modern than FORTRAN and COBOL. It also added many ambitious new features including exception handling and multitasking.

In 1963 IBM and a user's group for scientific applications formed the Advanced Language Development Committee and was given the task of specifying a programming language for systems, commercial, and scientific applications. Three members of each organization were selected to be on the committee. In a few months a proposal for FORTRAN VI was composed. After compatability with FORTRAN was rejected, a New Programming Language (NPL) was developed. Over the next several years the language was heavily revised. In 1965 the language was renamed PL/I to avoid confusion with the National Physical Laboratory in England. The first compilers appeared about this time. An ANSI standard was approved in 1976 and a standard for a "general-purpose subset" was approved in 1981.

Other institutions implemented their own versions of PL/I. Bob Morris and Doug McIlroy of Bell Laboratories developed EPL in which MULTICS was written. Digital Equipment Corporation (DEC) had a version called CPL. Several universities implemented compilers appropriate for educational as opposed to production purposes. Prominent among these was the Cornell University's PL/C. The C stood for "Conway," "Cornell," or "correcting." The compiler attempted to repair errors so that students who spent most of their time compiling and little of their time running programs could make maximum use of computing resources.

BASIC

BASIC (Beginner's All-purpose Symbolic Instruction Code) was designed for students at Dartmouth College by John G. Kemeny and Thomas E. Kurtz. The goals were to make an interactive language that was easy to learn, quick to compile, and easy to debug.

Variables in BASIC were consisted of a single letter or a single letter followed by a single digit, something that seemed appropriate for composing quick programs. Like FORTRAN, variables are not declared and there is no distinction between integer and real numbers. A program is organized by line numbers as in the following BASIC program.

```
 10 REM     BASIC PROGRAM FOR TPK ALGORITHM
 20 DIM A(11)
 30 FOR I = 1 TO 11
 40 INPUT A(I)
 50 NEXT I
 60 FOR J = 1 TO 11
 70 LET I = 11 - J
 80 LET Y = A(I+1) + 5 * A(I+1)
 90 IF Y > 400.0 THEN 120
100 PRINT I+1, Y
```

```
110 GO TO 130
120 PRINT I, "TOO LARGE"
130 NEXT J
140 STOP
150 END
```

BASIC spread widely, aided by the personal computer revolution. The simplicity of BASIC appeals to the many people who want to use the computer, but do not wish to learn programming. The popularity of BASIC lead to multiple implementations of the language with vastly different characteristics. An ANSI standard for BASIC in 1978 did little to change the situation. In 1985 Kemeny and Kurtz produced an new version of BASIC, called True BASIC, with many new features including interactive graphics.

The programming language C

The programming language C was originally designed and implemented by Dennis M. Ritchie at Bell Laboratories in New Jersey in 1972. It was greatly influenced by the programming language B created by Ken Thompson for the first UNIX system on the PDP-11. B, in turn, was greatly influenced by BCPL, a systems-programming language developed for compiler writing.

After ten years of gradual growth, the decade of 1980s saw an enormous increase in the use of C. A large number of different compilers were written and implementations were ported to nearly every machine architecture and operating system. Both personal computer hobbyists and producers of commercial software were using C extensively. It is worth speculating why this happened. The competing languages were FORTRAN, COBOL, and Pascal. FORTRAN was and is still used by the scientific computing community. During the 1980s this group of users did not account for many of the new users of computers. COBOL is more appropriate for large data-processing operations, and, again, these operations did not increase notably in number. Pascal was much easier to learn than FORTRAN and COBOL and, in fact, was being taught to the next and large generation of new computer users. It is easier and safer to use than C, but its insulation from "real" computing makes it unsuitable for some applications. In particular, graphics and network programming require greater access to the hardware environment. These applications have been increasingly popular and important. C is ideal for these applications because it allows low-level access to words and bits of computer memory and because the `#include` facility permits the flexible addition of system-dependent definitions.

Eventually in 1989 an ANSI standard was established for C. Its most important change over the de facto standard by Ritchie and Brian W. Kernighan was the incorporation of the types of formal arguments in the type of a function. Figure 1.4 shows the TPK program in the C programming language using function prototypes.

```c
#include <stdio.h>     /* include header file for standard I/O   */
#include <math.h>      /* include header file for math functions */

double f (double x) {
    return (sqrt(fabs(x)) + 5.0*pow(x,3.0));
}

int main (int argc, char* argv[]) {
    double A [11], y;
    int i;

    /* Read in the values of the array A */
    for (i=0; i<11; i++) {
        scanf ("%lf", &A[i]);
    }

    /* Apply "f" to each value of A in reverse order */
    for (i=10; i>=0; i--) {
        y = f (A[i]);
        if (y > 400.0) {
            printf ("%d TOO LARGE\n", i);
        } else {
            printf ("%d %f\n", i, y);
        }
    }
    return (0);
}
```

Figure 1.4: The TPK algorithm in C

The use of curly braces where other languages use **begin**/**end** keywords gives the language a concise appearance.

1.6.2   Structured programming

In the decade of the 1970s there was consolidation and improvement. This decade saw the emergence of a number of influential languages: Pascal, Modula, and CLU.

Pascal

The programming language ALGOL had demonstrated the enormous range of possibilities. But all the intricacies had to be melded into a whole that had many competing requirements. Discipline was required and this was provided by Niklaus

Wirth, who first tried to influence the direction of ALGOL 68 with his proposal (ALGOL W) and then went his own way with the development of Pascal. The first draft of the language excluded dynamic arrays and recursive procedures and was implemented by a single graduate student in FORTRAN for the CDC 6000 in 1969.

A second version of the language, this time with recursion, was written in Pascal itself and bootstrapped. It was a single-pass compiler written using a recursive-descent parser. The published description of the language appeared in 1971. In that year Pascal was used in introductory programming courses at Eidgenössische Technische Hochschule in Zürich. Pascal has been widely used all over the world to teach programming to students. Standardization efforts in the late 1970s and early 1980s failed to stop the proliferation of implementations with their own extensions. Particularly troubling was the issue of dynamic arrays for which the need was obvious, but the solution was not.

A big contribution of the language was its philosophy of language design embodying simplicity and emphasizing data types. Wirth explains the significance of this new point of view toward data types in a retrospective twenty years later:

> Along with programmer-defined data types came the clear distinction between type definition and variable declaration, variables being instances of a type. The concept of strong typing—already present in Algol—emerged as an important catalyst for secure programming. A type was to be understood as a template for variables specifying all properties that remain fixed during the time-space of a variable's existence. Whereas its value changes (through assignments), its range of possible values remains fixed, as well as its structure. This explicitness of static properties allows compilers to verify whether rules governing types are respected. The binding of properties to variables in the program text is called *early binding* and is the hallmark of high-level languages, because it gives clear expression to the intention of the programmer, unobscured by the dynamics of program execution. [41, page 335]

Linked to the influence of Pascal was the structured approach to program methodology called *stepwise refinement* [39]. User-defined data types and structured program constructs like the `if` and `while` statements facilitated a new era in programming that started at a "higher-level" than previously possible. It was possible to start from the problem statement and refine it into the intermediate steps top-down until the problem was solved with a computer program.

Modula-2

As the decade of the 1970s progressed it was clear that Pascal and all other languages were inadequate for programming-in-the-large. Big programs are not structured purely hierarchically from a narrow top to a wide base at the bottom. Big programs often borrow chunks of code. The key problem, continuing to this day, is how to organize these chunks into units that can be written and borrowed clearly, efficiently, and seamlessly.

The programming language Modula was Niklaus Wirth's answer to these needs. The version of the language known as Modula-2 has achieved some popularity, although not as much as Pascal. The competition with other languages with modules (notably Ada), other popular languages like C and C++, and the ever present FORTRAN and COBOL, has left little room for Modula-2. Now, even Wirth has moved on with a new language Oberon [40] with typed object-oriented features.

1.6.3   Logic programming

In the 1970s an entirely new programming paradigm was born with the advent of PROLOG. PROLOG emerged out of a project in natural language translation headed by Alain Colmerauer at the University of Marseilles.

The first preliminary interpreter for PROLOG was written in the language ALGOL W in 1972 by Phillipe Roussel. The interpreter was just a prelude to a man-machine communication system that was then built in PROLOG. In 1973 three students wrote a new PROLOG interpreter in FORTRAN for the CII 10070 computer under Colmerauer and Roussel's direction. In the same year, it was ported to the IBM System/360. The FORTRAN version no longer had the "occurs check" but had all the basic features of modern PROLOG.

PROLOG was not designed as a theorem prover for a particular logical system. Rather it grew by capturing certain logical inferences that might implicitly be made in natural language. Robert Kowalski later proved that the approach is complete for what are known as Horn clauses.

We consider this approach to programming important enough to devote a chapter to PROLOG. There are other languages that might be judged to belong to the logic programming paradigm, but these are not as well known and tend to be specialized.

1.6.4   Object-oriented languages

Smalltalk

The progenitor of the object-oriented programming (OOP) paradigm is the programming system Smalltalk. It has an interesting and expansive genesis influenced by the social impact of cheap and powerful computers. In the words of Smalltalk's creator, Alan Kay:

> Though OOP came from many motivations, two were central. The large scale one was to find a better module scheme for complex systems involving hiding of details, and the small scale one was to find a more flexible version of assignment, and then to try to eliminate it altogether. [20, page 70]

The design of Smalltalk was influenced by the programming language SIMULA. SIMULA is unlike ALGOL, which allocates data structures in a last-in/first out, or stack manner. In SIMULA structures have a more independent existence. Each structure is like its own little computer.

> ... the B5000, Sketchpad, and finally Simula, all used the same idea of different purposes. Bob Barton, the main designer of the B5000 and a professor at Utah had said: The "basic principle of recursive design is make the parts have the same power as the whole." For the first time I thought of the whole as the entire computer and wondered why anyone would want to divide it up into weaker things called data structures and procedures. Why not divide it up into little computers, as time-sharing was starting to? But not in dozens. Why not thousands of them, each simulating a useful structure? [20, page 71]

It was not enough to have a language with computer-like objects; the objects needed to be visible as well. For this reason, Smalltalk was always more than a language and was inextricably linked to a bit-mapped display. Objects needed to have iconic representations on the display. This iconic programming later found popular expression in the products of the Apple Computer Corporation. Kay explains the many influences that led to this point of view:

> After reading Piaget and especially Jerome Bruner, I was worried that the directly symbolic approach taken by FLEX, LOGO (and the current Smalltalk) would be difficult for the kids to process since evidence existed that the symbolic state (or mentality) was just starting to switch on. In fact, all of the educators that I admired (including Montessori, Holt, and Suzuki) all seemed to call for a more figurative, more iconic approach. Rudolph Arnheim had written a classic book about visual thinking, and so had the eminent art critic Grombrich. It really seemed that something better needed to be done here. [20, page 77]

In the early 1970s at the Xerox Palo Alto Research Center (PARC) a personal computer system including both hardware and software were developed. The language of the system came to be called Smalltalk. In the words of Kay:

> In the summer of '71 I refined the KiddiKomp idea into a tighter design called miniCOM. It used a bit-slice approach, had a bit-map display, a pointing device, a choice of "secondary" storages, and a language I now called "Smalltalk"—as in "programming should be a matter of ..." and "children should program in ...". The name was also a reaction against the "IndoEuropean god theory" where systems were named Zeus, Odin, and Thor, and hardly did anything. I figured that "Smalltalk" was so innocuous a label that if it ever did anything nice people would be pleasantly surprised. [20, page 75]

From these early versions three major systems were designed and implemented at Xerox PARC. The first Smalltalk interpreter was a thousand-line BASIC program written in 1972. Under the direction of Dan Ingalls of the Software Concepts Group at Xerox PARC, successively more advanced versions were implemented which came to be known as Smalltalk-76 and Smalltalk-80.

In 1980 Smalltalk left the confines of Xerox. The formal description of Smalltalk-80 was reviewed and debugged by four companies: Apple Computer, Digital Equipment Corporation, Hewlett-Packard, and Tektronix. Each company implemented the system on their own hardware. Later an additional research license was granted to the University of California at Berkeley. The resulting experience was captured in a series of three books authored by Adele Goldberg and others, published by Addison-Weseley. Currently Smalltalk is available on a wide variety of platforms.

Smalltalk has a played a large role in spreading the object-oriented programming paradigm. This general paradigm, which has different meanings to different people, has an unclear relation to data abstraction. It is important to note that data abstraction was not the goal of Smalltalk. In Kay's words:

> This is probably a good place to comment on the difference between what we thought of as OOP-style and the superficial encapsulation called "abstract data types" that was just starting to be investigated in academic circles. ... The "official" computer science world started to regard Simula as a possible vehicle for defining *abstract data types* (even by one of its inventors), and it formed much of the later backbone of Ada. This led to the ubiquitous stack data-type example in hundreds of papers. To put it mildly, we were quite amazed at this, since to us, what Simula had whispered was something much stronger than simply reimplementing a weak and ad hoc idea. What I got from Simula was that you could now replace bindings and assignments with *goals*. The last thing you wanted any programmer to do is mess with internal state even if presented figuratively. Instead, the objects should be presented as *sites of higher level behaviors more appropriate for use as dynamic components.* [20, page 81]

The influence of Smalltalk is evident in the object-oriented terminology that is currently popular. *Objects* are the independent units of the program. *Classes*, a term taken from SIMULA, are a description of a collection of objects. An object is an *instance* of a class. Classes are organized in a *class hierarchy*. A class may *inherit* some properties from *super classes* higher up in the class hierarchy. Objects interact by sending *messages* to each other. The messages that an object reacts to are implemented by its *methods*. The hierarchical organization of classes and method suites can be exploited by some new kinds of software development tools. One category of such tools is called a *browser*. A browser allows the programmer to jump from class to class easily to view the associated code. This is a useful tool for tracing the execution of an object-oriented program.

The fact that Smalltalk is an entire programming system in and of itself is both a major advantage and disadvantage. One advantage is the integrated program development environment that gives the user great flexibility and control. One disadvantage is the large overhead in learning an entire system and difficulty of supporting such an multi-faceted system uniformly across diverse hardware platforms. Another programming language, C++, was built for a more conventional environment where a compiler takes an ASCII program in a file and produces an executable file.

C++

One currently popular object-oriented language is C++. Bjarne Stroustrup was motivated by SIMULA to add classes to the programming language C in a preprocessing step of the compiler. The success and the widespread use of C, coupled with the lack of any sort of support for abstract data types in C, has prompted widespread use of C++. In 1993 Stroustrup won the Grace Murray Hopper Award given by the ACM to an oustanding young computer professional for a single major technical contribution. At HOPL-II, the second conference on the history of programming languages, Stroustrup gave the following overview of the evolution of C++ [34]:

C with classes	1979–1983	adding classes with a preprocessor
Evolution of C++	1982–1985	first commercial release
Release 2.0	1985-1988	early commercial use
Growth in use	1987–	large-scale use
Standardization	1988–	

It is interesting to note that the language has become immensely popular before seemingly major language design issues, like exception handling and templates, have been resolved.

The name of the language C++ is pronounced "see plus plus" as all inveterate C programmers know. In 1984 Stroustrup

> asked for ideas for a new name and picked C++ because it was short, had nice interpretations, and wasn't of the form "adjective C." In C, ++ can dependent on context be read as "next," "successor," or "increment" though it is always pronounced "plus plus." The name C++ and its runner up ++C are fertile sources for jokes and puns—almost all of which were known and appreciated before the name was chosen. The name C++ was suggested by Rick Mascitti. [34, page 279]

Many people equate object-oriented programming with programming in C++, although just exactly what is meant by object-oriented programming is unclear. It seems the predication of one of the Smalltalk designers has come true.

> My guess is that object oriented programming will be in the 1980's what
> structured programming was in the 1970's. Everyone will be in favor
> of it. Every manufacturer will promote his products as supporting it.
> Every manager will pay lip service to it. Every programmer will practice
> it (differently). And no one will know just what it is. [30, page 51]

A new generation of object-oriented languages with theoretical foundations is emerging in which objects are akin to records. Languages in this class are Modula-3 and Oberon. We will have more to say about Modula-3 later.

1.6.5   Ada

Another significant event in the 1980s was the development of Ada. Starting in the mid-1970s the United States Department of Defense (DoD) supported an effort to reduce the mounting software costs caused by the multitude of languages used by the defense establishment.

> The technical requirements for the common language reflect six major
> goals: (1) that it be suitable for software in DoD embedded computer
> applications; (2) that it be appropriate for the design, development, and
> maintenance of reliable software for systems that are large, long-lived,
> and continually undergoing change; (3) that it be suitable as a com-
> mon language (i.e., complete, unambiguous, and machine-independent
> standards can be established); (4) that it will not impose execution
> costs in applications where it provides unused or unneeded generality;
> (5) that it provide a base around which a useful software development,
> maintenance, and support environment can be built; and (6) that it be
> an example of good current language design practice. [12]

In 1976, 23 already-existing programming languages were appraised in light of these goals. Since no existing language was found entirely satisfactory, a cycle of language specifications and design reviews was conducted to develop a new language. Eventually five companies contracted to make competing designs for the language. A team from Honeywell Bull of France led by Jean Ichbaih produced the design that was selected by the Department of Defense. The language was named Ada in honor of Ada Augusta, Countess of Lovelace, with the permission of her descendants. The countess is considered to be the first programmer for her work with Babbage's analytic engine. The language standard for Ada appeared in 1983. It can be obtained from the United States Government Printing Office and has been reprinted widely.

There are a number of noteworthy features in the language, including high-level constructs for concurrent execution and real-time programming. The language has some innovations in the organization of types that will be discussed in section 4.4. Ada also has a construct for aggregating data structures and subprocedures called a "package" and a mechanism for exception handling.

```
with text_io, math;
procedure tpk is

    package int_io is new text_io.integer_io (INTEGER);
    package real_io is new text_io.float_io (LONG_FLOAT);

    A : array (0 .. 10) of LONG_FLOAT;

    -- We assume a square root function in package math
    function f (x: LONG_FLOAT) return LONG_FLOAT is
    begin
        return (math.sqrt (ABS x) + 5.0*x**3);
    end f;

begin
    -- Read in the values of the array A
    for I in A'RANGE loop
        real_io.get (A (I));
    end loop;
    -- Apply "f" to each value of A in reverse order
    for I in reverse A'RANGE loop
        declare
            Y : constant LONG_FLOAT := f (LONG_FLOAT (I));
        begin
            if (400.0 >= Y)
            then
                int_io.put (I);
                real_io.put (Y);
                text_io.new_line;
            else
                int_io.put (I);
                text_io.put_line (" TOO LARGE");
            end if;
        end;
    end loop;
end tpk;
```

Figure 1.5: The TPK algorithm in Ada

Figure 1.5 shows a sample Ada program, the same TPK program we used to illustrate FORTRAN, ALGOL-60, BASIC, C, and Icon. Notice that the square-root operation is not an integral part of the language (as it is in FORTRAN).

Using the square-root function requires identifying an implementation-dependent library called `math`, learning an implementation-dependent system for managing these libraries, and linking them with the program. The `text_io` library is a standard part of any Ada implementation.

A revision of the Ada language is currently nearing completion. Intermetrics, Inc. of Cambridge, Massachusetts, has the contract to revise the language. The new language is currently known as Ada 9X. The major changes concern objects, data-oriented synchronization, and real-time programming. Backward compatibility with existing Ada code is a high priority. In early February of 1994, the Committee Draft for Ada 9X (ANSI/ISO CD 8652) passed both the ISO SC22 ballot and the ANSI canvass. A Draft International Standard will incorporate responses to comments received during the voting. By the end of 1994 the standard document defining Ada 9X could be approved.

1.7   Bibliography

[1] Abelson, Harold, and Gerald Jay Sussman. *Structure and Interpretation of Computer Programs*. MIT Press, Cambridge, Massachusetts, 1985.

[2] Babbage, Charles. "On the influence of signs in mathematical reasoning." *Transactions of the Cambridge Philosophical Society*, volume 2, 1827, pages 325–377.

[3] Backus, John. "The history of FORTRAN I, II, and III." In *History of Programming Languages*, edited by Richard L. Wexelblat, Academic Press, New York, 1981, pages 25–45.

[4] Beeson, Michael J. "Problematic principles in constructive mathematics." In *Logic Colloquium '80*, edited by Dirk van Dalen, D. Lascar and J. Smiley, North-Holland, Amsterdam, 1982, pages 11–55.

[5] Cajori, Florian. *A History of Mathematical Notations*. Two volumes. Open Court, Chicago, Illinois, 1928–29.

[6] Constable, Robert L., et al. *Implementing Mathematics with the NUPRL Proof Development System*. Prentice Hall, Englewood Cliffs, New Jersey, 1986.

[7] Dahl, Ole-Johan, and Kristen Nygaard. "The development of the SIMULA languages." In *History of Programming Languages*, edited by Richard L. Wexelblat, Academic Press, New York, 1981, pages 439–480.

[8] Driver, Godfrey Rolles. *Semitic Writing from Pictograph to Alphabet*. Oxford University Press, London, 1976.

[9] Dummett, Michael A. E. *Elements of Intuitionism*. Oxford Logic Series. Oxford University Press, London, 1977.

[10] Falkoff, Adin D., and Kenneth E. Iverson. "The design of APL." *IBM Journal of Research and Development*, July 1973, pages 324–334. Reprinted in *Programming Languages: A Grand Tour*, edited by Ellis Horowitz, 1987, pages 240–250.

[11] Falkoff, Adin D., and Kenneth E. Iverson. "The evolution of APL." In *History of Programming Languages*, edited by Richard L. Wexelblat, Academic Press, New York, 1981, pages 661–674.

[12] Fisher, David A. "DoD's common programming language effort." *IEEE Computer*, volume 11, number 3, March 1978, pages 24–33. Reprinted in *Tutorial, Programming Language Design*, edited by Anthony I. Wasserman, 1980, pages 316–325.

[13] Friedman, Daniel Paul, Mitchell Wand, and Christopher T. Haynes. *Essentials of Programming Languages*. MIT Press, Cambridge, Massachusetts, 1992.

[14] van Heijenoort, Jean, editor. *From Frege to Gödel: A Source Book in Mathematical Logic*. Harvard University Press, Cambridge, Massachusetts, 1977.

[15] Huskey, Vekna R., and Harry D. Huskey. "Lady Lovelace and Charles Babbage." *Annals of the History of Computing*, volume 2, number 4, October 1980, pages 299–329.

[16] Iverson, Kenneth E. *A Programming Language*. John Wiley & Sons, New York, 1962.

[17] James, Carol L., and Duncan E. Morrill. "The real Ada, Countess of Lovelace." *ACM SIGSoft Engineering Notes*, volume 8, number 1, January 1983, page 30.

[18] Jensen, Hans. *Sign, Symbol, and Script: An Account of Man's Efforts to Write*. Third revised and enlarged edition. George Allen and Unwin, London, 1970.

[19] Kamin, Samuel N. *Programming Languages: An Interpreter-based Approach*. Addison-Wesley, Reading, Massachusetts, 1990.

[20] Kay, Alan C. "The early history of Smalltalk." *SIGPLAN Notices*, volume 28, number 3, March 1993, pages 69–96.

[21] Knuth, Donald Ervin. "Ancient Babylonian algorithms." *Communications of the ACM*, volume 15, number 7, July 1972, pages 671–677. Errata, volume 19, number 2, February 1976, page 108.

[22] Knuth, Donald Ervin, and Luis Trabb Pardo. "The early development of programming languages." In *Encyclopedia of Computer Science and Technology*, Marcel Dekker, New York, 1977, pages 419–496.

[23] Lindsey, Charles H. "A history of ALGOL 68." *SIGPLAN Notices*, volume 28, number 3, March 1993, pages 97–132.

[24] Mackenzie, Charles E. *Coded Character Sets, History and Development*. The systems programming series. Addison-Wesley, Reading, Massachusetts, 1980.

[25] Madsen, Ole Lehrmann, Birger Møller-Pederson, and Kristen Nygaard. *Object-Oriented Programming in the Beta Programming Language.* Addison-Wesley, Wokingham, England, 1993.

[26] Moore, Doris Langley. *Ada, Countess of Lovelace.* Harper & Row, New York, 1977.

[27] Naveh, Joseph. *Early History of the Alphabet: An Introduction to West Semitic Epigraphy and Palaeography.* Magnes Press, Jerusalem, 1982.

[28] Perlis, Alan J., and Klaus Samelson. "Preliminary Report—International Algebraic Language." *Communications of the ACM*, volume 1, number 12, December 1958, pages 8–22.

[29] Perlis, Alan J., and Klaus Samelson. "Report on the Algorithmic Language Algol." *Numerische Mathematik*, volume 1, January 1959, pages 41–60.

[30] Rentsch, Tim. "Object oriented programming." *SIGPLAN Notices*, volume 17, number 9, September 1982, pages 51–57.

[31] Schmandt-Besserat, Denise. "The earliest precursor of writing." In *Language, Writing, and the Computer*, W. H. Freeman, New York, 1986, pages 31–40.

[32] Shu, Nan C. *Visual Programming.* Van Nostrand Reinhold, New York, 1988.

[33] Slater, Robert. *Portraits in Silicon.* MIT Press, Cambridge, Massachusetts, 1987.

[34] Stroustrup, Bjarne. "A History of C++: 1979–1991." *SIGPLAN Notices*, volume 28, number 3, March 1993, pages 271–297.

[35] Stroustrup, Bjarne. *The Design and Evolution of C++.* Addison Wesley, Reading, Massachusetts, 1994.

[36] Struik, D. J., editor. *A Source Book in Mathematics, 1200–1800.* Harvard University Press, Cambridge, Massachusetts, 1969.

[37] Wexelblat, Richard L., editor. *History of Programming Languages.* Academic Press, New York, 1981.

[38] Williams, Michael Roy. *A History of Computing Technology.* Prentice Hall, Englewood Cliffs, New Jersey, 1985.

[39] Wirth, Niklaus Emil. "Program development by stepwise refinement." *Communications of the ACM*, volume 14, number 4, April 1971, pages 221–227.

[40] Wirth, Niklaus Emil. "From Modula to Oberon." *Software—Practice and Experience*, volume 18, number 7, 1988, pages 661–670.

[41] Wirth, Niklaus Emil. "Recollections about the development of Pascal." *SIGPLAN Notices*, volume 28, number 3, March 1993, pages 333–342.

[42] Wirth, Niklaus Emil, and Charles Antony Richard Hoare. "A contribution to the development of ALGOL." *Communications of the ACM*, volume 9, number 6, June 1966, pages 413–431.

[43] Zemanek, Heinz. "Al-Khorezmi: His background, his personality, his work and his influence." In *Algorithms in Modern Mathematics and Computer Science*, edited by Andreĭ Petrovitch Ershov and Donald Ervin Knuth, Springer-Verlag, Berlin, 1981, pages 8–81.

Chapter 2

Syntax and grammars

Before examining concepts that are found in programming languages, this chapter looks at some notions from the general study of formal languages and grammars. This is useful for a number of reasons:

1. It is important to the study of programming languages to be familiar with the terminology and some aspects of formal languages and grammars.

2. The study of formal language provides the opportunity to introduce the dichotomy between meta-language and language, and between name and denotation.

3. Some techniques important in the study of programming languages, for example, structural induction, inductive proof, and inductive definition, can be illustrated.

4. Generally, familiarity with formalisms more powerful than context-free grammars is limited to Turing machines, so we introduce two other powerful formalisms: attribute grammars and Post systems.

2.1 The study of language

Traditionally the study of language is divided into three areas: syntax, semantics, and pragmatics. The syntax of a language encompasses the form, format, well-formedness, and compositional structure of the language. For example, the sentence

   Painted two desk.

is syntactically incorrect in English.

However, there is more to language than just syntax. Contrast the following examples used by Noam Chomsky [3]:

> Revolutionary new ideas appear infrequently.
> Colorless green ideas sleep furiously.

Both sentences are syntactically correct, but the second is vividly meaningless! The problem is not with its syntax, because it has the same syntax as the first sentence, but with its semantics.

The semantics of a language concerns the meaning and interpretation of the language. Syntax and semantics are often difficult to separate. Consider these sentences [6, pages 9–10]:

> Time flies like an arrow.
> Fruit flies like a banana.

As these examples illustrate, the meaning of words in a sentence is closely intertwined with the syntactic structure of the sentence.

The pragmatics of a language concerns everything else: the origin, uses, and effects of the language. Sometimes the pragmatic issues are very important, but they are difficult to study systematically. For example, the influence of APL was limited by its need for a nonstandard keyboard to enter the symbols of the language.

We will begin this chapter and open the study of programming languages with some lessons about the design of programming languages. The rest of the chapter will deal only briefly with syntax, as the formalization of syntax is familiar to many. The success of grammars is well known. Many books deal with this subject and only a few aspects of the study of syntax will appear here. In particular we introduce attribute grammars, which, while important to programming languages, have not received good coverage. The formalization of semantics, one of the important topics in programming languages, will be the subject of the last chapters.

Computer science is different from linguistics in that the study of programming languages is prescriptive or normative; linguistics is descriptive. Linguists are stuck with natural languages, but programming languages we can build. We can build bad ones, or we can build good ones.

2.1.1   Programming language design

What are the criteria with which we analyze the medium of communication? What makes good (or bad) programming languages? The experience of designing programming languages has led to some general conclusions about language design. Unfortunately, most of these conclusions are easier to recognize when they have been violated than to apply in designing good languages.

Abstraction   It is desirable to have constructs that factor out recurring patterns, e.g., subprocedures.

Orthogonality   Basic features should be separately understandable and free from unexpected interaction. An example in which this principle is violated can be found in Pascal, where **val** and **var** parameters combine the type of use of parameters (i.e., input or output) with the parameter-passing mechanism (i.e., call-by-value or call-by-reference).

Simplicity The fewer concepts to understand in a language the better.

Regularity The few exceptions to the rules the better. This is sometimes formulated by saying that the only reasonable numbers are zero, one, and infinity. For example, FORTRAN had three, but not higher, dimensional arrays. Although this made it possible for the compiler to better optimize subscripting, such a restriction is quite easy for a programmer to overlook.

Consistency Similar constructs should look similar. And conversely, different constructs should appear differently. Compare, for example, the syntax of array subscripting A(I) with the syntax of function calls F(I) in FORTRAN or Ada. The reader is helped enormously by the use of square brackets A[I] in subscripting.

Translation A translator for the language that runs quickly and produces efficient object code is obviously desirable.

2.2 Grammars

The syntax of a language has a profound effect on the ease of use of a language. All C programmers have suffered the deleterious effects of using the assignment operator = when the relational operations equals == was meant. PL/I programmers must be wary of the **end** keyword that can close *any* number of **begin** constructs.

Another example of this is the deliberate decision of the FORTRAN designers to make spaces insignificant in that language. From the perspective of the coders in those days who left the actual punching up of the card decks in the hands of others, this decision made sense. But in conjunction with other features of the language, this decision about the syntax undoubtably led to errors. Part of the folklore of programming languages is the apocryphal story that the following program fragment contributed to the destruction of a rocket during launch:

```
    DO 10 I = 1.5
       A(I) = X + B(I)
10  CONTINUE
```

Presumably a comma, not a period, was meant to separate 1 and 5. The problem is that, since FORTRAN ignores spaces, the DO statement was interpreted as the assignment statement:

```
DO10I = 1.5
```

Instead of a loop, an assignment (to an undeclared variable) was performed. The story is totally false. Ceruzze [2] documents that FORTRAN was not involved.

Another story relating to language design concerns the nationwide blockage of telephone traffic in the United States in 1990 [17]. A contributing factor to that problem has been reported to be a `break` statement in a C program. This statement causes execution of the program to leave the most closely nested iteration construct containing the `break` statement. The `break` statement also applies to the `switch` statement, but not to the `if` statement, the only other compound statement for control flow. While there is good reason that `break` does not apply to an `if` statement (presumably that would be equivalent to omitting the remaining statements in that branch of the conditional), it is easy to believe that changing a `while` statement to an `if` statement, for example, could cause a programming error.

Some persuasive evidence has been established about various aspects of programming language syntax. For example, the use of punctuation as a terminator as opposed to a separator has been supported by experiments conducted by Gannon and Horning [5]. In some languages, like Turing and ML, the semicolon as a separator of items is optional.

Another issue is that of keywords. Keywords are fixed symbols of the language, such as `if` and `do`. Should they be reserved words? Reserved words are keywords that are illegal as identifiers. Pascal, Ada, and COBOL all set aside reserved words; PL/I does not. Here are some confusing statements that are possible in PL/I:

```
IF IF=THEN THEN THEN=ELSE; ELSE ELSE=IF
IF IF THEN THEN=ELSE; ELSE ELSE=0;
```

The trend appears to be reserving all keywords. The only problem with this is that the unsuspecting programmer may unintentionally use a keyword in a language (like Ada) that has many keywords. The error message from the compiler about the resulting syntactically incorrect program may not direct the programmer to the true cause of problem.

There are other issues of syntax, some of which have caused great controversy. One issue is that of comments [7]. There are several ways to indicate comments in programming languages, including

1. a comment column, like in FORTRAN,

2. the rest of the line after a certain delimiter, like in many assembly languages, and `--` in Ada,

3. "`comment ...;`," like in ALGOL and SIMULA, and

4. opening and closing brackets, like "`/* ... */`" in C.

The relative virtues of these approaches are not infrequently discussed. We do not enter in any of these disputes, leaving to common sense and experience what is best.

We remain neutral by studying the tools to describe syntax: formal languages and grammars.

In particular, three mechanisms for describing formal languages are important to the design of programming languages: regular expressions, BNF, and attribute grammars. The next sections cover these topics.

2.2.1 Definition of language

A *formal language* is a set of finite strings of atomic symbols. The set of symbols is called the *alphabet*. Strings of symbols are written one symbol after another, just as one might expect. One string that should not be overlooked is the *empty string*. It is denoted by "". Some strings belong to a particular language, the others (if any) do not. The strings that belong to the language are sometimes called *sentences* or *words* of the language.

Here are some examples of languages over the alphabet $\{a, b\}$:

$$L_1 = \{a,\ b,\ ab\}$$

$$L_2 = \{aa,\ aba,\ abba,\ abbba,\ \ldots\}$$

We may choose to pick symbols for an alphabet that are composed of more than one sign. For example, we may include the keyword **begin** as a single element of an alphabet, although it obviously is made up of several letters of the English alphabet. The language L_3, defined below, is over the alphabet $\{\textbf{begin}, x, |, \textbf{end}\}$.

$$L_3 = \{\textbf{begin}\,x\,\textbf{end},\ \textbf{begin}\,x \mid \textbf{end},\ \textbf{begin}\,x \mid\mid \textbf{end},\ \ldots\}$$

The language L_1 is finite; it has just three strings belonging to it. The other languages are infinite. The reader must intuit the form of strings that belong to the language from the sequence of strings provided explicitly. One can see that more precise methods for defining languages are desirable than just using "$\ldots$". The next section takes up one such way.

2.2.2 Definition of regular expressions

Regular expressions were invented by the mathematical logician Stephen Kleene, and their first appearance was in a Rand Corporation report about 1950.

A *regular expression* over A denotes a language with alphabet A and is defined by the following set of rules:

1. Empty. The symbol $\emptyset$ is a regular expression, denoting the language consisting of no strings $\{\}$.

2. Atom. Any single symbol of $a \in A$ is a regular expression denoting the language consisting of the single string $\{a\}$.

3. Alternation. If r_1 is a regular expression and r_2 is a regular expression, then $(r_1 + r_2)$ is a regular expression. The language it denotes has all the strings from the language denoted by r_1 and all the strings from the language denoted by r_2.

4. Concatenation. If r_1 and r_2 are regular expressions, then $(r_1 \cdot r_2)$ is a regular expression. The language it denotes is the set of all strings formed by concatenating a string from the set denoted by r_1 to the end of a string in the set denoted by r_2.

5. Closure. If r is a regular expression, then r^* is a regular expression. The language it denotes consists of all strings formed by concatenating zero or more strings in the language denoted by r.

Note that the plus, dot, asterisk, the empty set symbol, and parentheses are part of the notation for regular expressions, not part of the languages being defined. Note also that the definition is recursive. In practice, the common rules of precedence are used to avoid parenthesizing regular expressions fully. If we take the alphabet A to be $\{a, b\}$, then $(a + b)^*$ and $(b^* \cdot \emptyset)$ are regular expressions.

The definition defines a structure, the syntax of regular expressions, as well as an associated set of strings. We can be formal and make the function explicit. We will call the function $\mathcal{D}$ for "denotes," and it maps regular expressions to languages.

$$
\begin{aligned}
\mathcal{D}[\![\emptyset]\!] &= \{\} \\
\mathcal{D}[\![a_1]\!] &= \{a_1\} \\
&\vdots \\
\mathcal{D}[\![a_n]\!] &= \{a_n\} \\
\mathcal{D}[\![(RE_1 + RE_2)]\!] &= \mathcal{D}[\![RE_1]\!] \cup \mathcal{D}[\![RE_2]\!]
\end{aligned}
$$

To describe the function $\mathcal{D}$ for concatenation we need an operator that concatenates two strings; i.e., a new string is formed by taking the characters of the second string and placing them immediately after the characters of the first string. The symbol we choose to denote this operator is "$\cdot$" (the centered dot). This is the same symbol we used to denote the concatenation of regular expressions. This is quite natural, since the operations are closely related. Any possible confusion can be avoided by looking at the operands. Here then is the case of concatenation of regular expressions:

$$
\mathcal{D}[\![(RE_1 \cdot RE_2)]\!] = \{x \cdot y \mid x \in \mathcal{D}[\![RE_1]\!] \ \& \ y \in \mathcal{D}[\![RE_2]\!]\}
$$

In the equation above, the "$\cdot$" on the right-hand side denotes concatenation of strings.

The final case of the definition of $\mathcal{D}$ requires an operation to concatenate a set with itself any number of times. The set S concatenated with itself i times is denoted S^i and is defined recursively as follows:

$$S^0 = \{""\}$$
$$S^{i+1} = \{x \cdot y \mid x \in S \,\&\, y \in S^i\}$$

Using this definition the final case of $\mathcal{D}$ can be given:

$$\mathcal{D}[\![RE^*]\!] = \bigcup_i (\mathcal{D}[\![RE]\!])^i$$

Using the definition of $\mathcal{D}$ it is possible to see that the regular expression $(a+b)^*$ stands for all strings of a's and b's, and $(b^* \cdot \emptyset^*)$ stands for all strings of b's.

Here are some examples of regular expressions used to define what sequences of ASCII characters make up a legal identifier. We let l stand for the regular expression denoting any lowercase or uppercase letter, and d stand for the regular expression denoting any decimal digit. The table below defines the syntax of identifiers in three languages.

Modula-3	$l \cdot (l + d + \_)^*$
ML	$l \cdot (l + d + \_ + ')^*$
Ada	$l \cdot (l + d)^* \cdot (\_ \cdot (l + d) \cdot (l + d)^*)^*$

In Modula-3 identifiers begin with a letter and continue with any number of letters or digits. In ML the apostrophe is a legal constituent of an identifier. In Ada the underscore character cannot appear twice in a row.

It is easy to decide if a given string belongs to a language defined by a regular expression. There are even programs that take a regular expression as input and produce a program to recognize the strings of the language. One such program is Flex, a widely available scanner generator.

Here is an example of Flex input that defines a regular expression for indefinite length identifiers. The first two lines define regular expressions for white space and letters. These regular expressions are combined to define a regular expression for identifiers.

```
LETTER [a-zA-Z_]
WHITE [ \\n\\t]

LETTER ([0-9] | LETTER)* : { /* return identifier token */ }
WHITE                    :   /* do nothing!              */
```

Figure 2.1 shows how the Flex program is used. The input, like the lines above, are examined by Flex and a program is produced that recognizes the longest possible occurrences of these regular expressions in an input stream of characters. In this

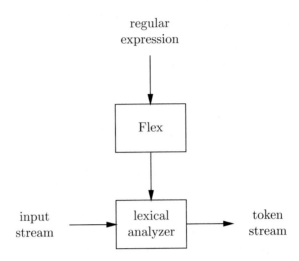

Figure 2.1: How Flex is used to recognize regular expressions

case a token is returned for every identifier, and white space is ignored. This Flex
program does not explicitly take care of the situation where the input characters
do not match one of the two cases.

What is the problem with regular expressions? Why don't we use them to
describe the syntax of programming languages? The major shortcoming of regular
expressions, as far as the description of programming languages is concerned, is that
bracketing is not expressible. Bracketing is indispensable. For example, arithmetic
expressions require opening and closing parentheses. Sequences of statements are
often bracketed by **begin**/**end** pairs. The next section gives another mechanism
for describing languages capable of handling bracketing.

2.2.3   BNF

A notation was invented to describe the syntax of ALGOL 60. This notation (and
some related variations) is known as BNF, for Backus-Naur Form in honor of John
Backus and Peter Naur, who developed the notation [10]. In the context of BNF
definitions we usually think of defining the sequences of tokens that make up the
language. By tokens we mean identifiers, numbers, keywords, punctuation, etc.
that constitute the language. These are the members of the alphabet of the formal
language being defined even if they themselves have a microsyntax, as identifiers
and numbers do. A BNF definition is used to specify that the sequence of tokens
say,

is legal in some language, but the sequence of tokens

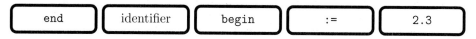

is not.

A BNF definition consists of a number of rules. Each rule has a left-hand side and a right-hand side. The left-hand sides are *syntactic categories*. A syntactic category is a name for a set of token sequences. The right-hand sides are sequences of tokens and syntactic categories.

$$\langle name \rangle \quad ::= \quad \text{sequence of tokens and syntactic categories}$$

There may be many rules with the same left-hand side. A token sequence belongs to a syntactic category if it can be derived by taking the right-hand sides of rules for the category and replacing the syntactic categories occurring in right-hand side with any token sequence belonging to that category.

The notation for the rules of a BNF definition typically contains the following meta-symbols:

- "::=" meaning "is defined to be,"

- "⟨ ⟩" to delimit syntactic categories, and

- "|" meaning "or."

Strictly speaking, the symbol for "or" is not necessary, but it is convenient for combining multiple right-hand sides for the same syntactic category.

Here is a simple BNF definition for nested **begin**/**end** pairs:

$$\langle nested \rangle \quad ::= \quad \epsilon$$
$$| \quad \text{begin } \langle nested \rangle \text{ end}$$

We use ϵ to "show" that nothing, no sequence of tokens, is on the right-hand side. Among the sequences of tokens belonging to the syntactic category "nested" are:

ϵ (the empty sequence)
```
begin end
begin begin end end
begin begin begin end end end
```

and so on. Notice that the definition of ⟨*nested*⟩ is recursive: it is used in one of its own right-hand sides.

Examples of BNF

Here is an example using BNF to describe the syntax of regular expressions over the alphabet $\{a, b\}$:

$$\langle RE \rangle \quad ::= \quad \emptyset \mid a \mid b \mid (\langle RE \rangle + \langle RE \rangle) \mid (\langle RE \rangle \cdot \langle RE \rangle) \mid \langle RE \rangle^*$$

This is to be read as:

> The syntactic category of regular expressions is defined to be either the symbol $\emptyset$, or the symbol a, or the symbol b, or an opening parenthesis, followed by a regular expression, followed by a plus sign followed by another regular expression, followed by a closing parenthesis, and so on.

The set of tokens used in this definition is $\{\emptyset, a, b, (,), +, \cdot, {}^*\}$. As we have already seen $(a + b)^*$ and $(b^* \cdot \emptyset)$ are regular expressions by the definition in section 2.2.2. Both these sequences of symbols belong to the language defined by the BNF description for $\langle RE \rangle$.

Here is another example of using the BNF notation. This time we use it to describe the ALGOL 60 **for** construct.

$$
\begin{aligned}
\langle \textit{for statement} \rangle \quad &::= \quad \langle \textit{for clause} \rangle \langle \textit{statement} \rangle \\
&\mid \quad \langle \textit{label} \rangle : \langle \textit{for statement} \rangle \\
\langle \textit{for clause} \rangle \quad &::= \quad \textbf{for } \langle \textit{variable} \rangle := \langle \textit{for list} \rangle \textbf{ do} \\
\langle \textit{for list} \rangle \quad &::= \quad \langle \textit{for list element} \rangle \\
&\mid \quad \langle \textit{for list} \rangle , \langle \textit{for list element} \rangle \\
\langle \textit{for list element} \rangle \quad &::= \quad \langle \textit{arith expr} \rangle \\
&\mid \quad \langle \textit{arith expr} \rangle \textbf{ step } \langle \textit{arith expr} \rangle \textbf{ until } \langle \textit{arith expr} \rangle \\
&\mid \quad \langle \textit{arith expr} \rangle \textbf{ while } \langle \textit{boolean exp} \rangle
\end{aligned}
$$

Here are some sample **for** statements in ALGOL 60.

for $i := j$ **step** 1 **until** n **do** $\langle statement \rangle$
A: B: **for** $k := 1$ **step** -1 **until** n, $i + 1$ **while** $j > 1$ **do** $\langle statement \rangle$

The BNF definition makes it clear that these are syntactically legal `for` statements. The meaning of these statements is quite another matter. The definition of ALGOL 60 itself was not clear about when loop variables were evaluated, tested, and incremented.

Variations on BNF

Several extensions to BNF have been proposed to to make BNF definitions more readable. Two popular extensions are square brackets for optional syntax, and curly braces for zero, one, or more instances. We call the formalism that uses these constructs *extended BNF*. Actually these extensions do not add to the expressive power of the formalism, just to the convenience (see exercise 2.8).

Here is an example from the syntax of Modula-3. The BNF definition for a list of statements is given below. The syntactic category ⟨*statement*⟩ is not given, but derives the usual variety of assignment and control statements. Notice that a list of statements can be empty.

$$\langle list\ of\ statements \rangle \quad ::= \quad \epsilon$$
$$| \quad \langle statement \rangle\ \{\ ;\ \langle statement \rangle\ \}$$
$$| \quad \langle statement \rangle\ \{\ ;\ \langle statement \rangle\ \}\ ;$$

The section grouped in curly braces can be omitted or repeated any number of times. A consequence of this formulation of a list of statements is that the semicolon is either a terminating symbol *or* a separating symbol. Both styles are accommodated by the syntax.

The Ada reference manual uses extended BNF. It also uses a different convention to distinguish syntactic categories from terminals. The syntactic categories are denoted by simple identifiers possibly containing underscores (with no angle brackets). Keywords and punctuation are in bold face. Here is an example of a block from the Ada reference manual §5.6.

$$block \quad ::= \quad [block\_identifier\ :]$$
$$[\mathbf{declare}\ \{declaration\}]$$
$$\mathbf{begin}\ statement\ \{statement\}$$
$$[\mathbf{exception}\ handler\ \{handler\}]$$
$$\mathbf{end}\ [block\_identifier]\ ;$$

Notice that the beginning identifier and the ending identifiers (if present) must be the same, but this property cannot be easily expressed using BNF, so the Ada reference manual resorts to English. In general it is not possible to express constraints like the following in BNF: a function must be called with the same number of arguments with which it was defined.

BNF notation is a slightly different form of what are called context-free grammars. These grammars and others were developed independently by Chomsky. We look briefly at the subject of grammars in the next section in order to have the necessary concepts and nomenclature for the discussion on attribute grammars.

2.2.4   Definition of grammar

A grammar is a 4-tuple $\langle T, N, P, S \rangle$, where T is the set of terminal symbols, N is the set of nonterminal symbols $T \cap N = \emptyset$, S, a nonterminal, is the start symbol, P are the productions of the grammar. A production has the form $\alpha \rightarrow \beta$ where α and β are strings of terminals and nonterminals ($\alpha \neq \epsilon$).

We say $\gamma\alpha\delta \Rightarrow \gamma\beta\delta$ (derives in one step) whenever $\alpha \to \beta$ is a production. We use $\alpha\overset{*}{\Rightarrow}\beta$ as the reflexive and transitive closure of the $\Rightarrow$ relation.

A string ω of terminals is in the language defined by grammar G if $S\overset{*}{\Rightarrow}\omega$. In this case the string ω is called a *sentence* of G. If $S\overset{*}{\Rightarrow}\alpha$ where α may contain nonterminals, then we say α is a *sentential form* of the grammar G.

The well-known Chomsky hierarchy relates the power of the different types of grammars. A completely arbitrary grammar defines the largest possible class of languages, called type 0 languages. It takes the full power of a Turing machine to determine if a string belongs to such a language. Attribute grammars and Post systems, formalisms we will study later in this chapter, are equally powerful.

	name	machine	grammar
0	unrestricted	Turing machines, Post systems	
1	context-sensitive	linear-bounded automata	$\|\beta\| \geq \|\alpha\|$
2	context-free	pushdown automata, BNF	$\alpha \in N$
3	regular	finite automata, regular expressions	$A \to \omega B,\ A \to \omega$

By restricting the form that productions $\alpha \to \beta$ can take, four distinct classes of formal languages emerge. Regular languages are those that can be defined using grammars with productions limited to at most one left-hand side nonterminal and right-hand sides consisting of nonterminals. Context-free grammars are restricted to productions with left-hand sides that are nonterminals. And context-sensitive grammars require that the left-hand side be longer than the right-hand side.

2.2.5   Parsing

From the point of view of implementing programming languages the interesting problem concerning grammars is how to efficiently recognize when a string is a sentence of a grammar. This is the *parsing* problem. Because it is of such practical importance, the parsing problem has been extensively studied [1].

Parsing of natural languages is difficult due to the ambiguity of language. Consider the following sentences used as examples by Terry Winograd [20]:

He saw that gasoline can explode.

The chickens are ready to eat.

Each sentence can be understood in two different ways depending on how the words or interpreted.

One well-known example of this sort of ambiguity has occurred in programming languages. It is the so-called dangling `else` problem. ALGOL 60 introduced the `if-then` and the `if-then-else` statements that naturally lead to an ambiguous grammar.

$$S \quad \to \quad \textbf{if } C \textbf{ then } S \mid \textbf{if } C \textbf{ then } S \textbf{ else } S \mid S'$$

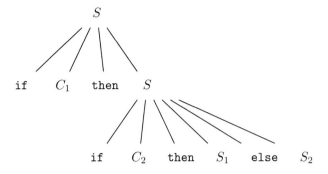

Figure 2.2: A parse tree for nested `if` statements

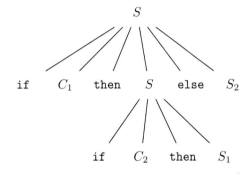

Figure 2.3: Another parse tree for nested `if` statements

A sequence of tokens of the form:

if C_1 **then** S_1 **else if** C_2 **then** S_2 **else** S_3

has only one interpretation. In contrast, the following string has two reasonable interpretations.

if C_1 **then if** C_2 **then** S_1 **else** S_2

These different interpretations of the same phrase are represented by the parse trees in figure 2.2 and in figure 2.3.

A formal definition of a parse tree for a context-free grammar is possible (see [12, 4]), but it is not illuminating. But the trees in the figures are suggestive. Each production used in the derivation of a string appears as a subtree in the diagram. The left-hand-side nonterminal appears as a node, and all the grammar symbols in the right-hand side of the production appear as children of this node.

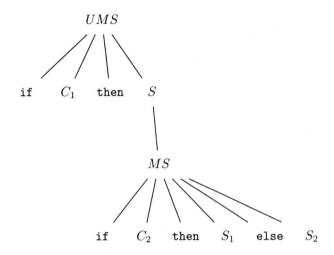

Figure 2.4: A parse tree in an unambiguous grammar for nested `if` statements

ALGOL 60 prohibited the nested `if` statement, as it could always be avoided by using the `begin/end` statement. PL/I and Pascal adopted the solution of matching the dangling `else` to the nearest unmatched `if` statement. This last solution can be formalized by the following unambiguous grammar:

$$
\begin{aligned}
S &\rightarrow MS \mid UMS \\
MS &\rightarrow \textbf{if } C \textbf{ then } MS \textbf{ else } MS \mid S' \\
UMS &\rightarrow \textbf{if } C \textbf{ then } S \mid \textbf{if } C \textbf{ then } MS \textbf{ else } UMS
\end{aligned}
$$

Here S is either a matched statement MS or an unmatched statement UMS. A S' is any statement other than an **if** statement. The parse tree in figure 2.4 is the only one possible for the example of nested **if** statements using this unambiguous grammar.

ALGOL 68 introduced the keyword **fi**, which also solves the dangling **else** problem. Ada solves the problem in essentially the same way with **end if**. The "terminating keyword" solution appears to be generally favored over the "nearest unmatched" solution in more recent programming languages.

2.3   Attribute grammars

A context-free grammar is a description mechanism for formal languages that is easy to comprehend. This accounts for its popularity (often in the guise of BNF) as a descriptive tool. On the other hand, there are a number of apparently simple languages that are not context-free, although they are seemingly quite close. Often such languages are best described by giving a context-free grammar and noting the exceptions or restrictions. One such example is the syntax of the Ada block statement that (slightly simplified) looks like this:

$$\langle block \rangle \quad ::= \quad \langle block\ identifier \rangle :$$
$$\textbf{begin}\ \langle statement \rangle\ \{\langle statement \rangle\}$$
$$\textbf{end}\ \langle block\ identifier \rangle\ ;$$

The Ada reference manual adds the restriction that the second block identifier must be equal to the first block identifier. Since this restriction is not difficult to express, it would be convenient if it were easily formalizable without resorting to context-sensitive grammars. One approach is to augment the context-free production above with an attribute OK that will be set to true if the production is used correctly. The constraint might be expressed in the following form:

$$\langle block \rangle.OK := \langle block\ identifier \rangle_1.value = \langle block\ identifier \rangle_2.value$$

We have used subscripts to distinguish between the two occurrences of identifiers in the rule.

In this section we will formalize this approach of augmenting a context-free grammar with attributes. This approach will attach additional information to each node of a parse tree. It will be useful to allow two types of information: information synthesized from the subtree below the node and information inherited from the subtree above the node (see figure 2.5). An attribute grammar definition will associate some functions to compute the value of the attributes with each production in the grammar. If these functions are carefully organized, it is possible to use the functions to decorate any parse tree of the grammar. In other words, these local definitions associated with each production of the grammar define the values of the attributes for all parse trees. Given the definitions and a parse tree, algorithms exist to compute the attributes of all the nodes in the tree.

We start with the underlying context-free grammar $G = \langle N, T, P, S \rangle$. For every production p in P, the number of terminal and nonterminal symbols in string α is denoted $n(p)$. If α is the empty string, then $n(p) = 0$. Sometimes we will find it necessary to consider each symbol of a production individually. For all productions $p \in P$ we write $A \to \alpha$ or

$$p_0 \to p_1\ p_2\ \cdots\ p_{n(p)}$$

Thus p_0 is the left-hand side nonterminal of the production p, and p_1 is the first terminal or nonterminal symbol on the right-hand side (if there are any), and so on.

An attribute grammar is a context-free grammar augmented by attributes and semantic rules. The set of attributes will be denoted At. For each attribute

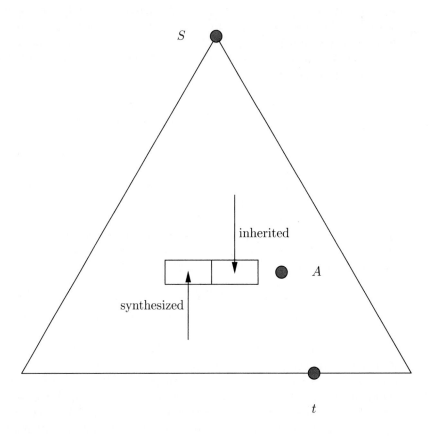

Figure 2.5: An arbitrary parse tree with attributes for A

$a \in At$ we associate a set of values $Domain(a)$. An attribute is just a name for a set of values. The set of attributes is divided into two disjoint classes, the inherited attributes In and the synthesized attributes Syn. (We have $At = In \cup Syn$ and $In \cap Syn = \emptyset$.) To every grammar symbol $x \in N \cup T$ we associate a set of attributes $At(x) \subset At$. We can think of $At(x)$ as additional information about the symbol x. And we set

$$In(x) = \{a \in At(x) \mid a \in In\}$$

$$Syn(x) = \{a \in At(x) \mid a \in Syn\}$$

We require that $In(S) = \emptyset$ for the start symbol S, since the start symbol can inherit no information. For all $t \in T$ we must have $Syn(t) = \emptyset$, for there is no structure beneath a terminal from which to synthesize information.[1] We could, without loss of generality, assume that $In(x)$ and $Syn(x)$ are singleton sets, for any set of attributes can be considered a single attribute.

Now consider productions. It is possible for the same attribute to be associated with different symbols appearing in the same production. For example, take the production $S \to AB$ in some appropriate grammar. We could have the case that S, A, and B all have the inherited attribute **int** associated to them, $In(S) = In(A) = In(B) = \{\textbf{int}\}$. Thus we cannot consider the set of attributes associated with all the symbols of a production without losing track of which attributes appear more than once. Even more confusing are productions that have a nonterminal appearing more than once, as in $S \to ASA$. Hence we introduce the notion of an *attribute occurrence* of a production p, which is an ordered pair of attributes and natural numbers $\langle a, j \rangle$ representing the attribute a at position j in production p. Naturally this notion is well defined only when we have $a \in At(p_j)$ and $0 \le j \le n(p)$. For a particular production $p \in P$ an attribute occurrence at j will be written $p_j.a$ when we wish to be completely formal. The set of attribute occurrences for a production p is defined as follows:

$$AO(p) = \{p_j.a \mid a \in At(p_j),\ 0 \le j \le n(p)\}$$

The set of attribute occurrences for a production is divided into two disjoint subsets. The *defined occurrences* for a production p is defined as follows:

$$DO(p) = \{p_0.s \mid s \in Syn(p_0)\} \cup \{p_j.i \mid i \in In(p_j),\ 1 \le j \le n(p)\}$$

The *used occurrences* for a production p is defined as follows:

$$UO(p) = \{p_0.i \mid i \in In(p_0)\} \cup \{p_j.s \mid s \in Syn(p_j),\ 1 \le j \le n(p)\}$$

To see what these sets mean intuitively, consider a parse tree in which the production p has been used. The set $UO(p)$ represents the information flowing into the node of the parse tree labeled p_0 and $DO(p)$ represents the information flowing out. Figure 2.6 shows the information flow in a parse tree in which the production $S \to AB$ has been used. The used attribute occurrences, the information flowing in, are $In(S)$, $Syn(A)$, and $Syn(B)$. These attribute occurrences are shaded in figure 2.7. The defined attribute occurrences, the information flowing out, are $Syn(S)$, $In(A)$, and $In(B)$. These occurrences are the ones shaded in figure 2.8.

For every attribute occurrence $v \in DO(p)$ we must have a defining semantic function $f_{p,v}$. The semantic functions define values for attributes in $DO(p)$ in terms of the values of the attributes in $UO(p)$. This is a function that produces a value for the attribute a from values of the attributes of $UO(p)$. We can make this precise

---

[1] Aho, Sethi, and Ullman [1] allow synthesized attributes for terminals, since they assume their attribute grammar system sits on top of a lexical analyzer that provides the attribute information for terminals. For example, the terminal "real" may have its value as an attribute.

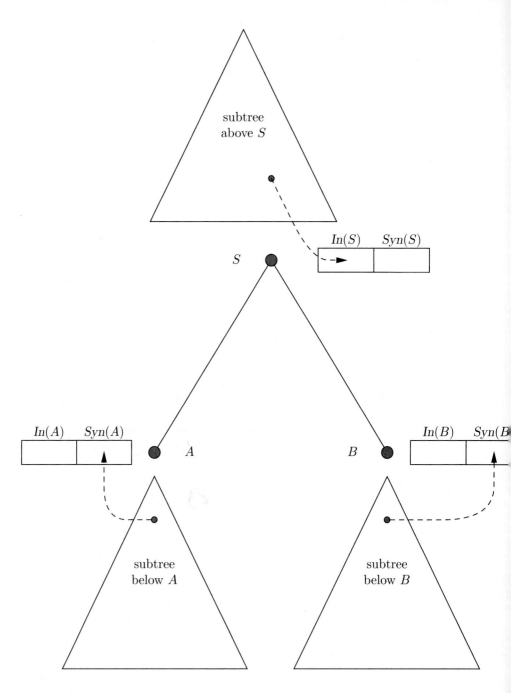

Figure 2.6: Information flow for the production $S \rightarrow AB$ used in a parse tree

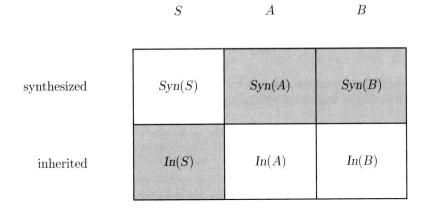

Figure 2.7: The used attribute occurrences for the production $S \rightarrow AB$ (the shaded boxes in the figure)

	S	A	B
synthesized	Syn(S)	Syn(A)	Syn(B)
inherited	In(S)	In(A)	In(B)

Figure 2.8: The defined attribute occurrences for the production $S \rightarrow AB$ (the shaded boxes in the figure)

by extending the notation of domains to attribute occurrences. For $v = p_j.a$ we set $Domain(v)$ to be $Domain(a)$. Thus the type of the semantic function $f_{p,v}$ is

$$f_{p,v} : Domain(v_1) \times \ldots \times Domain(v_k) \rightarrow Domain(v)$$

where $v_1, \ldots, v_k$ are attribute occurrences from the set $UO(p)$.

There is no requirement that the semantic function $f_{p,v}$ use all the attribute occurrences of $UO(p)$ in its computation. The set of attribute occurrences that it does use is called the *dependency set* of $f_{p,v}$ and is denoted $D_{p,v}$. The dependency set $D_{p,v}$ is a subset of $UO(p)$. It is entirely possible that $D_{p,v}$ is empty. In this case the value of the attribute must be computed without any other additional information, so the function $f_{p,v}$ is a constant.

Now we are in a position to define an attribute grammar as a context-free grammar with two disjoint sets of attributes (inherited and synthesized) and semantic functions for all defined attribute occurrences. Oddly, the language defined by an attribute grammar is usually of no interest, so we do not give a definition here. It is the values in the decorated parse tree that are usually of interest.

2.3.1   Binary digits example

Consider the following context-free grammar generating strings of binary digits. We have labeled the four productions p, q, r and s.

$$
\begin{aligned}
p : B &\rightarrow D \\
q : B &\rightarrow D\,B \\
r : D &\rightarrow 0 \\
s : D &\rightarrow 1
\end{aligned}
$$

We now give an attribute grammar based on the preceding context-free grammar. The purpose of the attribute grammar will be to define the value represented by the binary numbers generated by the context-free grammar. We begin by describing the attributes we wish to use. The nonterminal B will have synthesized attributes *pos* and *val* and the nonterminal D will have inherited attribute *pow* and synthesized attribute *val*. The two terminal symbols 0 and 1 will have no attributes. The attribute *val* will be used to accumulated the value of the binary numbers. The attributes *pow* and *pos* will be used to keep track of the position, and hence what power of 2, in the binary number we are currently considering.

	B	D
synthesized	*pos, val*	*val*
inherited	(none)	*pow*

From this information we can compute the defined and the used occurrences for each production. Take, for example, production q. The defined occurrences of q are the synthesized attributes of $q_0 = B$. These are $q_0.pos$ and $q_0.val$. To these attribute occurrences we add the inherited attributes of all the grammar symbols on the right-hand side. In this case there is only one: $q_1.pow$. The used occurrences of q are the remaining attribute occurrences, namely, $q_1.val$, $q_2.pos$, and $q_2.val$. For greater clarity, it would be convenient to write the attribute occurrence $q_0.pos$ as *B.pos*, but this would create a problem, since $q_2.pos$ would also be written *B.pos*.

$$
\begin{aligned}
p: \quad B \quad &\rightarrow \quad D \\
&\quad B.pos := 1 \\
&\quad B.val := D.val \\
&\quad D.pow := 0 \\[4pt]
q: \quad B_1 \quad &\rightarrow \quad D\, B_2 \\
&\quad B_1.pos := B_2.pos + 1 \\
&\quad B_1.val := B_2.val + D.val \\
&\quad D.pow := B_2.pos \\[4pt]
r: \quad D \quad &\rightarrow \quad 0 \\
&\quad D.val := 0 \\[4pt]
s: \quad D \quad &\rightarrow \quad 1 \\
&\quad D.val := 2^{D.pow}
\end{aligned}
$$

Figure 2.9: Attribute grammar definition of binary numbers

This is the very reason attribute occurrences were introduced in the first place. In order to get the best of both worlds, we agree to add subscripts from left to right to all grammar symbols that occur more than once. Using this convention we can write all attribute occurrences with the grammar symbol and not the position in the production. The following table uses this convention to list the defined and the used attribute occurrences for each of the four productions.

	Defined	Used
p	$B.pos$, $B.val$, $D.pow$	$D.val$
q	$B_1.pos$, $B_1.val$, $D.pow$	$B_2.pos$, $B_2.val$, $D.val$
r	$D.val$	$D.pow$
s	$D.val$	$D.pow$

To complete the description of an attribute grammar based on underlying context-free grammar and the attributes given above, we must give function definitions for the eight defined attribute occurrences. We give definitions in figure 2.9 that compute the value of the binary numbers in the language. The productions of the context-free grammar have been augmented by assignments that are meant to define the semantic functions. Every assignment defines one semantic function. Take, for example, this assignment associated with production q:

$$B_1.val := B_2.val + D.val$$

This is a definition of the semantic function $f_{q,v}$, where v is the attribute occurrence $B_1.val$ (or $q_0.val$). The definition of this function is necessary by virtue of that fact that $q_0.val \in DO(q)$, since $val \in Syn(B)$. Notice that attribute occurrences $B_2.val$ and $D.val$ are in $UO(q_0)$, since they are synthesized attributes occurring on the right-hand side. The assignment is to be read "the value of attribute $B_1.val$ is the sum of the values of $B_2.val$ and $D.val$."

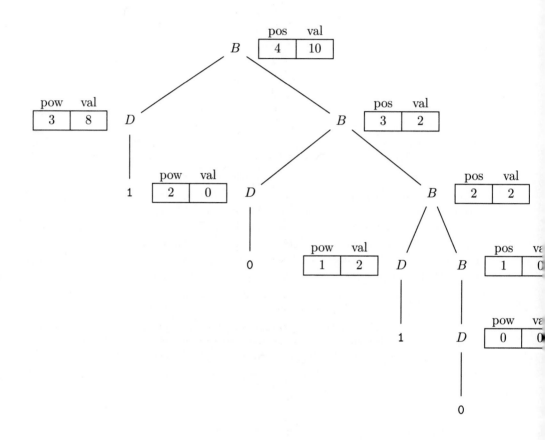

Figure 2.10: Evaluation of parse tree for 1010

This completes the description of the attribute grammar for binary numerals. Notice that we specified only how the values of the attributes are to be evaluated for each production. We did not give any mechanism to compute the values of all attributes for a given parse tree. In most cases this is easy. Figure 2.10 shows a parse tree for the string 1010 with the values for all the attributes.

2.3.2   Expression language example

Now we consider an example of evaluating expressions of a simple expression language. Here is the underlying context-free grammar.

$$S \;\rightarrow\; E$$

$$E \;\rightarrow\; 0 \mid 1 \mid I \mid \mathbf{let}\ I = E\ \mathbf{in}\ E\ \mathbf{end} \mid (E + E)$$

For example, 1+1 is an expression in the language, and its value is intended to be 2. Also,

```
let x=1 in x+x end
```

is an expression of this language, and its value is also 2. In this section we design an attribute grammar to give the definition of the value for all expressions in this language. Our attribute grammar to evaluate expressions will have two attributes: *val* a synthesized attribute computing the value of the expression, and *env* an inherited attribute containing the bindings formed by **let** expressions. The following table summarizes the choice of attributes.

	S	E
synthesized	(none)	*val*
inherited	(none)	*env*

The value of an expression will be an integer. Thus we take $Domain(val)$ to be the set of integers. An environment is not a simple data type, but a list of bindings. Each binding is name/value pair. We assume that we have some helpful functions that operate on environments. We need a function $LookUp$ that determines the value belonging to a name in some environment. We need a function $Update$ that adds a binding to the environment. Finally we need some initial environment, which we may take as the empty list of bindings.

Figure 2.11 presents the attribute grammar to compute the value of expressions. Notice that the environment is not some global data structure accessed by the rules, but is constantly passed around where needed. Programs that evaluate attribute grammars may try to avoid excessive copying. This approach has good potential as these "copying" productions are common, and large data structures, like the environment in this example or the symbol table in more realistic examples of languages, are common as well.

Figure 2.12 shows the result of computing all the attributes for a particular parse tree. We do not give any techniques for computing the values of the attributes. In general, this can be quite complex and involve many passes through the parse tree. For the simple **let** language a strategy can be easily devised. For some attribute grammars, usually pathological, it is not possible to compute the values of all the attributes. In the next section we examine this possibility.

$$
\begin{aligned}
S \quad &\rightarrow \quad E \\
&\qquad E.env := InitialEnv \\[4pt]
E \quad &\rightarrow \quad 0 \\
&\qquad E.val := 0 \\[4pt]
E \quad &\rightarrow \quad 1 \\
&\qquad E.val := 1 \\[4pt]
E \quad &\rightarrow \quad I \\
&\qquad E.val := LookUp(I, E.env) \\[4pt]
E_1 \quad &\rightarrow \quad \textbf{let } I = E_2 \textbf{ in } E_3 \textbf{ end} \\
&\qquad E_2.env := E_1.env \\
&\qquad E_3.env := Update(E_1.env, I, E_2.val) \\
&\qquad E_1.val := E_3.val \\[4pt]
E_1 \quad &\rightarrow \quad (E_2 + E_3) \\
&\qquad E_1.val := E_2.val + E_3.val \\
&\qquad E_2.env := E_1.env \\
&\qquad E_3.env := E_1.env
\end{aligned}
$$

Figure 2.11: Attribute grammar definition of the `let` language

2.4   Post systems

Grammars are examples of formal systems. They are useful in describing certain aspects of programming languages. Other formal systems are useful in the study of programming languages. For instance, the lambda-calculus is a formal system that is useful for models of programming languages. Deductive formal systems are useful in various capacities in reasoning about programming languages. Deductive systems are rarely presented as grammars; they are more often given as Post systems, named after Emil Post, who first used them. So before we finish the current topic of syntax, we examine Post systems.

2.4.1   Definition of Post systems

A *Post system* consists of a list of signs, a list of variables, and a finite set of productions. The signs form the *alphabet* of the canonical system. A *term* is a string of signs and variables, a *word* is a string of signs, and a *production* is a figure of the form

$$
\frac{t_1 \quad t_2 \quad \cdots \quad t_n}{t}
$$

where $t, t_1, \ldots, t_n$ $(n \geq 0)$ are all terms. The t_i are called the *premises* and t the *conclusion* of the production. A production without premises $(n = 0)$ is

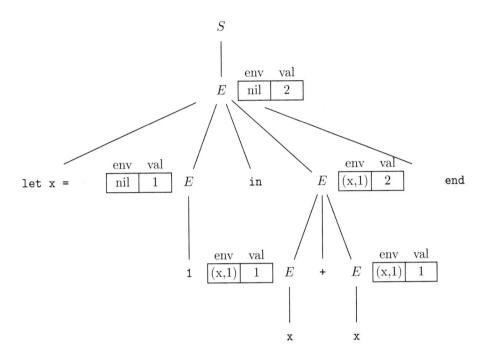

Figure 2.12: Evaluation of parse tree for `let x=1 in x+x`

called an *axiom*. An *instance* of a production is obtained from a production by substituting strings of signs for all the variables, the same string being substituted for all occurrences of one and the same variable.

Given a Post system, we shall define inductively the notion of a *proof* of a word.

1. An instance of an axiom is a proof of the conclusion.

2. If Pr_1, Pr_2, ..., Pr_n are proofs of a_1, a_2, ..., a_n, respectively, and

$$\frac{a_1 \quad a_2 \quad \cdots \quad a_n}{a}$$

is an instance of a production, then

$$\frac{Pr_1 \quad Pr_2 \quad \cdots \quad Pr_n}{a}$$

is a proof of a.

A term is *provable* in a Post system if we can find a proof of it. The set of words provable from a Post system forms the language derived by the system.

Sometimes it is necessary to consider the language derived by a Post system to be the set of strings from a subset of the signs that are provable.

2.4.2   Simple examples of Post systems

In this section we give some examples of Post systems.

The first example is tally notation. The signs we shall use are $\{N, |\}$. We need just one variable, x. There are two productions:

$$\frac{}{N} \qquad \frac{Nx}{Nx\,|}$$

Clearly this Post system derives the word N. Other words can be derived from N using the second production. An instance of the second production is:

$$\frac{N}{N\,|}$$

Here the variable x has been replaced by the empty string. This instance can be used in the proof of $N\,|$:

$$\frac{\overline{N}}{N\,|}$$

Hence, this Post system derives strings of the form $N\,|\,\ldots\,|$.

The following Post system makes use of the tally notation for natural numbers previously introduced. This Post system derives addition equations of the form $x + y = z$. It uses the variables x, y, and z, and the signs $\{N, |, +, =\}$.

$$\frac{}{N} \qquad \frac{Nx}{Nx\,|} \qquad \frac{Ny}{+y=y} \qquad \frac{x+y=z}{x\,|\,+y=z\,|}$$

The last two rules reflect the recursive definition of addition in terms of the successor function (concatenating $|$ to a string is like adding one). From this Post system correct equations are derivable like $2 + 2 = 4$:

$$\frac{\dfrac{\dfrac{\dfrac{\overline{N}}{N\,|}}{N\,\|}}{\dfrac{+\,\|=\|}{\dfrac{|\,+\,\|=\||}{\|\,+\,\|=\||}}}}{}$$

Other interesting Post systems can be built using just a few rules. The **MIU** system of Hofstadter [8] can be framed in terms of a Post system.

$$\frac{}{\mathbf{MI}} \qquad \frac{x\mathbf{I}}{x\mathbf{IU}} \qquad \frac{\mathbf{M}x}{\mathbf{M}xx} \qquad \frac{x\mathbf{III}y}{x\mathbf{U}y} \qquad \frac{x\mathbf{UU}y}{xy}$$

This Post system produces strings beginning with **M** and containing **I** and **U**. Is the string **MU** derivable (see exercise 2.22)?

The productions in all the previous examples had the following two properties:

1. each production has at most one premise, and

2. a variable occurs at most once in a premise.

Adhering to these two restrictions makes the Post system particularly easy to understand. Relaxing these restrictions appears to provide much more flexibility, namely, proof trees and pattern matching. Surprisingly, the restrictions do not diminish the power of Post systems as Post himself proved. A proof of this result can be found in a book by Marvin Minsky [16, Chapter 13].

Here is an example in which one rule has two premises.

$$\overline{N} \qquad \frac{Nx}{Nx\,|} \qquad \frac{Nx \quad Ny}{x+y=xy}$$

This Post system generates all the correct equations of the form $x + y = z$, just like a previous example. This system makes use of the fact that concatenation is addition for tally notation.

2.4.3 Connection with grammars

A Post system is nothing more or less than another formalism for an unrestricted grammar. Post systems live today in the formalism and terminology of formal logical systems. We will see it again in the typing rules of section 4.5.3 and the rules for Hoare logic in chapter 9.

Post systems are good for pattern matching—something that is difficult to capture easily in grammars. For example, the following axiom

$$\frac{xax}{xxx}$$

applies only to strings that have the pattern "x" appearing twice, separated by the terminal symbol a. Simulating this with grammars is not easy.

Here is a comparison of the terminology for formal systems and grammars:

formal system	grammar
alphabet	alphabet
well-formed formula	string
axiom	start symbol
rule of inference	production
theorem	sentential form

We leave it as an exercise (2.23) at the end of this chapter to prove the equivalence of these two formal systems.

2.4.4 A Post system for propositional logic

Propositional logic consists of a collection of propositions P, R, Q, etc., and statements about these propositional symbols using various connectives. For example, $\neg P$, $P \& Q$, $P \Rightarrow Q$.

The Post system uses the set $\{P, |, N, C, F, Th\}$ as signs and $\{x, y, z\}$ as variables.

We have two productions for propositions.

$$\frac{}{P} \qquad \frac{Px}{Px\,|}$$

The words of the form Px provable in the Post system are concrete representations of propositions. This set of words is particularly simple. It is just the set

$$\{P,\ P\,|,\ P\,||,\ \ldots\}$$

For formulas we have three productions.

$$\frac{Px}{FPx} \qquad \frac{Fx}{FNx} \qquad \frac{Fx \quad Fy}{FCxy}$$

The words of the form Fx provable in the Post system are concrete representations of formulas of the propositional logic. Strings of the form FNx, correspond to negated formulas and strings of the form $FCxy$ correspond to implications. The prefix notation is convenient, since no parentheses are required.

For theorems we have four productions. The first three productions correspond to three "axioms" of propositional logic.

$$\frac{Fx}{ThCCNxxx} \qquad \frac{Fx \quad Fy}{ThCxCNxy}$$

$$\frac{Fx \quad Fy \quad Fz}{ThCCxyCCyzCxz}$$

Curiously these productions are not axioms in the Post system because of the well-formedness conditions that are the premises of the productions. These conditions are needed to ensure that if a term has the form Thx then Fx is a formula. The last production corresponds to *modus ponens*.

$$\frac{ThCxy \quad Thx}{Thy}$$

Modus ponens is one of the classic laws of thought. But we can form whatever Post system we want. We can accept or reject this production as we judge most appropriate. This is reminiscent of Lewis Carroll's clever story "What the Tortoise said to Achilles." In this story, the Tortoise deftly leads Achilles down an infinite path of prior assumptions. In the end the exasperated Achilles remarks that logic will take the Tortoise by the throat and force it to accept the law of *modus ponens*. We give a sample proof of a word of the form *Thx*:

$$\frac{\dfrac{\dfrac{\dfrac{\overline{P}}{FP}}{FNP}\quad\dfrac{\overline{P}}{FP}}{FCNPP}\quad\dfrac{\overline{P}}{FP}\quad\dfrac{\dfrac{\overline{P}}{P\,|}}{FP\,|}}{ThCCCNPPPCCPP\,|\,CCNPPP\,|}\quad\dfrac{\dfrac{\overline{P}}{FP}}{ThCCNPPP}}{ThCCPP\,|\,CCNPPP\,|}$$

The law of *modus ponens* is used but once. The language defined by words of the form *Thx* cannot be described as easily as that of propositions and formulas. The next section gives some insight.

Semantics

The collection of words of the form *Thx* is not just a random collection of symbols. We are compelled to accept them as useful, because they appear to be true. But what does it mean for a string of the form *Thx* to be true? In this section we answer this question by giving the usual semantics to propositional logic.

We require, first, a notion of assignment. An *assignment* is a function σ from propositions to the set $\{\top, \bot\} = Bool$, or equivalently from the natural numbers to *Bool*. If $\sigma(i) = \top$, then P_i is a true proposition. The set of all possible assignments is denoted by Σ.

For convenience we associate with each proposition a nonnegative integer in the following manner:

1. $\mathcal{N}[\![P]\!] = 0$

2. $\mathcal{N}[\![Px\,|\!]\!] = \mathcal{N}[\![Px]\!] + 1$

So we can view assignments $\sigma \in \Sigma$ as functions from natural numbers to boolean values.

The semantics for propositional logic is given by a function $\mathcal{M}$ from Σ to *Bool*:

1. $\mathcal{M}[\![FPx]\!]\sigma = \sigma(\mathcal{N}[\![Px]\!])$

2. $\mathcal{M}[\![FNx]\!]\sigma = \top$, iff $\mathcal{M}[\![Fx]\!]\sigma = \bot$

3. $\mathcal{M}[\![FCxy]\!]\sigma = \top$, iff $\mathcal{M}[\![Fx]\!]\sigma = \bot$ or $\mathcal{M}[\![Fy]\!]\sigma = \top$.

We say that a formula Fx of the propositional logic is *valid* if $\mathcal{M}[\![Fx]\!]\sigma = \top$ for all assignments σ.

Theorem 1 *The term Thx is derivable in the Post system for propositional calculus if, and only if, the formula represented by Fx is valid.*

Proof. The three axioms are valid, and *modus ponens* preserves validity, so all derivable formulas are valid. The proof that all valid formulas are derivable is harder.   ∎

2.5   Abstract syntax

We will not be further interested in issues of concrete syntax. We wish to ascend to a higher level of abstraction. We will not be interested in how to parse constructs or how convenient the constructs are. These pragmatic issues are important to compiler writers and those concerned with user-friendliness; we want to focus on other issues and concepts. We take a view focusing on the underlying significance of the constructs. This perspective we call *abstract syntax* [14]. In this section we illustrate the perspective using a simple programming language and introduce constructors, a notion that appears in several contexts, like functors in PROLOG and patterns in ML.

2.5.1   Definition of abstract syntax

BNF notation and context-free grammars are used to describe a programming language in a *synthetic* manner. Namely, they describe how the various kinds of programs are built up from their parts. Sometimes it is useful to describe a language in an *analytic* manner. This is an *abstract* syntax description. It is abstract in that it is independent of the notation used to represent the language constructs. It only affirms that they can be built, recognized, and taken apart. Functions used to build the constructs are sometimes called *constructors*. Functions used to recognize constructs are sometimes called *recognizers*, and functions used to take constructs apart are called *destructors* or *selectors*. Note that the level of abstractness is subjective. What is abstract for one purpose may be too concrete for another. Different levels of abstractness may be possible.

2.5.2   Abstract syntax of `while` programs

Consider for a moment a simple programming language. The concrete syntax of this language is given by the following BNF definition.

$$
\begin{array}{lll}
W & ::= & I := E \\
W & ::= & \texttt{if } B \texttt{ then } W \texttt{ else } W \\
W & ::= & \texttt{while } B \texttt{ do } W \\
W & ::= & W \texttt{ ; } W
\end{array}
$$

We may not be interested in such concrete matters of syntax such as:

- whether the assignment operator is := or something else,

- whether the conditional statement has a terminating delimiter or not, or

- whether semicolons are separators or terminators.

But the definition using BNF requires that these issues be resolved.

Furthermore, notice that the grammar is ambiguous. There are two interpretations of the program:

$$\texttt{while } B \texttt{ do } W_1 \texttt{ ; } W_2$$

If we were building a parser, this would be a significant issue. Since we are not, we will ignore this issue and study others. In this case, a more abstract representation may be appropriate.

At some point we must choose some representation to proceed with the example. We can represent the constructs of the $\texttt{while}$ programming language with four constructors: *Assignment*, *Block*, *While*, *If*. The constructors have the following form:

$$Assignment(I, E)$$
$$Block(W_1, W_2)$$
$$While(B, W)$$
$$If(B, W_1, W_2)$$

where I represents identifiers, E expressions, B boolean-valued expressions, and W other $\texttt{while}$ program fragments. The ambiguous program above would be rendered in one of the following two ways:

$$While(B, Block(W_1, W_2))$$
$$Block(While(B, W_1), W_2)$$

and the program is unambiguous when constructed this way. Thus the representation we choose is not unlike a parse tree.

To manipulate the abstract representation of the programs we require selectors to access the subpieces of the constructed program: *Ident*, *LHS*, *FirstOfBlock*, *SecondOfBlock*, *WhileCond*, *WhileBody*, *IfCond*, *ThenStmt*, *ElseStmt*. These selectors extract the indicated parts of the program.

2.6   Exercises

2.1 Give a regular expression for the language $L = \{""\}$.

2.2 Is there any regular expression besides $\emptyset$ that denotes the completely empty language? Is there any BNF definition that specifies the completely empty language?

2.3 Give a BNF definition (do not use extended BNF) of a language of balanced parentheses. The only two tokens in the language are (and). For example, ()() and ((()))()((()())) are in this language, while (((() is not.

2.4 Give a BNF definition for the `for` statement in Ada, and Modula-3. (You may assume an appropriate syntactic category for expressions, statements, etc., in each language.)

2.5 The syntax of the `if` statement in Ada is as follows:

> if_statement ::= **if** condition **then** sequence_of_statements
>
> { **elsif** condition **then** sequence_of_statements }
>
> [**else** sequence_of_statements]
>
> **end if**;

The syntax is the same in Modula-2 and Modula-3 except that the ending keyword is simply **end**, not **end if**. Any number of **elsif** clauses are allowed to avoid deeply nested **if** statements when the program performs a series of tests, only one of which will succeed. The keyword **elsif** might be considered aesthetically repugnant. What would the consequences be of replacing **elsif** with the two keywords **else if**?

2.6 The set of valid BNF definitions is itself a context-free language. Give a BNF definition of the BNF notation (without the extensions). Be careful with the meta-symbols ::=, ⟨, ⟩, and |. You will have to adopt some convention to distinguish their use in the definition from their use in the language being defined. Carefully state your convention.

2.7 What happens to the white space (spaces, tabs, newlines, etc.) when a BNF grammar is used to recognize a legal program?

2.8 An extended BNF definition can be transformed to an ordinary BNF definition.

(a) Describe informally an algorithm to transform a definition given in extended BNF into ordinary BNF without "or."

(b) What result do you get with the following extended BNF definition?

$$\langle S \rangle \quad ::= \quad \langle A \rangle \,[\,b\,] \mid \langle A \rangle \,[\,\langle B \rangle\,]\,[\,c\,] \mid \langle B \rangle \,[\,a\{\,\langle A \rangle\,\}\,]$$
$$\langle A \rangle \quad ::= \quad a \,\{\,\langle B \rangle\,\}$$
$$\langle B \rangle \quad ::= \quad b$$

2.9 Convert the extended BNF definition of a block in Ada to an unextended BNF definition; i.e., one that does not use square brackets or curly braces.

2.10 (From Loeckx, Mehlhorn, and Wilhelm [12, page 79].) Give a context-free grammar for the language $L = \{a^i b^j c^k \mid i, j, k \geq 0\}$. Make this an attribute grammar with an attribute attached to the start symbol that is true iff $i = j = k$.

2.11 What if production q of the attribute grammar for binary digits in section 2.3.1 were changed from $B \to DB$ to $B \to BD$. Design an attribute grammar for this new set of production to define the value of a binary string of digits.

2.12 Suppose $A \to ABB$ is a production in the underlying context-free grammar of an attribute grammar. Furthermore, let the following attributes be associated with the non-terminals A and B: $In(A) = \{i\}$, $Syn(A) = \{s\}$, $In(B) = \{j\}$, and $Syn(B) = \{t\}$. Give the defined *and* used attribute occurrences of the production.

2.13 Give a context-free grammar for regular expressions. Make this an attribute grammar with a set-valued attribute attached to the start symbol that is the language denoted by the regular expression.

2.14 Consider the following incomplete attribute grammar with nonterminals A, B, C, and terminals d and e. The start symbol is A. The attributes *abel*, *boole*, *cantor*, *descartes*, *euler*, *fermat*, and *gauss* are assigned to these grammar symbols as indicated by the table below.

	A	B	C	d	e
synthesized	abel, boole	cantor	descartes	(none)	(none)
inherited	(none)	euler	fermat	gauss	(none)

The underlying context-free grammar has the following four productions labeled p, q, r, and s.

$$
\begin{aligned}
p: & \quad A   & \to & \quad Bd \\
q: & \quad B   & \to & \quad CA \\
r: & \quad B_1 & \to & \quad B_2 e C \\
s: & \quad C   & \to & \quad dA
\end{aligned}
$$

To complete this definition of an attribute grammar requires that the defined attribute occurrences be defined using the used attribute occurrences. For each production, list the defined attributes occurrences and list the used attributes occurrences.

2.15 Consider the following attribute grammar. Every nonterminal symbol of this grammar has a synthesized attribute m that can take the value of any positive real number.

$$
\begin{array}{lll}
S & \rightarrow & B\,p\,F \\
  &   & S.m := B.m + F.m \\
D & \rightarrow & a \\
  &   & D.m := 0.0 \\
D & \rightarrow & b \\
  &   & D.m := 1.0 \\
D & \rightarrow & c \\
  &   & D.m := 2.0
\end{array}
\qquad
\begin{array}{lll}
B_1 & \rightarrow & B_2\,D \\
    &   & B_1.m := 3 \times B_2.m + D.m \\
B & \rightarrow & D \\
  &   & B.m := D.m \\
F & \rightarrow & D \\
  &   & F.m := D.m/3 \\
F_1 & \rightarrow & D\,F_2 \\
    &   & F_1.m := (D.m + F_2.m)/3
\end{array}
$$

What is the value of the attribute m for the start symbol S in the parse tree of the string $bapcb$?

2.16 Complete the following attribute grammar description of **goto** programs S:

$$
\begin{array}{lll}
S & \rightarrow & L : \mathbf{skip} \\
S & \rightarrow & \mathbf{if}\ E\ \mathbf{goto}\ L \\
S & \rightarrow & A \\
S_1 & \rightarrow & S_2\ ;\ S_3
\end{array}
$$

where L are labels, E are boolean expressions, and A are basic actions. We are not further interested in the structure of L, E, and A. The problem is that the context-free grammar above permits jumps to undefined labels and permits unnecessary labels. You are to add attributes to the grammar to prevent this. Include a synthesized attribute *Check* of type boolean for the nonterminal S that is true if the **goto** program represented by S has no undefined labels and no unnecessary labels. (You need not detect multiply defined labels.)

2.17 Prove that an L-attributed grammar is absolutely noncircular.

2.18 (Aho, Sethi, and Ullman [1, page 79].) Answer the following two questions.

(a) Show that all binary strings generated by the following grammar have values divisible by 3.

$$
N \quad \rightarrow \quad 11\ |\ 1001\ |\ N\,0\ |\ N\,N
$$

(b) Does the grammar generate all binary strings with values divisible by 3?

2.19 Add two productions to the following Post system to derive strings of the form $n! = m$, where n and m are non-negative numbers in tally notation. If the string $n! = m$ is derivable, then m must be the factorial of n. The Post system has signs $\{N, |, \cdot, !, =\}$ and productions:

$$\frac{}{N} \qquad \frac{Nx}{Nx\,|} \qquad \frac{Nx}{x\cdot =} \qquad \frac{x\cdot y = z}{x\cdot y\,|= xz}$$

Give a derivation of $|||! =||||||$.

2.20 Consider the following Post system.

$$\frac{}{N} \qquad \frac{Nx}{Nx\,|} \qquad \frac{Nx}{x\cdot\ =} \qquad \frac{x\cdot y = z}{x\cdot y\,|= xz} \qquad \frac{x\,||\,\cdot y\,||= z}{z}$$

The signs of this Post system are $\{|, N, \cdot, =\}$ and the variables are $\{x, y, z\}$. Describe in fewer than ten words the set of words provable in this Post system that contain only the sign $|$ (i.e., ignore the words containing the signs $\{N, \cdot, =\}$).

2.21 Consider the Post system over the alphabet $\{^2, |, =\}$ given by the following two rules:

$$\frac{}{2 =} \qquad \frac{x^2 = y}{x\,|^2 = yxx\,|}$$

(a) Prove by induction (on integers) that for any integer i, the string

$$\underbrace{|\cdots|}_{i}{}^2 = \underbrace{|\cdots|}_{i^2}$$

is derivable from the Post system.

(b) Prove by induction that if the string

$$\underbrace{|\cdots|}_{i}{}^2 = \underbrace{|\cdots|}_{j}$$

is derivable in the Post system, then $j = i^2$.

2.22 Is **MU** derivable in the formal system **MIU** of Hofstadter? Why, or why not? (*Hint:* No, it is not derivable. Find some property possessed by all axioms of the system, but not by **MU**. Prove that all the inference rules preserve this property.)

2.23 Prove that any language definable by a Post system can be defined by an unrestricted grammar, and vice versa. Be sure to use the fact that any Post system can be written without multiple premises and with distinct variables in the premise. Also crucial is the fact that some of the signs in a Post system can be excluded from the terminal strings.

2.24 This question requires knowledge about inductive sets as can be found in Gallier [4]. The following is the BNF description of a simple language.

$$
\begin{array}{lcl}
\langle statement\rangle & ::= & \text{while } b \text{ do } \langle statement\rangle \\
\langle statement\rangle & ::= & \text{if } b \text{ then } \langle statement\rangle \text{ else } \langle statement\rangle \\
\langle statement\rangle & ::= & \text{if } b \text{ then } \langle statement\rangle \\
\langle statement\rangle & ::= & \langle statement\rangle \text{ ; } \langle statement\rangle \\
\langle statement\rangle & ::= & x{:=}e
\end{array}
$$

The symbols b, x, and e are terminals, as well as the usual keywords.

(a) Show that the set of strings derivable from the definition is an inductive set.

(b) Is the inductive set in part (a) freely generated or not?

(c) Prove *carefully*, i.e., exhibit clearly the structure of the proof, that all strings derivable from the definition have the same number or greater of **then** keywords as **else** keywords.

2.25 The question requires knowledge about inductive sets as can be found in Gallier [4].

(a) Explain how a context-free grammar with one nonterminal can be viewed as defining a language that is an inductive set.

(b) What is the importance of the restriction to one nonterminal?

(c) Explain how a context-free grammar with one nonterminal can be viewed as defining an inductive set of *derivations*.

(d) Are all such sets freely generated?

2.7   Bibliography

[1] Aho, Alfred Vaino, Ravi Sethi and Jeffrey David Ullman. *Compilers: Principles, Techniques, and Tools.* Addison-Wesley, Reading, Massachusetts, 1986, chapter 5.

[2] Ceruzze, Paul E. *Beyond the Limits: Flight Enters the Computer Age.* MIT Press, Cambridge, Massachusetts, 1989.

[3] Chomsky, Noam. *Aspects of the Theory of Syntax.* MIT Press, Cambridge, Massachusetts, 1965.

[4] Gallier, Jean H. *Logic for Computer Science: Foundations of Automatic Theorem Proving.* Harper & Row, New York, 1986.

[5] Gannon, John D. and J. J. Horning. "Language design for programming reliability." *IEEE Transactions on Software Engineering*, volume SE–1, number 2, June 1975, pages 179–191.

[6] Higman, Bryan. *A Comparative Study of Programming Languages*. American Elsevier, New York, 1967.

[7] Hoare, Charles Antony Richard. "Hints on programming language design." In *SIGACT/SIGPLAN Symposium on Principles of Programming Languages*, October 1973. Reprinted in *Programming Languages: A Grand Tour*, edited by Ellis Horowitz, 1987, 35–40.

[8] Hofstadter, Douglas R. *Gödel, Escher, Bach: An Eternal Golden Braid*. Basic Books, New York, 1979.

[9] Holt, Richard C. Design goals for the Turing programming language. CSRI–187, Computer Systems Research Institute, University of Toronto, August 1986.

[10] Knuth, Donald Ervin. "Backus Normal Form vs. Backus Naur Form." *Communications of the ACM*, volume 7, number 12, December 1964, pages 735–736.

[11] Knuth, Donald Ervin. "Semantics of context-free languages." *Mathematical Systems Theory*, volume 2, number 2, June 1968, pages 127–145. A corrigendum appears in volume 5, number 1, pages 95–96.

[12] Loeckx, Jacques J. C., Kurt Mehlhorn and Reinhard Wilhelm. *Grundlagen der Programmiersprachen*. Teubner, Stuttgart, 1986.

[13] McGettrick, Andrew D. *The Definition of Programming Languages*. Cambridge Computer Science Texts, volume 11. Cambridge University Press, Cambridge, 1980.

[14] McCarthy, John. "Towards a mathematical science of computation," In *Information Processing 1962*, edited by Cicely M. Popplewell, North-Holland, Amsterdam, 1963, pages 21–28.

[15] Martin-Löf, Per. *Notes on Constructive Mathematics*. Almqvist & Wiksell, Stockholm, 1970.

[16] Minsky, Marvin L. *Computation: Finite and Infinite Machines*. Prentice Hall, New York, 1967.

[17] Neumann, Peter G. "Some reflections on a telephone switching problem." *Communications of the ACM*, volume 33, number 7, July 1990, page 154.

[18] Popek, G. J., James J. Horning, Butler W. Lampson, James G. Mitchell and Ralph L. London. "Notes on the design of EUCLID." *SIGPLAN Notices*, volume 12, number 3, March 1977, pages 11–18.

[19] Richard, Frederic and Henry F. Ledgard. "A reminder for language designers." *SIGPLAN Notices*, December 1977, pages 73–82.

[20] Winograd, Terry A. "Computer software for working with language." In *Language, Writing, and the Computer*, W. H. Freeman, New York, 1986, pages 61–72.

[21] Wirth, Niklaus Emil. "On the design of programming languages." In *Information Processing 74*, edited by Jack L. Rosenfeld, North-Holland, Amsterdam, 1974, pages 386–393.

Chapter 3

Location, reference, and expressions

In this chapter we begin the examination of programming languages with *conventional* or *imperative* programming languages. Conventional languages are those that require the programmer to move data values around in storage locations in order to compute. This paradigm has dominated programming language design until recently. In this chapter we examine the basic constructs of the paradigm and some of the consequences.

3.1 Assignment

The dominant feature of conventional languages is the assignment statement. The assignment statement is the action that causes some value to be placed in a location. An empirical study of FORTRAN programs by Knuth published in 1971 [7] showed 51 percent of the punchcards had an assignment statement in them. The purpose of a program is to cause particular assignments to take place. All the other actions are just a means of reaching that goal. The action of assignment is apparently quite intuitive, as most people are comfortable with it.

Assignment only makes sense if there is some container that holds different things at different times. We use the term "location" for this container instead of the word "variable," because "variable" has a particular use in mathematics. Another possibility is "address," but that word has a hardware connotation.

3.1.1 Forms of the assignment statement

The assignment statement has several different forms in different languages. The following table shows most of the forms that the statement has assumed.

`A := 3`	Pascal, Ada, Icon, ML, Modula-3, ALGOL 68
`A = 3`	FORTRAN, PL/I SNOBOL4, C
`A <- 3`	Smalltalk, Mesa, APL
`J =. 3`	J
`3 -> A`	BETA
`MOVE 3 TO A`	COBOL
`(SETQ A 3)`	LISP

Most modern languages use the infix form for assignment with the asymmetrical `:=` operator. This distinguishs assignment from the ubiquitous "=" sign used in mathematics and programming languages for the test of equality.

3.1.2   Use-mention problem

It is possible in some languages to write `X=X+1`. This is troubling notation, because it seems to suggest that something can be equal to something different from itself. For this reason many languages have adopted asymmetric notation suggesting the action of transferring a value. But this does not change the fact that the `X` on the left-hand side means something different from the `X` on the right-hand side. This subtle distinction is similar to the use-mention problem in language.

Typically when we use a proper noun in a sentence, we use it to refer to some particular object, as in the following sentence:

Dallas is a populous city.

The word "Dallas" is used to refer to the city of that name. Now consider the next sentence.

"Dallas" has two syllables.

In this case the word "Dallas" does not refer to the city at all, but rather to the English language name of the city. In writing we make the distinction between use and mention of a word by enclosing the word in quotation marks when meaning of the sentence demands the word itself and not the thing to which it refers.

To understand programming languages one must be careful with the distinction between entities and names for these entities. Logicians, who have been studying formal languages for 100 years, are used to this. (See the passage from *Through the Looking Glass* by Lewis Carroll in figure 3.1.) Very rarely in informal speech do we make such distinctions, although in one case we do. In English we make the distinction between the word "number" and the word "numeral." Numerals are names for the Platonic entities, numbers. The situation in programming languages is complicated by the fact that there are names for objects and names for locations of objects.

Objects manipulated in computer programs written in conventional languages are schizophrenic. They have two attributes: location and value. The `X` on the left-hand side of the assignment `X:=X+1` refers to the location of X; the `X` on the

"You are sad," the Knight said in an anxious tone: "let me sing you a song to comfort you."

"Is it very long?" Alice asked, for she had heard a good deal of poetry that day.

"It's long," said the Knight, "but it's very, *very* beautiful. Everybody that hears me sing it—either it brings the *tears* into their eyes, or else—"

"Or else what?" said Alice, for the Knight had made a sudden pause.

"Or else it doesn't, you know. The name of the song is called *"'Haddocks' Eyes'*."

"Oh, that's the name of the song, is it?" Alice said, trying to feel interested.

"No, you don't understand," the Knight said, looking a little vexed. "That's what the name is *called*. The name really *is 'The Aged Aged Man'*."

"Then I ought to have said 'That's what the *song* is called'?" Alice corrected herself.

"No, you oughtn't: that's quite another thing! The *song* is called *'Ways And Means'*: but that's only what it's *called*, you know!"

"Well, what *is* the song, then?" said Alice, who was by this time completely bewildered.

"I was coming to that," the Knight said. "The song really *is 'A-sitting On A Gate'*: and the tune's my own invention."

Figure 3.1: The white Knight's song by Lewis Carroll

right-hand side refers to the value of X. We call the location attribute of an identifier the *l-value* and the value attribute the *r-value*, because we are so accustomed to having identifiers stand for their value on the right-hand side and for their location on the left-hand side [13].

Some languages explicitly distinguish between the l-value and the r-value. BLISS and ML are two such languages.

```
X := .X + 1    BLISS
X := !X + 1    ML
```

These languages have an explicit *dereferencing* operator that finds the contents of an l-value; in other words, given a reference to a value the operator yields the value. An l-value can be coerced to an r-value when necessary, as is the case in the right-hand side of assignments.

3.1.3   Assignment constructs

The updating assignment

Often the assignment statement is used to increment some value, as for instance in the assignment: $l := l + e$. Many languages provide a special notation for such assignments. Here are some of the forms of this type of assignment:

INC(l,e)	Modula-3
l += e	C
ADD e TO l	COBOL
l +:= e	ALGOL 68

The updating assignment is an example of the "principle of information preservation," since the useful fact that the l-value appears both on the left and right side of the equation is preserved. The compiler can generate code to evaluate the l-value once, which might result in considerable savings if the l-value computation were complex.

But the assignment $l := l + e$ is equal to l +:= e only in the absence of side effects. Compare A[f(x)]:=A[f(x)]+2 with A[f(x)]+:=2. If the function f computes different values for f(x), then these two assignments may have completely different results.

The multiple target assignment

Some languages permit more than one location to be given a value at the same time.

$$l_1, l_2, \ldots, l_n := e \quad \text{ALGOL 60, PL/I}$$

This is a minor convenience when initializing several variables to the same value.

The multiple assignment statement

Using this form of the assignment, the operation of swapping the values of two variables can be written x,y := y,x, saving the introduction of a temporary variable. This form of the assignment statement does not appear in programming languages that have actually been implemented. But it is often used in written descriptions of algorithms, because this form of the assignment can be given a clean mathematical semantics (see exercise 9.21). The semantics is noncontroversial when the expressions on the left-hand side denote different l-values. But consider the multiple assignment a[i],a[j] := 2,3 when $i = j$. This assignment has no obvious, unambiguous effect.

L-valued expressions

Most languages permit a wide variety of expressions to denote r-values, for example, x+2 or a[2*i]**2. We discuss these expressions in more detail in a subsequent section. Languages often have expressions other than identifiers for l-values, though often these are less common and come in a smaller variety than r-valued expressions. Clearly, every l-valued expression has an r-value, but not every r-valued expression has an l-value as the previous examples show.

The expression `a[i+1]`, like the identifier `x`, denotes both an l-value and an r-value. Besides array subscripting, record selection may be used in an l-valued expression, for instance, `r.f` and `a[j].f`. Some languages permit conditional l-valued expressions, as in:

```
(if i=3 then a[j] else x) := 2
```

In C++ and ML user-defined functions can be included in l-valued expressions. In the following example the function `f` returns an l-value. The type of the return value is `int&`, a reference to an integer.

```
// Example of l-value as result of function call in C++
int a[10];                    // declare an array
int& f(int i) {return (a[i]);}   // define a function f
f(5) = 17;                    // a[5] := 17
```

Here is an example in the programming language ML.

```
(*  Example of l-value as result of function call in ML   *)
val x = ref 1;              (*  declare a variable  *)
val y = ref 2;              (*  declare a variable  *)
fun f (n) = if (n mod 2)=0 then x else y;
f(3) := 4;                  (*  y := 4              *)
```

Again the type of the return value is `int ref`, a reference to an integer.

Two l-valued expressions may denote the same location, in which case they are called *aliases* for that location. A construct for aliasing exists in FORTRAN, namely, the `EQUIVALENCE` construct. This construct allows computer memory to be reused, something that is important when memory is scarce. Likewise aliases are purposely introduced with the `union` construct in C. But for the most part aliasing causes problems because it makes reasoning about programs difficult. And aliasing often arises unexpectedly when using pointers and in parameter passing.

3.2 Control

A great part of imperative programming is arranging the order in which assignment statements are executed to cause the desired values to be left at the appropriate addresses. A single programming language construct, the test-and-branch, is capable of controlling the flow of execution to all conceivable ends. The `goto` construct is a special case, an unconditional branch. In the typical computer architecture the program is a sequence of instructions stored in memory (as is the data). Nothing is simpler than implementing a branch, as it is a change in the next instruction to fetch. Since the underlying machine supports the operation it is not surprising that programming languages should contain a `goto` construct.

However, programming with `goto` statements is unstructured, because they reveal little about the programmer's intent. This was obvious from the beginning, as FORTRAN provided the first structured control flow construct, the `DO` statement. From it has evolved the `for` construct. The `for` construct has the following syntax in Ada:

```
for i in lb .. ub loop
    ⟨sequence of statements⟩
end loop;
```

This causes execution of the statements beginning with `i` equal to the lower bound *lb* through every value of *i* up to and including the upper bound *ub*. Because of the importance of arrays in imperative programming, the `for` construct is useful to indicate an action to perform on each element in the array. (In languages with concurrency it is sometimes possible to perform the action simultaneously on all elements of the array.) So the following form of the loop is a common idiom with benefits to the compiler and programmer alike.

```
for i in A'RANGE loop
    ⟨sequence of statements⟩
end loop;
```

In Ada the `RANGE` attribute yields a discrete subrange from the lower bound to the upper bound of an array. In Modula-3 the programmer would write:

```
FOR i := FIRST(A) TO LAST(A) DO
    ⟨sequence of statements⟩
END;
```

The loop index needs no declaration in Ada or Modula-3. And it is visible only within the loop construct.

Other structured control-flow constructs have emerged. The primitive test-and-branch `IF` statement of FORTRAN has evolved into the modern `if` constructs that textually delimit the alternative possibilities. The following is the syntax of the `if` construct in Ada:

```
if ⟨condition⟩ then
    ⟨sequence of statements⟩
elsif ⟨condition⟩ then
    ⟨sequence of statements⟩
else
    ⟨sequence of statements⟩
end if;
```

Closely related to the if construct is the case statement that chooses among several discrete possibilities. Most languages have such a construct. In C, programmers are sometimes caught unaware that a branch falls through to the next branch unless control is transferred explicitly out of the construct with the break statement.

Another common form of control is repeated execution until some boolean condition holds. If the test of the condition is at the beginning of the loop, then we have the while loop. In Ada it has the following form:

```
while ⟨condition⟩ loop
    ⟨sequence of statements⟩
end loop;
```

Some languages (not Ada) have loops with the test at the end. This is usually called a repeat/until loop. Both this and the while loop are special cases of the more general loop construct:

```
loop
    ⟨sequence of statements⟩
    exit when ⟨condition⟩;
    ⟨sequence of statements⟩
end loop;
```

In this Ada loop construct, control is passed to the end of the loop, if the condition ever holds. If the first sequence of statements is empty, then the loop is equivalent to the repeat/until loop. If the last sequence of statements is empty, then the loop is equivalent to the while loop (but the condition must be negated). In Ada several nested loops can be exited by an exit statement that names the outer loop. Such a general loop construct and exception handling (see section 5.5) make the use of goto unnecessary.

A letter to the *Communications of the ACM* by Dijkstra [2] touched off a furious controversy about the use of goto. Eventually, the widespread acceptance of structured control flow emerged to a level of near dogma. A satirical contribution to the elimination of goto's is the COME FROM [1]. The COME FROM can best be understood by an example.

```
10   J = 1
11   COME FROM 20
12   WRITE (6,40) J
     STOP
13   COME FROM 10
20   J = J+2
40   FORMAT (I4)
```

In this program, J is set to 1 by statement 10. Control then passes to statement 20 because of the COME FROM 10 and then to statement 12 because of the

COME FROM 20. The variable J is written and the program stops; J is equal to 3 at the end.

An important set of control constructs have been devised by Dijkstra around *guarded commands* [3]. A guarded command is a boolean expression followed by a statement or statements. The statements are executed only if the guard is true. If one of many guarded commands is chosen, then this is like an **if** statement. If the guarded commands are repeatedly chosen until none are true, this is like a **while** statement. The order of the guarded commands is irrelevant. If the guard of a statement is true, it could be chosen. If more than one guard is true, then one is nondeterministically selected.

The following example uses two guarded commands.

if $x \geq y \rightarrow m := x$
$[] \; y \geq x \rightarrow m := y$
fi.

This program fragments set m to be the maximum of x and y. If x is equal to y, then both guards are true, and either statement could be executed. But regardless of which one is executed m is set to the maximum. Should no guard be true in a **if/fi** construct, then the program fails or aborts.

The following program fragment computes the greatest common divisor of X and Y using a **do/od** construct. The guarded commands are repeated executed until all the guards are false in which case the program terminates normally.

$x := X; y := Y;$
do $x > y \rightarrow x := x - y$
$[] \quad y > x \rightarrow y := y - x$
od.

The program terminates when x is equal to y, and this is the value of the greatest common divisor.

3.3   Binding

The assignment statement is really an instance of a more general phenomenon of attaching various kinds of values to names. The association of a name to an attribute is called a *binding*. For example, the execution of an assignment statment binds a value to a location. Identifiers are bound to locations, types, and other attributes at various points in the translation of a program. To make matters worse, in many programming languages locations can be both names (things that get bound) and values (things bound to names). Furthermore, bindings happen at different and invisible points after the programmer submits a program for execution. In this section we look at some of the issues surrounding bindings.

The binding of names or identifiers to locations (and other attributes) is done by *declarations*. In ALGOL 68 a declaration may be very explicit. Here is an example of a declaration:

```
ref real x = loc real
```

The declaration is interpreted as: "A location able to hold a real number is created and a reference to it is given the name x." This declaration can, however, be abbreviated as `real x`, which is the syntax used in most programming languages. This declaration makes several bindings. The identifier x is bound to some location (known to the compiler, but not the programmer) and to the type `real`.

Binding times

Anyone that has written a compiler knows the confusion between all those things to keep track of now and all those things to generate code to take care of later. This is the difference between compile time and run time. *Compile-time* decisions are those made during the language translation (especially in the early phases), like whether the actual argument to a procedure call has the same type as the formal parameter. *Run-time* decisions are the choices made during the execution of the program, like where a value is equal to zero. Actually there are several decision making "times" we can distinguish. These times form a spectrum from early to late.

1. compile time

2. link time

3. load time

4. run time

Generally speaking, the later the binding, the more flexible the language, the earlier the binding, the more efficient the language.

Occasionally we speak of load time, when the program is actually placed into the memory of the computer. At this time all the hypothetical addresses used by the compiler are actually bound to physical locations in the computer. Even this is simplistic, as operating systems with virtual memory may move pages of virtual memory around in "real" memory even as the program executes. This does not have any impact (except in performance) on the execution of the program or on the creation of the program. Consequently, it does not influence programming languages. More pertinent is link time. All parts of the program may not be compiled at the same time. This is even encouraged by designing languages so that separate compilation is safe and efficient. Powerful libraries of precompiled programs can be available to enhance programming. The separately compiled pieces must be linked together and reconciled. It is possible to bring two correctly compiled pieces that cannot work together. It is necessary for language designers to address this issue by declaring what the expectations are and by designing interfaces. This is one of the main purposes of modules in programming languages. Modules are studied in section 5.6.

Program parts can be linked during program execution as well as before. This is convenient in keeping the size of programs small. The linker must know all the parts of the program that may be used, but it does not know which parts will be used. If the parts are brought in as needed, this could result in considerable savings.

Scope and extent

The *scope* of a name is the section of the program text in which the name has the attributes established by the declaration. (So more accurately we should speak of the scope of a *declaration*.) The scope of name is usually determined by the structure of the program. We defer further discussion of this point until we introduce blocks.

The *extent* of a location in memory is that period of program execution in which the location can be accessed by some name or expression in the program. The extent of a location is determined by its *storage class*. There are three major categories, often known by different names in different languages:

- static (C), own (ALGOL 68);

- local, automatic (C, PL/I), loc (ALGOL 68);

- dynamic, based (PL/I), heap (ALGOL 68).

FORTRAN (originally) used *static storage* for all variables. In static storage all identifiers are bound to locations whose extent is the entire life of the program. Today most languages offer the other storage classes, and static variables are discouraged. If the extent of a variable is the lifetime of the program's execution, then the scope usually is a large part of the program text, and this is bad because the programmer cannot understand parts of the program in isolation. However, a static variable whose scope is local to a procedure is sometimes used to recall state from call to call. The following C program counts the number of times the subprocedure f is called.

```
void f () {
    static int count = 0;   /*  initialize count (once) to 0    */
    count++;                /*  increment each time f is called  */
}
```

Because the scope of the declaration for count is entirely within the subprocedure f, it is not possible for another procedure to maliciously or inadvertently alter the value of count. Because the extent of the location allocated for count is static, all calls to f throughout the life of the program are counted.

Local storage appears in ALGOL-like languages. During the execution of the program, procedures are invoked and eventually terminate. The extent of the locations for the identifiers declared locally to the procedure is only for the lifetime of the procedure activation. The compiler must ensure that storage is allocated for all the local variables of a procedure whenever the procedure is invoked. This storage is typically reclaimed after the procedure exits.

Dynamic storage is allocated and deallocated as needed depending on the course of the program's execution. Such storage may be explicitly allocated and deallocated by the programmer. This is the case with `new` in Pascal, and `malloc` and `free` in C. Sometimes dynamic storage may be required by recursive data structures, like lists in LISP. Each the program creates a list the run-time system implicitly allocates the appropriate storage. Dynamic storage cannot be allocated and deallocated in conjunction with procedure activation like local storage, so the run-time system of a language with both local and dynamic storage usually allocates dynamic storage in a separate and formless area called the heap. When the extent of a location allocated on the heap is up, i.e., when the programmer can no longer access a location, there is no guarantee that the programmer has deallocated the storage. This results in garbage or inaccessible storage. In some languages, e.g., Modula-3, *garbage collection* is performed by the run-time system. In other words, all the inaccessible storage is collected for future allocation by the program.

3.3.1 Storage models

Declarations and assignments are actually quite similar operations as can be seen by a detailed analysis of their semantics. In this section we look more closely at assignment and distinguish various kinds of assignment operations.

Figure 3.2: The effect of the binding `let A = B`

We first look at what we call a "let" binding. Figure 3.2 shows the bindings of A and B. Before the new binding takes place, A is bound to the value 2 and B is bound to 3. The statement `let A=B` causes a new binding, which eclipses the previous binding to A, and the current bindings of A and B are both to the value 3. This sort of binding is appropriate for integers. Integers are an example of an immutable value. An *immutable* object is one that no operation can change.

Adding one to an integer does not change it; the result is simply another integer. On the other hand, we typically view the updating of an element of an array A or a field of a record as changing A, not creating a new array. Thus an array is a *mutable* object, an object that "has a state which may be modified by certain operations without changing the identify of the object" [9]. This requires another type of binding.

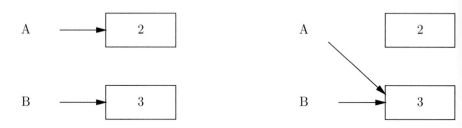

Figure 3.3: The effect of `A:-B` (pointer assignment)

If the program has bindings to mutable objects and changing one object effects the others, then these objects exhibit *pointer semantics*. This is illustrated in figure 3.3. This semantics is used, for example, in the assignment of objects in SIMULA (for this reason we use the SIMULA notation `:-` for this kind of assignment) and CLU. Of course, it is the semantics of pointers.

The semantics of the usual assignment operation in imperative languages is something different still. The semantics in which the object denoted by the target of the assignment is treated as a box. This is illustrated in figure 3.4 and is called *storage semantics*. Notice that if the object is immutable then pointer semantics is the same as storage semantics. If it is not possible to mutate the object, then the program cannot tell if assignment is effected by copying pointers or by copying the entire value.

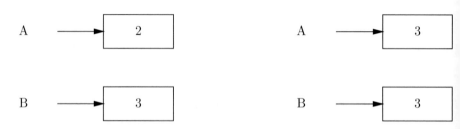

Figure 3.4: The effect of `A:=B`

The let binding has the most simple semantics. It can be modeled using the notion of an environment. An *environment* is a mapping from names to values:

$$\rho : \text{Ident} \rightarrow \text{Nat}$$

or, to be more concrete, from identifiers to natural numbers. An environment can be used to model the let binding in figure 3.2. Before the binding we have an initial environment ρ_0 such that $\rho_0(A) = 2$ and $\rho_0(B) = 3$. After the binding `let A = B` we have a new environment ρ_1 much like ρ_0 except that $\rho_1(A)$ now has the value $\rho_0(B)$. We denote this $\rho_1 = \rho_0[A \mapsto \rho_0(B)]$. This is called *value semantics*.

To model pointer semantics and storage semantics we need a more complex model. In the first place identifiers are no longer bound directly to values, but to locations. And, in addition to the environment, we need the *state*, which maps locations to their values:

$$\rho : \text{Ident} \rightarrow \text{Loc} \qquad \sigma : \text{Loc} \rightarrow \text{Nat}$$

where *Loc* is some set of locations. In this model it is easy to define aliasing. We say two identifiers A and B are *aliases* if $\rho(A) = \rho(B)$.

The assignment $A:=B$ in pointer semantics changes the environment, but not the state. If ρ_0 and σ_0 are the initial environment and state, respectively, then after the assignment the resulting environment and state are $\rho_1 = \rho_0[A \mapsto \rho_0(B)]$ and $\sigma_1 = \sigma_0$. So except for the addition of states, this transformation is the same as in value semantics.

The assignment $A:=B$ in storage semantics changes the state, but not the environment. If ρ_0 and σ_0 are the initial environment and state, respectively, then after the assignment the resulting environment and state are $\rho_1 = \rho_0$ and $\sigma_1 = \sigma_0[A \mapsto \sigma_0(\rho_0(B))]$. The particular assignment $A:=A+1$ has the effect of changing the state to $\sigma_0[\rho(A) \mapsto \sigma_0(\rho_0(A)) + 1]$.

Pointer semantics and storage semantics sometimes appear unexpectedly in programing languages. Both are used in the assignment to references in C++. Consider this example adapted from Ellis and Stroustrup (reference [3, page 80] in chapter 5).

```
void f () {
    int i=1, j=2;    // Declare two integer variables i and j
    int& r = i;      // Declare int reference and initialize
    r = j;           // Assign contents of j to r
}
```

Because the assignment `r=i` appears in the declaration, the language specifies that pointer semantics is to be used, and so `r` points to the same location as `i`. Because the assignment `r=j` is not an initialization, storage semantics is used. So the value referred to by `r` and `i` is changed to 2. The following table traces the effects of this C++ program.

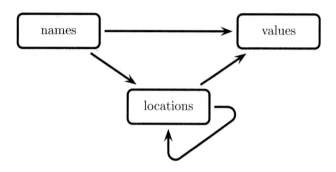

Figure 3.5: Storage model of a typical programming language

	int i,j	i=1; j=2	int& r=i	r=j
$\rho(\text{i})$	α_1	α_1		
$\rho(\text{j})$	α_2	α_2		
$\rho(\text{r})$			α_1	α_1
$\sigma(\alpha_1)$		1	1	2
$\sigma(\alpha_2)$		2	2	2

The initialization r=i changes $\rho(\text{r})$, the assignment r=j changes $\sigma(\rho(\text{r}))$.

As we mentioned, declarations are not unlike assignments. The ALGOL declaration we used earlier **ref real** x = **loc real** means $\rho[\text{x} \mapsto \alpha]$ where α is some new location for a real number. If x is initialized to r, the new state would be $\sigma[\alpha \mapsto r]$. A declaration is a binding of an identifier to a location and is similar to a binding in value semantics.

Modeling assignment is more comprehensible when locations are simply in the range of environments and the domain of states. But in languages with pointers, locations are also in the range of states. Pointers are discussed in the next section. This extra loop (see figure 3.5) greatly complicates understanding the bindings of names to values.

3.4 Pointers

When a storage location is not just denotable (by l-expressions), but can be a value (r-value) itself, then we have what is known as a *pointer*. Pointers may be declared statically, but the storage locations may be created and disposed dynamically under the control of the program. Pointers often have a special value, called nil, that represents a pointer that does not point to any valid location.

It is possible to create inaccessible locations with pointers: `new(p); p:=nil`. Here we request that the pointer p point to a new storage location, and then we lose all access to it by destroying the contents of p. Whatever storage location was obtained for the program is now unusable and said to be garbage. Inaccessible locations can be detected by the run-time system and returned to a pool of free storage locations. For this and other reasons some languages need garbage collection. And some language definitions require that an implementation perform garbage collection at run time.

Pointers are most often used to create data structures like lists, trees, and graphs. C. A. R. Hoare [4], among others, has argued:

> There are many reasons to believe that the introduction of references
> into a high-level language is a seriously retrograde step.

The alternative in many cases, is for programming languages to have provision for recursive data types.

To compare the two approaches we consider the data structure of a binary tree in ML, a language with recursive data structures, and in C, a language that relies on pointers. In ML the data type **tree** is defined in terms of itself.

```
datatype tree = empty | node of int * tree * tree
```

This declares that a **tree** may be the special element **empty** or (the vertical bar | separates the cases) it is a triple consisting of an integer and two trees.

In C the type definition might be rendered as:

```
struct tree {
    int n; struct tree *left; struct tree *right;
};
```

This is not recursive. The language C does not care if the identifier **tree** appearing in the structure has been, is, or will be declared. All pointers to **struct** types are treated alike.

The empty tree in ML is denoted simply by:

```
emtpy
```

In C the nil pointer to a tree can be written

```
(struct tree*) 0
```

However, the big difference appears in constructing a nonempty tree. In ML the expression:

```
node (3, empty, empty)
```

implicitly constructs a tree. In C the program must explicitly allocate storage on the heap and then assign the appropriate parts.

```
t       = (struct tree *) malloc (sizeof struct tree);
t->n    = 3;
t->left = t->right = (struct tree*) 0;
```

If that particular storage area is no longer needed, then the programmer must explicitly return it to the heap in C.

Pointers are nuisance because it is easy to make mistakes in the storage management of all the data structures that appear in any program of significance. In the next section we discuss storage insecurities. One reason that pointers are difficult to manage is that they are hard to reason about. One interesting contribution to the subject of pointers is considered in the section on collections.

3.4.1   Storage insecurities

Uninitialized variables may cause a problem. If accidentally used at run time, an uninitialized variable may cause the program to become unpredictable. In Ada, for example, such a program is allowed to do anything, perhaps accessing memory locations thought to be protected. Modula-3 requires that the initial value of a variable be of the appropriate type, even if an initial value for the variable is not provided. So the program will not halt abnormally (for this reason), but will execute with a value chosen by the implementation. Presumably an uninitialized variable is a mistake in the program and should be avoided.

A *dangling reference* is a pointer to a location that has potentially been used for another purpose. In other words, the extent of the location ended before all ways of accessing the location have ended.

Can you get a dangling reference in Pascal? Not in the original definition of the language. Dangling references were carefully excluded by avoiding any construct that could return a pointer to the unused portion of the heap. But some implementations of Pascal have such a construct.

```
var p,q: ^integer;
begin
    new(p);
    q:=p;
    dispose(p)
    (* q may point to garbage now *)
end;
```

Another way in which a dangling reference may be caused is through the implicit release of storage on the stack when a procedure activation record is popped. Any pointers that pointed to values stored on that portion of the stack now point to memory than may be reused for other purposes. This cannot happen in Pascal because all pointers point to the heap. But some languages allow pointers to values on the stack through the use of a construct to get the address of any value. C has & and, PL/I and ALGOL 68 have `ADDR`. Here is how an address operator can cause a dangling reference.

```
var p: ^integer;
procedure q;
    var i: integer;
begin
    p:= ADDR(i)
end;
```

When procedure `q` returns, the location allocated for `i` may be reused by another procedure's activation record. Yet the global variable `p` still holds the location of `i`.

3.4.2 Collections

Several languages have constructs to aggregate like pointers into what is called a *collection*. A collection is like an array. A programmer may very well want more than one collection of the same elements, if they are used for disjoint purposes. The similarity of collections and arrays is not accidental and reflects the formal semantics of mutable objects. By partitioning the heap into collections is possible to reason more accurately about pointers than would be the case when reasoning about the heap as one large mutable object.

The programming language Turing [5] is one language with collections. Turing is greatly influenced by Euclid, which also has collections. These languages were designed with program reliability and verification in mind. Figure 3.6 is a simple Turing program fragment that illustrates the use of collections. In it a singly linked list of records for names of persons is defined. The operation `new` creates an element of the given collection. In the program we allocate a name, set it to `Turing`, and append it to the list. The head of the list is kept in the global variable `first`. Then we free the item and try to access the element again. The compiler does not detect this illegal access, but at run time the error is caught.

If a new collection was defined in addition to `list`, even if it had the same structure, then the compiler would prevent the pointers to elements of one collection to be used to as pointers into the other collection.

The collection does not appear to be particularly useful. At least, it is not part of many languages. This may be attributed to the fact that pointers, unlike arrays, of the same type are most often used for the same purpose. Arrays of like type, say, arrays of integer values, are commonly used for different purposes, even in the same program.

```
% FIFO, singly linked list of names
var list: collection of
    record
        next: pointer to list
        name: string(30)
    end record

var first, last: pointer to list := nil(list)

% Usual operation of appending to end of list
procedure append (p: pointer to list)
    if first = nil(list) then
        first := p
    else
        list(last).next := p
    end if
    last := p
    list(p).next := nil(list)
end append

var item: pointer to list   % declare list element called "item"
new list, item              % allocate a list element called "item"
list(item).name := "Turing" % set the name field
append(item)                % add "item" to FIFO data structure
free list, item             % free the list element called item
list(item).name := "Neuman" % Turing detects error at run time
```

Figure 3.6: Turing program illustrating collections

3.5   Expressions

There are many types of values or objects that can be manipulated in a programming language. Usually a language has a rich collection of expressions that are used to denote these values. The simplist expressions are identifiers. Identifiers are the names of values. The syntax of identifiers differs slightly from language to language, but usually consists of alphanumeric characters beginning with a letter. Languages with modules often have names with a prefix that chooses the module followed by an identifier that selects the desired module component. These are called selected components in Ada. For example, `math.sqrt` refers to the procedures `sqrt` in the module `math`. In some language identifiers are syntactically divided into separate categories forming different *name spaces*. For example, in ML type variables are

365	typical integer
5.11E-8	typical real number in "scientific" notation
170_234	integer in Ada
TRUE	boolean value in Modula-3
'A'	typical character
$a	character in Smalltalk
#symbol	symbol or atom in Smalltalk
'atom	atom in LISP
"string"	typical string
5HHELLO	old "Hollerith" string in FORTRAN
[]	empty list in PROLOG and ML
()	unit in ML

Figure 3.7: Various literals in different languages

identifiers beginning with the apostrophe and so cannot be confused with the names of types that cannot begin with an apostrophe. In Haskell all types must begin with a capital letter.

In the rest of this section we look at ways other than names to represent values.

3.5.1 Literals

A *literal* is a constant expression whose value can be immediately determined. Literals come in a wide variety. Several literals from different programming languages are shown in figure 3.7. Some kinds are well known, others less common.

One unusual feature is the use of underscores in Ada numeric literals. Underscores are intended to be used like commas to separate groups of digits. Since the comma could be confused with the use of commas to separate different numeric literals, the underscore is used instead. It is possible to have several different literals representing the same integer. For example, 1E3, 1_000, 1000, and 1_0_0_0 all represent one thousand.

Numeric literals for non-whole numbers are a problem. There may be literals that do not have a corresponding representation on some particular machine or even any machine. Maybe two distinct (and conceptually different) literals have the same underlying representation. Possibly some representations do not have a corresponding literal available for the programmer's use. The IEEE floating-point standard requires a representation of a value obtained from invalid operations like division by zero. This value "NaN" is not a number, and the programmer does not need a literal representing it.

The programming languages Smalltalk, PROLOG and LISP have literals for atoms. These literals are identifiers—names—that stand for themselves and are like the members of a potentially infinite enumerated type.

3.5.2   Constants

A *constant* is an identifier whose r-value does not change at run time. If the value of a constant can be determined at compile time, it is said to be a *static constant*, sometimes called a *compile-time constant* or *manifest constant*. Static constants are useful to the compiler for constant folding and other optimizations.

Ada does not require that the values of constants be determined at compile time. The following example is from section 3.2.1 §20 of the Ada reference manual. Constant declarations in Ada differ from variable declarations with initialization only by the addition of the keyword `constant`.

```
LIMIT       : constant INTEGER := 10_000;
LOW_LIMIT : constant INTEGER := LIMIT/10;
TOLERANCE : constant FLOAT   := DISPERSION(1.15);
```

The value of the first constant can easily be determined at compile time, since its value is given as a literal. The value of the second constant can also be determined at compile time. This requires noting that `LIMIT` is a static constant, and performing a division at compile time. This can become a lot of effort for the compiler, especially when division by zero is taken into account. So, many languages have strict requirements on constant expressions. The value of a constant in Ada need not be an expression known at compile time, as in the third constant, `TOLERANCE`, which is computed by a user-defined function `DISPERSION`.

There are good reasons to have nonstatic constants. Assigning to an Ada constant (or passing an Ada constant as an `in out` or `out` parameter, see section 5.4.8) is flagged by the Ada compiler. This protects the programmer from accidently modifying values that are meant to be read-only. Writing and reading a program with constants is much easier than using literals throughout and much safer than declaring them to be changeable quantities.

The purpose of a constant as a read-only quantity is not identical with the purpose of declaring an identifier as a quantity known at compile time (e.g., one that the compiler can use in optimizations). We have already mentioned the initialization of constants with run-time values—a quite useful case. Another case that occurs occasionally in system programming is the association of a read-only identifier with a hardware address. Its value might be changed by the external world. In this case the compiler may not assume that the value does not change just because it determines that no user code can change it. In fact, the compiler may not even assume that the value it placed in a register is still valid for another reference, and so it is not an ordinary variable at all. The ANSI standard definition of the programming language C makes provisions for these possibilities by providing `const` and `volatile` as qualifiers to variable declarations.

	Ada		
and	1	†	conjunction
or	1	†	disjunction
xor	1	†	exclusive or
and then	1		conditional and
or else	1		conditional or
=	2	†	equality
/=	2		inequality
<	2	†	less than
<=	2	†	less or equal
>	2	†	greater than
>=	2	†	greater or equal
in	2		membership
not in	2		not member
+	3	†	addition
-	3	†	subtraction
&	3	†	concatenation
*	4	†	multiplication
/	4	†	division
mod	4	†	modulus
rem	4	†	remainder
**	5	†	exponentiation
abs	5	†	absolute value
not	5	†	negation

	Modula-3	
OR	1	conditional or
AND	2	conditional and
NOT	3	negation
=	4	equality
#	4	inequality
<	4	less than
<=	4	less or equal
>	4	greater than
>=	4	greater or equal
IN	4	membership
+	5	addition
-	5	subtraction
&	5	concatenation
*	6	multiplication
/	6	real division
DIV	6	integer division
MOD	6	modulus

† can be overloaded

Figure 3.8: Language-defined operators and their precedence

3.5.3   Operators

Functions that operate on constants, locations, and the values of other functions enrich the class of expressions in a programming language. Many such operators are built in to the language definition, or its particular environment. Figure 3.8 shows a complete list of language-defined operations in two languages. Operations with higher precedence bind more tightly.

Almost every language permits the programmer to define additional functions. Implementations of Ada and Modula-3 come with standard modules that expand the list of known functions. In Modula-3 no functions may be overloaded, so only the operators listed in figure 3.8 may be used in infix form. And they will have their language-defined interpretations. In Ada only the listed operators may be used in their infix form. It is not possible to change the "fixity" or precedence in Ada. But, like functions in general, these operators may be overloaded by the user. So the programmer must pick one of these operators in order to have an infix operator.

One class of operators present in some programming languages is used to control the evaluation of expressions. Consider the following program fragment:

```
if x<>0 and y/x < 1 then ... else ...
```

In Pascal, for example, this could lead to trouble when x has the value zero, for the language requires that the programmer assume the expression y/x may be evaluated. In Pascal the order of evaluation is left unspecified. Here is a selection from the Pascal report, page 21:

> The rules of Pascal neither require nor forbid the evaluation of the second part in such cases. This means that the programmer must assure that the second factor is well-defined, independent of the value of the first factor.

In Pascal the fragment above should be rewritten with two conditional statements. This could be considered verbose, so *short-circuit* operators are present in some languages that evaluate the second operand only if necessary.

Sometimes these operators are called **cand** and **cor**, for "conditional and" and "conditional or." The programming language Ada has the keywords **and then**, **or else**. ML has **andalso**, **orelse** written as one word each. C has **&&** and **||**. All these languages do not define the order of evaluation in expressions, but for the short-circuit operators these languages do define that the operand on the left-hand side is evaluated first and the operand on the right-hand side is evaluated only if necessary. Sometimes the programmer wants everything evaluated (for side effects); sometimes it is more convenient and more efficient to evaluate only as much as needed. In Ada the language definition permits the best of both worlds. If the implementation can determine that evaluation of an operand of a conditional expression has no effect on the program, then the evaluation of the operand may be omitted. Thus, the statement

```
if TRUE and y/x < 1 then ... else ... end if;
```

can be executed as if it were:

```
if y/x < 1 then ... else ... end if;
```

Of course, it is not possible in general to determine which operands need not be evaluated.

3.5.4   Expression languages

In some languages like C, APL, LISP and ALGOL 68 assignments are expressions (with side effects). The value of an assignment statement is typically the value of the right-hand side, so i=j=k=1 as in C sets all three variables to the same value.

Sometimes every command construct in the language has an r-value. An *expression language* is one in which "every executable statement or group of statements can (at least potentially) deliver a value" [14].

The comma operator in C ensures that side effects can be fit in as many parts of the language as possible. Here is part of the function `reverse(s)`, which reverses the string `s` in place, given in [6, page 63]:

```
for (i = 0, j = strlen(s)-1; i < j; i++, j--)
    c = s[i], s[i] = s[j], s[j] = c;
```

3.5.5   Referential transparency

We have noted that side effects, aliasing, and the order of evaluation cause subtleties that can lead the unwary programmer into making mistakes. These are examples of cases where the language does not reveal the true effect of its constructs. A language without contingencies in its meaning is said to be *referentially transparent*. The phrase "referential transparency" was first used by Whitehead and Russell in *Principia Mathematica* to compare the following two syllogisms:

All men are mortal;
Socrates is a man;
Therefore Socrates is mortal.

Everything Xenophon said about Socrates is true;
Xenophon said: "Socrates is mortal";
So Socrates is mortal.

The second syllogism is significantly different from the first. In the first the argument is irrefutable because of the force of its structure. The second is less satisfying because it depends on the nature of Xenophon's belief.

Willard Quine [12] uses the phrase slightly differently to refer to the substitutivity of identities. For example, in the sentence

Tully was a Roman.

the word "Tully" may be replaced by "Cicero," which was another name of the same man. But the phrase

William Rufus was so-called because of the colour of his hair.

becomes untrue if we replace "William Rufus" by another description of the same man, "King William II." Likewise, the sentence

Peter the Great was so-called because of his exploits.

becomes untrue if we replace "Peter the Great" by another name of the same man, "Ivan Ivanovitch."

We see the same idea reflected in Frege's *Über Sinn und Bedeutung*:

The meaning of a sentence must remain unchanged when a part of the sentence is replaced by an expression having the same meaning.

A language in which the context does not affect the meaning of expressions is said to be *referentially transparent*. Of course, this is not a precise statement, as context and meaning are both ill-defined. The notion of referential transparency is significant, as it captures the property taken for granted in mathematical language, that expressions denote the same values regardless of context. This property is violated in imperative programming languages because of the central importance of locations shifting values over time.

3.6   Exercises

3.1   (From reference [21, problem 4.3] of chapter 4.) Show that the multiple assignment $l_1, l_2 := e$ is not the same as the two assignments

    (a) $l_2 := e; l_1 := l_2$, or

    (b) $l_1 := e; l_2 := l_1$.

3.2   (From reference [21, problem 4.4] of chapter 4.) Is it always the case, say in Pascal, that the r-value of l after executing the assignment $l := e$ is equal to the r-value of e before executing the command?

3.3   Knuth [8] argues that in some contexts a program using goto's is better than one without. The following C program implements an in-order traversal of a binary tree.

```
int main (int argc, char* argv[]) {
    const int max = 100, empty = 0, nil = -1, root = 0;
    int St[max], top=0;     /* A stack implemented by an array */
    int A[] = {0,1,2,3,4,5,6};              /* nodes of tree          */
    int L[] = {1,3,5,nil,nil,nil,nil};  /* indices of left ...*/
    int R[] = {2,4,6,nil,nil,nil,nil};  /* and right subtrees */
    int t=root;
  l1:
    if (t == nil) goto l5;
    St[top++]=t; t=L[t]; goto l1;
  l2:
    t = St[--top];      /* decrement top before accessing stack */
    printf ("%d\n", A[t]);
    t = R[t];
    goto l1;
  l5:
    if (top!=empty) goto l2;
    return (0);
}
```

Write this program in C without using any goto's.

3.4 Consider the following ALGOL-like code fragment:

```
i := 1;
A [i+:=1] := A [i+:=1] + 2;
```

Describe several possible interpretations of the second assignment statement using storage semantics. You may assume that A[1], A[2], and A[3] have locations α_1, α_2, and α_3, respectively.

3.5 Consider the following Pascal fragment.

```
type A = 1..10;
procedure P;        (* Start a nested scope *)
   type B = ^A;
        A = record F1: char; F2: B; end;
   ...
```

(a) Which type does the name A in the declaration of B refer to?

(b) Describe the applicable scope rule in English.

(c) Propose a change to the language that makes scope rules easier to understand. *Hint:* Consider how mutually recursive procedures are declared in ISO standard Pascal (or in Ada).

3.6 What differences are there between the scope rules of Ada and Modula-3? Consider the following declarations:

```
declare                         VAR
      x: INTEGER := y;                x: INTEGER := y;
      y: INTEGER := 0;                y: INTEGER := 0;
   begin                          BEGIN
      -- x,y visible here            (* x,y visible here *)
   end                            END
```

3.7 Consider the following declarations in Modula-3 which are suggestive of a doubly linked list.

```
TYPE
    Elem = RECORD back, forw: REF Elem END;

VAR
     a := NEW (REF Elem, back := NIL, forw := b);
     b := NEW (REF Elem, back := a, forw := NIL);
```

(a) Do any of the declarations produce a compile-time error in Modula-3?

(b) What is wrong with the initialization of a and b?

3.8 Consider the following two declarations in ANSI C.

```
int const A;    /*  First declaration of A  */
const int A;    /*  Second declaration of A */
```

(a) What, if any, are the differences between the two declarations of A?

(b) Are these declarations legal in C++?

(c) What are the differences between const declarations in C++ and ANSI C?

3.9 Consider the following program in ANSI C.

```
struct ListStr { int n; struct ListStr *next; };

int main () {
    struct ListStr *a, *b;
    struct ListStr  u,  v;
    const struct ListStr *e, *f;
    struct ListStr const *r, *p;
    struct ListStr * const x, y;
    /* ... */
}
```

For each of the assignments below explain what the compile-time and run-time consequences are, if each of the following fragments were substituted into the program above.

(a) e = u;

(b) r = u;

(c) x = u;

(d) *e = u;

(e) *r = u;

(f) *x = u;

(g) a = b->next;

(h) *a = *(b->next);   a->n = 9;

(i) *a = *b->next;

(j) a->next = a->next->next;

(k) b->n = 6;

(l) a = u;

(m) `b = &u;`

(n) `a->next = &u;`

(o) `b->next = &b;`

(p) `a = e;`

(q) `a = x;`

(r) `e = a;`

(s) `p = p->next;`

(t) `*p = *r;`

(u) `y = y->next;`

(v) `y = &x;`

(w) `*y = *x;`

3.10 What is the next number in the sequence 8, 5, 4, 9, ...? What does this have to do with referential transparency?

3.11 (From [10].) Exhibit a declaration of a function e in an ALGOL-like language that takes no arguments and returns an integer value such that the conditional expression

```
if e=e then 0 else 1 end if;
```

evaluates to 1. What does this have to do with referential transparency?

3.12 (From [10].) Exhibit a simple context into which either of the phrases (1+2) or (2+1) can be substituted so that in essentially all programming languages the resulting substitutions yield different results. *Hint:* This is a trick question! What does this say about substitution?

3.7 Bibliography

[1] Clark, R. Lawrence. "A linguistic contribution to GOTO-less programming." *Datamation*, volume 19, number 12, 1973, pages 62–63. Reprinted in *Communications of the ACM*, volume 27, number 4, April 1984, pages 394–395.

[2] Dijkstra, Edsger Wybe. "Go to statement considered harmful." *Communications of the ACM*, volume 11, number 3, March 1968, pages 147–148. Reprinted in *Tutorial, Programming Language Design*, edited by Anthony I. Wasserman, 1980, pages 102–103.

[3] Dijkstra, Edsger Wybe. "Guarded commands, nondeterminacy and the formal derivation of programs." *Communications of the ACM*, volume 18, number 8, August 1975, pages 453–457. Reprinted in *Tutorial, Programming Language Design*, edited by Anthony I. Wasserman, 1980, pages 165–169.

[4] Hoare, Charles Antony Richard. "Recursive data structures." *International Journal of Computer and Information Sciences*, volume 4, number 2, June 1975, pages 105–132.

[5] Holt, Richard C., and James R. Cordy. "The Turing programming language." *Communications of the ACM*, volume 31, number 12, December 1988, pages 1410–1421.

[6] Kernighan, Brian W., and Dennis M. Ritchie. *The C Programming Language.* Prentice Hall software series. Second edition. Prentice Hall, Englewood Cliffs, New Jersey, 1988.

[7] Knuth, Donald Ervin.   "An empirical study of FORTRAN programs." *Software—Practice and Experience*, volume 1, 1971, pages 105–133.

[8] Knuth, Donald Ervin. "Structured programming with go to statements." *Computing Surveys*, volume 6, December 1974, pages 261–301. Reprinted in *Tutorial, Programming Language Design*, edited by Anthony I. Wasserman, 1980, pages 104–144.

[9] Liskov, Barbara H., Alan Snyder, Russell Atkinson, and J. Craig Schaffert. "Abstraction mechanisms in CLU." *Communications of the ACM*, volume 20, number 8, August 1977, pages 564–576.

[10] Meyer, Albert R. Puzzles in programming logic. MIT, November 1985.

[11] Nicholls, John E.   *The Structure and Design of Programming Languages.* Addison-Wesley, Reading, Massachusetts, 1975.

[12] Quine, Willard Van Orman. *Word and Object.* MIT Press, Cambridge, Massachusetts, 1960.

[13] Strachey, Christopher. "Towards a formal semantics." In *Formal description of languages for computer programming*, edited by Thomas B. Steel, Jr., North-Holland, Amsterdam, 1966, pages 198–220.

[14] Tanenbaum, Andrew S. "A tutorial on ALGOL 68." *Computing Surveys*, volume 8, number 2, June 1976, pages 155–190. Reprinted in *Programming Languages: A Grand Tour*, edited by Ellis Horowitz, 1987, pages 69–104.

Chapter 4

Data types

Expressions in a programming language represent the objects or values of computation. These values can be grouped according to their nature. At the machine level the bit representations of values must be manipulated by the correct operations. Usually there are distinct machine operations for integer and real arithmetic (possibly with various different precisions), bit-wise arithmetic, and character manipulation. A high-level programming language usually provides more abstract collections of values. Most of the time the abstract objects provided by a high-level programming language are the ones with which the programmer prefers to compute. But sometimes the programmer wants or needs to manipulate the words and bytes of the underlying machine. This is the case in systems programming and numerical analysis. The language designer may chose to allow direct and efficient access to words and bytes. The programming language C is a good example of this. Adding two numbers may actually be carried out by the execution of a single machine add instruction. Other languages may have special provisions for this access but try to segregate its destruction of abstraction from the rest of the program. All high-level languages try to give expression to objects at a more abstract level. For example, the programming language Ada requires that the implementation detect integer overflow. As a consequence, adding two numbers may require the computer to execute several instructions. Of course, this version of the integers is barely more abstract than the first, and hardware support for overflow is nearly universal. The programming language Scheme, on the other hand, typically has an "infinite" precision version of integers and this requires the language implementation to support a representation of integers that is likely unknown to the programmer.

But integers are just the tip of the iceberg. Arrays, records, lists, and graphs are all worthy objects of computation. A challenging aspect for programming language design is to find the right mechanisms to allow the programmer to create and manipulate objects appropriate to the problem at hand. Naturally, this must be accomplished while considering all the competing pressures of programming

	homogeneous	heterogeneous
static		record
dynamic	array	

Figure 4.1: Range of composite data structures

language design: simplicity, efficiency, generality, etc. This chapter looks at some of the issues concerning the organization of values into data types.

4.1   Kinds of types

The introduction of types opens up the possibility of static type-checking (i.e., at compile time). If a type is seen as an approximation to the value of some expression, it is especially useful that the programmer, and the compiler, know the approximation at compile time. At run time everything is known about a value, so an approximation is not useful. A language is said to be *strongly typed* if all type checking can be done at compile time. As a result there are fewer programming errors, and the compiler can produce better code for the language. Pascal was one of the languages that helped introduce this point of view of programming languages.

A language is said to be *type complete* [13] if all the objects in the language have equal status. In some languages objects of certain types are restricted. For example, in Ada it is not possible to pass objects of function types as parameters, but one can pass records and arrays. In Pascal, for example, it is not possible to declare variables of function types. Functions usually have inferior status in ALGOL-like languages; we will examine this issue more closely in section 5.2.1.

4.1.1   Structured and unstructured types

A *scalar type* is a type whose elements consist of indivisible entities. These types are sometimes called *base types* or *primitive types* or *unstructured types*. For example, integer, real, boolean, complex, character, string, atoms (formal symbols), and pointers (addresses) are unstructured types. A *structured type* is a compound type. For example, arrays, records, tuples, lists, sets, functions, and pointers (to objects of a type) are structured types.

There are two kinds of structured types: *heterogeneous*, whose elements are of different types, and *homogeneous*, whose elements are of the same type. Arrays have homogeneous elements, but dynamic (known only at run time) selectors, called indices, and records have heterogeneous elements, but static field selectors. The situation is depicted in figure 4.1. These two cases are natural because the compiler can determine the type of an element of the data structure. If the selection is dynamic, then the elements must be homogeneous because the compiler will not

ML	`{x:int, y:real}`
C	`struct {int x; float y;}`
ALGOL 68	`struct (int x, real y)`
Pascal	`record x: int; y: real; end`
Modula-3	`RECORD x:INTEGER; y:REAL END`

Figure 4.2: A record type in various languages

know which one will be selected at run time. But if the selection is static, then the elements need not be homogeneous. The case of homogeneous elements and static selection is uninteresting, since it is just a special case of records. The case of heterogeneous elements and dynamic selection is more interesting. Several languages without compile-time type checking have data structures of this kind. Examples include tables in Icon and association lists in LISP. These data structures associate a value of any type to a dynamically computable key. They abandon constant time access to the elements in favor of dynamically changing size.

In this chapter we will often look at types in the Ada programming language because of its several interesting features. The general form of a type definition in Ada is:

type identifier is type_definition ;

Some simple Ada type definitions follow:

```
type MONTH_TYPE is
  (Jan, Feb, Mar, April, May, June, July, Aug, Sept, Oct, Nov, Dec);
type INT_POINTER is access INTEGER;
type COORD is record x: INTEGER; y: FLOAT end;
type TABLE is array (1 .. 5) of INTEGER;
type MATRIX is array (INTEGER range <>, INTEGER range <>) of FLOAT;
```

The first type is an enumerated type of the months in the year. The second is a pointer type. Notice that pointer types are called access types in Ada and are defined using the keyword `access`. The next type is a two-component record type. (Figure 4.2 shows the same record type in several other languages.) The last two type definitions are array types.

The range of index values of an array is not part of the type and may be left unspecified as in `MATRIX`. This is expressed in Ada using the "<>" keyword. In this way the size of arrays need not be specified when writing subprograms taking arrays as arguments. In Ada a formal parameter may be declared to have type `MATRIX` and arrays of different sizes are possible arguments. These sorts of arrays are sometimes known as *flexible arrays*. Also the size of arrays need not be determined at compile time. The following is a block in Ada with an array whose size may be different each time the block is invoked:

ML	`int*real->bool`	`int->unit`
Haskell	`(Int,Float)->Bool`	`Int->()`
ANSI C	`int f (int x, float y)`	`void f (int x)`
ALGOL 68	`proc (int, real) bool`	`proc (int) void`
Modula-3	`PROCEDURE(x:INTEGER,y:REAL):BOOLEAN`	`PROCEDURE(x:INTEGER)`

Figure 4.3: Procedure types in various languages

```
A: declare
    u1: constant INTEGER := input (1,20);   -- get value from user
    u2: constant INTEGER := input (1,50);   -- get value from user
    m:  MATRIX (1..u1, 1..u2);  -- use previous def of type MATRIX
begin
    for i in m'RANGE(1) loop
        for j in m'RANGE(2) loop
        --  m(i,j)
        end loop;
    end loop;
end A;
```

Arrays whose size is not determined until block entry are said to be *semidynamic*. Ada does not, however, permit the array bounds to be changed during the lifetime of the array. Once the array m in block A is allocated, its size is fixed. Assignment between array types is possible, but only if the sizes are appropriate. ALGOL 68 has *dynamic arrays* or *flex arrays* introduced by the keyword `flex`. The size and, hence, the bounds of these arrays can be changed. The extra flexibility is rarely useful except that strings are often considered equivalent to dynamic arrays. A string might be a five-character array `"queue"` at one point in the program and then changed to a one-character array `"q"` by deleting all the vowels. Strings in Ada, however, are semidynamic arrays. A type for strings is predefined in the Ada language:

```
subtype POSITIVE is INTEGER range 1 .. INTEGER'LAST;
type STRING is array (POSITIVE range <>) of CHARACTER;
```

This has the consequence that strings have a length that is independent of the contents. Given the declaration

```
word: STRING := "queue";
```

the array `word` will always have five elements, i.e., `word'LENGTH` is 5. It is not possible to delete any positions, but, of course, the contents of any character could be changed.

Figure 4.3 shows how the types of two procedures would be expressed in ML, Haskell, ANSI C, ALGOL 68 and Modula-3. Procedural types play only a small role in most imperative languages. The programming language Ada does not have procedural types. The first example in the figure is of a function with two arguments that returns a boolean value. (C does not have a built-in type for boolean values.) The second example is of a procedure with one integer argument that does not return a value. Several languages have an explicit type for "no value." In ANSI C it is void. Functional languages do not have "no value." Every function must return some value, so in the cases where no value is significant, then a type with one value, unit in ML and () in Haskell, is used.

The functional languages ML and Haskell have procedural types indicated by the arrow operator "->." On the left-hand side of the arrow comes the type of the arguments; on the right-hand side comes the type returned by the function. Some languages have procedural types that enclose the types of the arguments in parentheses. ML uses the symbol * for the cartesian product; int*real is a pair whose first element is an integer and whose second element is a real number, int*real*string is a triple, and so on. Notice also that C, alone among the languages in figure 4.3, requires the name of the function to appear as part of the function type. This makes it impossible to express the type of a collection of similar functions.

4.1.2 Constructors of structured types

It is possible in Ada, and some other languages, to construct arrays and records all at once, and not just piece by piece. The expressions that use constructors are called *aggregates* in Ada. Syntactically aggregates are a parenthesized list of values.

Consider the following record type in Ada:

```
type Date is
    record
        Day:    INTEGER range 1 .. 31;
        Month: MONTH_TYPE;
        Year:   INTEGER range 0 .. 4000;
    end record;
```

Then the following are all legal record aggregates.

```
A: DATE := (4, July, 1776);                    -- positional association
B: DATE := (Day => 4, Month => July, Year => 1776);
C: DATE := (Month => July, Day => 4, Year => 1776);
D: DATE := (2+2, MONTH_TYPE'SUCC(June), 3552/2);
```

All four record variables are initialized with the same record value. In the first one the record is initialized in the order in which the fields appear in the type definition. In the next two the field names are used so that the order does not matter. The last record demonstrates that the aggregates are not necessarily static. They are constructors of records and their values may be computed at run time. It is also worth emphasizing that these record aggregates are expressions like any other; they are not confined to use as just initializers. They can appear wherever a record is needed—in an assignment, a return statement, and so on.

The following examples illustrate the use of Ada array aggregates in the initialization of some variables of type TABLE used previously.

```
A: TABLE := (1..5 =>0);
B: TABLE := (11, 14, 10, 16, 11);            -- positional association
C: TABLE := (5=>11; 1=>11; 2=>14; 3=>10; 4=>16);
D: TABLE := (1 | 3 | 5 => 2, others => 3)
E: TABLE := (1..5 => f)
```

In each case, a five-element array is allocated, and the individual elements are initialized. The components may be initialized by position or by index. In Ada, if one component is initialized, all components must be initialized.

4.2   Type insecurities

The purpose of a compile-time type system is to avoid interpreting the bits in computer memory incorrectly at run time without encoding the type of every object in those bits. This requires careful design of the language. For example, if a language permits untyped pointers, then this will prevent type checking at compile time. PL/I is a language in which there is a data type for pointers regardless of the type of the data element. The following PL/I program illustrates the problem.

```
POINT:  PROCEDURE OPTIONS (MAIN);
     DECLARE
          1 NODE BASED (P),
               2 INFO FIXED,
               2 LINK POINTER,
          1 STUDENT BASED (Q),
               2 NAME CHARACTER (30),
               2 GPA FLOAT,
          X POINTER;
     ALLOCATE NODE;    /* P points to new record object  */
     ALLOCATE STUDENT; /* Q points to new record object  */
     X = P;
     X->GPA = 3.75;    /* X points to a node, not a student! */
END POINT;
```

This program declares two records NODE, STUDENT, and a pointer X. The pointer X may point to either record; the compiler cannot tell which. So the compiler is unable to report that in the program above the access to the GPA field is incorrect as X points to a record of a different structure.

This problem does not occur in Pascal.

```
program Main (input, output);
    var p: ^integer;  q: ^real;  x: ^integer;
begin
    new (p);  new (q);  x := p;  x^ := 3.75 {  Illegal!  }
end.
```

Programmers must declare pointers *to* some particular type. Improper use of the pointers can be detected by the compiler, as in attempting to assign 3.75 to an integer pointer.

While Pascal was one of the first languages to espouse compile-time type checking, it is not possible to do all the type checking of Pascal at compile time. We will look at three constructs in the original definition of Pascal that prevent compile-time type checking.

4.2.1 Subranges

One difficulty in type checking in Pascal concerns subranges. The following program fragment illustrates the situation:

```
var
    wide: 1 .. 100;  narrow: 10 .. 20;  farout: 150 .. 300;
begin
    narrow:=farout;  wide:=narrow;  narrow:=wide
end
```

Because the variables `narrow` and `farout` come from disjoint subranges, no assignment between them is legal. The compiler can detect this. The assignment `wide:=narrow` is legal as the subrange for `wide` includes every value in the subrange 10..20. But the assignment `narrow:=wide` is a problem. If the value in `wide` is not between 10 and 20, then the assignment is illegal and otherwise it should be permitted. As there is no way the compiler can determine the value in the variable `wide`, it cannot check whether the assignment should be allowed or not.

In Ada the solution to the problem of subranges is to not introduce a new compile-time *type* for every subrange. There is no subrange type in Ada. Ada has a means for checking the value at run time to see whether it is in a certain range or not. See section 4.4.1.

4.2.2 Variant records

A variant record in Pascal is similar to a record. But it has a variant part that depends on a special component of the record, called the discriminant or tag. Here is a declaration of the variant record type `vrt`.

```
type
    option = (a,b);              (* enumerated type with two options *)
```

```
vrt = record case tag: option of        (* variant record type *)
    a: (f1: real);
    b: (f2: integer)
end
```

Variant records introduce another type insecurity. A variable of type `vrt` can be used as if it has an `f1` or an `f2` field without regard to the value of the `tag` field. And the value of the `tag` field can be changed at any time. Thus the programmer can access a value as if it were an integer when in fact it was stored as a real number.

```
var x: vrt
begin
    x.f1  := 12.65;
    x.tag := b;
    if x.f2 = 32 then (* ... *)
end
```

It is not possible to detect such breeches of type security at compile time in Pascal. It must be pointed out that this was a deliberate decision to permit access to the data representation of a value as whatever type desired. This is occasionally useful, and so some languages provide an explicit mechanism to circumvent the type system. Modula-3 isolates such potentially dangerous machinations in "unsafe" sections.

It is possible to have a strongly typed language with variant record structures that change dynamically. The language Euclid, which was conceived to improve Pascal, ensures type-safe access to variant records. In Euclid there are two ways of declaring a variable to have a variant type. First, one can specify the value of the discriminant when the variable is declared. This is like Pascal `new(p,t)`. No assignment to the tag field is possible after the variable is initialized, and the record is not variant at all. Second, one can specify the value of the discriminant to be "any." This recovers the advantage of changing the tag at run time. To be able to type check at compile time, a special form of the case statement was added to Euclid.

```
var x : vrt(a);
var y : vrt(b);
var z : vrt(any);
z := x;
case discriminating w = z on tag of   { implicit declaration of w }
  a => {  we can use w here as if it were declared vrt(a) }
  b => {  here we can use w as if it were declared vrt(b) }
end case
```

The `case` statement introduces a new identifier to refer to the variant record. Within the individual cases of the `case` construct it is safe to assume the identifier refers to the record with the indicated variant, because a run-time test was performed on the discriminant to determine which case to take.

The same result is achieved within an entirely different framework in ML. The comparable variant record type would be declared as follows:

```
datatype vrt = f1 of real | f2 of int;
```

In ML `f1` and `f2` are two constructors of the type `vrt`. The constructor `f1` constructs an element of type `vrt` given a `real` number, `f2` constructs one given an integer. A case analysis must be used at run time to determine if a value `x` has been constructed using `f1` or `f2`. ·

```
case x of f1 r => (* ... r:real ... *) | f2 i => (* ... i:int ... *)
```

In the one branch of the `case` construct `r` is a real number. The compiler knows this and the implementation ensures this by testing `x` at run time. In the other branch `i` is an integer.

Ada has variant records similar to Pascal. Like Pascal, and unlike Euclid and ML, it is possible for the programmer to write a program for which the compiler cannot tell if the access to the variant part will be legal at run time. But it is possible to program in a way that guarantees that the access to fields does not cause a run-time problem. Figure 4.4 is an Ada program that illustrates a number of different situations. The major difference in Ada over Pascal is that the direct assignment to the tag of a variant record is forbidden. The whole record must be assigned. This maintains the internal consistency of the data. But the compiler does not know in general which variant will be in a variable, and so run-time checks are still required.

4.2.3   Function types

A third problem with Pascal's type system concerns function types. Pascal permits one to pass procedures and functions as parameters to other procedures and functions. The method of specifying that a parameter is a function requires only the return type; it says nothing about the number or types of the arguments. Here are some procedure specifications in Pascal whose second argument is a functional parameter:

```
procedure P (x: integer;   procedure F;   y: real);
procedure P (x: integer;   function F: real; y: real);
```

Modern versions of Pascal require that formal functional arguments specify the number and type of their arguments. For example:

```
procedure P (x: integer;   procedure F(a: real; b: char);   y: real);
procedure P (x: integer;   function F(c: real): real; y: real);
```

```
procedure vr is
-- variant record for a mailing address (from N. Cohen, page 329)
type Mailing_Address_Type (US_Address: Boolean := true) is
    record
        Name, Street, City : STRING (1..30);
        case US_Address is
            when true =>
                State    : STRING (1..2);
                Zip_Code : INTEGER range 0 .. 99999;
            when false =>
                Country  : STRING (1..20);
        end case;
    end record;

Address1: Mailing_Address_Type (US_Address => true);
Address2: Mailing_Address_Type (US_Address => false);
Address3: Mailing_Address_Type;  -- no value required, type has default

begin
    Address1.US_Address := false; -- not legal; cf. Ada Ref Man 3.7.1(9)
    Address3.US_Address := true;  -- can't assign directly to discriminant

    -- legal, the compiler can determine that a run-time
    -- CONSTRAINT_ERROR will always be raised; cf. RM 5.2(4)
    Address1 := Address2;

    -- legal, but at run time if value of the discriminant in Address3
    -- is false, then must raise CONSTRAINT_ERROR
    Address1 := Address3;

    -- It is perfectly legal to copy any address into Address3.  No
    -- run-time error is possible, so no run-time check is necessary.
    Address3 := Address2;

    Address1.State := "TX";  -- legal, no run-time check is necessary
    Address2.State := "TX";  -- will raise run-time error; cf. RM 4.1.3(8)
    Address3.State := "TX";  -- run-time check is necessary in general

    Address3 := Address1;    -- another legal copy into Address3

    -- Below is the type-safe way to access variant record Address3;
    -- a good compiler can avoid issuing the run-time checks.
    case Address3.US_Address is
        when true  => Address3.Zip_Code := 76203;
        when false => Address3.Country  := "Canada              ";
    end case;
end vr;
```

Figure 4.4: Ada program with variant record

The following program [24] illustrates that meaningful programs can be written that would be illegal if procedure specifications are required.

```
program Main (input, output);
    procedure Print (x: integer; procedure P);
    begin
        if x=1 then P (2.1) else P (3.2, 9.3);
    end { Print };
    procedure Print1 (x: real);
    begin
        writeln ('Print1: x = ', x);
    end { Print1 };
    procedure Print2 (x, y: real);
    begin
        writeln ('Print2: x = ', x, 'y = ', y);
    end { Print2 };
begin { Main }
    Print (1, Print1);  Print (2, Print2);
end.
```

This program would run perfectly well. If the first argument to `Print` is one, then a procedure with one argument is called; if the first argument is two, then a procedure with two arguments is called. The unscrupulous programmer might, however, pass a one-argument procedure when the first argument is two. Since that compiler cannot know what values the first argument may have at run time, it cannot ensure that the formal parameter `P` will be called with suitable procedures. Therefore the compiler requires that the parameter specification be given for all formal procedure arguments. Once such a specification is given, programs such as `Main` are illegal because the formal procedure arguments are not used consistently.

4.3   Type equivalence

ALGOL and Pascal introduced structured types and user-defined types. It is time to consider just exactly what a type is, and, in particular, when types are equivalent. For example, the Pascal user manual [15] requires that assignment be between expressions which have "identical types." Also, formal parameters must have same types as the actuals in procedure and function calls. But what does identical mean? The Pascal manual does not give any definition. In fact, different Pascal implementations have used different definitions of equivalence.

Consider for a moment the following Ada-like program fragment [8]:

```
declare
    type BLACK is INTEGER;
    type WHITE is INTEGER;
    B: BLACK;  W: WHITE;  I: INTEGER;
```

```
begin
    W := 5;  B := W;  I := B;
end;
```

Which of the assignments are legal? Are types BLACK and WHITE identical? Are they the same as INTEGER? Answers in both the affirmative and the negative are reasonable.

We will distinguish between two broad categories of type equivalence: *name equivalence*, types with the same name, and *structural equivalence*, types with the same structure. Under the interpretation of structural equivalence, all of the previous assignments are legal. The types of the variables B, W, and I, regardless of what they are named, are all integers. Under the interpretation of name equivalence, none of the previous assignments are legal. Also there is some question about the type of the constant 5. If the name of the type of the expression 5 is INTEGER, can it be coerced to type WHITE?

We do not give a precise definition of name equivalence. Such a definition would have to take into account the notion of the scope of an identifier. A precise definition of scope is more trouble than it is worth. Consider the following program fragment in the syntax of Ada:

```
Outer: declare
    type BLACK is INTEGER;
    B: BLACK;
    Inner: declare
        type BLACK is FLOAT;
        A: BLACK;
    begin
    B := A;
    end Inner;
end Outer;
```

The type of A and B have the same name, namely, BLACK, but the type definitions occur in different scopes. Thus their types are different even though they have the same name. Under the interpretation of name equivalence, A and B do not have the same type.

Structural equivalence has problems of its own, as seen in this example [8] written in Ada-like syntax:

```
type T1 is record
    X: INTEGER;
    N: access T1;  -- pointer to T1
end record;
```

The type T1 is the type of a list of integers implemented using a link to the next element. The pointer N points to the data structure itself. This gives rise to several structurally equivalent variants, T2, T3, and T4, shown in figure 4.5.

```
type T2 is record              type T4 is record
    X: INTEGER;                    X: INTEGER;
    N: access T2;                  N: access T2;
end record;                    end record;

type T3 is record              type T5 is record
    X: INTEGER;                    N: access T5;
    N: access record              X: INTEGER;
        X: INTEGER;            end record;
        N: access T3;
    end record;                type T6 is record
end record;                        Y: INTEGER;
                                   N: access T6;
                               end record;
```

Figure 4.5: Structural equivalence of types with records and pointers

Record type T2 just renames T1 to T2. Under structural equivalence the name chosen for the type does not change the type, so T1 and T2 are structurally equivalent. Record type T3 looks different, but it has merely substituted the structure of T3 for the name T3. So it is structurally identical to T1 and T3. (It is not legal in Ada, however. Pointer types must be given a name; an expression is not permitted.) Record type T4 just substitutes names, so it, too, is equivalent to the others. Finally, the last two types may or may not be considered equivalent. If the order is not important (as in ALGOL 68 union types or ML records), then T5 is equivalent to the others. If the fields names are part of the structure (and usually they are), then T6 is not type equivalent to the others.

The previous examples suggests that testing structural equivalence is not easy. C uses structural equivalence, but when this becomes difficult, i.e., with **struct**, C uses name equivalence. C++ uses name equivalence (but bear in mind that **typedef** does not introduce a new type name, just a synonym). Name equivalence is sometimes favored because it is simpler and safer. (But see the interesting counter arguments in [1].) Consider:

```
type point   is record first, second: real end record;
type complex is record first, second: real end record;
```

These types are distinct in name equivalence, thus in the scope of

```
var p:point; z: complex;
```

both z:=p and p:=z are wrong. It may be just an accident that the two types are structurally similar. The programmer or programmers may have made these declarations separate because conceptually they represent completely different data structures. For this reason name equivalence is popular in modern programming languages.

On the other hand, name equivalence is not always clear, because the types of some objects do not have a user-defined or a language-defined name. For example, (from [21, page 191]) all the following types are structurally equivalent, but none of the types of the variables have names:

```
type
    T = record a: integer; b: char end;
var
    x,y: array [1..2] of record a: integer; b: char end;
    z:   array [1..2] of T;
    u,v: array [1..2] of record a: integer; b: char end;
```

In some versions of Pascal the types of x and y are equivalent and the types of u and v are equivalent, but no others are equivalent. This sort of name equivalence is termed *declaration equivalence* (called *occurrence equivalence* by some). Notice that if we declare names for all these anonymous types, one name for each distinct type expression, we get a different result.

```
type
    T = record a: integer; b: char end;
    Anon1 = array [1..2] of record a: integer; b: char end;
    Anon2 = array [1..2] of T;
var
    x,y: Anon1;
    z: Anon2;
    u,v: Anon1;
```

Here the types of x, y, u, and v are all equivalent.

We have switched to Pascal-like syntax, because the analogous declarations are syntactically illegal in Ada:

```
X: array (1..2) of record a: INTEGER; b: CHAR; end record;--illegal!
Y: record a: INTEGER; b: CHAR; end record;              --illegal!
```

The Ada reference manual (3.2 §9 and 3.3.2 §2) requires that the type of an object always be a name or a constrained array. In general, the language requires type names to be used except in a few situations. This avoids the problem of anonymous type names. On the other hand, the programmer may have to invent a few type names that may be otherwise unnecessary.

In a few cases an analogous situation can arise in the Ada programming language. In these cases the other sort of equivalence is used.

```
type T is record a: INTEGER; b: CHAR; end record;
X,Y : array (1..2) of T;
```

Ada interprets this declaration *exactly* as:

```
type T is record a: INTEGER; b: CHAR; end record;
X : array (1..2) of T;
Y : array (1..2) of T;
```

Each type expression has its unique anonymous name. Of course, the types of X and Y are compatible, one can assign one to the other in Ada, so the difference is not important, *except* if there are side effects in the evaluation of the array bounds.

The strict interpretation of name equivalence forces the programmer to add a few new type names, in order to ensure that certain variables have the same type. And there are other consequences. Consider this example from [17, page 278]:

```
declare
    N: INTEGER;
    type INDEX is INTEGER range 1..10;
    I : INDEX;
begin
    N := I;      -- illegal, different types
    I := I+1;    -- illegal, + is for type INTEGER not INDEX
end;
```

We may want an INDEX type to convey the intention that the value of the variable I will be a subset of the integers. Yet we may wish to use I as if it were an integer. Declaring I to be of type INDEX prevents its use as an integer.

Even the cautious type security that name equivalence provides can be circumvented in certain cases. Consider again the example of type **point** and **complex**.

```
declare
    type point   is record first, second: real end record;
    type complex is record first, second: real end record;
begin
    z := p            -- not type correct
    z.first := p.first; z.second := p.second;   -- same effect
end;
```

This illustrates the need for abstract types. We discuss this subject in section 5.6.

4.4 Types in Ada

The programming language Ada has chosen name equivalence, yet we have pointed out several problems with name equivalence. Ada has two innovative type constructs to avoid the problems mentioned in the previous section. These innovations are subtypes and derived types. We look at each of these constructs in turn.

4.4.1 Subtypes

The Ada solution to the subrange problem is to introduce subtypes, which are not really types at all. The example earlier would be written using subtypes.

```
declare
    N: INTEGER;
    subtype INDEX is INTEGER range 1..10;
    I : INDEX;
begin
    N := I;
    I := N;      -- possible run-time error, but type correct
    I := I+1;
end;
```

A subtype declaration in Ada does not introduce a new type at all. As far as the compiler is concerned INDEX is just another name for the *same* type INTEGER. The purpose of an Ada subtype is the run-time guarantee that the program will notice if the value is out of range.

Subtypes are a way of constraining the values that variables can take at run time. Here is another example:

```
type Month = (Jan,Feb,Mar,April,May,June,July,Aug,Sept,Oct,Nov,Dec);
subtype Fall is Month range Oct .. Dec;
M : Month;   F : Fall;
```

The variables M and F have the same type, but assigning June to F will cause the predefined exception CONSTRAINT_ERROR to be raised.

```
F := June;     -- type correct, but causes run-time error.
```

4.4.2 Derived types

A useful way of defining new types has been provided in Ada, called *derived types*. Derived types create an isomorphic copy of another type. For example, consider the following type definitions and variable declarations:

```
type Centimeters is new INTEGER;   -- type definitions
type Meters is new INTEGER;

Length1: Meters;                   -- variable declarations
Length2: Centimeters;
```

Expressions of these types: INTEGER, Meters, Centimeters, cannot be mixed together. That is, the expression

```
Length1 + Length2
```

is not legal in Ada given the declarations above. All three types have the same operations defined for their respective elements: plus, times, etc. A new operation for `INTEGER` will apply to elements of all three types. Thus the statement

```
Length1 := 5 + 2 * Length1;
```

is perfectly legal. Notice that the constants 2 and 5 in the example above are literals of type `INTEGER` and `Meters` and `Centimenters`. Functions and constants can be overloaded in Ada (Ada reference manual 3.5.4 §8). Only through *overload resolution* can the proper operation be found. In overload resolution the compiler chooses from among different alternatives for the code to run for some operation. This is different from coercion, where the compiler provides for the conversion at run time of one data type for another. Overload resolution is particularly difficult in Ada, since the user can overload operations as well. But good algorithms exist [2]. For example, we can define the functions to add meters and centimeters as follows:

```
function "+" (cm: Centimeters, m: Meters) return Centimeters is
begin
    return (cm + Centimeters(100 * INTEGER(m)));
end "+";

function "+" (m: Meters, cm: Centimeters) return Centimeters is
begin
    return (cm + Centimeters(100 * INTEGER(m)));
end "+";
```

These functions make use of explicit conversion routines (denoted by the type names) that exist among values of derived types (for conversion of derived types see section 4.6 §9 of the Ada reference manual). Implicit coercions are not allowed in Ada. In the first function we used `Centimeters`, which converts numbers of type integer to type centimeters. We could have also used:

```
return (cm + Centimeters(100 * m));
```

Here `Centimeters` converts numbers of type meters to numbers of type centimeters.

Not only can built-in, infix operators, like `+`, be overloaded in Ada, but any identifier can be overloaded by simply giving two functions definitions for the same identifier. The types of the two functions must be distinct (for otherwise the compiler could not tell which one was meant). The situation is similar in C++. But functions differing in only the return type may not have the same name. Here is a simple example of overloading the function `f` in C++:

```
int    f (int i1, int i2)    { return (8); }   // f 1
double f (int i1, double d2) { return (3.5); } // f 2
```

The previous definitions might be used in the following initializations of the variables x, y, and z:

```
int    x = f (1, 2);           // f 1
double y = f (1, 2.0);         // f 2
int    z = f (1.3, 2);         // f 1 (an implicit coercion to int)
```

It is possible in C++ as in Ada to overload the predefined infix operators.

4.5   Polymorphism

An important purpose of programming language design is to find the right abstractions that permit the clear expression of algorithmic ideas and their reuse in more complex constructions. It is tedious and error-prone to repeat the same algorithmic content with small variations—for example, writing a separate Pascal function for arrays of different size, or writing the C code first for linked lists of one type and again for another type. It ought to be possible to write the procedure once and generalize. There are various possibilities and intricacies that we now investigate under the subject heading of polymorphism.

If a subprogram or function can assume more than one type, it is said to be *polymorphic*. For example, the identity function

$$f(x) = x$$

is a good candidate for a function that could be considered to have more than one type. Any of the following Pascal declarations seem to suit it.

```
function f(x:int): int;
function f(x:boolean): boolean;
function f(x:real): real;
```

Although each function performs the same action, return its argument, one would be forced to write all three functions if the function were to be used on arguments of all three types.

Another good example is the length function. Here is the definition of the `length` function in ML:

```
fun length (x) = if null (x) then 0 else 1 + length(tl x)
```

The function does not take advantage of the structure of its argument x, except that it must know if the list x is empty (`null`) and it must be able to find the rest of the list (`tl`). From this we conclude the function should apply to all lists regardless of the type of the elements; e.g., lists of integers, lists of real numbers, lists of records, lists of lists, etc. Indeed, the type system and implementation of ML permit this.

In the next two sections we examine various aspects of polymorphism including generics in Ada and the ML type system. We conclude the discussion by looking at the polymorphic type system of the programming language Amber.

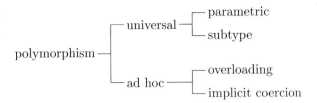

Figure 4.6: Kinds of polymorphism

4.5.1 Universal and ad hoc polymorphism

Polymorphism has been divided into *ad hoc polymorphism* and *universal polymorphism* [7]. Roughly speaking, ad hoc polymorphism is distinguished from universal polymorphism by having different code for the different manifestations of the operators. With ad hoc polymorphism the compiler chooses from an ad hoc and finite number of choices for the correct code to generate. With universal polymorphism the appropriate arguments to a procedure must be from a uniform (but possible infinite) collection of data structures. The same code works, regardless of the type of the arguments.

Ad hoc polymorphism (see figure 4.6) can be divided into two kinds: *overloading* and *implicit coercion*. Overloading occurs when the same name is used for different functions, like "+" in Ada. The function "+" is used for integer and real numbers, and, as we have seen, it can be used again for user-defined types.

Implicit coercion occurs when values of one type are routinely converted to another so that a value will have a type appropriate for the context. Many languages permit "mixed-mode" expressions like:

```
822.34 + 4
```

Such an expression is usually interpreted as requiring a conversion of 4 from type integer to type real. PL/I is infamous in this regard, as it converts nearly any type into any other type, sometimes with surprising results. Consider the expression 1/3 + 25. In PL/I this expression has the value 5.33333333333. Why? One-third is computed to 15 digits of precision, 14 to the right of the decimal point. Then 25 is coerced to the same precision, losing the most significant digit 2! This does raise an error in PL/I, but the default is to ignore it. This first appeared in print in [3], where it is given as a violation of a folk law of language design: "the law of least astonishment."

Coercion is less astonishing when there is a natural mapping to the target type. For example, if n is an integer and the context requires a real number, then there is an obvious mapping that loses no information. Such coercions are called

```
// Example of user-defined type conversion, Stroustrup 1986, p. 174
#include <stream.h>
class tiny {
    char v;
    int assign (int i)
        { return (v=(i&~63) ? (cerr << "range error",0) : i); }
public:
    tiny (int i)                    { (void) assign (i); }
    tiny (tiny& t)                  { v = t.v; }
    int operator =(tiny& t)         { return (v = t.v); }
    int operator =(int i)           { return (assign (i)); }
    operator int()                  { return (v); }     // tiny to int
};

int main () {
    tiny c1 = 2;
    tiny c2 = 62;
    tiny c3 = c2 - c1;      // c3 = 60
    tiny c4 = c3;           // range check avoided
    int i = c1 + c2;        // c1, c2 converted to int; i = 64
    c1 = c2 + 2 * c1;       // c1, c2 converted to int; range error
    c2 = c1 - i;            // c1 converted to int; range error
    c3 = c2;                // range check avoided
}
```

Figure 4.7: Type coercion in C++

widenings or *promotions*. Going from a real number to an integer loses information, and there is more than one reasonable inverse mapping—rounding and truncating, in particular. Such a coercion is called a *narrowing*. PL/I demonstrates that implicit narrowing leads to confusion.

A common coercion is dereferencing of l-values. Another one is *voiding* in which the value is discarded. This occurs when functions are called for their side effects and the return value is discarded. Modula-3 has an explicit construct in the language for this purpose: EVAL *expr*.

The language C++ has implicit type coercion. In C++ all coercions are for user-defined types. This is illustrated by the definition of the class **tiny** in figure 4.7. In this program **tiny** is a one-byte integer data type or class. (More about classes can be found in section 5.6.4.) In any context expecting an integer, a value of type **tiny** can be used because the user has declared a conversion function from integers to **tiny**. The compiler automatically inserts the function wherever needed.

4.5.2   Parametric and inclusion polymorphism

Universal polymorphism can be divided into two kinds as well, *parametric polymorphism* and *inclusion polymorphism*. These types of universal polymorphism differ in what facet of data structures they take advantage of. Parametric polymorphism takes advantage of the fact that data structures are built out of other data structures. Thus any value is built from many layers of constructors. Not all the layers may be relevant to a particular function. Inclusion polymorphism takes advantage of the fact that not all fields of records may be relevant to a particular function. In both cases the part of the data structure that is not relevant to a function is permitted to be filled by different structures with different types. The type system of a polymorphic language permits variation in the types of actual arguments only so far as it does not interfere with the working of the function. The key, then, to language design is to find type systems that permit wide variation that the compiler can still implement uniformly.

The "parametric" in parametric polymorphism refers to a language in which functions have *type* parameters as well as ordinary value arguments. Here is a hypothetical function definition of the polymorphic identity function:

```
function id [T] (x: T) = return (x)
```

The identifier T is a type parameter. Notice that the type of the value argument x depends on it. In this syntax we put the type parameters in square brackets and the value arguments in parentheses. To use the function id we must first apply id to a type and then to a value of that type. Here are two examples:

```
id [Int] (3)
id [Real] (2.3)
```

Presumably the first evaluates to 3 and the second to 2.3.

A form of parametric polymorphism can be achieved in Ada using *generics*. For example, the polymorphic identity function is defined as follows:

```
generic
    type Type is private;
function Id (X : in Type) return Type is
begin
    return X;
end;
```

The identifier Type is a generic parameter—not a predefined type. So this Ada program is just a template; it is not executable. To create a function that is executable, the template must be instantiated with a particular type, as in:

```
function IntId is new Id (INTEGER);
```

This definition can go anywhere in an Ada program that a function definition could go. To use the Ada identity function on values of another type, first the template must be instantiated again:

```
function FloatId is new Id (FLOAT);
```

The function `FloatId` can be used on values of type `FLOAT`.

The Ada mechanism for generics does not generalize well. Suppose one wants to write a function to compute the length of a list in Ada. We will need a record declaration something like:

```
type GenericList is record
    Element: Type;
    Next: access GenericList;
end record;
```

where `Type` is again a generic parameter. Where do we put this declaration? We cannot put it inside the definition of the length function because `GenericList` is the type for the function argument. We cannot put it outside the function because it depends on the generic parameter `Type`. We can put both the type declaration and function definition in a package (see section 5.6.1), but the problem has mushroomed out of proportion.

4.5.3   Milner-style parametric polymorphism

A form of parametric polymorphism has been made popular by the programming language ML. The type system is carefully designed so that all the type parameters are inserted by the compiler. The programmer need not worry about parameterizing the function by type or about instantiating the functions for some particular type. Parametric polymorphism is best developed after the introduction of lambda expressions (chapter 7) and unification (section 6.4). Nevertheless, in this section we introduce a method for carefully defining what the type of an expression is. This is not a simple matter in the case of polymorphism, because expressions can have more than one type. This method uses Post systems.

We examine a much simplified programming language based on ML. For the sake of concreteness we call this language mini-ML. The type system of mini-ML is given by the following BNF definition:

$$\begin{array}{rcl}
\langle type \rangle & ::= & \langle type\ variable \rangle \\
& | & \texttt{int} \\
& | & \texttt{bool} \\
& | & \langle type \rangle \texttt{ -> } \langle type \rangle
\end{array} \tag{4.1}$$

Besides the two base types `int` and `bool`, the type system includes type variables. For type variables we will use the identifiers `'a` and `'b`. The type system also includes the type of functions indicated by the arrow `->` between the range and the domain. The mini-ML language itself has four constructs:

$$\begin{array}{rcl}
\langle expr \rangle & ::= & \langle identifier \rangle \\
& | & (\texttt{fn}\ \langle identifier \rangle\ \texttt{=>}\ \langle expr \rangle) \\
& | & \langle expr \rangle\ \langle expr \rangle \\
& | & \texttt{if}\ \langle expr \rangle\ \texttt{then}\ \langle expr \rangle\ \texttt{else}\ \langle expr \rangle
\end{array} \tag{4.2}$$

This grammar is ambiguous, so we will occasionally use additional parentheses to render the structure of expressions more clearly. Mini-ML has a conditional construct and function application (represented by the juxtaposition of the function and its one argument). Functions of one argument are defined using a syntactic construct of the form (fn ⟨identifier⟩ => ⟨expr⟩) where ⟨identifier⟩ is the formal parameter name and ⟨expr⟩ is the value returned. This expression may contain the formal parameter, hence the first production in the grammar for mini-ML. The fn construct is roughly equivalent to

```
function ⟨name⟩ ((⟨identifier⟩) is
    return ((⟨expr⟩));
end ⟨name⟩;
```

in Ada-like syntax but is *anonymous*. The programmer does not have to give the function a name in order to define it. For example, the identity function in mini-ML is (fn x => x). Mini-ML is nearly identical to the lambda expressions of chapter 7.

In mini-ML the polymorphic identity function has type int->int, and type real->real, and type 'a->'a. In fact, it has an infinite number of types, all instances of the type 'a->'a. Not all expressions in mini-ML have a type; if they do, they may have more than one.

Typing rules

We now consider how to define the type of an expression in the language mini-ML. The rules for the four constructs are what one would expect. The type of the function application $\langle expr \rangle_1\ \langle expr \rangle_2$ is the range of $\langle expr \rangle_1$, if type of $\langle expr \rangle_2$ is equal to the domain. The type of the conditional construct is the type of $\langle expr \rangle_2$ and $\langle expr \rangle_3$. Now the type of a variable must somehow be known from context. The type of (fn ⟨identifier⟩ => ⟨expr⟩) is more subtle. It is τ->σ where τ is the type of the domain and σ is the type of the expression returned by the function. The key is to make this intuition precise and polymorphic.

We will define the collection of types that an expression may assume by giving a Post system. The Post system will separate the "good" strings from the "bad" strings (see figure 4.8). If the expression does not have a type, then no derivation for the expression will have a conclusion in the set of "good" strings. It is possible that more than one type can be derived for an expression. In this case we say the expression is *polymorphic*. If it has exactly one type it is *monomorphic*.

To give the Post system for types, we require two definitions. First, the strings derived by the type system are called judgments. A *typing judgment* is a triple of

All strings of the form $A \vdash e : \tau$

Strings of the form $A \vdash e : \tau$ derivable from the mini-ML typing rules

Figure 4.8: Typing judgments in mini-ML

the form
$$A \vdash e : \tau$$
where A is a type assignment, e is an expression, and τ is a type. In this case, we say "expression e has type τ under the assignment A." The turnstile symbol $\vdash$ and the colon are used solely to separate the parts. (They are signs in the terminology of Post systems.) Second, a *type assignment*, which we shall denote by the letter A, is a set of pairs. It maintains the already established bindings of identifiers to their types.

A Post system of typing judgments for mini-ML is given by the four rules that follow. We begin with the typing rule for the conditional statement:

$$\frac{A \vdash e_1 : \texttt{bool} \qquad A \vdash e_2 : \tau \qquad A \vdash e_3 : \tau}{A \vdash (\texttt{if } e_1 \texttt{ then } e_2 \texttt{ else } e_3) : \tau}$$

In words this rule says: if e_1 has type $\texttt{bool}$, and e_2 and e_3 both have the same type (call it τ), then the whole $\texttt{if}$ construct has type τ. We insist that the two branches of the $\texttt{if}$ be reconcilable; otherwise we would have undesirable complications. If the type is e_2 is $\texttt{bool}$ and the type e_3 is $\texttt{int}$, what type should the $\texttt{if}$ construct have? We shall derive no type for it and say that it is not typable in the type system (4.1).

The type of an identifier x is determined by the context. For this reason a type assignment is necessary. If x has been bound by some $\texttt{fn}$ construct, as in the next rule, then x has some value in the assignment A. The value in A is the type of x. This is the content of the next rule in the deductive system.

$$\frac{}{A \vdash x : A(x)} \qquad \text{if } x \in \text{Dom}(A)$$

By this rule we mean: if x is one of the identifiers assigned a type by A, then the type of x is $A(x)$, the type associated to x by A; otherwise the rule does not apply.

The following rule is for function definitions:

$$\frac{A[x \mapsto \tau_1] \vdash e_1 : \tau_2}{A \vdash (\texttt{fn } x \texttt{ => } e_1) : \tau_1 \texttt{ -> } \tau_2}$$

The type assignment denoted by $A[x \mapsto \tau_1]$ is just like the assignment A, except that the value for the variable x is the type τ_1. This rule is understood to mean that if we can derive that the type of the function body is τ_2 under the assumption that the formal parameter has type τ_1, then the type of the function is $\tau_1\text{->}\tau_2$.

The following type rule is for the application of the expression e_1 to e_2.

$$\frac{A \vdash e_1 : \tau_2 \; \text{->} \; \tau \qquad A \vdash e_2 : \tau_2}{A \vdash e_1\, e_2 : \tau}$$

The type of the first expression e_1 must be a function. The type of the second expression must be equal to the domain of the type of e_1.

These four rules define what it means for an expression to have a type in mini-ML. Some typing judgments are derivable in the given Post system, some are not. For example, the typing judgment $\emptyset \vdash$ (fn x => x) : int->int is derivable. Here $\emptyset$ stands for the empty type assignment, the assignment with no bindings. The fact that the judgment is derivable means that the identity function has type int->int (among others). On the other hand, no typing judgment of the form $A \vdash$ (fn x => $x\ x$) : τ is derivable. This means the expression (fn x => $x\ x$) does not have a type in the type system defined for mini-ML by our Post system.

Next we give an example derivation for the type of the expression $f =$ (fn l=>if true then 0 else 1) using the typing rules for mini-ML. We require an initial environment or type assignment A_0 consisting of the types of the predefined function symbols. Let

$$A_0 = \{\langle \text{true}, \text{bool}\rangle, \langle 0, \text{int}\rangle, \langle 1, \text{int}\rangle\}$$

The expression true is associated with the type bool, and the expression 0 is associated with the type int, and so on. We view a type assignment as a finite set of pairs. In the deduction we will use the rule for function definition, and this will require another assignment that we call A_1. The type assignment A_1 is just like A_0 except that the identifier l is associated with the type bool. Thus

$$A_1 = \{\langle \text{l}, \text{'a}\rangle, \langle \text{true}, \text{bool}\rangle, \langle 0, \text{int}\rangle, \langle 1, \text{int}\rangle\}$$

The rule for function definition, and the rule for the conditional statement are each used once. The rule that looks up an identifier in the type assignment is used three times.

$$\frac{\dfrac{A_1 \vdash \text{true: bool} \qquad A_1 \vdash 0 : \text{int} \qquad A_1 \vdash 1 : \text{int}}{A_1 \vdash (\text{if true then 0 else 1}) : \text{int}}}{A_0 \vdash (\text{fn l => if true then 0 else 1}) : \text{'a->int}}$$

The conclusion is that the expression has type 'a->int. It is possible to derive other types for f using other type assignments. The choice for the type of l did not matter; we picked 'a, but int would have worked, as would any other type. This flexibility makes f polymorphic. That f is polymorphic is not unexpected. The argument l was not used, so why should its type matter? Fortunately, there is one best type, the type `'a->int`. This type is more general than all the other types capable of being derived for f. The others are all instances of the most general type. By replacing `'a` with some other type, all the other derivable types for f can be obtained.

The goal of *type reconstruction* is to determine the (canonical) type of expressions in the programming language by their use. The programmer is freed from specifying obvious or redundant information to the compiler. In mini-ML the type of the formal parameter in (`fn` ⟨*identifier*⟩ `=>` ⟨*expr*⟩) is *not* specified by the programmer, as it would be in Ada or Pascal. Rather the type analysis reconstructs the least restrictive type possible for the parameter. A key part of the process is letting type variables stand for any type whatever.

Type checking can be viewed as proving theorems in the deductive system defined by the four preceding rules. There is an algorithm or theorem prover for computing the type of expressions. We call the algorithm `TypeOf` (Milner called it W). The function `TypeOf` has two important properties expressed by the following theorems [18].

Theorem 2 (Milner) *If* `TypeOf`(A,e) *succeeds with* τ, *then* $A \vdash e : \tau$ *is derivable from the typing rules.*

Theorem 3 (Milner) *If* $A \vdash e : \sigma$ *is derivable from the typing rules, then* `TypeOf` (A,e) *succeeds with* τ *and* σ *is an instance of* τ.

The first theorem ensures that any type the function `TypeOf` finds for an expression is indeed one given by the typing rules. Hence the algorithm is correct. The second theorem ensures that if there is a type for an expression the algorithm will find it;s i.e., the algorithm is complete. Moreover, all the types derivable for an expression are instances of one, most general type.

Let construct in ML

The `let` construct is of vital importance to the type system in the programming language ML. To show this we extend mini-ML to include a `let` construct of the form:

$$\text{let } \langle identifier \rangle = \langle expr \rangle_1 \text{ in } \langle expr \rangle_2 \text{ end}$$

Computationally this is equivalent to:

$$(\text{fn } \langle identifier \rangle \text{ => } \langle expr \rangle_1) \, (\langle expr \rangle_2)$$

Consequently, one may be tempted to conclude that the `let` statement is not necessary at all, or perhaps that it is an insignificant syntactic convenience. This is far from the case, however. The `let` statement is *not* equivalent as far as type checking is concerned. In fact, it plays a crucial role in obtaining polymorphism and is a key innovation in ML.

To demonstrate the importance of `let` we consider the following simple example of the `let` statement. The body of this example is a pair, written in parentheses, that is part of the ML language (see exercise 10).

```
let f = (fn x => x) in (f 2, f true) end;
```

The function `f`, the identity function, is applied to an integer and to a boolean value. The result is the pair (2, true) and has type `int*bool`. The ML system successfully finds the type `int*bool` for the `let` expression but fails to find a type for the following expression, which is computationally equivalent:

```
(fn f => (f 2, f true)) (fn x => x)
```

The `let` statement permits the type variable `'a` in `'a->'a`, the type of `(fn x=>x)`, to be instantiated differently each time required, once in `(f 2)` and again in `(f true)`. Because of the way in which the typing rules for `fn` work, we must find *one* type for the domain of `f` which will work for both elements of the pair. This is impossible.

It is not an option to conclude from $e = $ (fn f =>(f 2, f true)) that f has type `'a->'b`. If this were the type of `f`, then we should be able to apply the function e to the function `(fn n=>n+1)`, say, of type `int->int`. This would cause a run-time type error, however, when it was applied to `true`.

A suitable typing system can be found for the `let` construct used this way, and the algorithm `TypeOf` can be extended to this case. The correctness and completeness theorems for mini-ML still hold in the extended system [10].

4.5.4 Case study of types in Amber

In this section we look at an experimental language with inclusion polymorphism, Amber [5]. While the language is not actually used, it employs concise notation for records and variant records. This provides a good setting for introducing inclusion polymorphism in other languages like Modula-3.

Amber has the usual assortment of unstructured types: `Int`, `Bool`, `String`, etc. It also has records, variant records, and functions. And it is these types we are most interested in here. We will order types in each of these three categories in a partial order called a subtype relation. The purpose of the subtype relation is to define a relaxed form of type compatibility. When a value of a certain type τ is expected, a value with type σ is acceptable as long as σ is a subtype of τ. It is as if a value with type σ also has type τ.

Record types are written in curly braces. For example,

```
{k: Int, l: String}
```

is a record with two fields k and l. Variant record types are written in square brackets. For example,

```
[k: Int, l: String, m: Bool]
```

is a variant record. Either it is an integer labeled **k**, a string labeled **l**, or a boolean value labeled **m**. Function types are written *dom->ran* where *dom* is the type of the domain of the function and *ran* is the type of the range. The types thus far have been relatively simple. Here are some type complex type definitions:

```
'( Tau is the type of a function from records to records.    )'
type Tau  = {k: Int, l: String} -> {m: Int};
'( Tau' is the type of a function from records to records.   )'
type Tau' = {k: Int} -> {m: Int, n: String};
'( Sigma is a record type with two fields, b and c.          )'
type Sigma  = {b: String, c: Tau};
'( Sigma' is a record type with three fields, a, b and c.    )'
type Sigma' = {a: Int, b: String, c: Tau'};
```

Notice that the type of a record field may be a function.

Field selection in Amber is only applicable to records, not variant records. Pascal programmers are accustomed to selecting fields from what are called variant records in that language. C programmers, too, are accustomed to "selecting fields" from what are called union types in C. Actually the dot notation indicates which of the variants the programmer expects to be occupying the union structure. Amber, like Euclid, uses the **case** statement to access variant records in a type-safe manner. The result of this is that the notation **x.f** in Amber (unlike Pascal and C) means that **x** is a record and cannot be a variant record.

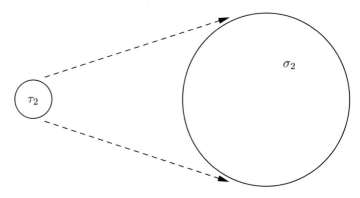

Figure 4.9: A function from type τ_2 to σ_2

The infinite collection of potential Amber types is organized in a hierarchy based on the structure of each type. There is no name equivalence in Amber. The whole scheme organizing types by structure is incompatible with name equivalence. We say that τ is a subtype of σ, written $\tau \leq \sigma$, if τ is equal to σ or one of the following three cases hold. A record r_1 is a subtype of r_2, if every field in r_2 is present in r_1 and for the fields common to both records the type of r_1's field is a

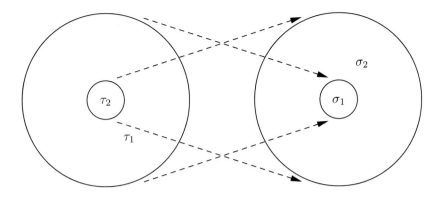

Figure 4.10: A function from type τ_1 to σ_1 compared to one from τ_2 to σ_2

subtype of r_2's field. We might write this as follows: $\{l_i : \tau_i\} \leq \{m_j : \sigma_j\}$ if for all l_i and m_j

$$m_j \in \{l_i\} \;\&\; (l_i = m_j \;\Rightarrow\; \tau_i \leq \sigma_j)$$

This means that additional fields are harmless. Suppose a subprocedure expects a record as an argument. All that subprocedure can do in Amber is select some fields from the argument. (Amber is a functional language—assignment to a field is not permitted.) If the subprocedure expects fields k and l, then it does not matter if the actual argument has extra fields. The extra fields can be ignored.

The subtype rule for variant records just turns the rule for records around:
[$l_i : \tau_i$] $\leq$ [$m_j : \sigma_j$] if for all l_i and m_j

$$l_i \in \{m_j\} \;\&\; (l_i = m_j \;\Rightarrow\; \tau_i \leq \sigma_j)$$

The only operation on a variant record is case analysis. Suppose a case statement is prepared for two cases, k and l, then the case analysis will work, if the variant record has these cases or a *subset* of them.

The subtype rule for function types goes both ways at once. The function type τ_1->σ_1 is a subtype of τ_2->σ_2 if

$$\sigma_1 \leq \sigma_2 \;\&\; \tau_2 \leq \tau_1 \tag{4.3}$$

The situation for function types is depicted in figures 4.9 and 4.10. If one is expecting a function from type τ_2 to σ_2, a function that will handle more arguments τ_1 and will produce results σ_1 within what is expected is acceptable. This rule is called *contravariant* because the relationship between the domains τ_1 and τ_2 is contrary to the ranges—an intriguing asymmetry.

If we add two fictitious types, one greater than all others called *top* and one less than all others called *bottom*, then the subtype relation forms a lattice. We write top with the symbol $\top$ and bottom with the symbol $\bot$. In figure 4.11 we show

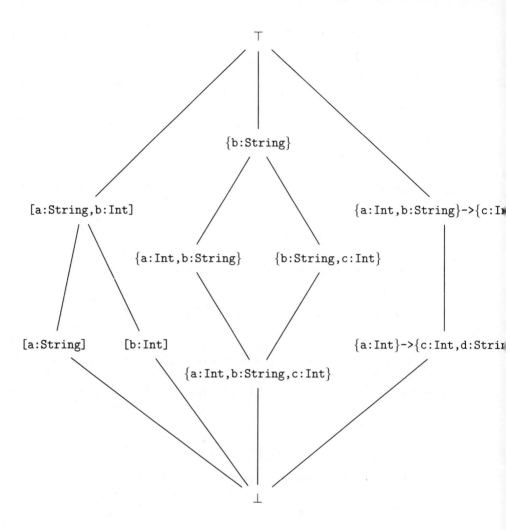

Figure 4.11: Some Amber types arranged in the type hierarchy

a few of Amber's types arranged in the lattice. Inclusion polymorphism means that a value with type τ can also be considered as belonging to any type higher than τ in the lattice.

4.5.5 Record model of object-oriented programming

It is possible to capture aspects of what are called object-oriented programming languages using inclusion polymorphism [4]. Objects are records; methods are fields with subprogram values. This approach is taken in Modula-3.

We consider an example in that language. The following Modula-3 program fragment [19] declares two kinds of objects. These data structures are defined using the keyword OBJECT. (Keywords in Modula-3, like the Modula family in general, are always in uppercase.) An OBJECT is a pointer to a record. In the declaration of an OBJECT the keyword METHODS separates the "ordinary" fields from the methods. The O1 objects have one integer field and a procedure m, which implicitly takes an O1 object as an argument. There are no other arguments, so m is declared as if it had no arguments. The O2 objects have an additional integer field as well as inheriting the fields and methods of O1. This is related to inheritance discussed in section 5.6.4. The method m of O2 objects may take advantage of the additional field. In the following Modula-3 segment procedures P and Q are attached to both kinds of arguments.

```
(*  Example of subtyping from Modula-3 Report.  *)
TYPE
    O1 =    OBJECT a: INTEGER METHODS m(); END;
    O2 = O1 OBJECT b: INTEGER END; (* Extend O1; O2 subtype of O1. *)


PROCEDURE P (self: O1) = BEGIN (* ... self.a ...            *) END P;
PROCEDURE Q (self: O2) = BEGIN (* ... self.a ... self.b ... *) END Q;


TYPE
    T1 = O1 OBJECT OVERRIDES m:=P END;
    T2 = O2 OBJECT OVERRIDES m:=Q END;
    T3 = O2 OBJECT OVERRIDES m:=P END;
    T4 = O1 OBJECT OVERRIDES m:=Q END;     (* Compile-time error.   *)


VAR
    v0 := NEW (O1);         (* Create an object with NIL method m.   *)
    v1 := NEW (O1, m:=P);   (* Override method m with procedure P.   *)
    v1 := NEW (T1);         (* Same effect as previous declaration.  *)
    v2 := NEW (O2, m:=Q);   (* Override method m with procedure Q.   *)
    v2 := NEW (T2);         (* Same effect as previous declaration.  *)
    v3 := NEW (O2, m:=P);   (* Procedure P is OK here, since O2<:O1. *)
    v3 := NEW (T3);         (* Same effect as previous declaration.  *)
    v4 := NEW (O1, m:=Q);   (* Compile-time error.                   *)
BEGIN
    v1.m();                 (* Invoke method m of v1. *)
END;
```

The procedure P may be used as the method m for objects of both kinds, since it may only use the field a. The procedure Q may not be used as the method m for O1 objects, since Q may use the fields a and b, but O1 objects have only the one field. This is an application of the contravariant rule for function subtying (4.3) with both methods having the same range.

Variables v0 through v4 are all instances of the objects O1 or O2. It is possible to dynamically associate a particular method with each of the variables. If many objects are to be created with the same methods, it is possible to define an object type with default methods already associated with it. Type T3 is an example in which m defaults to P, so object instantiation NEW(O2,m:=P) is exactly the same as NEW(T3).

4.6   Exercises

4.1   Is there any advantage in adding collections of pointers to Ada?

4.2   (From [9, pages 279–283].) Consider the following Ada subprogram specifications which overload the function identifier Max.

```
function Max (i1, i2: INTEGER) return INTEGER;       -- Max 1
function Max (i1: INTEGER; f2: FLOAT) return FLOAT;   -- Max 2
function Max (f1: FLOAT, i2: INTEGER) return FLOAT;   -- Max 3
function Max (f1, f2: FLOAT) return FLOAT;            -- Max 4
function Max (i1, i2: INTEGER) return FLOAT;          -- Max 5
function Max (f1, f2, f3: FLOAT) return FLOAT;        -- Max 6
```

Determine which of the following expressions are ambiguous or impossible (and hence illegal) given the following declarations:

```
n1, n2, n3: INTEGER;
x1, x2, x3: FLOAT;
```

Give all possible interpretations of each occurrence of the identifier Max.

(a) n1 := Max (n2,n3);

(b) x1 := Max (n1,n2);

(c) x1 := Max (n1, Max(x2,n2));

(d) x1 := Max (x2,Max(n1,n2),x3);

(e) x1 := Max (x2, Max(n1,n2));

(f) x1 := Max (x2, i2=>Max(n1,n2));

4.3 Overloading in Ada is permitted only if the procedure specifications are distinct. Formal parameter names and default parameters are not used in determining if the specifications are distinct. Which of following procedure specifications are distinct from the six specifications of Max in the previous exercise?

(a) `function Max (x1, x2, x3: FLOAT) return FLOAT;`

(b) `function Max (x1, x2: FLOAT := 0.0) return FLOAT;`

(c) `function Max (x1, x2: FLOAT := 0.0) return LONG_FLOAT;`

4.4 Rewrite the Ada block A on page 108 in Modula-3.

4.5 Consider the following type definitions in the programming language Ada used to define the three unrelated data structures R, V, and T.

```
type R is record
    a: INTEGER; b: BOOLEAN;
end record;

type V (tag: BOOLEAN := true) is record
    case tag is
        when true  => a : INTEGER;
        when false => b : BOOLEAN;
    end case;
end record;

type C = ('#', '/', '\', '^');
type N;
type T is access N;
type N (tag: C := '#') is record
    info : INTEGER;
    case tag is
        when '#'        => null;
        when '/' | '\' => sub : T;
        when '^'        => left : T;  right : T;
    end case;
end record
```

Give ML, or Haskell, type definitions that most naturally model these data structures.

4.6 Consider adding the following function:

```
function Insidious return STRING is
begin
    Address3 := Address2;              -- modify global variable!
    return ("TX");
end Insidious;
```

to the Ada program shown in figure 4.4. Consult the Ada reference manual to determine the effect of the assignment

```
Address3.State := Insidious;
```

when `Address3` has a discriminant with value `true`.

4.7   Determining structural type equivalence can be reduced to determining if two infinite trees are equal. Give an algorithm for structural type equivalence.

4.8   Give at least three more types for the identity function (`fn x => x`) in the type system (4.1) of mini-ML described on page 126.

4.9   Which of the following typing judgments are derivable from the typing rules for mini-ML given in section 4.5.3?

    (a) $\{\langle \mathtt{x}, \mathtt{bool}\rangle\} \vdash \mathtt{x} : \mathtt{bool}$

    (b) $\{\langle \mathtt{x}, \mathtt{'a}\rangle\} \vdash \mathtt{x} : \mathtt{int}$

    (c) $\{\langle 1, \mathtt{int}\rangle, \langle \mathtt{x}, \mathtt{bool}\rangle\} \vdash (\mathtt{if\ x\ then\ x\ else\ 1}) : \mathtt{'a}$

    (d) $\{\langle 1, \mathtt{int}\rangle, \langle \mathtt{y}, \mathtt{bool}\rangle\} \vdash (\mathtt{fun\ x\ =>\ 1})\,(\mathtt{y\ y}) : \mathtt{'a}$

4.10 Suppose we add pairs to mini-ML with the following syntax:

$$\langle expr\rangle \quad ::= \quad (\langle expr\rangle,\ \langle expr\rangle)$$
$$|\quad \ldots$$

The type of a pair is the cartesian product which we give the following syntax: $\tau * \sigma$. For instance, the pair (`1,true`) has type `int*bool`. Give a typing rule appropriate for pairs.

4.11 Does the expression (`fn x => x x`) have a type given the typing rules for mini-ML in section 4.5.3? If so, derive a type for it. If not, explain why not.

4.12 Give a concrete syntax of type assignments and design a proper Post system in which all judgments of the form $A \vdash x : \tau$ where the pair $\langle x, \tau\rangle$ is in the set of typing assignments A. Do not rely on any informal explanation of the rules of the Post system.

4.13 Suppose we add a `let` construct to the mini-ML language with the following form: `let` x `=` e_1 `in` e_2 `end`.

(a) Derive a typing rule for the `let` construct assuming it is equivalent to:
`(fn x => e`$_2$`) e`$_1$`.`

(b) Suppose we add the typing rule proposed in the previous part to the typing rules for mini-ML. Show that this new type system cannot derive a type for

`let f = (fn x => x) in (f 2, f true) end;`

under the type assignment $\{\langle 2, \mathtt{int}\rangle, \langle \mathtt{true}, \mathtt{bool}\rangle\}$.

4.14 Comment on the effect of adding the following typing rules to the type system of mini-ML:

(a)

$$\frac{}{A \vdash x : \tau} \qquad \text{if } x \text{ expression variable}$$

(b)

$$\frac{A \vdash e : \alpha}{A \vdash e : \beta} \qquad \text{if } \alpha, \beta \text{ type variables}$$

4.15 Not only is it possible to define the types of an expression using a Post system, it is possible to define the semantics of a language as well. Consider the `let` language of section 2.3.2. Suppose we were to define the semantics of the language using judgments of the form $E \vdash e \longrightarrow v$ where E is the environment of identifier/value pairs, e is an expression of the language, and v is the integer value to which the expression evaluates. The semantics would contain two axioms for the constants:

$$\frac{}{E \vdash 0 \longrightarrow 0} \qquad \frac{}{E \vdash 1 \longrightarrow 1}$$

The rule for the addition operator would be:

$$\frac{E \vdash e_1 \longrightarrow v_1 \quad E \vdash e_2 \longrightarrow v_2}{E \vdash (e_1 + e_2) \longrightarrow v}$$

where v is the sum of v_1 and v_2. Complete the semantics for the `let` language by giving a rule for the remaining two cases.

4.16 Give two subtypes of each of the following Amber types:

```
{a: Int, b: String}          '( record          )'
[a: Int, b: String]          '( variant record )'
{a: Int, b: String} -> Int   '( function type  )'
```

4.17 Consider the following pairs of types in Amber. Indicate if the first is a subtype of the second, the second a subtype of the first, both, or neither.

```
(a)   Int                                      Bool
(b)   Int                                      {l: Int}
(c)   {l: Int}                                 {l: Int}
(d)   {m: Int}                                 {m: String}
(e)   {a:Int,b:Bool}->{c:Int}                  {a:Int}->{a:Bool,c:Int}
(f)   {a:Int,b:Bool}->{c:Int,d:Bool}          {a:Int}->{c:Int}
(g)   {a:Int,b:Bool}                           {a:Int}
```

4.18 What possible types does the following Amber-like subprocedure have?

```
function f (x) = if true then x.a else x
```

4.19 Consider the following two typing rules:

$$\frac{A \vdash e : \tau}{A \vdash e : \sigma} \ \text{ if } \tau \leq \sigma \qquad \frac{A \vdash e : \tau}{A \vdash e : \sigma} \ \text{ if } \sigma \leq \tau$$

where $\leq$ is the subtype relationship. One of these two rules correctly captures inclusion polymorphism and is called the *subsumption rule*. Which rule is it? Explain.

4.20 The problem concerns overload resolution and the language defined by the following grammar.

$$
\begin{aligned}
P \ &\rightarrow \ \textbf{declare } D \textbf{ begin } S \textbf{ end} \\
D \ &\rightarrow \ I : T \text{ ;} \\
&\mid \ I : T \text{ ; } D \\
T \ &\rightarrow \ B \\
&\mid \ B -> B \\
B \ &\rightarrow \ \textbf{int} \\
&\mid \ \textbf{string} \\
&\mid \ \textbf{real} \\
&\mid \ \textbf{bool} \\
S \ &\rightarrow \ I \\
&\mid \ I \,(\, S \,)
\end{aligned}
$$

Not all syntactically correct programs are "legal." Some statements S have occurrences of undeclared identifiers, some may be ambiguous, and others may not be type correct. Give a reasonable definition of "legal" by defining an attribute grammar which does the type checking.

4.21 (From [21, page 207].) Bertrand Russell noticed the following inconsistency. Suppose that it were possible to define a set R whose elements are all the sets that do not contain themselves. That is, $R = \{S \mid S \notin S\}$. Is $R \in R$? If $R \in R$ then $R \notin R$, a contradiction. So, $R \notin R$, but then $R \in R$, again a contradiction.

This problem can be simulated in programming languages. Sets can be simulated by boolean-valued functions, called *characteristic functions*. The function representing a set of integers S will be declared like

```
function S (x: integer): boolean
```

and will return true exactly when the argument is in the set S. In a language like Pascal where functions can be passed as arguments it is possible to represent sets of sets. This makes it possible to try to represent the set R given above. (*Hint:* This problem has nothing to do with the set data type of Pascal.)

(a) Show that the set R may be simulated in the original definition of Pascal, which does not require specification of parameters of procedural parameters, by writing a Pascal program.

(b) Show that R is not expressible in versions of Pascal that require such specification.

4.22 (From [21, page 207].) In some languages (including ALGOL 68), it is possible to define procedural types and recursive types. Here is an example:

```
mode T = proc (T, int) int;
proc f = (T g, int n) int;
begin
     if n=0 then f:=1 else f:=n*g(g,n-1) fi
end
```

Here is the example again in a Pascal-like notation:

```
type T = function (T; integer): integer;
function f(g:T; n:integer): integer;
begin
     if n=0 then f:=1 else f:=n*g(g,n-1)
end;
```

(a) What is the type of the function `f`?

(b) What is the value of `f(f,`i`)` for $i \geq 0$?

(c) Is the function definition of `f` recursive?

(d) Simulate Russell's paradox of the preceding exercise by giving a well-typed program using the notation of this exercise. What would happen if an attempt were made to compute the analog of $R \in R$?

4.23 Write the function f from exercise 4.22 and the analog of $R = \{S \mid S \notin S\}$ from exercise 4.21 in completely legal ANSI C with function prototypes.

4.7   Bibliography

[1] *Anonymous.* "Chapter 8: How the language got its spots." In *Systems Programming with Modula-3* edited by Greg Nelson. Prentice Hall, Englewood Cliffs, New Jersey, 1991.

[2] Baker, T. P. "One pass algorithm for overload resolution in Ada." *ACM Transactions on Programming Languages and Systems*, volume 4, number 4, October 1982, pages 601–614.

[3] Barron, David William. *Comparative Programming Languages.* American Elsevier, New York, 1968.

[4] Cardelli, Luca. "A semantics of multiple inheritance." In *Semantics of Data Types*, edited by Gilles Kahn, David B. MacQueen, and Gordon Plotkin, Springer-Verlag, Berlin, 1984, pages 51–67.

[5] Cardelli, Luca. "Amber." In *Combinators and Functional Programming Languages*, edited by Guy Cousineau, Pierre-Louis Curien, and Bernard Robinet, Springer-Verlag, Berlin, 1986, pages 21–47.

[6] Cardelli, Luca. "Basic polymorphic typechecking." *Science of Computer Programming*, volume 8, number 2, April 1987, pages 147–172.

[7] Cardelli, Luca, and Peter Wegner. "On understanding types, data abstraction, and polymorphism." *ACM Computing Surveys*, volume 17, number 4, 1985, pages 471–522.

[8] Cleaveland, J. Craig. *An Introduction to Data Types.* Addison-Wesley, Reading, Massachusetts, 1986.

[9] Cohen, Norman H. *Ada As a Second Language.* McGraw-Hill series in software engineering and technology. McGraw-Hill, New York, 1986.

[10] Damas, Luis Manuel Martins, and Robin Milner. "Principal type-schemes for functional programs." In *Conference Record of the Ninth Annual ACM Symposium on Principles of Programming Languages*, 1982, pages 207–212.

[11] Demers, Alan J. "A simplified type structure for Ada." In *Jornadas en Computacion*, June 1982, pages 86–104.

[12] Demers, Alan J., and James E. Donahue. "Data types, parameters and type checking." In *Conference Record of the Seventh Annual ACM Symposium on Principles of Programming Languages*, 1980, pages 12–23.

[13] Demers, Alan J., and James E. Donahue. "'Type-completeness' as a language principle." In *Conference Record of the Seventh Annual ACM Symposium on Principles of Programming Languages*, 1980, pages 234–244.

[14] Demers, Alan J., James E. Donahue, and Glenn Skinner. "Data types as values: Polymorphism, type-checking, encapsulation." In *Conference Record of the Fifth Annual ACM Symposium on Principles of Programming Languages*, 1978, pages 23–30.

[15] Jensen, Kathleen, and Niklaus Emil Wirth. *Pascal: User Manual and Report.* Second edition. Springer-Verlag, New York, 1974.

[16] Lampson, Butler W., James J. Horning, Ralph L. London, James G. Mitchell, and G. J. Popek. "Report on the programming language EUCLID." *SIGPLAN Notices*, volume 12, number 3, February 1977.

[17] MacLennan, Bruce J. *Principles of Programming Languages: Design, Evaluation, and Implementation.* Holt, Rinehart and Winston, New York, 1983.

[18] Milner, Robin. "A theory of type polymorphism in programming." *Journal of Computer and System Science*, volume 17, number 3, December 1978, pages 348–375.

[19] Nelson, Greg, editor. *Systems Programming with Modula-3.* Prentice Hall series in innovative technology. Prentice Hall, Englewood Cliffs, New Jersey, 1991.

[20] Tennent, R. D. "Another look at type compatibility in Pascal." *Software—Practice and Experience*, volume 8, 1978, pages 429–437.

[21] Tennent, R. D. *Principles of Programming Languages.* Prentice Hall, Englewood Cliffs, New Jersey, 1981.

[22] United States Department of Defense. *Reference Manual for the Ada Programming Language.* United States Government Printing Office, Washington, D.C., 1983.

[23] Welsh, Jim, J. Sneeringer, and Charles Antony Richard Hoare. "Ambiguities and insecurities in Pascal." *Software—Practice and Experience*, volume 7, number 6, 1977, pages 685–696. Reprinted in *Tutorial, Programming Language Design*, edited by Anthony I. Wasserman, 1980, pages 284–295.

[24] Winkler, J. F. H. "Some improvements of ISO Pascal." *SIGPLAN Notices*, volume 19, 1984. Reprinted in *Programming Languages: A Grand Tour*, edited by Ellis Horowitz, 1987, pages 123–153.

[25] Wirth, Niklaus Emil. "The programming language Pascal." *Acta Infomatica*, volume 1, number 1, 1971, pages 35–63.

[26] Wirth, Niklaus Emil. "An assessment of the programming language Pascal." *IEEE Transactions on Software Engineering*, June 1975, pages 192–198. Reprinted in *Programming Languages: A Grand Tour*, edited by Ellis Horowitz, 1987, pages 117–122.

Chapter 5

Blocks, procedures, and modules

In this chapter we examine structures of programs that are bigger than expressions and statements. These include blocks, procedures, and modules. We also discuss related topics: the implementation of block-structured languages, procedure calling, exception handling, abstract types, and classes and inheritance in C++.

5.1   Blocks

The fundamental difference between the modern, mainstream, ALGOL-like languages and the first programming language, FORTRAN, is the block. A *block* has two intertwined meanings. First, a block is the scope-defining unit of the language. Second, a block is a sequence of executable statements that are treated as a unit. Subprocedures in most languages are blocks in both senses of the word. In Pascal the *only* scope-defining unit is the procedure. In contrast, ALGOL and Ada have other scope-defining constructs called blocks. In these languages, the syntax for blocks uses the keywords `begin` and `end`. For example, in Ada the form of a block is as follows:

```
B: declare
    -- declarations
begin
    -- executable code
end B;
```

where B is the name of the block. The declarations in the declaration section are visible throughout the executable part (and not outside the block).

Sometimes the keywords `begin` and `end` are used as part of the syntax of control structures. Pascal, for instance, uses them to delimit branches of an `if` statement or the body of a `while` loop. For example, a `while` loop with one statement looks like:

`while` *expression* `do` *statement*

But with more than one statement the statements must be grouped with the keywords `begin` and `end` like this:

```
while expression do
begin
     sequence of statements
end
```

In Pascal no local declarations can be introduced in these group of statements. Since Ada uses a syntax for control constructs that clearly delimits the control flow, there is no need for a construct solely to group executable statements together. And so Ada uses the keywords `begin` and `end` for scope-defining units only.

A block-structured programming language permits the hierarchical nesting of blocks. Although this organization is mostly taken for granted, it is important. Blocks limit the context of the program that someone must consider in understanding the program. Good use of blocks (including subprocedures) make programs easier to read and understand. Variables can be introduced and initialized close to where they are used.

Some languages have scope-defining units other than the block. In C for example, variables declared outside the scope of any procedure are visible in the rest of the file. They can become visible in another file if they are imported using an `extern` declaration. Many languages use a less arbitrary construct for aggregation. These are usually called modules. Not only do they delimit the scope of variables local to the module, but these languages often provide a mechanism for exporting and importing a set of variables and for separate compilation.

We have previously introduced declarations, bindings, and environments (section 3.3). An environment is a set of identifier bindings. A block introduces an environment and all of the bindings have approximately the same scope (see exercise 3.6). From the perspective of same point in the program, the *local environment* is the collection of bindings declared in current block. The *nonlocal environment* is the collection of all the variables not declared in the current scope.

The nested structure of scoping can be represented pictorially via contour diagrams [7] or nested boxes as in figure 5.1. The local environment of every block appears in a box. The nonlocal environment comprises all the variables in surrounding boxes. This rule corresponds to *implicit inheritance*; i.e., variables declared in outer blocks are visible to inner blocks. Variables in declared in inner blocks are not visible. If a nested block introduces an identifier declared in an outer block, then the outer declaration is eclipsed and there is a hole in its scope for the scope of the inner block. Almost all language use implicit inheritance, although Euclid does not.

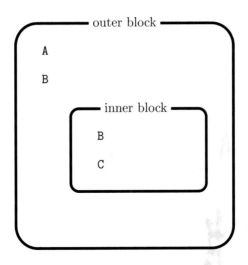

Figure 5.1: Contour diagram of nested blocks

Ada scope rules eliminate holes in scope. Variables hidden by an intervening declaration of the same name are accessible by giving an explicit path of block names called an *expanded name* in Ada and is written using a dot between the names. This is sometimes called *dot notation* or *prefix notation*. Of course, expanded names do not give access to variables in inner scopes. The following example is taken from the Ada reference manual 8.3 §19.

```
Outer: declare
    A, B: INTEGER;
    Inner: declare
        B: INTEGER;           --  Hides Outer.B
        C: INTEGER;
    begin
        B := A;               --  means Inner.B := Outer.A
        C := Outer.B          --  means Inner.C := Outer.B
    end Inner;
begin
    A := B;                   --  means Outer.A := Outer.B
    A := Inner.C;             --  ILLEGAL
end Outer;
```

Note that if `Inner.B` had been declared to be a variable of a different type, the inner declaration would still hide the outer one. In Ada a variable cannot be overloaded. The visibility rules for enumeration literals and subprocedures are different because overloading is permitted.

The contour rule also incorporates static scoping. *Static scoping* or lexical scoping means that a procedure is called in the environment of its definition. The dynamic calling of procedures results in another possibility for resolving nonlocal variables. A procedure is defined in one place in the program, but may well be called in an entirely different environment or environments. If a procedure is called in the environment of its caller, then we have *dynamic scoping*, sometimes known as dynamic binding, or fluid binding. This is the most recently occurring and still-active binding of a variable.

To illustrate the difference between static and dynamic scoping, we consider two nested blocks in Ada-like syntax.

```
Outer: declare
    b: Boolean := true;        -- 1st decl of variable b
    procedure P is
    begin
        print (b);             -- variable b not local to P
    end P;
begin
    Inner: declare
        b: Boolean := false;   -- 2nd decl of variable b
    begin
        P;                     -- call procedure P
    end Inner;
end Outer;
```

The key ingredients are a procedure that accesses a nonlocal variable and two different declarations for the variable. One of these declarations is visible where the procedure is declared; the other is visible where the procedure is invoked. In the case of `Outer` and `Inner` above, the first declaration of `b` is visible where the procedure `P` is defined. Hence, under static binding, the program fragment prints `true`. If dynamic scoping were used, the second declaration would be the one visible when the procedure `P` is called, and so the program prints `false`.

The example of blocks `Outer` and `Inner` show that it is impossible to statically type-check programming languages that use dynamic scoping. If the types of the two declarations of `b` were different, it would be impossible for the compiler to know (in general) if all nonlocal uses of `b` were consistent with the declarations that would be applicable during the execution of the program. The same use of `b` in procedure `P` may well refer to different declarations under dynamic scoping, say, if `P` were called in block `Outer`.

There are some situations where dynamic scoping is useful. Consider the following situation. Define a function `F` using nonlocal function `G`. Call `F` in environments where `G` is bound to different functions. This may happen because a bug was found in `G`. So `G` is fixed. Then you call `F` again. Under static binding `F` still exhibits the old error in G because that is the environment in which F was defined. In dynamic scoping F would pick up the new, bug-free version of G.

Dynamic scoping was first used by LISP, where it was achieved by accident. Most modern dialects of LISP (e.g., Scheme, Common LISP) have abandoned dynamic scoping in favor of static scoping, as the disadvantages of dynamic scoping are severe. It is possible to break code that works perfectly by choosing the wrong name for an identifier. The following example is from [11]. In this tragic scenario two programmers are working together to compute the roots of a quadratic equation. One programmer writes the function roots, which works perfectly in the context of first definition of the function discr. (Notice that the identifier discr is free in the definition of roots.) The second programmer uses roots in a different context in which there is a second definition of the function discr.

```
declare
    function discr (a,b,c: FLOAT) returns FLOAT is
    begin return (b**2 - 4*a*c); end discr;
    procedure roots (a,b,c: FLOAT; r1,r2: out FLOAT) is
        d: FLOAT := discr (a,b,c);
    begin
        -- body of procedure roots
    end roots;
begin
    -- a call to "roots" here works as expected
    declare
        function discr (x,y,z: FLOAT) returns FLOAT is
        begin return (math.sqrt (x**2 + y**2 + z**2)); end discr;
    begin
        -- with dynamic scoping, a call to "roots" here
        -- does NOT work as expected
    end;
end;
```

If dynamic scoping were used, the function roots would suddenly fail. If either programmer renamed their function discr, then the program would mysteriously work. This demonstrates that in dynamic scoping the choice of the name for a variable can make or break a program.

Of course, static type checking is impossible with dynamic scoping. A procedure with a global variable would be correct only if every call was in the context of declarations of the right types. This is impossible to verify in general. So the following implications of static binding are significant. One, a strongly typed language is possible. Two, all references can be resolved from the text of program, because the connection between the declaration and the use is static. This is important to the implementation.

5.2   Implementation of block-structured languages

The implementation of block-structured languages has an important impact on programming language design and even on hardware design. In particular, restrictions on procedural parameters are a result of the traditional stack-based implementation of these languages. In this section, we look at implementing access to data values and the implications of using a stack for data values local to blocks.

Originally, management of data in FORTRAN was simple, since only one active invocation of a subprocedure is possible. Local variables can be found in some fixed place associated with the subprocedure. All the other variables are global, and fixed places in memory can be allocated for them, too. With the introduction of recursion to programming languages we can have multiple invocations of the same subprocedure. The fixed strategy for managing local variables precludes recursion, since we would then have more than one procedure active at one time.

To capture the state of a procedure invocation, we need a data structure containing:

- the code

- where we are in the code

- values of all the variables

- what to do when we are through

This data structure is called an *activation record*.

With clever management all the information in an activation record can be reduced to:

- the instruction pointer, which designates the current instruction

- local variables (since every variable is local to some procedure or block)

- the environment pointer, which defines the nonlocal environment

Since the code executed by a procedure does not change from invocation to invocation, we do not need all the code in each activation record. We can factor out all the code to all the procedures and put it in one place. In the activation record we need only put a pointer, the instruction pointer, to the current instruction being executed.

The compiler generates code to manipulate these activation records at procedure invocation and exit. This is one of the management tasks common to all (or most) programs written in a language. We call these tasks the *run-time system* or the run-time support of the language. The run-time system is usually linked with the programmer's code to create a viable unit ready for execution.

The run-time system organizes the activation records. It is natural to implement this organization with a stack: call a procedure, push the activation record, exit a procedure, pop the activation record off the stack. By putting all the activation records in a stack, procedure exit is handled easily. No explicit dynamic link to the calling procedure is required; we just pop the current activation record off the stack. The activation record now on the top of the stack resumes.

Since the statically enclosing blocks are represented by activation records present on the run-time stack, the nonlocal environment can always be found somewhere on the stack. The trick is to link the statically enclosing blocks on the stack according to their nesting in the program.

Are the dynamic link and static link the same? No, they are not. Consider the following program fragment.

```
Main: declare
    procedure P is
        procedure Q is
        begin
            -- call P
        end Q;
    begin
        -- call P again recursively sometimes
        -- call Q sometimes
    end P;
begin
    -- call P
end Main;
```

The main procedure calls P. The subprocedure calls itself recursively. For the sake of this illustration assume that thereafter it calls Q. The subprocedure is statically nested in P and also calls P. The *call graph*, a graph of procedures and the subprocedures they call, of the program main is depicted in figure 5.2.

The execution of the program main may proceed as follows: P is called, P calls P, P calls Q, Q calls P, and so on. The portion of the execution of the program is depicted in figure 5.3. Each time a procedure is called an activation record is pushed into the stack. In figure 5.3 the stack grows at the top. After the procedure finishes execution the activation record is popped off the stack. The dynamic link of each activation record is implicit (it would point to the activation record immediately below). The static link of each activation record, however, is not evident in the structure of the stack, so it is drawn explicitly in figure 5.3. Each pointer points to the activation record of the procedure where the search for nonlocal variables begins. Since Q is statically nested inside P, the static link for Q always points to an activation record for P. The values of any variables declared in P and used in Q would be found in P's activation record. If Q uses nonlocal variables not declared in P, these would be found in the main program's activation record. Variables visible in Q can be found only in Q, P, or Main.

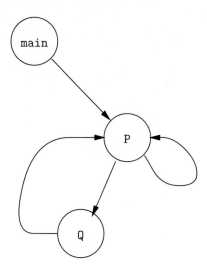

Figure 5.2: Call graph of program `Main`

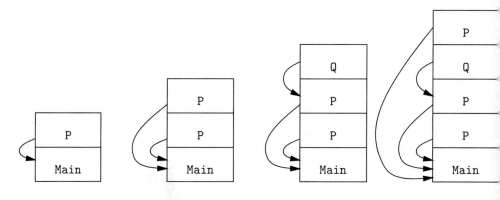

Figure 5.3: Run-time stack during execution of program `Main`

A key observation about this run-time organization is that two values pinpoint a variable in static binding. One, the *static distance* is the difference in static nesting between a variable use and its declaration. The *static nesting* is how deeply nested a declaration or variable use is. Two, *offset* is a more or less arbitrary displacement within an activation record locating where the variable is stored. At compile time this information can easily be stored in the symbol table and used to generate code to access the local or nonlocal variable. A local variable (static distance equal zero) is located in the current activation recored. A nonlocal variable is located n hops (where n is the static distance) along the static chain. This fetch can be done in constant time if the static links are kept in an array.

5.2.1 Procedural parameters

It is uncommon in ALGOL-like languages to pass procedures as parameters. In Ada, for example, it is illegal. In many languages it is legal to pass a procedure down to a subprocedure as an argument, but returning procedures as the values of functions is illegal. In this section we see that the motivation for these language design decisions is based on the stack implementation of the run-time environment for these languages.

The following Modula-3 program serves as an example of a program in an ALGOL-like language in which procedures are passed as arguments. Both subprocedures P and T are passed as arguments to the procedure Q. The types of subprocedures P and T are the same, and this type is given the name F in the program.

```
MODULE Main;
    TYPE F = PROCEDURE (x: INTEGER); (* procedure type *)
    PROCEDURE P (x: INTEGER) = BEGIN (* ... *) END P;
    PROCEDURE Q (fp: F) = BEGIN fp(5) END Q;
    PROCEDURE R () =
        PROCEDURE T (x: INTEGER) = BEGIN (* ... *) END T;
    BEGIN
        Q(P); Q(T);
    END R;
BEGIN
    R();  (* call subprocedure R *)
END Main.
```

The run-time execution of the program is illustrated in figure 5.4. The main program calls R, R calls Q, once with the subprocedure P as an argument and again with subprocedure T as an argument. P is defined in Main, so its static link points to Main. T is defined in R, so its static link points to R.

The compiler writer must figure out how to implement a call to formal procedural parameters. This breaks into two questions. In the context of the example above, we must know:

1. What gets passed to Q to represent P or T?

2. What code must be emitted to implement the call fp(5)?

An answer to the second question will suggest a solution to the first. For any procedure call we must:

1. transmit the parameters,

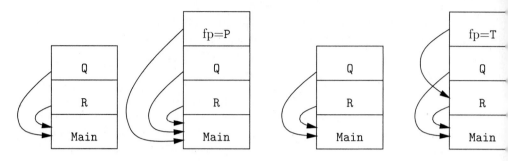

Figure 5.4: Run-time stack of program with procedure argument

2. save the return address,

3. set the dynamic link,

4. start the execution of the new procedure, and

5. set the static link.

The first three of these are no different in the case of calling a formal procedure argument. Hence the same protocol must be followed. But the last two require an address and a pointer to the statically enclosing block of the procedure being called. Usually, this information is known to the compiler. A procedure, like other identifiers, has all the information necessary to the compiler stored in the symbol table. But a formal procedure parameter stands (potentially) for more than one procedure, and so this information is not fixed at compile time. This suggests that procedural parameters be represented at run time by the two pieces of information missing at compile time. This pair of pointers, to the instructions and to the static link, is called a *closure*. It is a closure, then, that is passed as the value of a parameter when a procedure is passed as an argument to subprogram. From the closure, the correct adjustments can be made to the run-time stack to complete the call to a formal procedure argument.

It is natural to assume that if a subfunction returns a procedure value as its result, then a closure should be the procedural value. But functions that pass functions back as result values break the stack model. Consider modifying program Main so that R is a function, a function that returns a procedure. For example, the function R might return procedure P or procedure T.

```
MODULE Main;
    TYPE F = PROCEDURE (x: INTEGER); (* procedure type *)
    PROCEDURE P (x: INTEGER) = BEGIN (* ... *) END P;
    PROCEDURE R (): F =
        PROCEDURE T (x: INTEGER) = BEGIN (* ... *) END T;
```

```
    BEGIN
        IF ... THEN RETURN P ELSE RETURN T END;
    END R;
BEGIN
    EVAL R();  (* call subprocedure R; throw away result *)
END Main.
```

Returning subprocedure P causes no problem. But suppose R returns a subprocedure T, which is local to R. The environment in which T is defined points to R, but when R returns, T's environment pointer points to a part of the stack that is no longer in use. The stack model is inadequate for this use of activation records. In Modula-3 nested subprocedures like T cannot be passed back by functions, so the compiler issues a fatal error message.

5.3 Calling procedures

In this section we look at procedure calls in general. First, we clarify the distinction between actual and formal parameters: *actual parameters* are the arguments passed to a procedure, and *formal parameters* are place holders used in the procedure or function definition.

For the most part programming languages use a *positional correspondence* between actuals and formals. The value passed for the first formal parameter is the value computed by evaluating the first actual parameter, and so on for all the parameters. Of course, you must have the same number of actual parameters and formal parameters. This is so obvious and natural to anyone that has programmed before that it is difficult to conceive of anything else. We mention it here because another kind of association used in some programming languages is not so well known. This other association is *name association*. This requires that the calling program know the names of the arguments; the names are the formal parameters.

In addition to name association of parameters, Ada also has *default parameters* (cf. Ada reference manual §6.4.2). Default parameters may be completely omitted in the actual call to the procedure.

```
-- An example procedure declaration
procedure ACTIVATE (PROCESS : in PROCESS_NAME;
                    AFTER   : in PROCESS_NAME := NO_PROCESS;
                    WAIT    : in DURATION := 0.0;
                    PRIOR   : in BOOLEAN := FALSE);
```

The following Ada procedure calls illustrate some ways the procedure ACTIVATE can be called.

```
-- Some legal calls to ACTIVATE
ACTIVATE (X);
```

```
ACTIVATE (X, AFTER => Y);
ACTIVATE (X, WAIT => 60.0, PRIOR => TRUE);
ACTIVATE (X, Y, 10.0, FALSE);
```

The programming language C++ has default parameters, but not name association. Here is a simple example in that language.

```
void f (int a = 1, int b = 2, int c = 3) {
   //  Body of function f
}

main () {
     f (5,6,7);  // Usual positional correspondence
     f (5,6);    // Formal argument c defaults to the value 3
     f (5);      // Formal arguments b and c get their default values
     f ();       // Parens are necessary
}
```

The following procedure specification is illegal in C++. If one parameter is given a default value, all the subsequent parameter must have default values. Suppose C++ did not have this restriction.

```
void h (int a = 1, int b = 2, int c)  // Illegal!
```

A procedure call such as h(5,6) would be ambiguous. It could mean a:=5, b:=2 (its default value), and c:=6, or possibly a:=1 (its default value), b:=5, and c:=6. A further method of parameter correspondence was introduced by the programming language HOPE and used in the programming language ML. In these languages subprocedures all have one argument, but the argument can be a pattern. One pattern is a tuple. Syntactically, a tuple is a comma-separated list of arguments. This, then, is positional correspondence. Another pattern is a labeled record. Syntactically, a record is a comma-separated list of label, argument pairs. This, then, is name correspondence, as the order of the list is immaterial.

```
fun f (x,y)       = x+y;  f (1,2);       (* Tuple pattern in ML  *)
fun g {a=x, b=y} = x+y;   g {b=2, a=1};  (* Record pattern in ML *)
```

Tuples and records are but some of the patterns. Patterns can be made of any predefined or user-defined constructors. The most common constructors are "nil" and "cons," both of which construct lists. The actual argument is matched against the pattern to see if it is constructed in a manner consistent with the pattern. In ML function definitions can have different cases for different patterns. Identifiers in the pattern (the formal parameters) are associated with the corresponding substructures of the actual argument. This approach provides a uniform way to define selectors (or destructors) for all data structures (even user-defined data structures).

5.4 Parameter passing

How do we associate actuals and formals? This question appears to be simple, but it is actually a subtle issue in programming languages.

We can categorize parameter passing into roughly two approaches. One approach is to consider the implementation of parameter passing. This approach is best illustrated by FORTRAN. The motivating factor in FORTRAN is finding some efficient way of accomplishing the job. The ensuing method of association is known as call-by-reference. As a reaction and refinement to call-by-reference come some of the other methods we will look at in this section: call-by-value, copy-in/copy out, etc. The other approach is cerebral. A bunch of people sit down and think about what the association should mean. This is the ALGOL 60 approach. The resulting parameter association is call-by-name. It is difficult to implement but is "correct" in a sense discussion in chapter 7.

No discussion of parameter passing can be complete without a famous story about Niklaus Wirth [15], the Swiss designer of the languages Pascal, Modula, and Oberon. True or not, it bears repeating. Wirth's name is one that is confusing for English speakers to pronounce. When asked how to pronounce his name, he is said to have answered that if you call him by name, it is "virt" (the German pronunciation), and if you call him by value, it is "worth" (the American pronunciation).

5.4.1 Call-by-reference

Call-by-reference is the parameter-passing mechanism used by the first programming language FORTRAN. This method of parameter passing is implemented by passing the l-value of each actual parameter to the subroutine. The pointer (address of the actual) is stored in a known location. The formal parameter refers to the actual via that address or pointer.

Not all actual arguments necessarily have an l-value. Consider passing the constant 2 using call-by-reference. If you pass the address of some location holding the constant two, then there is the risk that a program would change the "constant." An actual implementation of FORTRAN had this problem [6, page 189]. The obvious solution is to assign a temporary l-value to the actual arguments that do not have l-values already.

Aliasing is a problem with call-by-reference. It makes the subprograms difficult to understand, if you must take into account the possibility that different names refer to the same location. Aliasing causes problems for optimization as well as for understanding.

The following Ada-like subprocedure detects aliasing if the parameters are passed using call-by-reference.

```
procedure P (x,y: INTEGER) is
    t : INTEGER := y;
begin
```

```
    x := y+2;
    if y=t then "no aliasing" else "aliasing" end if;
end P;
```

The variable `y` may be changed if the call to `P` has uses the same actual argument twice, as in `P(a,a)`. In this case `x` and `y` are aliases; both refer to `a`.

5.4.2 Call-by-value

A response to the difficulties in understanding subprocedures using call-by-reference is the parameter-passing mechanism known as call-by-value. Call-by-value is implemented by initializing a variable local to the subprocedure with the r-value of the actual parameter. This has a mathematically clean semantics.

It appears that call-by-value cannot be the only parameter-passing mechanism in a language. With call-by-value it is not possible to affect the calling program through the parameters. (This was the property that makes it desirable.) It is not possible to update a location or swap two values. So languages often have call-by-reference parameters and call-by-value parameters. Yet the programming language C uses call-by-value exclusively. Because it is possible to compute the l-value of identifiers (using the `&` operator), the l-values can be passed by value. Thus the programmer can simulate call-by-reference any time it is desired.

A disadvantage of call-by-value is that the initialization of a local variable with a copy of the actual argument is expensive if the argument is a large structured object like an array.

5.4.3 Copy-out

The parameter-passing mechanism copy-out is the converse of call-by-value. Its sole purpose to change something in the calling program. A variable local to the subprocedure is created, and when the subprocedure terminates its value is copied back to the corresponding actual parameter. No information flows to the subprocedure through any copy-out parameter. So it is not suitable as the only parameter-passing mechanism in a language. Clearly, the actual argument must be an l-valued expression like a variable.

Ada uses call-by-result for the `out` parameters in the subprocedure below.

```
procedure roots (a,b,c: FLOAT; r1,r2: out FLOAT) is
    d: constant FLOAT := math.sqrt (b**2.0 - 4.0*a*c);
begin
    r1 := (-b + d) / (2.0*a);
    r2 := (-b - d) / (2.0*a);
end roots;
```

The formal arguments `r1` and `r2` are set, but not used. Their initial values are undefined by the language. The procedure is normally called like `roots(1.0,2.0,3.0,` x,y). If it is called like `roots(1.0,2.0,3.0,x,x)`, then the effect is undefined, because the order in which `r1` and `r2` are copied back is not specified by the language definition.

If the l-value of a copy-out parameter is changed during the execution of the subprocedure, then it makes a difference when the l-value is computed.

```
declare
    A: array 1..10 of INTEGER;
    i: INTEGER := 1;
    procedure P (x: out INTEGER) is
    begin
        i := 2;  x := 3;
    end P;
begin
    P (A[i]);
end;
```

In Ada the l-value is computed at the beginning of the procedure invocation. Thus the program fragment sets `A[1]` to 3. In ALGOL W, which also uses copy-out, the l-value is computed at the end of the procedure. Thus the analogous program would set `A[2]` to 3.

5.4.4 Copy-in/copy-out

The parameter-passing mechanism known as copy-in/copy-out is a combination of call-by-value and copy-out. Like call-by-value, an internal location is initialized with the r-value of the actual argument at the beginning of the procedure call. After the procedure call, the r-value in the internal location is copied back into the location indicated by the l-value of the actual argument. Clearly, actual arguments passed copy-in/copy-out must have l-values and cannot be expressions without l-values like `2` or `2+x`. This parameter-passing mechanism is sometimes known as *value-result* or *copy-restore*.

Copy-in/copy-out can be different from call-by-reference because of abnormal termination (like exceptions) or because of aliasing. Since the l-value denoted by an actual argument may change during the course of the execution of the subprocedure, it is important to know when the l-value is determined. Although the l-value is not needed until after the subprocedure is finished, it is usually determined at the time of the procedure call. In this way the initial value of the argument is in fact the value stored at the location that is used in copying back the result.

5.4.5 Text substitution

The remaining three parameter-passing methods are defined by the effect of a procedure invocation, not by how the association of the actual argument to the formal parameter is implemented. The compiler writer is free to implement a procedure call in any manner desired as long as the effect of the call is consistent with the definition. This has the advantage that procedure invocation can be defined from a high-level and logical point of view rather than operationally.

The first of these parameter-passing mechanisms is called *text substitution* and is found in the `#define` directive in the preprocessing step of the C language. Text substitution, as it names implies, requires the effect of inserting the body of the subprocedure at the place of the call and that every formal parameter be replaced by the actual argument.

Here is an example in the programming language C.

```
#define P(x,y) temp=x;x=y;y=temp

main () {
    int temp, a=1, b=2;
    P(a,b);                 /* Produces legal code    */
    P(2*a,2);               /* Produces illegal code  */
}
```

After the macro P is expanded we get:

```
main () {
    int temp, a=1, b=2;
    temp=a;a=b;b=temp ;
    temp=2*a;2*a=2;2=temp ;
}
```

This effect is not even legal. The simplicity of macros is their unswerving adherence to the text. This is also their downfall as a parameter-passing mechanism—the scope rules of the language and even the syntax of the language are ignored.

5.4.6   Call-by-name

The parameter-passing mechanism known as *call-by-name* is based on the *copy rule*. This rule says that a procedure can be replaced by its body with the actuals substituted for the formals (just like text-substitution). If necessary variables must be renamed. There are two types of clashes that require renaming.

1. If a formal argument uses an identifier that is also used locally to the subprocedure, then the local identifier must be consistently renamed to something else.

2. Identifiers that are defined in the context in which the subprocedure is called and are also free identifiers in the body of the subprocedure must be renamed throughout that context to something else.

This is a definition of the effects of a procedure invocation, not an implementation of a parameter-passing mechanism. For recursive procedures the definition still works. The effect of executing each call is given by the definition. The definition does not have to, nor can it, define the effect of the whole execution.

To illustrate the substitution process, consider the following Ada-like procedure definition remotely like the previous `roots` procedure.

```
procedure roots (a: FLOAT) is
    d: FLOAT;
begin
    d := discr (a,a,a);
end roots;
```

We assume that the procedure `discr` is already defined somewhere. Suppose the mechanism used to pass the parameter `a` is call-by-name. The call `roots (2.3)` will have the effect of the block:

```
roots: declare
    d: FLOAT;
begin
    d:= discr (2.3, 2.3, 2.3);
end square;
```

provided that `discr`, a free identifier in the procedure definition, has the same meaning.

Now consider the invocation `roots(d)` in the context of

```
ctx: declare
    d: FLOAT;
    function discr(x,y,z: FLOAT) return FLOAT is begin ⋯ end discr;
begin
    -- The call "roots (d)"
end ctx;
```

Without the proper identifier substitutions the invocation would be replaced by the following program text:

```
roots: declare
    d: FLOAT;
begin
    d := discr (d,d,d);
end roots;
```

Now two problems arise:

1. a conflict with `d` as actual parameter and as local identifier of the procedure definition, and

2. a conflict between the occurrence of `discr` in the procedure definition and the context of the procedure invocation.

The problems are solved by systematically renaming the variables that conflict. The following is the resulting program text after the substitutions.

```
ctx: declare
    d: FLOAT;
    function newdiscr(x,y,z:FLOAT) return FLOAT is begin···end discr;
begin
    -- Calls to "discr" here are renamed to newdiscr.
    -- The call "roots(d)":
    roots: declare
        newd: FLOAT;
    begin
        newd := discr (d,d,d);
    end roots;
    -- Calls to "discr" here are renamed to newdiscr.
end ctx;
```

The first conflict is resolved by renaming the local variable `d` in `roots` to `newd`. The second conflict is resolved by renaming the subprocedure `discr` declared in the block `ctx`. It is important that every call to `discr` refer to the proper subprocedure. Since we assume that the procedure `roots` is visible in the block `ctx` (after all, the procedure is called from there), then `discr` must also be visible in that block, too. So the assignment `newd:=discr(d,d,d)` refers to the correct definition of `discr`, which is declared somewhere outside of `ctx`. All calls to the local subprocedure `discr` have been renamed to `newdiscr` along with all the calls present in the block `ctx`, so there is no longer any conflict concerning the two procedures originally named `discr`. It is tempting to rename the *other* procedure `discr`, but this would entail changes in an even a larger context.

Despite the confusing renamings required in this setting, call-by-name has elegant foundation in the beta-reduction rule of the lambda calculus (see section 7.5). And call-by-name can be useful and natural. The following example was given by Dijkstra [2]:

```
real procedure Sum (index, lb, ub, x);
  value lb, ub;
  integer index, lb, ub;  real x;
  begin  real temp;  temp := 0;
    for index:=lb step 1 until ub do
      temp := temp + x;
    Sum := temp;
  end;
```

This ALGOL 60 program is intended to act like the mathematical summation operator. The call `Sum (i,1,n,A[i])` can be used to compute $\sum_{i=1}^{n} A[i]$. This call to `Sum` makes use of what is called *Jensen's device* (named after Jørn Jensen of Copenhagen [2]). One of the actual parameters `A[i]` is an expression using another parameter `i`. The following table shows some more procedure calls to `Sum`.

$\sum_{i=1}^{n} A[i]$	`Sum (i,1,n,A[i])`
$\sum_{i=1}^{n} B[i,i]$	`Sum (i,1,n,B[i,i])`
$\sum_{i=1}^{m} \sum_{j=1}^{i} j \times B[j,i]$	`Sum (i,1,m,j*Sum(j,1,i,B[j,i]))`

In fact, a slight generalization of the procedure `Sum`, call it `GPS`,

```
real procedure GPS (I,N,Z,V); real I,N,Z,V;
   begin for I:=1 step 1 until N do Z:=V; GPS:=1 end;
```

can be used to compute any computable function using a single assignment statement [8].

Another use of call-by-name is to allow programmers to avoid the evaluation of one or more of their actual parameters.

```
procedure cand (p,q)
   boolean p,q;
   if p then cand := q else cand := false;
```

Here the procedure `cand` first evaluates the parameter `p`, but only if the parameter evaluates to true is the parameter `q` evaluated.

On the other hand, SWAP does not work using call-by-name [4].

```
procedure swap (x,y: integer);
   var temp: integer;
   begin  temp := x; x:= y; y:= temp end;
```

Using call-by-name the procedure call `swap (i, a[i])` has the effect:

```
temp := i;  i := a[i];  a[i] := temp;
```

Since `i` is changed during the course of executing the body of the subprocedure, the l-value of `a[i]` in the assignment `a[i]:=temp` may not refer to the location used before.

5.4.7 Call-by-need

A variation of call-by-name is call-by-need. The evaluation of the actual parameter is deferred until the value of the formal parameter is first needed. This value is saved for any subsequent uses of the formal parameter. This parameter-passing mechanism is more efficient and, in the absence of side effects, has the same effect as call-by-name.

5.4.8   Parameter passing in Ada

The programming language Ada separates the question of how parameter passing is implemented from the question of the programmer's intent in using the parameters.

Ada has three *modes*: in, out, and in/out.   The mode in is default.   A subprocedure that looks at a parameter, but does want to change it would declare it an in parameter. A subprocedure that generates a value to be passed back to the caller would declare the parameter to be an out parameter. And if information is both passed in and back out through the same parameter it would be declared an in out parameter, as the following subprogram specifications illustrate.

```
procedure Use (x: in INTEGER) is ···
procedure Produce (x: out INTEGER) is ···
procedure Modify (x: in out INTEGER) is ···
```

The compiler can choose (sometimes) whether to use copy-in/copy-out or call-by-reference. Thus the programmer can choose the mode of the argument according to how it will be used, and the compiler can choose the best way to implement it.

5.5   Exception handling

Exception handling was introduced first in the programming language PL/I. There were 22 so-called ON conditions for abnormal events such as overflow, conversion errors, dividing by zero, etc. When a condition occurs a standard system action is invoked, but these actions can be overridden by the programmer. An ON unit is a parameterless procedure that returns to the place the interrupt occurred—either to the same statement or the next statement depending on the type of condition. But, of course, the programmer can jump out of the ON-unit, making it difficult to understand.

More recent languages like CLU, Ada, Modula-3, and ML have moved toward a block-structured mechanism for exception handling. We examine exception handling in Ada as the representative of this trend.

5.5.1   Exception handling in Ada

Ada has the ability to catch certain run-time anomalies like constraint errors or numeric overflow. This is generalized to a mechanism of raising and catching exceptions. User-defined exceptions can be raised just like exceptions that are generated by the underlying hardware or by the run-time system. The following Ada block illustrates a system-defined exception and a user-defined exception.

```
A: declare
     I, J, K: INTEGER;
     singular: exception;    -- declare user-defined exception
begin
```

```
    I := J * K;              -- overflow could cause NUMERIC_ERROR
    if det = 0 then raise singular;  -- raise user-defined exception
    F := June;               -- causes exception CONSTRAINT_ERROR
exception
    when NUMERIC_ERROR =>  -- deal with NUMERIC_ERROR
    when singular =>       -- deal with user-defined exception
end A;
```

An exception that is not caught (like CONSTRAINT_ERROR above) is propagated to the dynamically enclosing block.

Here is an extensive example illustrating the propagation of exceptions.

```
procedure P is
    ERROR: exception;       --  declare ERROR as an exception name

    procedure R;            --  stub of R for forward reference

    procedure Q is
    begin
        R;
        -- if ERROR raised here, situation (1)
    exception
      when ERROR =>          --  exception handler E1
    end Q;

    procedure R is
    begin
      -- if ERROR raised here, situation (2)
    end R;

begin
    -- if ERROR raised here, situation (3)
    Q;
exception
    when ERROR =>              -- exception handler E2
end P;
```

The following situations can occur:

1. If the exception ERROR is raised in the sequence of statements of procedure Q, execution of the body of Q immediately halts. The handler E1 provided within Q is then executed and Q terminates normally. Control will be returned to the point of call of Q upon completion of the handler.

2. If the exception ERROR is raised in the body of R, called by Q, the execution of R is abandoned and the same exception is raised in the body of Q. The handler E1 is then used to complete the execution of Q, as in situation (1).

3. If the exception ERROR is raised in the sequence of statements of the outer procedure P, the handler E2 provided within P is used to complete the execution of P.

At first it seems that abandoning the execution of a block when an exception is raised is too drastic. The programmer may want to "patch" a problem and continue on with the normal execution of a block. This may lead one to wish for a construct to allow the flow of execution to jump back to the place where the exception is raised as in PL/I ON conditions. In the first place, jumping back may be fraught with ambiguities caused by the different context of two points in the program. And furthermore, a separate construct is not needed. The granularity of a block can be controlled to circumscribe the effect of exception handling, just as it can be used to control the scope of variables.

Consider the problem of handling overflow caused by multiplication in an expression such as I*J*K. It is a mistake to try to handle overflow in a block *surrounding* the expression. The solution is to approach the problem from *within* the expression. This is possible even for the built-in operators. Here is how a "safe" multiplication operation could be defined.

```
procedure "*" (N, M: INTEGER) return INTEGER is
begin
    return (STANDARD."*" (N, M));
exception
    when NUMERIC_ERROR => return (SYSTEM.MAX_INT);
end "*";
```

Of course, it is not necessary to replace the predefined operator for multiplication— another name could have been chosen. This function requires the usual multiplication operation in its definition. Using simply * would result in a recursive call (and an infinite loop). The usual operation is found in a predefined package called STANDARD and is accessible using dot notation.

It is possible to catch unnamed exceptions. This is useful to regain control despite any exceptional event that occurs during the execution of a procedure body. Then some clean-up could be performed, e.g., closing files. These actions are sometimes called "final wishes."

The following block has two exception handlers, including one that catches all exceptions not explicitly mentioned. This includes those that could not be mentioned by name because the handler is not in the static scope of the exception.

```
declare
    procedure P is
```

```
        E: exception;
    begin   raise E;   end P;
begin
        P;                              -- call P
exception
    when NUMERIC_ERROR =>               -- handle a particular exception
    when others => clean_up; raise; -- clean up, and re-raise except
end;
```

The keyword **others** introduces the clause that catches all other unnamed exceptions.

5.5.2   Exception handling and recursive procedures

The next Ada program illustrates a confusing case of identity. When a recursive procedure defines a local exception, is the exception the same in all invocations of the subprocedure?

```
procedure F(N: INTEGER) is
    E: exception;
begin
    if N=1 then raise E; else F(N-1); end if;
exception
    when E => PUT ("Got it"); raise;
    when others => null;
end F;
```

According to the Ada reference manual 11.1 §3: "if an exception declaration occurs in a recursive subprogram, the exception name denotes the same exception for all invocations of the recursive subprogram." So the call **F(3)** prints **Got it** three times, not once.

The programming language ML, which has an exception-handling mechanism quite similar to Ada's, chooses differently on this point. In ML, an exception identifier declared locally in a subprogram is local to the subprogram just like any other identifier and so is distinct from exceptions (of the same name) in other invocations of the subprogram. In Modula-3, nested exception declarations are illegal.

Another special rule in Ada pertains to generics. Again quoting from the reference manual: "If a generic unit includes an exception declaration, the exception declarations implicitly generated by different instantiations of the generic unit refer to distinct exceptions (but all have the same identifier)."

Exceptions are usually declared like other identifiers, so they naturally follow the same static scope rules. Exception propagation, on the other hand, follows the dynamic chain of execution. This means exceptions can propagate to places in the program where the exception name is not visible.

5.5.3 More about exceptions

CLU, Modula-3, and ML permit exceptions to have parameters. This allows some information to be passed along with the exception. In Modula-3 for example, you might declare an IO exception

```
VAR   IO_error: TEXT;
```

with a string argument. The string argument could be used to give more details about the circumstances in which the exception was raised. For example, a Modula-3 program might raise the exception this way:

```
RAISE IO_error ("File not found");
```

or this way:

```
RAISE IO_error ("Don't have permission to open file");
```

In Ada, the procedure specification gives no indication about the possible exceptions that may passed back to any caller of the procedure. Some languages, like CLU and Modula-3, require procedures to specify all exceptions that are permitted to propagate from a procedure. Here is an example of a procedure specification in Modula-3 which may raise the exception IO_error:

```
PROCEDURE (a: INTEGER): BOOLEAN RAISES {IO_error}
```

A procedure may not propagate an exception that is not in its "raises" set. Here is an example of a procedure specification in CLU:

```
P (a:int, b: real) returns (int)
    signals (zero(int), overflow, bad(string))
```

The procedure named P explicitly lists the three exceptions (signals) that may propagate to any program calling P. Other exceptions get changed to the special signal failure that is implicitly declared for every procedure.

5.6   Encapsulation

The aggregation of program components into larger units is called *encapsulation*. Among these components are typically types, constants, variables, and subprocedures. We call the programming language construct for encapsulation a *module*. Encapsulation is useful logically, i.e., for the benefit of programmers, and practically, i.e., for the benefit of program compilation. Logically, a module provides the opportunity to gather related program pieces to a single textual location. This allows the programmer to build and describe a high-level entity. In some languages this unit can be named and manipulated further itself to build yet other components. Practically, a module provides the opportunity for the implementation to produce an easy-to-use unit that does not incur the cost of recompilation. This unit might be made available to different programmers, or to entirely different projects. A collection of these units is often called a *library*. In many cases, modules reduce the cost of repeatedly compiling large programs.

The implementations of C and FORTRAN often provide the ability to compile parts of the program separately (*separate compilation*). But unlike many modern programming languages, these languages do not provide any programming language support for modules. In languages like Modula, ML, and Ada it is more difficult to misuse separately compiled modules because the language makes more checkable requirements about the use of modules.

The notion of an *abstract type* is related to a module in that it implies encapsulation. In particular, it implies that one type is collected with its relevant operations. But it goes further and requires that representation of the type be hidden from the programmer who knows only some specification. This information-hiding idea was expressed many years ago by Parnas [14, page 334]:

> The important feature of this specification is that it provides sufficient information to use a module which is correctly implemented according to any of these methods, *without the user having any knowledge of the method.*

An abstract type is a type bundled together with a fixed number of procedures. These procedures are the only way to manipulate elements of the abstract type.

The program may choose to use a module to implement one abstract type, but in general a module may provide many types and unrelated functions. Moreover, the representation of these types may or may not be hidden. Languages with modules usually provide some mechanism to hide the representation of data structures. Hence we are led to make the following definitions:

- A type whose structure is hidden is called an *opaque type*.

- A type whose structure is not hidden is called a *transparent type*.

Furthermore, we say that a module that provides an abstract type is a *server*, a program that uses the abstract type is said to be a *client*.

In the next few sections we examine the constructs used in various languages to provide modules.

5.6.1   Packages in Ada

Abstract data types in Ada are implemented with help of *packages*. Figure 5.5 is an example of a package for rational numbers. There are three operations explicitly defined for rational numbers: `Equal`, `"+"` and `"*"`. The binary infix operators `+` and `*` are thereby overloaded. Only by the types of the operands can Ada choose between addition and multiplication defined by the package `RationalNumbers` for rational numbers and predefined operations for other types (`INTEGER`, `FLOAT`, etc.).

```
package RationalNumbers is
    type Rational is
        record
            Numerator: INTEGER;
            Denominator: INTEGER range 1 .. INTEGER'LAST;
        end record;
    function Equal (x, y: Rational) return BOOLEAN;
    function "+"   (x, y: Rational) return Rational;
    function "*"   (x, y: Rational) return Rational;
end RationalNumbers;

package body RationalNumbers is
    procedure SameDenominator (x, y: in out Rational) is
        NewDenominator: INTEGER := x.Denominator * y.Denominator;
    begin
        x.Numerator   := x.Numerator * y.Denominator;
        y.Numerator   := y.Numerator * x.Denominator;
        x.Denominator := NewDenominator;
        y.Denominator := NewDenominator;
    end SameDenominator;

    function Equal (x,y: Rational) return BOOLEAN is
        u: Rational := x;  -- modifiable copy of x
        v: Rational := y;  -- modifiable copy of y
    begin
        SameDenominator (u,v);
        return (u.Numerator = v.Numerator);
    end Equal;

    function "+" (x,y: Rational) return Rational is
        u: Rational := x;  -- modifiable copy of x
        v: Rational := y;  -- modifiable copy of y
    begin
        SameDenominator (u, v);
        return ( (
            Numerator =>   u.Numerator + v.Numerator,
            Denominator => u.Denominator) );
    end "+";

    function "*" (x,y: Rational) return Rational is
    begin
        return ( (
            Numerator   =>  x.Numerator * y.Numerator,
            Denominator => x.Denominator * y.Denominator) );
    end "*";
end RationalNumbers;
```

Figure 5.5: Ada module for rational numbers

Both the package specification and implementation begin with the keyword `package`. The implementation is distinguished from the specification by the additional keyword `body`. Three functions are specified in the package specification, but four functions are defined in the implementation. The fourth function `SameDenominator` can be used only in the package implementation itself; no client can access it. All the specified entities must be implemented, but additional variables, constants, exception, types and subprocedures are permitted for internal use. Executable code to initialize the package is permitted (none is needed for the rational number package). This code would be executed before the main program begins execution.

The implementation details of some type in the package specification may be irrelevant to its use outside the package. These details can be hidden from the user by declaring such a type with a private type definition in the package specification. This is accomplished as follows.

```
package P is
    type T is private;
private
    type T is ...;      -- The complete definition
end;
```

Notice that the compiler still has access to the complete type definition. This is important in order to allocate storage for variables declared to be of a private type.

Private types have only the operations of assignment and equality defined for them outside the package. Even these operations can be disallowed by declaring the type to be `limited private`.

Modula-2 also has transparent types and opaque types as in Ada. The definition of opaque types appear in the implementation module; only the name appears in the definition module. Files depending of the definition module do not have to be recompiled if the structure of the type changes. But there is a cost associated with the advantage. Opaque types must be pointer types in Modula-2 because pointer types usually take the same amount of storage regardless of the type they point to. Thus the size of an opaque type is known even if its definition is not.

5.6.2   Modules in Modula-3

Figure 5.6 shows how to implement a module for rational numbers in Modula-3. The module implements one type that, according to Modula-3 conventional practice, is named `T`. Clients of the module would normally refer to the type as `Rational.T`. At the beginning of the program any executable statements between the `BEGIN` and the `END` of the module would be executed. This can be used for initializing data structures and the like. In the case of the module for rational numbers no such code is required, and so nothing appears between the `BEGIN` and the `END`. The `BEGIN` cannot be omitted as in Ada.

```
INTERFACE Rational;
    TYPE T = RECORD Numerator:=0; Denominator: [1..LAST(INTEGER)]:= 1; END;
    PROCEDURE Equal (READONLY x,y: T): BOOLEAN;
    PROCEDURE Plus  (READONLY x,y: T): T;
    PROCEDURE Times (READONLY x,y: T): T;
END Rational.

MODULE Rational;
    PROCEDURE SameDenominator (VAR x, y: T) =
    VAR
        NewDenominator := x.Denominator * y.Denominator;
    BEGIN
        x.Numerator   := x.Numerator * y.Denominator;
        y.Numerator   := y.Numerator * x.Denominator;
        x.Denominator := NewDenominator;
        y.Denominator := NewDenominator;
    END SameDenominator;

    PROCEDURE Equal (READONLY x,y: T): BOOLEAN =
    VAR
        u := x;  v := y;  (* modifiable copies of x and y *)
    BEGIN
        SameDenominator (u,v);
        RETURN (u.Numerator = v.Numerator);
    END Equal;

    PROCEDURE Plus (READONLY x, y: T): T =
    VAR
        u := x;  v := y;  (* modifiable copies of x and y *)
    BEGIN
        SameDenominator (u, v);
        RETURN (T {
            Numerator   := u.Numerator + v.Numerator,
            Denominator := u.Denominator});
    END Plus;

    PROCEDURE Times (READONLY x, y: T): T =
    BEGIN
        RETURN (T {
            Numerator   :=  x.Numerator * y.Numerator,
            Denominator := x.Denominator * y.Denominator} );
    END Times;
BEGIN END Rational.
```

Figure 5.6: Modula-3 module for rational numbers

The module in figure 5.6 implements a transparent type. An opaque type, like in Modula-2, must be a pointer type. The type name appears in a subtype declaration in the specification module, for instance:

```
TYPE T <: REFANY  (* T is a subtype of any reference type. *)
```

The use of inclusion polymorphism (see section 4.5.4) in opaque types is uncommon and innovative. The "revelation" or implementation of the type appears in the implementation module:

```
REVEAL
    T = BRANDED REF RECORD
        Numerator:  INTEGER := 0;
        Denominator:  [1..LAST(INTEGER)] := 1;
    END;
```

Opaque types must be "branded" to ensure that structurally identical types are distinct. (Modula-3 uses structural equivalence.) Revelations can be partial $T<V$. In this case T is a subtype of V, but the entire structure of T is not known and must be disclosed later.

References to records are called objects in Modula-3 and have special significance in the language. As we have see earlier (section 4.5.5) objects can have methods associated with them. Using objects and subtyping it is possible to have abstract types that are partially opaque and partially transparent. As an example, suppose we want to define a graphic object that is capable of being translated by some horizontal and vertical amount. The specification module declares the public protocol with method `translate`. The type `Graphic` is subtype of `PublicProtocol`; this reveals that an object of type `Graphic` has the `translate` method, but nothing else about the object.

```
TYPE
    PublicProtocol = OBJECT METHODS translate (h,v: INTEGER) END;
    Graphic < PublicProtocol;
```

In the implementation module all (or some) of the remaining structure is revealed.

```
REVEAL
    Graphic = PublicProtocol BRANDED OBJECT
        x,y: Point.T
    END;
```

In this case the structure contains two points x and y. These fields are known only to the implementation module and cannot be used by the client.

5.6.3 Modules in ML

We look at the module construct in a third language, ML [12]. In ML the specification is called a signature for, just as in algebra, a specification gives the type of

```
signature RationalNumbersSig =
sig
    type Rational
    val Eq:   Rational * Rational -> bool
    val Add:  Rational * Rational -> Rational
    val Mult: Rational * Rational -> Rational
end

structure RationalNumbers : RationalNumbersSig =
struct
    type Rational = {Numerator: int, Denominator: int}
    fun Num ({Numerator=x, Denominator=_}:Rational) = x
    fun Den ({Numerator=_, Denominator=x}:Rational) = x

    fun Eq (x,y) = (Num(x)*Den(y) = Num(y)*Den(x))

    fun Add (x,y): Rational =
        {Numerator   = Num(x)*Den(y) + Num(y)*Den(x),
         Denominator = Den(x)*Den(y) }

    fun Mult (x,y): Rational =
        {Numerator=Num(x)*Num(y), Denominator = Den(x)*Den(y)}
end
```

Figure 5.7: ML module for rational numbers

the function symbols. In figure 5.7 we show how the example module for rational numbers would appear in ML. In between the keywords **signature** and **end** appear a type declaration and three function specifications. The signature is given a name, **RationalNumbersSig**. In between the keywords **structure** and **end** appear a type definition and five function definitions. The type **Rational** is defined to be a record. Records in ML are written with curly braces. The whole collection of definitions is given the name **RationalNumbers**. The line

```
structure RationalNumbers : RationalNumbersSig =
```

restricts the structure to have the signature **RationalNumbersSig**. This hides the auxiliary functions **Num** and **Den** from any user of the **RationalNumbers** structure.

To make an opaque type the keyword **structure** is replaced with keyword **abstraction**. Now the structure of the type **Rational** would not be available to a client. This would leave no way for a client to create an element of that type. So we should add a constructor to the structure:

```
fun Rational (n,d) = {Numerator=n, Denominator=d}
```

Unlike Ada and Modula-3, where modules and interfaces come primarily in pairs linked by their common name, structures and signatures in ML are more independent. They can be given names or be anonymous, they can be associated which each other in multiple ways, and they can even be treated in limited respects like values and types. For example, ML `functors` can be created that take structures as arguments to create other structures.

5.6.4 Classes in C++

The programming language C++ extends the language C by introducing a construct called a *class*. A class is a generalization of the C `struct` construct (the syntax for records in C uses the keyword `struct`). A class declaration in C++ provides an interface of fields and member functions like the module constructs in other languages. The fields and member functions are divided into private and public parts (and protected parts that are germane to derived types). The public parts are visible to any client of the class. Private fields and functions may be used only in the implementation of the class.

Classes in C++ are not really abstract data types, but a set of restrictions on the visibility of identifiers. This reflects the origins of C++ as a preprocessor for C. The programming challenge lies in ensuring that expressions have access to the correct parts of the data structures they need. C++ has various access-granting mechanisms. One of these is the `friend` mechanism. A friend of a class is a function that is not a member of the class but is nevertheless permitted to use its private and protected fields and functions.

A class declaration in C++ is somewhat like a module specification in other languages. The top part of figure 5.8 is a class declaration for rational numbers. In it are the declarations of the fields and functions comprising the class. Often the definitions of functions are part of the declaration when these definitions are short. (An example is the function `Rational` in figure 5.8.) The whole declaration is usually put in a file by itself. This file ends with the characters `.h` by convention, just like header files in the C programming language. In C++ you "import" the class declaration by including the header file in any file that wishes to use the class. The programmer cannot make use of all the details in a `.h` file, but the compiler can. The compiler then knows the size of the class and can replace functions inline if their definition is part of the declaration. The implementation of the class is usually in another file (or files). An implementation file must include the class definition file and provide the definitions for the functions that do not have them.

In figure 5.8 we have define a C++ module for rational numbers. The top part of the figure is the class declaration, and the bottom part is the implementation of the class. The procedure `SameDenominator` is not part of the class declaration, so it is not available to any clients of the class `Rational`. So it might be more properly declared as private member function of the class. We have overloaded the infix, binary operators `==`, `+`, and `*`. This requires the keyword `operator`. Special rules

```
/*  file rn.h -- declaration of class Rational in C++ */
class Rational {
  private:
    int Numerator, Denominator;
    friend void SameDenominator (Rational *x, Rational *y);
  public:
    // Constructor Rational has a default argument.
    // Since this constructor can be called with one argument it can
    // be used as an implicit coercion from int to the class Rational
    Rational (int n, int d = 1) { Numerator = n; Denominator = d; }
    friend int operator == (Rational x, Rational y);
    friend Rational operator + (Rational x, Rational y);
    friend Rational operator * (Rational x, Rational y);
};

/*  file rn.cc -- implementation of class Rational */
#include "rn.h"

void SameDenominator (Rational *x, Rational *y) {
    int NewDenominator = x->Denominator * y->Denominator;
    x->Numerator   *= y->Denominator;
    y->Numerator   *= x->Denominator;
    x->Denominator = y->Denominator = NewDenominator;
}

int operator == (Rational x, Rational y) {
    SameDenominator (&x, &y);
    return (x.Numerator == y.Numerator);
}

Rational operator + (Rational x, Rational y) {
    Rational Sum (0);                       // declare variable Sum
    SameDenominator (&x, &y);
    Sum.Numerator   = x.Numerator + y.Numerator;
    Sum.Denominator = x.Denominator;
    return (Sum);
}

Rational operator * (Rational x, Rational y) {
    Rational Product (0);                   // declare variable Product
    Product.Numerator   = x.Numerator * y.Numerator;
    Product.Denominator = x.Denominator * y.Denominator;
    return (Product);
}
```

Figure 5.8: C++ module for rational numbers

govern the overloading of binary operators (cf. [3, §13.4]). Another difficulty with the binary operations exists. The usual case in which a member function implicitly accesses the fields and methods of a class does not hold. In the implementation of the rational number operations, we require access to the private fields (`Numerator` and `Denominator`) of two rational numbers given explicitly as arguments. The class `Rational` grants this permission to the three binary functions by designating them as "friends."

Here is a sample main program that uses the module for rational numbers given in figure 5.8.

```
#include "rn.h"
int main () {
    Rational r1 = Rational (1,2);
    Rational r2 = Rational (7);      // default denominator is 1
    Rational r3 = 3;                 // implicit coercion to Rational
    r1 = r1 + r2;                    // operator += is NOT deduced
    r2 = 4 + r1;                     // rational addition
    return 0;
}
```

Classes are designed to be cloned into new, similar data structures called derived classes. These classes are said to *inherit* methods from the base classes when they implicitly offer their clients the same methods as the base classes. While on the subject of C++, we look at some of the different ways real code is associated with these implicit methods in C++. In figure 5.9 a class `base` is used in defining another class `derived`. The derived class inherits all the methods of class `base`. All of these methods are public, so there are available to any user of the class. Any private methods would not be inherited. Using the `protect` mechanism it is possible to have methods that are inherited by derived classes yet not publicly accessible.

The base class defines three member functions `m1`, `m2`, and `m3`. The derived class inherits the three methods of the base class. But the situation is different in each. The method `m1` is left as it is, the method `m2` is overridden by a different function definition, and method `m3` is a virtual method. The meaning of a call to a virtual function depends on the type of the object not the type of the pointer or reference denoting the object. An object that is supposed to point to class `base`, but actually points to a derived class, like R in figure 5.9, will use the methods in `base` unless they are virtual. An object of type `derived`, like P in the figure, will use its own methods for `m2`, and `m3`.

The importance of base classes with virtual functions is explained this way [3, pages 208–209]:

> Derived classes and virtual functions [are] the key to the design of many C++ programs. A base class defines an interface for which a variety of implementations are provided by derived classes. A pointer to an object

```
/*  Some examples of inheritance.  */
#include <stream.h>

/* A base class */
class base {
public:
            void m1 () { cout << "base::m1\n"; }
            void m2 () { cout << "base::m2\n"; }
    virtual void m3 () { cout << "base::m3\n"; }
};

/* A derived class */
class derived : public base {
public:
            void m2 () { cout << "derived::m2\n"; }
            void m3 () { cout << "derived::m3\n"; }
            void m4 () { cout << "derived::m4\n"; }
};

int main () {
    base      0;
    derived  P;
    base     *Q = new derived;
    derived *R = new base;      /*  compile-time error  */

    0.m1();        //  calls base::m1
    0.m2();        //  calls base::m2
    0.m3();        //  calls base::m3
    0.m4();                     /*  compile-time error  */

    P.m1();        //  calls base::m1
    P.m2();        //  calls derived::m2
    P.m3();        //  calls derived::m3
    P.m4();        //  calls derived::m4

    P.base::m3();  //  calls base::m3

    Q->m1();       //  calls base::m1
    Q->m2();       //  calls base::m2
    Q->m3();       //  calls derived::m3
    Q->m4();                    /*  compile-time error  */

    Q->base::m3(); //  calls base::m3

    return 0;
}
```

Figure 5.9: Inheritance in C++

of a class can be passed into a context where the interface defined by one of its base classes is known but where the derived class is unknown. The virtual function mechanism ensures that the object is still manipulated by the functions defined for it (and not just by the functions defined for the base class).

5.7 Exercises

5.1 Consider the following nested blocks in Ada-like syntax:

```
Main:  begin
    One:   declare
        X: INTEGER := 1;
    begin
        null;
    end One;
    Two:   declare
        X: INTEGER;
    begin
        if x=1 then
            --   1 left over
        else
            --   implicit reinitialization
        end if;
    end Two;
end Main;
```

What should be the result of the test x=1? Why?

5.2 Describe in general terms an algorithm to associate an actual argument to every formal parameter in subprocedure calls for a language with positional and named parameters and with default parameters. Assume that the subprocedure names cannot be overloaded.

5.3 Give an ALGOL-like program that demonstrates the difference between call-by-reference and copy-in/copy-out.

5.4 Give an ALGOL-like program that distinguishes the parameter-passing mechanism call-by-name from call-by-reference.

5.5 Give an ALGOL-like program that distinguishes the parameter-passing mechanism call-by-reference from copy-in/copy-out. Also, the subprocedure cannot modify its arguments.

5.6 Consider the following function:

```
function F (x,y: integer) return integer is
begin
    x:=x+1; y:= y+1; return (x-y);
end F;
```

Show by one or more examples of calls on procedure F that call-by-name, call-by-value/result and call-by-reference are different parameter-passing methods. That is, show calls that produce different results for the different binding rules.

5.7 A program fragment of a statically scoped programming language is given below. Suppose that the parameter-passing mechanism used to pass the argument of procedure P is call-by-name. Give the effect of the procedure call P(a) in the program below by rewriting the main begin/end block.

```
main: declare
    a, b: integer;
    procedure S is begin ... end S;
    procedure P (x: integer) is
        a: integer;
    begin
        x := b;   S;   x := a;
    end P;
begin
    inner: declare
        procedure S is begin ... end S;
    begin
        S;   P (a);   S;
    end inner;
end main;
```

5.8 (From [5, pages 156–157].) To get the swap function to work correctly using call-by-name, we need somehow to bind the l-value and r-value of the arguments simultaneously. Consider the following implementation of the swap procedure:

```
procedure swap (x,y: INTEGER) is
    function w is
        z: INTEGER := x;
    begin
        x:=y;
        return (z);
    end w;
begin
```

```
        y := w;     -- call w
   end;
```

  (a) Assume x and y are passed using call-by-name. What is the effect of the
      call swap(i,A[i])?

  (b) Find an example in which swap fails to swap the two values of its argu-
      ments.

5.9 Consider the following Pascal program.

```
program Main (input, output);

    procedure Recurse (i: integer; procedure P);
        procedure Print;  begin  write(i)  end;
        begin {Recurse}
            if i>0
                then Recurse (i-1, Print)
                else begin  Print;  P end
        end; {Recurse}

    procedure Skip;  begin end;

begin  {Main}
    Recurse (2, Skip)
end.
```

  (a) What is the output of this program?

  (b) Show the run-time stack throughout the entire course of execution of this
      program. Draw a picture of the stack each time the stack is changed.
      For each activation record show only the name and the static link.

  (c) Would the output of this program be different if Pascal used dynamic
      scoping instead of static scoping? If different, what would the output
      be?

  (d) What is the value that is passed to a subroutine as the value of a
      procedure? In particular, describe how this value is determined for the
      procedural parameter Print in the procedure call Recurse (1, Print)
      that occurs during the execution of the above program.

5.10 What does the following Ada program output with the PUT statement?

```
declare
    E: exception;
    procedure P (n: INTEGER) is
```

```
        F: exception;
    begin
        text_io.put ("Call P");
        if n=2 then raise E end if;
        if n=3 then raise F end if;
    exception
        when E => text_io.put ("E1");
        when others => text_io.put ("others1");
    end P;
begin
    P(1);  P(2);  P(3);  P(4);
exception
    when E => text_io.put ("E2");
    when others => text_io.put ("others2");
end;
```

5.11 What do the following two Ada programs print?

```
(a) declare
        E1, E2: exception;
        procedure P (n: INTEGER) is begin raise E1; end P;
        function F (n: INTEGER) return INTEGER is
        begin
            raise E2;
        exception
            when E1 => text_io.put ("handler 1"); return (1);
            when E2 => text_io.put ("handler 2"); return (2);
        end F;
    begin
        P (F (0));
    exception
        when E1 => text_io.put ("handler 3");
        when E2 => text_io.put ("handler 4");
    end;
(b) declare
        E1, E2: exception;
        procedure P (n: INTEGER) is
        begin
            raise E2;
        exception
            when E1 => text_io.put ("handler 1"); return (1);
            when E2 => text_io.put ("handler 2"); return (2);
        end P;
        function F (n: INTEGER) return INTEGER is
```

```
        begin raise E1; end F;
    begin
        P (F (0));
    exception
        when E1 => text_io.put ("handler 3");
        when E2 => text_io.put ("handler 4");
    end;
```

5.12 In a functional language with exception handling (like ML), write a function **prod** to compute the product of a list of numbers. The function **prod** must return zero as soon as zero is encountered in the list and not do any extra multiplications.

5.13 Consider the problem of initializing values in one module using values from another module. In C++ we may have these values in different files. Suppose the following situation occurs:

```
// file1:
extern int y;
int x = y+1;

// file2:
extern int x;
int y = x+1;
```

In Ada the analogous program is written using packages:

```
with Package_Y;
package X is
    X : Integer := Package_Y.Y+1;
end X;

with Package_X;
package Y is
    Y : Integer := Package_X.X+1;
end Y;
```

Compare the semantics of C++ and Ada with respect to these programs.

5.14 Implement the following Modula-3 interface for tables. These tables hold a set of key-value pairs. For the sake of concreteness both keys and values are integers.

```
INTERFACE IntIntTable;
```

```
TYPE T <: REFANY;        (* Type T is a pointer of some kind. *)
EXCEPTION not_found;

PROCEDURE New (initial:CARDINAL := 64): T RAISES {};
PROCEDURE Get (table:T; key:INTEGER): INTEGER RAISES {not_found}
PROCEDURE Put (table:T; key:INTEGER; value:INTEGER) RAISES {};
PROCEDURE Delete (table:T; key:INTEGER) RAISES {};

END IntIntTable.
```

5.15 What would the `package` specification for the abstract data type `IntIntTable` of the previous exercise look like in the programming language Ada?

5.8   Bibliography

[1] Barnes, John Gilbert Presslie. *Programming in Ada.* Second edition. International computer science series. Addison-Wesley, London, 1984.

[2] Dijkstra, Edsger Wybe. "Defense of ALGOL 60." *Communications of the ACM*, volume 4, number 11, November 1961, pages 502–503.

[3] Ellis, Margaret A., and Bjarne Stroustrup. *The Annotated C++ Reference Manual.* Addison Wesley, Reading, Massachusetts, 1990.

[4] Fleck, A. C. "On the impossibility of content exchange through the by-name parameter transmission mechanism." *SIGPLAN Notices*, volume 11, number 11, November 1976, pages 38–41.

[5] Gelernter, David Hillel, and Suresh Jagannathan. *Programming Linguistics.* MIT Press, Cambridge, Massachusetts, 1990.

[6] Gries, David. *Compiler Construction for Digital Computers.* John Wiley & Sons, New York, 1971.

[7] Johnston, John B.. "The contour model of block structured processes." *SIGPLAN Notices*, volume 6, number 2, February 1971, pages 55–82.

[8] Knuth, Donald Ervin, and Jack N. Merner. "ALGOL 60 Confidential." *Communications of the ACM*, volume 4, number 6, June 1961, pages 268–272.

[9] Liskov, Barbara H. "Exception handling in CLU." *IEEE Transactions on Software Engineering*, November 1979, pages 545–558. Reprinted in *Tutorial, Programming Language Design*, edited by Anthony I. Wasserman, 1980, pages 403–415.

[10] Liskov, Barbara H., and Stephen N. Zilles. "Programming with abstract data types." *SIGPLAN Notices*, volume 9, number 4, April 1974, pages 50–59. Reprinted in *Tutorial, Programming Language Design*, edited by Anthony I. Wasserman, 1980, pages 189–198.

[11] Marcotty, Michael, and Henry F. Ledgard. *The Programming Language Landscape: Syntax, Semantics, and Implementation.* Second edition. Science Research Associates, Chicago, 1986.

[12] Milner, Robin, Mads Tofte, and Robert Harper. *The Definition of Standard ML.* MIT Press, Cambridge, Massachusetts, 1990.

[13] Morris, James H., Jr. "Protection in programming languages." *Communications of the ACM,* volume 16, number 1, January 1973, pages 15–21.

[14] Parnas, David Lorge. "A technique for software module specification with examples." *Communications of the ACM,* volume 15, number 5, 1972, pages 330–336.

[15] Pournelle, Jerry. "Computing at Chaos Manor: Come to the Faire." *BYTE,* volume 10, number 7, July 1985, pages 309–339.

[16] Stroustrup, Bjarne. *The C++ Programming Language.* Addison-Wesley, Reading, Massachusetts, 1986.

Chapter 6

PROLOG

The programming language PROLOG was developed at the University of Marseilles, France, in the early 1970s. The language is called PROLOG (PROgrammation en LOGique) because it is based on Robinson's resolution principle. The resolution principle is a single rule of inference for deducing true formulas of predicate logic. We study PROLOG because it is the founding and quintessential member of the logic programming paradigm.

PROLOG is an example of what is called a nonprocedural language. A *nonprocedural language* does not convey step by step how to compute a result, but specifies what properties the result should possess. Execution of the specification finds the solution. Consider the problem of sorting an array. In a procedural language the programmer would have to give an algorithm, say, Quicksort, to find the answer. In a nonprocedural language the programmer may need only specify that a permutation of the array in nondecreasing order is required. This is an attractive approach to problem solving when the general mechanisms provide the solution in an efficient manner.

The prospect is appealing, but the difficulty is to design specifications that can be translated into executable instructions. Both set theory and predicate logic have been explored as the framework for these executable specifications. The programming language SETL allows programmers to specify and manipulate sets in expressing computation. PROLOG relies nearly exclusively on formulas of predicate logic to express computation.

Next we give an example to illustrate nonprocedural specification of computation in the language SETL. Consider the problem of sorting a graph in topological order. A program written in SETL for sorting a graph is given in figure 6.1. Of particular interest in this program is the `while` loop, which chooses a node n, *any* n with the appropriate properties. The choice of n is not controlled by the programmer as would be necessary in a procedural language. Any n in the set `nodes` satisfying the specification `n notin range G` will work. How the choice of n

```
$ topological sort in SETL from
$    Schwartz, et al., Programming with Sets, page 408

$ the input G is a graph represented by a set of ordered pairs
$ the output t is a total order represented by an ordered tuple
proc top (G);
    nodes := (domain G) + (range G); $ set of all nodes of graph
    t := [];                          $ initially nothing in order

    $ pick an n in nodes such that n is not in range of G
    (while exists n in nodes | n notin range G)
        t with := n;                  $ n is next in total order
        G lessf := n;                 $ remove pairs with 1st elem n
        nodes less := n;              $ remove n from nodes
    end while;
    return t;
end proc top;
```

Figure 6.1: Topological sort program in SETL

is made is entirely up to the implementation. An efficient way of choosing is to keep a count of the number of predecessors of each node that have not been put into the order. And this is how it is usually written in a procedural language, but this is not prescribed in the SETL program in figure 6.1. In PROLOG it is possible to specify the desired solution in using predicate logic, and the PROLOG system will find the solution automatically. In this chapter we introduce PROLOG programming and discuss some interesting aspects of the language: its search technique, means of controlling the search, matching with uninterpreted function symbols, and the relationship to predicate logic.

6.1   Programming in PROLOG

Programming in PROLOG involves

   (a) *objects*, which include indivisible entities called atoms or actors, and

   (b) *relationships* between objects.

Each distinct name (identifier) represents an individual atom or relationship. Programming in PROLOG consists of an interactive dialog between the user and the PROLOG system in which the user can

   1. declare facts about objects and relationships,

2. define rules about objects and relationships, and

3. ask questions about objects and relationships.

Actually, as we will see in this chapter, the first one of these is a special case of the second. And all these actions can be represented uniformly by special logical formulas called Horn clauses (see section 6.5).

The following are examples of declaring facts.

```
Valuable (Gold).          /*  Gold is valuable.          */
Valuable (Money).         /*  Money is valuable.         */
Father (John, Mary).      /*  John is the father of Mary. */
Gives (John, Book, Mark). /*  John gives the book to Mark. */
King (John, France).      /*  John is the king of France. */
Iam.                      /*  I am.                      */
```

In these examples we have capitalized the relation symbols Valuable, Father, Gives, King, and Iam. We have also capitalized the atomic objects Gold, Money, John, Book, Mark, and France. Variables, which will be introduced shortly, will always begin with lowercase letters. We use the convention throughout most of this chapter despite the fact that the opposite convention is used in most implementations of PROLOG. We do so to draw attention to the fact that a convention is being used. The response of the PROLOG system to a declaration of fact is not important, and we assume that there is no response.

Syntactically a fact ends with a period. The period indicates that the phrase is a declaration (and not a question). In the syntax of a fact, all the identifiers found inside the parentheses are atoms. This is so because we make the simplifying assumption that relationships cannot be the objects of other relations. Hence we can tell by context which identifiers stand for relationships and which for objects.

Now we give the definition of a literal. If P is a n-ary relation symbol and $t_1, \ldots, t_n$ are $n \geq 0$ terms representing objects, then $P(t_1, \ldots, t_n)$ is said to be a *(positive) literal*. The only terms we have introduced thus far are atoms, but others will come later. If n is equal to zero, then we have a nullary relation symbol as in Iam above. A fact is an assertion that a single literal is true.

All facts involve exactly one relationship. It does not make any sense to omit the relationship and assert an atom as fact.

```
Chair.                    /*  Nonsense (but syntactically legal).  */
```

In the syntax of a fact, the relation name appears first, outside the parentheses. We can view a fact as a predicate, in the philological sense, with a subject and verb. The relation symbol is the verb expressing some action or state, for instance, "giving." Just as a sentence is not complete without a verb, no assertion of a fact in PROLOG can omit the relation. This philological view of PROLOG is often quite useful. Since Frege's subtle but important shift from this 2,000-year-old point of view to one including the notion of an argument, we have a clearer view of a relation in set-theoretic terms. Indeed, that is why we chose the term *relation*. We can view the facts asserted above as enumerating the elements of the relation `Valuable`. Thus PROLOG has important and close ties with relational databases.

The interpretation of the facts above, or the reason these statements are asserted, is entirely up to the programmer. The choice of names is meant to be suggestive of their possible interpretation, and the comments indicate the intended interpretation. But the PROLOG system does not take advantage of this. What is significant to PROLOG is the order of the arguments. The declaration of the fact

```
Father (John, Mary).
```

is not the same as

```
Father (Mary, John).
```

The list of asserted facts comprises a database over which we may pose questions. Queries are literals, just as facts are, so we distinguish them from facts by using a question mark instead of a period. Here is an example.

```
Greek (Socrates)?
no
```

This query asks if `Greek(Socrates)` is in the list of facts asserted by the programmer in the current interactive session. The response can be either yes or no. Indeed `Greek(Socrates)` is not among the six facts asserted above, so PROLOG would give a negative response in this case. PROLOG is not an oracle; the response means that `Greek(Socrates)` is not in the list of facts, rather than that Socrates is not Greek. On the other hand, if we ask:

```
Valuable (Gold)?        /* Is Gold valuable?  */
yes
```

then we get a positive response, because the literal `Valuable(Gold)` does appear in the list of six facts.

Atoms are not the only terms. Variables are terms as well. By the convention used here variables will begin with lowercase letters to distinguish them from relation symbols and atoms. Using variables it is possible to formulate more sophisticated questions. For example, to ask "Who is the father of Mary?" we formulate the query as:

```
Father (x, Mary)?
x=John
```

The PROLOG system gives the response x=John. PROLOG treats the variables as unknowns and tries to find objects, which, when substituted for the variables, give a literal that appears in the list of facts. In this case picking the variable x to be `John` results in a match because we have previously asserted the literal `Father(John,Mary)`. Here is another example. This time we ask "Of whom is John the father?"

```
Father (John, x)?
x=Mary
```

We see by this example that relations are not functions. There are no specially designated input and output variables.

What if a query matches one or more facts? Each match is a potential answer. For example:

```
Valuable (x)?
x=Gold
x=Money
```

PROLOG implementations usually allow you to choose if you want to continue after every answer. It may be a waste of time to find more than one answer, if the user is satisfied by the first answer.

To find out if two or more facts are true simultaneously, queries are permitted to have a list of literals separated by commas. The following query asks if John gives anything valuable to Mark.

```
Gives (John, x, Mark), Valuable (x)?
```

Put less idiomatically the query is: does John give x to Mark and x is valuable? So the list of literals acts like a conjunction. The variable x means the same throughout the query but has no connection with any x appearing in any other query. The response to the query is negative because there is no object x such that both literals `Gives(John,x,Mark)` and `Valuable(x)` appear in the database of six facts asserted above. Thus this query is completely different from

```
Gives (John, x, Mark)?
x=Book
Valuable (x)?
x=Gold
x=Money
```

which are two separate queries.

It is possible to have variables in assertions as well as questions. These variables mean the literal is to be taken as fact for *all* objects.

```
Beautiful (x).    /* Everything is beautiful. */
```

There is no need to have a conjunction for asserting facts, because each literal could just as well be asserted individually. What is needed is a mechanism for asserting facts based conditionally on other circumstances. Assertions of this kind are called *rules*. Rules have two parts: the head and tail separated by a symbol ":-" called a turnstile.

```
Iam :- Ithink.    /* If I think, then I am. */
```

This rule asserts the nullary relation `Iam`, if the nullary relation `Ithink` can be established. The head of a rule is a single literal, but the tail can be a conjunction if desired. A conjunction is expressed by a list of literals separated by commas.

Using variables and implication we can capture in PROLOG the classic syllogism concerning mortality.

```
Mortal (x) :- Man (x).        /*  All men are mortal.  */
Man (Socrates).               /*  Socrates is a man.   */
Mortal (Socrates)?
yes
```

PROLOG deduces that Socrates is mortal given that Socrates is a man.

Assume for the moment some database of parenthood consisting of facts about people in a `Parents` relation. We express, for example, that `Victoria` is the mother of `Edward` and `Albert` is the father of `Edward` with the clause `Parents(Edward,Victoria,Albert)`. Here is an example of a rule that defines the paternal grandfather relation in terms of the `Parents` relation:

```
Grandfather (g,c) :- Parents (c,m1,f), Parents (f,m2,g).
```

Note the different uses of the variables in this rule. The variables `g` and `c` appear in the head of the clause have the effect of making this rule a definition of the grandfather relation *in general*, rather than for specific cases. The variables `m1` and `m2` are "don't care" variables. Some PROLOG systems permit variables used like this to be replaced with a special anonymous variable symbol such as `_`. The variable `f` is used to form a connection between the two `Parents` literals.

From

```
Parents (George, Alexandra, Edward).
Parents (Edward, Victoria, Albert).
```

PROLOG concludes that `Grandfather (Albert, George)`. To extend the definition of the grandfather relation to both paternal and maternal lines, we assert two rules:

```
Grandfather (g,c) :- Parents (c,m1,f), Parents (f,m2,g).
Grandfather (g,c) :- Parents (c,m1,f), Parents (m1,m2,g).
```

PROLOG tries all possible ways to establish a literal, so both definitions are employed. Hence two rules with the same head act like choices.

It is possible and useful to define relations in PROLOG in terms of themselves. For example, the "ancestor" relation could be defined:

```
Ancestor (a,c) :- Parents (c,m,a).
Ancestor (a,c) :- Parents (c,a,f).
Ancestor (a,c) :- Parents (c,m,f), Ancestor (a,m).
Ancestor (a,c) :- Parents (c,m,f), Ancestor (a,f).
```

Colloquially expressed, your parents are your immediate ancestors and their ancestors are also your ancestors. The first two rules serve as the base cases. Without them it would be impossible to establish any `Ancestor` literal.

6.1.1 Search strategy

Now we examine how PROLOG uses a collection of rules (which constitutes a PROLOG program) to answer queries. We consider an example about royal English parentage from Clocksin and Mellish [5, page 16].

```
1   Male (Albert).
2   Male (Edward).
3   Female (Alice).
4   Female (Victoria).
5   Parents (Edward, Victoria, Albert).
6   Parents (Alice, Victoria, Albert).
7   Sister (x,y) :- Female(x), Parents (x,m,f), Parents (y,m,f).
```

At each step in the process of answering a query we maintain a list of goals and variables we have instantiated. The original query becomes the first goal, and we search for an appropriate fact or rule that matches the first clause of the goal. If a fact matches the clause, we continue the search to satisfy the remaining clauses. If a rule matches the clause, we add the rule's preconditions to the list of goals. If no fact or rule matches the first clause of the goal, then the last choice is undone and the remaining possibilities are systematically considered. If there are no more clauses left in the goal, then PROLOG has succeeded in satisfying the original query. The answer can be found in the chain of variable instantiations made by all the matchings. If no possibilities remain to be explored, the search fails. This search strategy is sometimes called *backward chaining* because it starts from the solution and works backward to justify it.

We illustrate the search strategy by tracing it on the following query:

`Sister (Alice, Edward)?`

The search process takes the following steps:

- Original goal: `Sister (Alice, Edward)`
  Matches head of rule (7): `Sister (x,y)` if x=Alice, y=Edward

- New goals: `Female(Alice), Parents (Alice,m,f), Parents (Edward,m,f)`
  First clause matches fact (3): `Female (Alice)`

- Left with two clauses: `Parents(Alice,m,f), Parents(Edward,m,f)`
  First clause matches fact (6): `Parents (Alice, Victoria, Albert)`
  if m=Victoria, f=Albert

- Left with one clause: `Parents (Edward, Victoria, Albert)`
  Matches fact (5): `Parents (Edward, Victoria, Albert)`

Each goal has been replaced by its prerequisites or removed when it has been fulfilled. No clauses remain, so the original goal is satisfiable. We have established that Alice and Edward both have the same parents, Victoria and Albert.

Here is another example query using the database of royalty.

`Sister (Alice, x)?`

Notice that the variable x in the rule for `Sister` may refer to (possibly) different objects from the variable x in the query. So we must be careful not to confuse them. The search proceeds as follows:

- Original goal: `Sister (Alice, `x_1`)`
  Matches head of rule (7): `Sister(`x_2`,y)` if x_2=`Alice`, and x_1=y

- New goals: `Female (Alice)`, `Parents (Alice,m,f)`, `Parents (y,m,f)`
  First clause matches fact (3): `Female (Alice)`

- Left with two clauses: `Parents (Alice,m,f)`, `Parents (y,m,f)`
  Matches fact (6): `Parents (Alice, Victoria, Albert)` if m=`Victoria`, f=`Albert`

- Left with one clause: `Parents (y, Victoria, Albert)`
  Matches fact (5): `Parents (Edward, Victoria, Albert)` if y=`Edward`

No clauses remain, so the search succeeded. This time there is a variable x in the query. Tracing through the execution we conclude that x=x_1=y=`Edward`, so x=`Edward`.

The systematic approach has found a solution. But not all possibilities have been exhausted. Continuing the same way may turn up other solutions. The last choice was the choice of fact 5. We can now continue as if that choice had failed. There is no point in checking rules 1 through 4 again, as that was done already. But matches on rules 6 through 7 are still possible. In fact, 6 does match if we take y=`Alice`. And we immediately find another solution. Thus, by this definition of "sister," Alice is her own sister.

Undoing a choice after it has been made is called *backtracking*. Undoing one choice may entail undoing other choices, if a replacement rule is not found immediately, and so on. The next section further examines backtracking.

6.1.2 Backtracking

We consider an example that uses nothing but nullary relation symbols, so that we can concentrate on the backtracking and simplify the matching. Section 6.4 will examine the issue of matching more closely.

We look at an example PROLOG program from Cohen [6] with the following six PROLOG assertions.

```
1   A :- B,C,D.
2   A :- E,F.
3   B :- F.
4   E.
5   F.
6   A :- F.
```

For a particular database such as this, every query gives rise to a tree of all explored approaches called the search space. We build the tree by making a node for the original goals. We make a new node and a new arc everywhere the head of some rule matches the first goal. The new node is like the old node except that the first goal is replaced by the tail of the rule. We check all the assertions in the database in order for all matches. Creating the search space in this manner reflects the usual way in which PROLOG is implemented. The key decisions that affect the shape of the search space are:

1. matching against the *first* of the goals,

2. trying the rules *in order*, and

3. placing the tail *at the beginning* of the goals after a match.

The search space for the query A,E? is shown in figure 6.2. The fan-out at each node is determined by number of facts and rules that have been asserted. The search algorithm employed by PROLOG is a depth-first search of this search space. A breadth-first search would be possible but would require considerable resources. The whole top portion of the search space would have to be stored throughout the algorithm. A depth-first search requires keeping only the path from the root to the current node at any point in the search.

The search space of a PROLOG program is not always as simple as the one in figure 6.2. Suppose we change rule 6 of that example to A:-F,A; then we would have an infinite search space with an infinite number of solutions. The node A,E would, after application of rule 6 and fact 5, yield the identical node A,E. And so this combination could be repeated over and over again. This is shown in figure 6.3 where instead of repeating the tree below A,E we have drawn an arrow back to A,E. The infinite search space is represented by a cyclic graph.

Now suppose we switch the order of rules in the last example and make rule 6 appear first. In other words, suppose the database looks like this:

```
1   A :- F,A.
2   A :- B,C,D.
3   A :- E,F.
4   B :- F.
5   E.
6   F.
```

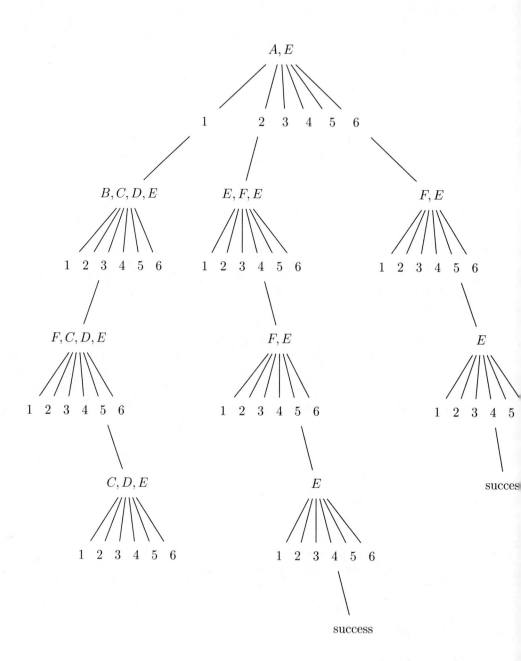

Figure 6.2: The search space for the query A,E?

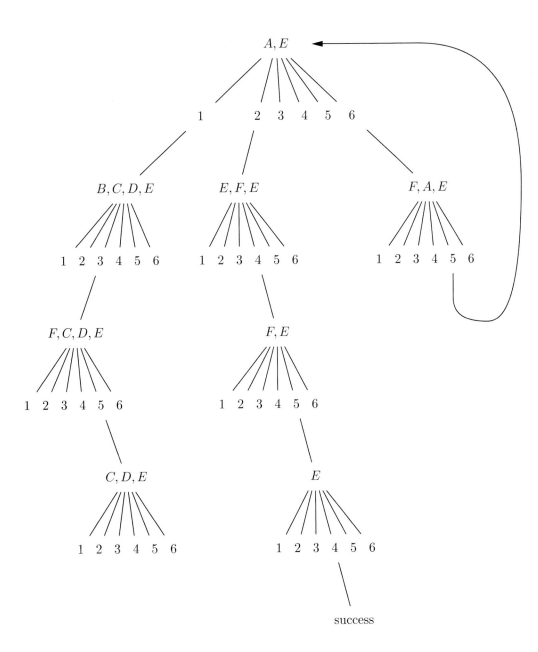

Figure 6.3: A search space with an infinite number of solutions

Now the PROLOG program will not terminate. The search always find the combination of rule 1 and rule 5 and continues endlessly around this loop. (See figure 6.4.) The algorithm never explores the consequences of applying rule 2. So despite the fact that there are an infinite number of solutions, none is found in a depth-first search. In a breadth-first search these solutions would eventually be found.

In summary, it is important to emphasize that the order in which facts and rules are asserted is significant, and PROLOG may fail to find solutions, even when some exist.

6.2   `fail` and "Cut"

One special clause permitted in PROLOG is `fail`. This clause never succeeds. Such a clause seems pointless. Consider any rule with `fail`, say:

```
A :- B, C, fail, D, E.
```

The clause A can never be satisfied by this rule, no matter what B, C, D, and E are. In the absence of side effects, the rule might as well be left out. A use for `fail` emerges after we introduce "cut."

The search space can be controlled somewhat by the use of *cut*. Syntactically, cut is indicated by a predicate ! with no arguments. It has the effect of committing the system to all choices made since the rule was selected. This prunes the search space. The placement of the ! in the rule is important. Backtracking is cutoff in satisfying all literals *before* the !. After the ! backtracking is unaffected. In all cases the choice of the rule is fixed.

Consider the example illustrated by the search space in figure 6.5. The program is as follows:

```
1   A :- C,!,C.
2   A.
3   B :- A.
4   B :- C.
5   C.
6   C :- D.
```

The part of the search space pruned by the use of cut is shown by an arc drawn through the path. These possibilities are not explored by PROLOG for the query B? and the given program. Placing ! after the first literal of rule 1 has the effect of freezing the choices of rules 1 and 5 in satisfying the goals A and C. PROLOG does not look for another way to satisfy these goals. As evident in figure 6.5 the use of cut may prune off a portion of the search space containing a solution. Cut cannot introduce any solutions where there are none to begin with.

Cut can be used to improve the efficiency of mutually exclusive cases. Suppose `P1(x)` and `P2(x)`. If `P1(x)` is true we may want to try `A(x)`, and there is no point in trying to establish `P2(x)`.

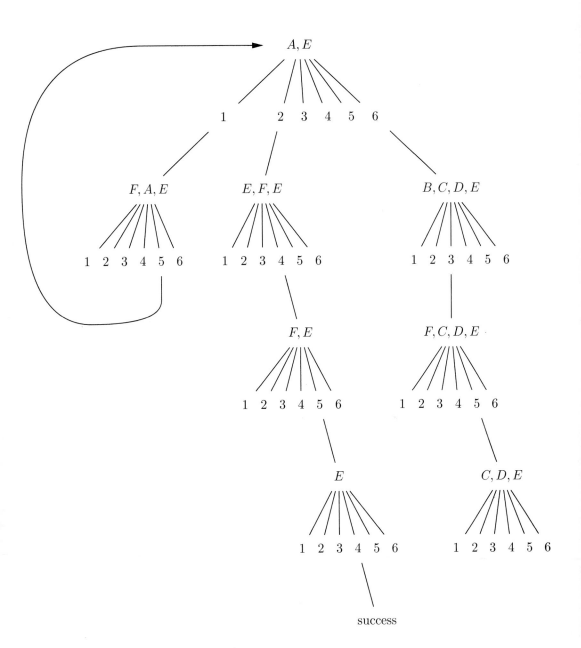

Figure 6.4: A search space in which a depth-first search finds no solutions

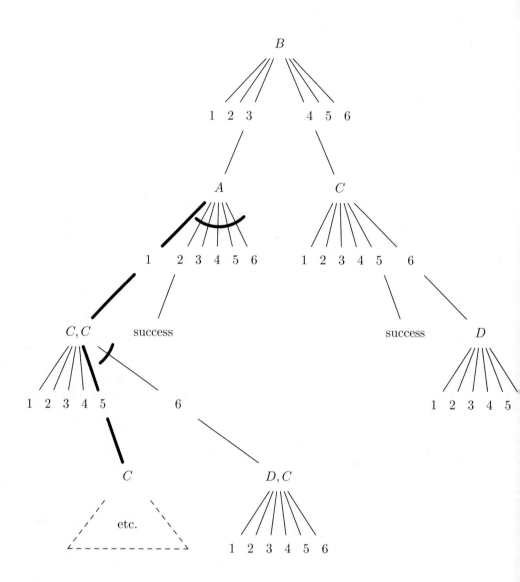

Figure 6.5: The search space for the query B?

```
Q(x) :- P1(x), !, A(x).
Q(x) :- P2(x), B(x).
```

Cut is also used in conjunction with `fail`. This makes it possible to make exceptions to general rules. For example, the next PROLOG program expresses the general rule that birds can fly. But penguins are an exception.

```
Bird (Eagle).
Bird (Sparrow).
Bird (Penguin).
Fly (x) :- Bird (Penguin), !, fail.
Fly (x) :- Bird (x).
```

Notice that the order of the `Fly` rules is crucial; the exceptions must come first.

Under certain circumstances the fact the PROLOG fails to prove a literal is true may be taken as proof the literal is false. This is the *closed-world assumption*. Most PROLOG systems provide a meta-logical or extra-logical relation `not` that succeeds only when its argument fails. Meta-logical predicates are those like `not` that take relations as arguments.

However, the meaning of `not` in PROLOG is problematic. The closed-world assumption assumes that all relevant facts are positively expressed by the PROLOG rules and that those assertions that do not follow are indeed false. If the domain of discourse is finite, then it may be reasonable to do so. But consider the following:

```
P(a).
Q(b) :- not (P(x)).
```

The query `Q(b)?` succeeds because the goal `P(b)` fails. The reasoning is that if `P(b)` is to hold, then it must be among the positively asserted facts about P; therefore `P(b)` does not hold. Consequently, neither does `Q(b)`. Yet the formula $P(a) \& (\forall x \, \neg \, P(x) \implies Q(b))$ does not logically imply $Q(b)$. This formula does not necessarily hold *if* there is some object x such that $\neg \, P(x)$. If we accept the closed-world assumption, then there is no such x.

6.3   Functors

The objects we have considered thus far have been atoms and variables. Other objects can be created in PROLOG using functors. Functors are uninterpreted function symbols. Functors are like the constructors of abstract syntax. Using functors one can build data structures. For example:

```
Book (WutheringHeights, Author (Emily, Bronte))
Book (Ulysses, Author (James, Joyce))
```

These examples are intended to represent just objects, not assertions. Notice there is no period. The only use of objects is to stand in relations. For example, we use a relation `Owns` to relate people (represented by atoms) and books (represented by objects formed with the functor `Book`).

```
Owns (John, Book (WutheringHeights, Author (Emily, Bronte))).
Owns (John, Book (x, Author (Emily, Bronte)))?
x = WutheringHeights
```

Terms are not just constants, but they can be built using functors as well. What we have been calling objects are sometimes called *ground terms*.

In some implementations of PROLOG there are no types, so total nonsense is legal as long as it is syntactically correct. The following, for example, is syntactically correct:

```
Book (Author (Emily, Bronte), Book (Alice, Victoria))
```

Turbo PROLOG [2] is more reasonable in this regard. In Turbo PROLOG it is possible to declare domains.

```
domains
    authors = author(symbol,symbol)
    books = book(symbol,authors)
```

And it is possible to type predicates

```
predicates
    owns(symbol,books)
```

This prevents the most egregious errors and enforces a more consistent use of functors and predicate symbols.

Lists are a predefined data type in PROLOG with a special notation. They actually fit into the framework of objects built out of functors. Just two functors are needed for all list objects. One is the functor `[]` denoting the empty list. The other functor, which is represented by a dot, builds lists from other lists. The dot is the "cons" (to use LISP terminology) functor, or the operator that concatenates an element to the head of a list of elements. So, the list with the single element `A` is written `.(A,[])`, or, since dot is an infix functor, as `A.[]`. The list consisting of the elements `A`, `B`, and `C` is written `A.(B.(C.[]))`, or, since the dot functor is right associative `A.B.C.[]`. Here is an example of a list containing another list as an element.

```
A . x . B . (y . z . []) . C . []
```

Since these lists are difficult to read, lists are given a special syntax. For example, the last two lists mentioned above can be written as follows:

```
[A,B,C]
[A,x,B,[y,z],C]
```

This notation pertains only to lists of a fixed length. A comma separates each element of the list. In PROLOG the notation [x|y] stands for x.y, and [A,x|y] stands for A.x.y.

Here is an example of simple PROLOG program to append two lists. This program illustrates the use of the notation for lists as well as the typical pattern for writing "functions" for recursive datatypes.

```
Append ([], x, x).
Append (head.tail, x, head.list) :- Append (tail, x, list).
```

The predicate Append has three arguments. We have in mind that the first two are the "input" arguments and the last one is the "output" list. The assertion Append ([], x, x). means that appending the empty list to anything yields the same list back. The second assertion means that if tail appended to x yields the list list, then tail with head on the front of the list appended to x yields the list with head on the front. This second assertion can also be written as follows:

```
Append ([head|tail], x, [head|list]) :- Append (tail, x, list).
```

The query

```
Append ([A], [B,C,D], x)?
```

computes the result of appending the lists [A] and [B,C,D]. Any list x satisfying the query is the result of appending the two given lists. There is exactly one such list and it is computed using the two rules for Append. To satisfy the goal Append([A],[B,C,D],x) we need to satisfy Append([],[B,C,D],x_2) where x=[A|x_2]. Taking x_2=[B,C,D] satisfies this, so the answer is x=[A,B,C,D].

6.4 Unification

Thus far we have dealt informally with the matching that takes places in PROLOG between the first goal and the head of a rule in the database. There are certain special cases of matching that are so compelling that they need no explanation. For example, syntactically identical objects match, but unlike objects do not match.

term	term	result
Female (Alice)	Female (Alice)	matches
Female (Alice)	Female (Victoria)	fails
Female (Alice)	Male (Albert)	fails

However, these are just a few of the possible situations. In this section we formalize the meaning of matching for a general collection of terms with variables.

Adding functors to PROLOG does not make matching substantially harder. For example, when x is Charlotte the literal

```
Owns (Kay, Book (JaneEyre, Author (x, Bronte)))
```

matches the following literal:

Owns (Kay, Book (JaneEyre, Author (Charlotte, Bronte)))

All atoms (actually nullary functors), functors (Book and Author), and the relation symbol Owns appear in corresponding places. Actually as far as matching is concerned there is no difference in the treatment of atoms, functors, and relation symbols. The difference that is crucial is between variables and these nonvariables. So in this section we ignore relation symbols and use the more general designation "term" without specific reference to PROLOG.

We give some more complex examples of matching terms than we have used thus far.

term	term	result
C(x,C(y,C(z,N)))	C(He,C(She,C(It,N)))	x=He,y=She,z=It
C(We,N)	C(x,y)	x=We,y=N
C(They,C(You,N))	C(You,C(x,N))	fails
C(x,C(She,C(It,N)))	C(He,C(She,C(y,N)))	x=He,y=It

These examples are thinly veiled examples of lists where N is the empty list and C is the binary cons constructor. We can rewrite the terms using the bracket notation of PROLOG.

term	term	result
[x,y,z]	[He,She,It]	x=He,y=She,z=It
[We]	[x|y]	x=We,y=[]
[They,You]	[You,x]	fails
[x,She,It]	[He,She,y]	x=He,y=It

In order to comprehend how the matching is done, the lists, whether or not they are written with bracket notation, must be understood as terms written with functors. Figure 6.6 shows a pair of terms in the previous table written as trees to show their structure. For matching, the terms act like templates. The constants are etched in the template, and when two templates are superimposed the two must agree. As long as the variables are distinct, they act as holes in the templates. The result of matching two templates is the set of terms that captured in each variable's window.

The matching gets more difficult when the variables are not distinct. Consider the following two terms:

$$A(x,B,y)   A(z,z,z)$$

To define PROLOG's matching we introduce the definition of unification in the general setting. In particular, we now use the customary mathematical convention that the letters a, b, c, etc., are constants (i.e., nullary term constructors); f, g, h, etc., are function symbols (i.e., non-nullary constructors of terms); and x, y, z are variables.

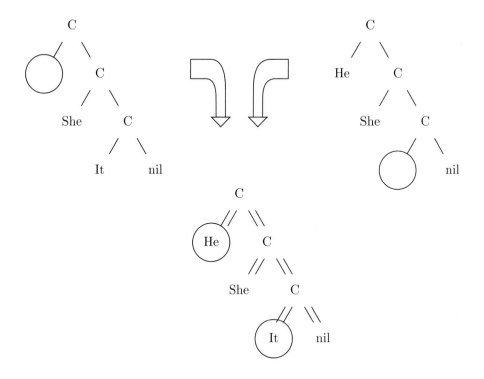

Figure 6.6: Matching two terms

Let σ be a list of ordered pairs. Each pair consists of a variable and a term (different from the variable). We call σ a *substitution* or *assignment*. A substitution can be viewed as a function with finite domain. The domain of the substitution is written $\text{Dom}(\sigma)$. The value of a term t under the substitution σ, denoted $t\sigma$, is the result of replacing the variable x by $\sigma(x)$ everywhere it occurs in t, for every x in the domain of σ. For example, let t be

$$f(x, g(y, z))$$

and let σ be

$$\{\langle x, h(a, b)\rangle, \langle z, f(c, d)\rangle\}$$

where x, y, and z are variables. Then the value of t under σ is

$$f(h(a, b), g(y, f(c, d))).$$

Other examples of terms under σ are given in the following table.

t	$t\sigma$
x	$h(a,b)$
y	y
$g(a,b)$	$g(a,b)$
$h(f(c,z),x)$	$h(f(c,f(c,d)),h(a,b))$

The composition of two substitutions σ and ρ is written $\rho \circ \sigma$ and is defined to be the substitution τ with domain equal to $\mathrm{Dom}(\sigma) \cup \mathrm{Dom}(\rho)$ such that $\tau(x) = \rho(x)$ for $x \in \mathrm{Dom}(\rho) \setminus \mathrm{Dom}(\sigma)$, and $\tau(x) = \rho(\sigma(x))$ for all other x.

Two terms are said to unify if there is a substitution such that the value of the terms are equal under the assignment.

$$t\sigma = s\sigma$$

We call σ a *unifying substitution*.

Each match PROLOG makes results in a substitution. The composition of all the substitutions made by PROLOG from the initial goal until all the goal clauses have been eliminated is the "answer" to the query.

If t and s can be unified, then there exists a *most general unifying substitution*. If σ is the most general unifying substitution, and τ is any other unifying substitution, then there exists a substitution ρ such that $\tau = \sigma \circ \rho$. For example, the terms $f(x, g(y, c))$ and $f(a, g(b, z))$ unify under the substitution

$$\{\langle x, a \rangle, \langle y, b \rangle, \langle z, c \rangle\}.$$

This is the most general unifying substitution for the two terms. However, not all pairs of terms can be unified. For example, the constant a cannot unify with the constant b no matter what substitution is chosen.

The terms $f(x)$ and $f(g(x))$ do not unify either. The substitution $\sigma = \{\langle x, g(x) \rangle\}$ does not unify them, because $f(x)\sigma = f(g(x)) \neq f(g(g(x))) = f(g(x))\sigma$. Some implementations of PROLOG do not check for substitutions of the form $\langle x, f(x) \rangle$. The check for self-referential substitutions is called the *occurs check*. Because unification is used so often in PROLOG, the added inefficiency of the occurs check was considered too costly. However, there are linear time algorithms for unification (with the occurs check) [15], and near-linear time algorithms that perform quite well [14].

The absence of the occurs check renders the deduction unsound, although there are possible interpretations of systems without the occurs check. In practice, the absence of the occurs check will occasionally result in infinite structures which will cause the interpreter to loop when printing them.

6.5   Resolution

In this section we relate PROLOG to logic and theorem proving. We have already seen that PROLOG captures some logical expression, like implication, conjunction, and universal quantification, easily. For example, the PROLOG clause

```
IndoEuropean (English) :- Germanic (English).
```

expresses the logical statement that "if English is a Germanic language, then it is Indo-European." And more generally,

```
IndoEuropean (x) :- Germanic (x).
```

expresses the logical statement that "for all x if x is a Germanic language, then x is Indo-European." But some logical expression, namely, negation and disjunction, seems more difficult. In fact, not all formulas for first-order logic can be captured in PROLOG clauses but can be captured by a more general form.

We define a *clause* to be of the form:

$$P_1, \ldots, P_n \Leftarrow Q_1, \ldots, Q_k$$

where the P's and Q's are literals. The arrow pointing to the left $\Leftarrow$ is to be understood as meaning "is implied by." And the whole clause is understood to mean that Q_1, and Q_2, and so on, imply P_1, or P_2, and so on. In more customary logical notation:

$$(Q_1 \& \cdots \& Q_k) \Rightarrow (P_1 \vee \cdots \vee P_n)$$

Any variables in the clause are understood to stand for any object; i.e., the clause is understood to be universally quantified.

All formulas of first-order predicate logic (including universal and existential quantification) can be put into the clausal form. The following table of examples suggests how this might be done.

$A \vee B$	$A, B \Leftarrow \top$
$A \vee \neg B$	$A \Leftarrow B$
$\neg A$	$\bot \Leftarrow A$
$A \& B$	$A \Leftarrow \top$
	$B \Leftarrow \top$
$(A \& B) \Rightarrow (C \vee D)$	$C, D \Leftarrow A, B$
$\neg A \vee \neg B \vee C \vee D$	$C, D \Leftarrow A, B$

Here $\top$ stands for an atomic formula representing "true" and $\bot$ stands for "false." The only significant difficulty is the elimination of existential quantification. This is overcome by "skolemization." For a complete discussion of the translation to clausal form see [5].

The general resolution principle is a single rule of inference with which all valid formulas of first-order predicate logic can be proved. This is the general resolution principle:

$$\frac{Q_1, Q_2, \ldots, Q_n \Leftarrow P_1, P_2, \ldots, P_k \qquad R_1, R_2, \ldots, R_m \Leftarrow S_1, S_2, \ldots, S_l}{(Q_1, Q_2, \ldots, Q_n, R_2, \ldots, R_m)\sigma \Leftarrow (P_2, \ldots, P_k, S_1, S_2, \ldots, S_n)\sigma}$$

where P_1 and R_1 unify under the most general unifying substitution σ. (Variables in the two clauses should be renamed as the same variable name in different clauses may refer to different objects.) Choosing the two clauses with which to do resolution is a challenge. The search for two clauses to put in the hypothesis of the resolution principle out of all the clauses derivable from a given set of clauses is like looking for a needle in a haystack. Therein lies the advantage of Horn clauses.

What we have called a fact in PROLOG is a special case of a clause in which $n = 1$ and $k = 0$. A rule is the special case where $n = 1$. A query is the special case where $n = 0$. PROLOG requires clauses to have $n = 0$ or $n = 1$; such clauses are called *Horn clauses*. The resolution principle for Horn clauses simplifies to:

$$\frac{\Leftarrow Q_1, Q_2, \ldots, Q_n \qquad P_0 \Leftarrow P_1, \ldots, P_k}{\Leftarrow (P_1, \ldots, P_k, Q_2, \ldots, Q_n)\sigma}$$

where Q_1 and P_0 unify under the most general unifying substitution σ. (Again variables may have to be renamed.)

As long as there is but one headless Horn clause $\Leftarrow Q_1, Q_2, \ldots, Q_n$ among the set of derived clauses, then the only freedom in applying the resolution principle for Horn clauses is in the selection for the second hypothesis. Choosing the first hypothesis to be the result of the last step is called *linear resolution*. Taking any one of the clauses from the database (as opposed to any clauses derived along the way) as the second clause is called *input resolution*. The fan-out in the search space in PROLOG is for a suitable hypothesis $P_0 \Leftarrow P_1, \ldots, P_k$ among the original facts and rules. Note that k may be zero, in which case the resulting formula is shorter than the previous one.

The crucial fact about the search is that it always works. A proof can be found in [8, 12, 13].

Theorem 4 *Linear input resolution is complete for Horn clauses, i.e., the search strategy will find a derivation if one exists.*

Not all formulas of first-order predicate logic can be put into *Horn* clause form. Nevertheless, it is still possible to compute all computable functions with Horn clauses [20]. However, no practical programming is done with the pure Horn clause PROLOG described here. Most implementations of PROLOG have many meta-logical predicates and predicates that cause specific side effects. These are often used in substantive PROLOG programs.

6.6   Exercises

6.1   Assume the following PROLOG facts about languages.

```
IndoEuropean(x)  :- BaltoSlavic(x).
IndoEuropean(x)  :- Germanic(x).
IndoEuropean(x)  :- IndoIranian(x).
NigerCongo(x)    :- Bantu(x).
```

```
NigerCongo(x)    :- Kwa(x).

BaltoSlavic (Lithuanian).
Germanic     (Luxemburgish).
IndoIranian (Magahi).
IndoIranian (Maithili).
Bantu (Makua).
Bantu (Swahili).
Kwa   (Yorba).
Bantu (Zulu).
```

What would be the results of the following PROLOG queries?

   (a) `IndoEuropean (Zulu)?`

   (b) `IndoEuropean (Luxemburgish)?`

   (c) `IndoEuropean (Letzebuergesch)?`

   (d) `IndoEuropean (x)?`

   (e) `IndoEuropean (x), NigerCongo (x)?`

   (f) `IndoEuropean (x), NigerCongo (y)?`

6.2 Write a PROLOG program to reverse the elements of a list. You may use the PROLOG definition for `Append`.

6.3 Write a simple PROLOG program that has an infinite number of solutions.

6.4 PROLOG is often used in parsing natural language. Context-free rules can be captured quite naturally in PROLOG. Usually a predicate is defined for each syntactic category. Each predicate verifies that a list of words belongs to the category. That a noun phrase and a verb phrase make up a sentence is an example of a rule in what linguists call a *phrase-structure grammar*. Consider the following two formulations of this rule:

```
Sentence (11) :- NP (12), VP (13), Append (12,13,11).
Sentence (11) :- Append (12,13,11), NP (12), VP (13).
```

The predicate `Sentence` succeeds if the list of tokens can be divided between NP and VP. In the first, we generate all the legal noun and verb phrases and then check to see if they form a sentence. In the second, we generate all word breaks and check if each phrase is legal. This illustrates a common PROLOG technique called *generate and test*. Which of the two formulations is more efficient?

6.5 A *difference list* is a representation of lists that make some PROLOG programs more efficient by avoiding costly appends. The key is to keep a reference to the whole list as well as a suffix. It is convenient to define a data structure for this: `DL(whole,suffix)`.

Parsing lists of tokens is a good application for difference lists. Here is a snippet of a natural language grammar.

$$
\begin{array}{rcl}
\langle sentence \rangle & ::= & \langle noun\ phrase \rangle \ \langle verb\ phrase \rangle \\
\langle noun\ phrase \rangle & ::= & \langle adjective \rangle \ \langle noun \rangle \\
\langle verb\ phrase \rangle & ::= & \langle verb \rangle \ \langle adverb \rangle \\
\langle adjective \rangle & ::= & \textbf{flying} \\
\langle noun \rangle & ::= & \textbf{planes} \\
\langle verb \rangle & ::= & \textbf{can be} \\
\langle adverb \rangle & ::= & \textbf{dangerous}
\end{array}
$$

(a) Avoid using **Append** as in the previous exercise and express this grammar with seven PROLOG predicates that recognize the appropriate difference lists. The query

```
Sentence (DL ([Flying, Planes, Can, Be, Dangerous], []))?
```

should succeed.

(b) Using your knowledge of English grammar add new phrases to the grammar so that the previous sentence can be parsed in another way that reflects the sentence's *other* meaning.

6.6 Given a relationship expressed as a predicate `R(x,y)`, define a PROLOG predicate `P(x,y)` that is the transitive closure of it. How does `P(x,y)` work on:

```
R(A,B).
R(B,A).
```

6.7 Write a PROLOG predicate `QuickSort (list, sorted)` that sorts a list using QuickSort. QuickSort picks an element from the list, divides the remaining elements into lists of the smaller and larger elements, sorts the two sublists, and then appends the results together.

6.8 Write a PROLOG definition of the 3-ary predicate `Eval` to evaluate expressions in the simple `let` language (see section 2.3.2) defined by the constructors:

```
Var (x)      /* Atom x is a variable.              */
Z            /* Constant Z stands for zero.        */
S (x)        /* The successor function.            */
Plus (x,y)   /* The addition function.             */
Let (x,v,b)  /* Let variable x have the value v in body b. */
```

So, for example,

```
Eval ([], Let (Var (X), S(Z), Plus (Var (X), Var (X))), x)?
```

yields x equal to S(S(Z)). As far as possible, the second argument should be simplified to a number of the form S(S(S(...(Z)))).

6.9 (Bratko [3].) Consider the following program:

```
F (1, One) .
F (S (1), Two) .
F (S (S (1)), Three) .
F (S (S (S (x)))), n) :- F (x, n) .
```

The symbol 1 is a constant symbol, S is a functor, and F is a predicate. How will PROLOG answer the following four queries? Whenever several answers are possible, give at least two.

```
F (S (1), x) ?
F (S (S (1)), Two) ?
F (S (S (S (S (S (S (1)))))), y) ?
F (z, Three) ?
```

6.10 Write a PROLOG program to compute the factorial function. Represent numbers using the "tally" notation introduced in the previous exercise.

6.11 Prove that PROLOG is Turing complete.

6.12 Is there any circumstance under which it is useful to have a rule with two cuts in it? Explain.

6.13 What is the composition of the substitution $\sigma = \{\langle x, f(y)\rangle\}$ and the substitution $\rho = \{\langle y, g(x)\rangle\}$? Can the resulting substitution ever unify anything?

6.14 A substitution S is *idempotent* if $S = SS$. Show that if S is the most general unifier of two terms, then it is idempotent.

6.15 Answer the questions given the following PROLOG program.

```
1   A :- B,A.
2   A :- B.
3   B.
```

(a) Show the *entire* search space for the query A,B?.

(b) Now switch the order of the first rule and the second rule. Now show the search space for the PROLOG query A,B?.

6.16 Give a simple PROLOG program in which the omission of the occurs check causes PROLOG to conclude that there is a solution when none exists.

6.17 Find the most general unifier for the following pairs of terms (x, y, and z are variables), if it exists.

$$
\begin{array}{ll}
f(a, x) & f(b, x) \\
f(a, x) & g(a, b) \\
f(a, x) & f(a, y) \\
f(a, b) & f(a, b) \\
f(a, x) & f(a, h(x)) \\
g(f(a, b), h(x, y)) & g(f(z, b), h(b, b)) \\
g(f(a, x), h(x, b)) & g(f(a, b), h(a, b)) \\
g(f(a, x), h(x, b)) & g(f(a, b), h(b, b)) \\
g(f(a, x), h(y, b)) & g(z, y) \\
g(f(a, x), h(y, b)) & g(z, x)
\end{array}
$$

6.18 (Clocksin and Mellish [5].) Write a PROLOG program Negate to produce the negation of a propositional expression. Propositional expressions are built up from atoms, the unary functor Not, and binary functors And, Or, and Implies. The negated expression should be in simplest form, where Not is only applied to atoms. For example,

```
Negate (Implies (P, And (Q, Not (R))), x)?
x = And (P, Or (Not Q, R))
```

Do not assume that the input is in simplest form. (*Hint:* You will need the built-in predicate Atom(x), which succeeds if x is an atom. The entire program is ten lines long.)

6.19 Write a reasonably efficient program in PROLOG to prove theorems in propositional logic. Use Lukasiewicz's axiomatization of propositional logic with the connectives "not" and "implies." A "reasonably efficient" program will find a proof of Implies(P,P). Here is a PROLOG program that defines Lukasiewicz's system.

```
ProofOf (Ax1(x),Implies(Implies(Not(x),x),x)) .
ProofOf (Ax2(x,y),Implies(x,Implies(Not(x),y))) .
ProofOf (Ax3(x,y,z),
     Implies(Implies(x,y),Implies(Implies(y,z),Implies(x,z)))) .
ProofOf (MP(x,y),z) :- ProofOf (x,Implies(w,z)), ProofOf (y,w) .
```

This program serves only as a proof checker, not a theorem prover. On the query

```
ProofOf (x, Implies(P,P)) ?
```

this program goes into an infinite loop. Not only is an unbounded search a problem, but the absence of the occurs check in PROLOG is a problem. Please solve both of these problems.

6.20 Answer the following questions about the occurs check and the programming language ML.

(a) What is the significance of the occurs check in ML?

(b) If the occurs check were omitted in ML, what problems would arise? How could these problems be overcome?

(c) If the occurs check were omitted in ML, what useful things would then be permitted?

6.21 Consider the following assumptions used by Sir Bedever in *Monty Python and the Holy Grail* to argue that the girl is a witch.

```
Witch (x) :- Burns (x), Woman (x).
Woman (Girl).
Burns (x) :- IsMadeOfWood (x).
IsMadeOfWood (x) :- Floats (x).
Floats (Duck).
Floats (y) :- Floats (x), SameWeight (x, y).
SameWeight (Duck, Girl).
```

(a) Describe the important features of the PROLOG search space for the query Witch(Girl)?.

(b) What is the response of PROLOG to the query Witch(Girl)?; i.e., is the girl a witch?

(c) Does the response PROLOG give follow *logically* from the assumptions? If so, give a tautology representing the deduction. If not, explain in what way PROLOG deviates from first-order predicate logic.

(d) Could cut be used somewhere in the assertions above to improve the program? Explain.

6.7 Bibliography

[1] Baxter, Nancy H., Ed Dubinsky, and Gary Marc Levin. *Learning Discrete Mathematics with ISETL*. Springer-Verlag, New York, 1989.

[2] Borland International, Inc. *Turbo PROLOG Owner's Handbook*. 1986.

[3] Bratko, Ivan. *Prolog Programming for Artificial Intelligence*. Second edition. Addison-Wesley, Wokingham, England, 1990.

[4] Chang, Chin-Liang, and Richard Char-Tung Lee. *Symbolic Logic and Mechanical Theorem Proving*. Academic Press, New York, 1973.

[5] Clocksin, William F., and Christopher S. Mellish. *Programming in PROLOG*. Second edition. Springer-Verlag, Berlin, 1984.

[6] Cohen, Jacques. "Describing PROLOG by its interpretation and compilation." *Communications of the ACM*, volume 28, number 12, December 1985, pages 1311–1324.

[7] Davis, Ruth E. "Logic programming and PROLOG: A tutorial." *IEEE Software*, volume 2, number 5, September 1985, pages 53–62. Reprinted in *Programming Languages: A Grand Tour*, edited by Ellis Horowitz, 1987, pages 493–502.

[8] Genesereth, Michael R., and Nils J. Nilsson. *Logical Foundations of Artificial Intelligence*. Morgan Kaufmann, Los Altos, California, 1987.

[9] Horn, Alfred. "On sentences which are true of direct unions of algebras." *Journal of Symbolic Logic*, volume 16, number 1, March 1951, pages 14–21.

[10] Knight, Kevin. "Unification: A multidisciplinary survey." *Computing Surveys*, volume 21, number 1, March 1989, pages 93–124.

[11] Kowalski, Robert A. "Algorithm = Logic + Control." *Communications of the ACM*, volume 22, number 7, July 1979, pages 424–436. Reprinted in *Programming Languages: A Grand Tour*, edited by Ellis Horowitz, 1987, pages 480–492.

[12] Lloyd, John Wylie. *Foundations of Logic Programming*. Springer-Verlag, Berlin, 1984.

[13] Maier, David, and David S. Warren. *Computing with Logic: Logic Programming with PROLOG*. Benjamin Cummings, Menlo Park, California, 1988.

[14] Martelli, Alberto, and Ugo Montanari. "An efficient unification algorithm." *ACM Transactions on Programming Languages and Systems*, volume 4, number 2, April 1982, pages 258-282.

[15] Paterson, M. S., and M. N. Wegman. "Linear unification." In *Proceedings of the Eighth Annual Symposium of Theory of Computing*, 1976, pages 181–186.

[16] Robinson, John Alan. "A machine-oriented logic based on the resolution principle." *Journal of the ACM*, volume 12, number 1, January 1965, pages 34–41.

[17] Robinson, John Alan. *Logic, Form and Function: The Mechanization of Deductive Reasoning.* North-Holland, New York, 1979.

[18] Robinson, John Alan. "Logic programming—past, present, and future." *New Generation Computing*, volume 1, 1983, pages 107–124.

[19] Schwartz, Jacob T., Robert B. K. Dewar, Ed Dubinsky, and E. Schonberg. *Programming with Sets: An Introduction to SETL.* Texts and Monographs in Computer Science. Springer-Verlag, Berlin, 1986.

[20] Tarnlund, S. A. "Horn clause computability." *BIT*, volume 17, 1977, pages 215–226.

Chapter 7

Lambda calculus

The theoretical basis of functional programming has its origins in the lambda calculus of Alonzo Church [4]. The lambda calculus was proposed as a theoretical model of computation in the same manner that Alan Turing proposed Turing machines. But Turing machines are uninspiring as a means of expressing computation and bear no useful relation to programming, imperative or otherwise. On the other hand, the lambda calculus captures the commonality of the functional programming paradigm. And thus the study of the lambda calculus is essential for further study about functional programming.

The lambda calculus as a notation is also valuable. In the study of mathematics the distinction between a function and the value of the function is often blurred. Frege criticized mathematicians for this in his lectures at Jena. This lack of precision has resulted in the lack of any consistent notation for representing functions. Lambda expressions can fulfill this purpose.

We present the lambda calculus as a formal game. We resist the temptation of "reasoning by analogy" condemned by Edsger Dijkstra [10, page 1399]. We hope to give in this, and the remaining, chapters a more elementary, fundamental explanation of programming language phenomena than is obtained by experiential means. Paradoxically most people are more comfortable with their informal experience than with formal systems; hence it seems backward to explain what is already experienced in unfamiliar, formal terms. Yet this is exactly what we must accomplish if we are to succeed in giving a satisfactory explanation of programming language phenomena.

One does not ask what the game of chess *means*. One begins to understand chess when one is in command of the rules. It is in this way we wish to approach the lambda calculus. Naturally this does not preclude the possibility of understanding chess or the lambda calculus in different, less formalistic ways. The scope of the present work does not permit the development of a "meaning" for lambda expressions. This intellectual triumph was accomplished by Dana Scott [24, 25, 26].

7.1   Syntax of lambda expressions

In the lambda calculus are a collection of terms built out of variables, function symbols, and other lambda expressions. We suppose we have a countably infinite set of variables (we usually use x, y, z, v, and so on, for variables), and an arbitrary set of function symbols (we usually use a, b, c, f, g, h, and so on, for function symbols). The only additional symbols used in the syntax of lambda expressions are the period, the Greek letter lambda λ, and parentheses.

The recursive definition of lambda expressions has four cases.

1. For all v in the set of variables, v is a lambda expression.

2. For all f in the set of function symbols, f is a lambda expression.

3. If v is a variable and l is a lambda expression, then $\lambda v \cdot l$ is a lambda expression.

4. If m and n are lambda expressions, then $(m\ n)$ is a lambda expression.

Function symbols are not actually necessary. But they correspond nicely to the collection of functions one generally perceives as being primitive or self-explanatory. And so we find it convenient to include them.

The following are examples of lambda expressions:

$$\lambda x \cdot \lambda y \cdot (x\ y)$$

$$(\lambda x \cdot x\ (f\ a))$$

$$((\lambda x \cdot b\ c)\ (f\ \lambda y \cdot c))$$

We call terms of the form $\lambda v \cdot l$ *abstractions*; the lambda expression l is said to be the *body* of the abstraction. Terms of the form $(m\ n)$ are called *applications*; the lambda expression m is in the *function position* of the application and n is in the *argument position* of the application. These terms suggest that the intended interpretation of lambda expressions is as function definitions and function-calling constructs. Indeed, this is correct.

We can give an alternate definition for the syntax of lambda expressions by presenting a context-free grammar for them. This is the grammar for lambda expressions:

$$
\begin{aligned}
V &\rightarrow\ x \mid y \mid z \mid v \mid\ \cdots \\
F &\rightarrow\ a \mid b \mid c \mid f \mid g \mid\ \cdots \\
L &\rightarrow\ V \mid F \mid \lambda V.L \mid (L\ L)
\end{aligned}
$$

This grammar is unambiguous. Expressions that can be derived by the grammar can be derived in only one way.

We can render the definition of lambda expressions as an ML type. From time to time in this chapter we will illustrate algorithms for lambda expressions in the programming language ML using this data structure.

```
type Variable   = string;  (* type abbreviation *)
type FuncSymbol = string;  (* type abbreviation *)

datatype LambdaExp =
  Var of Variable                   |
  Fun of FuncSymbol                 |
  Abs of Variable  * LambdaExp |
  App of LambdaExp * LambdaExp ;
```

The constructors `Var`, `Fun`, `Abs`, and `App` are constructors of the abstract syntax of lambda expressions.

We now write the three previous lambda expressions as ML expressions.

```
Abs ("x", Abs ("y", App (Var "x", Var "y")));
App (Abs ("x", Var "x"), App (Fun "f", Fun "a"));
App (App (Abs("x",Fun"b"), Fun"c"), App (Fun"f", Abs("y",Fun"c")));
```

The entire structure of the lambda expressions is displayed in these ML expressions much in the way the abstract syntax of `while` statements was represented in chapter 2. All the ML lambda expressions are already parsed, that is, decomposed, into their constituent components. There is no need for the Greek letter lambda or the dot, which are part of the concrete syntax for lambda expressions. In the ML definition there is no need for the parentheses either—at least as part of the syntax of lambda expressions. Parentheses are needed as part of the ML syntax, i.e., in the meta-language syntax, of constructor application. Writing lambda expressions out this way is generally too verbose, although it is sometimes useful in order to emphasize the structure of a lambda expression.

Even the unambiguous, concrete syntax given for lambda expressions is not entirely satisfactory, although it is more parsimonious than the ML representation. So we are led to take shortcuts. For example, in the lambda expression $(\lambda x \,.\, x \,(f \,a))$ we are tempted to get greater clarity by inserting parentheses around the abstraction obtaining $((\lambda x \,.\, x) \,(f \,a))$. In fact, parentheses are often used willy-nilly in lambda expressions. This suggests the following syntax for lambda expressions.

$$L \;\rightarrow\; V \mid F \mid \lambda V.L \mid L\,L \mid (L)$$

The grammar is ambiguous, but parentheses can be used wherever deemed necessary to make a lambda expression more readable. This approach is often taken.

As a compromise we follow the established conventions about parentheses, but in a consistent and predictable manner. These conventions are: (1) the body of a lambda abstraction includes everything up to the first unmatched closing parenthesis (or the rest of the lambda expression) and (2) function application is left-associative. The effect of these conventions is to modify the original syntax of lambda expressions by adding parentheses in certain cases for the sake of clarity, and leaving them out under other circumstances for the sake of brevity. We can summarize the modifications to the original concrete syntax of lambda expressions by the following two rules:

A. Leave out the parentheses around an application if it is the outermost constructor, if it is the body of an abstraction, or if it is in the function position of an application.

B. Insert parentheses around an abstraction if it is in the function or in the argument position of an application.

Or put another way, the modified syntax of lambda expressions is given by the following unambiguous grammar:

$$
\begin{aligned}
L &\;\rightarrow\; V \mid F \mid \lambda V. L \mid G\,A \\
G &\;\rightarrow\; V \mid F \mid (\lambda V. L) \mid G\,A \\
A &\;\rightarrow\; V \mid F \mid (\lambda V. L) \mid (G\,A)
\end{aligned}
$$

Here are some examples of lambda expressions in both the formal and informal syntax.

$\lambda x . b$	$\lambda x . b$	
$(f\,x)$	$f\,x$	leave outermost parentheses out
$(f\,(g\,x))$	$f\,(g\,x)$	
$(f\,\lambda x . b)$	$f\,(\lambda x . b)$	abstraction as argument
$((f\,x)\,y)$	$f\,x\,y$	application as function
$(\lambda x . b\,f)$	$(\lambda x . b)\,f$	abstraction as function
$((f\,y)\,(g\,x))$	$f\,y\,(g\,x)$	
$((f\,y)\,\lambda x . b)$	$f\,y\,(\lambda x . b)$	
$((g\,x)\,(f\,y))$	$g\,x\,(f\,y)$	
$(\lambda x . b\,(f\,y))$	$(\lambda x . b)\,(f\,y)$	
$\lambda y . (g\,x)$	$\lambda y . g\,x$	application as body
$\lambda y . \lambda x . b$	$\lambda y . \lambda x . b$	

From now on we will follow these conventions about parenthesizing lambda expressions and use the "informal" syntax.

All this discussion about syntax leaves a big question unanswered: what does a lambda expression mean or represent? We will see that $\lambda v . b$ can be interpreted as defining a function with a formal parameter v and with a function body b. The lambda expression $f\, a$ can be interpreted as applying the function f to the actual argument a. We will not give a formal meaning to lambda expressions here, but we want to give a computational meaning. This is developed in the next few sections.

7.1.1 Free variables

The set of free variables in a lambda expression e is defined as follows:

1. If the lambda expression e is a variable, say v, then $FV[v] = \{v\}$.

2. If the lambda expression e is a function symbol, say f, then $FV[f] = \emptyset$.

3. If the lambda expression e is of the form $\lambda v \,.\, b$, then $FV[\lambda v \,.\, b] = FV[b] \backslash \{v\}$. In other words, the free variables of $\lambda v \,.\, b$ are those of b except for v.

4. If the lambda expression e is of the form $l\, m$, then $FV[l\, m] = FV[l] \cup FV[m]$.

We say that the lambda expression e is *closed*, if $FV[e] = \emptyset$.

A particular variable can occur free at some place in a lambda expression and bound at another. For example, the variable x occurs both free and bound in the lambda expression $L = (\lambda x \,.\, x)\, x$. Note that $FV[L] = \{x\}$.

We define the abstraction that binds the variable occurrence v to be the innermost abstraction of the form $\lambda v \,.\, m$ containing the variable occurrence. If this abstraction exists, it is unique, and we call the formal parameter v the *binding occurrence* of all the occurrences of the variable v that become bound in $\lambda v \,.\, m$.

The names of variables in lambda expressions are quite immaterial. We could replace them by arrows to the place where they are bound. For example, the lambda expression:

$$\lambda x \,.\, (\lambda y \,.\, (\lambda x \,.\, x\, (x\, y))\, (\lambda z \,.\, f\, x\, z))\, (g\, x)$$

where x, y, and z are variables and f and g are function symbols, might be written:

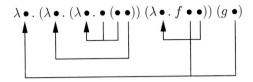

Such a syntax without names for variables is quite attractive when implementing lambda expressions in programs (cf. [21]).

7.1.2 Substitution

To motivate the definition of substitution we jump ahead of the story slightly. We know that when we apply an abstraction to an argument the formal parameter must be replaced by the actual argument. This is the act of substitution that we will define shortly. In the example above, we see that the function definition with formal parameter y has been applied to the actual argument $g\,x$. While we have the variables replaced by arrow, we will examine what happens when we substitute $g\,x$ for y. The resulting lambda expression looks like:

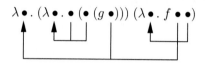

Putting the names back in and drawing the lines from variables to their binding occurrences yields the following:

$$\lambda x.\,(\lambda x.\,x\,(x\,(g\,x)))\,(\lambda z.\,f\,x\,z)$$

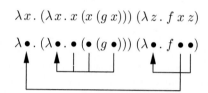

The arrows are drawn differently. The reason is that the use of the variable name x has caused a problem when substituting $g\,x$ for y in the lambda expression $\lambda x.\,x\,(x\,y)$, which has a binding of its own for the variable named x.

In the definition of substitution that follows we will avoid the clash-of-variables problem just illustrated by renaming variables when necessary.

Definition of substitution. If t and e are lambda expressions, and x is a variable, the function for substituting t for x in e (denoted $e[x := t]$) is defined as follows:

1. If the lambda expression e is a variable, then there are two possibilities.

   1a. If e is the variable x, then $x[x := t] = t$.

   1b. If e is a variable different from x, say v, then $v[x := t] = v$.

2. If the lambda expression e is a function symbol f, then $f[x := t] = f$.

3. If the lambda expression e is of the form $\lambda v.\,b$, then there are three possibilities.

   3a. If the variable v is equal to x or x does not occur free in b, then $(\lambda v.\,b)[x := t] = \lambda x.\,b$. In other words, the substitution makes no changes.

   3b. If the variable v is not equal to x and v does not occur free in t, then $(\lambda v.\,b)[x := t] = \lambda v.\,b[x := t]$.

3c. If the variable v is not equal to x but v does occur free in t, then

$$(\lambda v \, . \, b)[x := t] = \lambda z \, . \, (b[v := z])[x := t]$$

where z is a new variable that does not occur free in t or b. In other words, the bound variable v is renamed before performing the substitution.

4. If the lambda expression e is an application of the form $l \, m$, then $(l \, m)[x := t] = l[x := t] \, m[x := t]$.

7.2   Term rewriting

Given the informal interpretation of lambda expressions as functions and function applications, it is time that we search for the meaning of applying the function $\lambda v \, . \, l$ with the formal parameter v to the actual argument m. Clearly, we can say the answer is lambda expression $(\lambda v \, . \, l) \, m$, but this does not seem to be the most simple answer in all cases. For example, the lambda expression $(\lambda x \, . \, x) \, a$, which we take to mean the application of the identity function to the constant a, should evaluate in some sense to the answer a. In this section we examine this issue.

Already the mechanism for evaluation has been prepared for by substitution. Evaluation is performed by replacing one lambda expression with another. In particular, a lambda expression of the form $(\lambda v \, . \, l) \, t$ is replaced by the lambda expression $l[v := t]$. We now formalize the process of evaluation in the framework of term rewrite systems. The process of evaluation can also be viewed as proving two lambda expressions equal. This view can be formalized as a calculus of lambda expressions.

We first look at the terminology of term rewrite systems. We start by considering an arbitrary relation between lambda expressions called a contraction. A contraction is a binary relation between terms. We will use the symbol ">" for contractions. A contraction relates a redex with the contractum:

$$redex > contractum$$

Any element of the domain of the relation $>$ is said to be a $>$-redex, and a corresponding range element (not necessarily unique) is said to be a $>$-contractum of the redex.

For example, we can define a particular contraction $>_0$ for lambda expressions by the definition:

$$\lambda x \, . \, x >_0 i$$

where i is a function symbol. The relation, viewed as a set of ordered pairs, has one member: $\{\langle \lambda x \, . \, x, i \rangle\}$. Generally, we want to define relations with infinite numbers of pairs. Usually, these pairs have some pattern. For example, we might define a contraction $>_1$ by

$$M \, N >_1 N$$

where M and N are meta-variables standing for any lambda expression. This definition defines an infinite relation and is understood to mean: any lambda expression of the form $M \ N$, i.e., any application, is a $>_1$-redex and the corresponding contractum is the lambda expression in the argument position. The $>_1$ relation has an infinite number of pairs. It includes, for instance, the pair $\langle f \ x, x \rangle$ and the pair $\langle (\lambda x . x) (f \ a), f \ a \rangle$.

The contraction relation gives rise to another relation formed by taking the closure under the formation of lambda expressions. This relation $\rightarrow$, read "reduces in one step," is defined as follows.

1. If $A > B$, then $A \rightarrow B$.

2. If $A \rightarrow B$, then $\lambda x . A \rightarrow \lambda x . B$.

3. If $A \rightarrow B$, then $A \ C \rightarrow B \ C$ and $C \ A \rightarrow C \ B$.

We have defined this relation particularly for lambda expressions, but, of course, it could be defined for any collection of terms.

The reflexive, transitive closure of the relation $\rightarrow$ is the "reduces" relation. This relation, denoted $\overset{*}{\rightarrow}$, is defined as follows.

1. If $A \rightarrow B$, then $A \overset{*}{\rightarrow} B$.

2. For all lambda expressions A, $A \overset{*}{\rightarrow} A$.

3. If $A \overset{*}{\rightarrow} B$ and $B \overset{*}{\rightarrow} C$, then $A \overset{*}{\rightarrow} C$.

Theorem 5 *The relation $\overset{*}{\rightarrow}$ is closed under the formation of lambda expressions.*

Proof. (Lemma 3.1.6 in Barendregt [3, page 52].) The proof is by induction on the generation of the relation $A \overset{*}{\rightarrow} B$. We must show $\lambda V . A \overset{*}{\rightarrow} \lambda V . B$, $A \ C \overset{*}{\rightarrow} B \ C$, and $C \ A \overset{*}{\rightarrow} C \ B$.

Suppose $A \overset{*}{\rightarrow} B$ because $A \rightarrow B$. The proof is immediate from the definition of the relation $\rightarrow$.

Suppose $A \overset{*}{\rightarrow} B$ because $A = B$. Using the fact that $\overset{*}{\rightarrow}$ is reflexive, we have immediately that $\lambda V . A \overset{*}{\rightarrow} \lambda V . A$, $A \ C \overset{*}{\rightarrow} A \ C$, and $C \ A \overset{*}{\rightarrow} C \ A$.

Suppose $A \overset{*}{\rightarrow} B$ because $A \overset{*}{\rightarrow} D$ and $D \overset{*}{\rightarrow} B$ for some D. By induction hypothesis and transitivity of $\overset{*}{\rightarrow}$, the conclusion follows immediately. ∎

Another relation generated by an arbitrary contraction is also of interest in some cases. This is the reflexive, symmetric, and transitive closure of the contraction, and is denoted $\equiv$. It is defined with the following four cases:

1. If $A \rightarrow B$, then $A \equiv B$.

2. For all lambda expressions A, $A \equiv A$.

3. If $A \equiv B$, then $B \equiv A$.

4. If $A \equiv B$ and $B \equiv C$, then $A \equiv C$

7.3 Rewriting lambda expressions

In considering lambda expressions there are three contractions of particular interest. First there is the alpha contraction, defined by the following schema

$$\lambda V . L >_\alpha \lambda W . (L[V := W]) \tag{7.1}$$

where W is a variable that does not occur free in L. The beta contraction is defined as follows:

$$(\lambda V . L) M >_\beta L[V := M] \tag{7.2}$$

for all lambda expressions L and M, and all variables V. The third contraction, the eta contraction, is defined by

$$\lambda V . L V >_\eta L \tag{7.3}$$

where V is a variable that does not occur free in L.

7.3.1 Alpha equivalence

In this section we examine the importance of the alpha contraction defined above. We will see that the alpha equivalence relation, $\equiv_\alpha$, induced by the alpha contraction formalizes the intuition that the choice of names of bound variables in lambda expressions does not matter. This reflects the more general characteristic of programming languages, namely, that the choice of names for formal parameters are not significant computationally. For example, the following Pascal procedures are computationally the same.

```
procedure P (x : integer);
begin
  if (x>0) then writeln ("Greater than zero.");
end
```

```
procedure P (y : integer);
begin
  if (y>0) then writeln ("Greater than zero.");
end
```

They differ only in the choice of the name of the formal parameter.

We look at some examples of lambda expressions in the $>_\alpha$, $\rightarrow_\alpha$, $\overset{*}{\rightarrow}_\alpha$, and $\equiv_\alpha$ relations. The lambda expression $\lambda x . x$ is an alpha-redex. There are many choices for the corresponding alpha-contractum: $\lambda y . y$, $\lambda z . z$, etc. For example,

$$\lambda x . x >_\alpha \lambda y . x[x := y] = \lambda y . y$$

The alpha-contraction relation is not reflexive (since we cannot always choose W to be V in 7.1 above), so neither is the relation $\rightarrow_\alpha$. But $\rightarrow_\alpha$ is closed under term formation, so we have

$$\lambda z . \lambda x . x \to_\alpha \lambda z . \lambda y . y$$

Note that $\lambda z . \lambda x . x$ does not stand in the $>_\alpha$ relation with $\lambda z . \lambda y . y$. Furthermore,

$$\lambda z . \lambda x . x \overset{*}{\to}_\alpha \lambda w . \lambda y . y$$

as

$$\lambda z . \lambda x . x \to_\alpha \lambda z . \lambda y . y \to_\alpha \lambda w . \lambda y . y$$

The alpha-contraction relation *is* symmetric.

$$\lambda V . L >_\alpha \lambda W . (L[V := W]) >_\alpha \lambda V . (((L[V := W]))[W := V]) = \lambda V . L$$

Hence the relations $\to_\alpha$ and $\overset{*}{\to}_\alpha$ are also symmetric. So the relation $\equiv_\alpha$ is the same as the relation $\overset{*}{\to}_\alpha$.

Consider equivalence classes of lambda expressions formed by the equivalence relation $\equiv_\alpha$. We can treat lambda expressions as representatives of their respective equivalence classes and rename the bound variables whenever we choose. This is because substitution is the most important operation we wish to perform on lambda expressions, and substitution respects equivalence classes. This is formally stated in Theorem 9. Furthermore, this explains why the choice of the variable name is immaterial in the substitution operation.

The proof of Theorem 9 requires the following lemmas.

Lemma 6 *For all lambda expressions L,*

$$\lambda W_1 . (L[V := W_1]) \equiv_\alpha \lambda W_2 . (L[V := W_2])$$

as long as the variables W_1 and W_2 do not appear free in L.

Proof. We begin by observing that

$$\lambda W_1 . (L[V := W_1]) >_\alpha \lambda W_2 . ((L[V := W_1])[W_1 := W_2])$$

as long as W_2 does not occur free in $L[V := W_1]$. So we prove that

$$(L[V := W_1])[W_1 := W_2] = L[V := W_2]$$

by induction on the structure of L for any variables W_1 and W_2 that do not appear in free in L.

If L is a variable or a function symbol, then substituting first W_1 for V and then W_2 for W_1 is the same as substituting W_2 directly for V.

If L is an application of the form $M\ N$, then W_1 and W_2 do not appear free in either M or N. Applying the induction hypothesis twice yields the desired conclusion.

Suppose L is an abstraction of the form $\lambda X_1 . M_1$. If X_1 is equal to V the result is trivial. If X_1 is not equal to V, then if W_1 and W_2 are not among free variables of $\lambda X_1 . M_1$, then they are not among the free variables of M_1. Applying the induction hypothesis to M_1 yields the desired conclusion.   ∎

Lemma 7 *For all lambda expressions L, M, and A, and all variables V, if L $\equiv_\alpha$ M, then L[V := A] $\equiv_\alpha$ M[V := A].*

Lemma 8 *For all lambda expressions L, A, and B, and all variables V, if A $\equiv_\alpha$ B, then L[V := A] $\equiv_\alpha$ L[V := B].*

The previous two lemmas, whose proofs we have omitted, yield the following theorem.

Theorem 9 *Substitution on alpha-equivalence classes is well defined:*

$$L \equiv_\alpha M \ \& \ A \equiv_\alpha B \ \Rightarrow \ L[V := A] \equiv_\alpha M[V := B]$$

Proof. The proof is a direct consequence of the previous two lemmas.

$$L[V := A] \equiv_\alpha M[V := A] \equiv_\alpha M[V := B]$$

(See Curry and Feys [8, pages 94–104].) ∎

7.3.2 Beta reduction

The occurrence of a subterm of the form $(\lambda v . b) \, t$ in a lambda expression is called a *beta redex*. We say e_1 reduces to e_2 in one step, $e_1 \to_\beta e_2$, if e_2 is the lambda expression obtained by replacing some beta redex by the appropriate contractum.

The beta-contraction relation can be interpreted as saying that a function $\lambda v . b$ applied to the actual argument t means the same as the body b where all occurrences of the formal parameter v have been replaced by t. The variable v is bound to t. This is essentially the call-by-name rule in ALGOL 60. Formal parameters must be renamed to avoid capturing variables in t.

Beta reduction is the process of repeatedly replacing beta redexes. It is so called, since the resulting lambda expression is generally more simple. A subterm of a lambda expression, a beta redex, is selected and replaced by $b[x := t]$. The selection and replacement continues until no beta redex is found. If an expression has no redexes, it is said to be in *normal form*, more precisely, in beta normal form.

We next give an example of the reduction of a lambda expression to normal form. The beta redex chosen at each step in the reduction is underlined. Notice that the function $\lambda x . x$ is used as an argument.

$$\begin{array}{c} (\lambda y . \lambda z . z \, y) \, c \, (\lambda x . x) \\ \underline{(\lambda y . \lambda z . z \, y) \, c} \, (\lambda x . x) \\ \hline (\lambda z . z \, c) \, (\lambda x . x) \\ \underline{(\lambda z . z \, c) \, (\lambda x . x)} \\ \hline (\lambda x . x) \, c \\ \underline{(\lambda x . x) \, c} \\ \hline c \end{array}$$

Now we look at another example. Let **S** and **K** stand for the following lambda expressions.

$$\mathbf{S} = \lambda x \,.\, \lambda y \,.\, \lambda z \,.\, x\, z\, (y\, z)$$

$$\mathbf{K} = \lambda x \,.\, \lambda y \,.\, x$$

Now then, applying beta reduction to the lambda expression **SKK** yields:

$$\mathbf{SKK} = (\lambda x \,.\, \lambda y \,.\, \lambda z \,.\, x\, z\, (y\, z))\,\mathbf{K}\,\mathbf{K}$$

$$(\lambda y \,.\, \lambda z \,.\, \mathbf{K}\, z\, (y\, z))\,\mathbf{K}$$

$$\lambda z \,.\, \mathbf{K}\, z\, (\mathbf{K}\, z)$$

$$\lambda z \,.\, (\lambda y \,.\, z)\,(\mathbf{K}\, z)$$

$$\lambda z \,.\, z$$

Hence the lambda expression **SKK** is the same as the identity function.

To illustrate the importance of renaming variables in substitution consider the following lambda expression, call it L:

$$(\lambda x \,.\, \lambda y \,.\, x\, y)\,(\lambda z \,.\, y)\, c$$

The lambda expression $\lambda x \,.\, \lambda y \,.\, x\, y$ represents the function that takes its first argument and applies it to its second argument. We expect that this lambda expression will return y, when applied to $\lambda z \,.\, y$ and c. Now we evaluate the lambda expression L, but we use a naive definition of substitution that does not rename variables at all.

$$\underline{(\lambda x \,.\, \lambda y \,.\, x\, y)\,(\lambda z \,.\, y)}\, c$$

The erroneous substitution yields:

$$\lambda y \,.\, x\, y[x := \lambda z \,.\, y] = \lambda y \,.\, (\lambda z \,.\, y)\, y$$

The free y in $\lambda z \,.\, y$ became captured. Continuing the evaluation yields the lambda expression c.

$$(\lambda y \,.\, (\lambda z \,.\, y)\, y)\, c$$

$$(\lambda z \,.\, y)\, y[y := c]$$

$$(\lambda z \,.\, c)\, c$$

$$c$$

The result c is surprising; intuitively the value should have been y. What happened is that the variable y is free in $\lambda z \,.\, y$, in the substitution of $\lambda z \,.\, y$ for x in $\lambda y \,.\, x\, y$, and the name conflicts with the name of the bound variable. Since we can change the name of a bound variable without changing the meaning of the lambda expression, we rename the bound variable y to some new variable, say v. The substitution thus becomes:

$$(\lambda y \,.\, x\, y)[x := \lambda z \,.\, y] = \lambda v \,.\, (\lambda z \,.\, y)\, v$$

The y in $\lambda z \,.\, y$ does not become captured because the outer $\lambda y.$ has been renamed. The beta reduction continues to the correct conclusion:

$$(\lambda v \,.\, (\lambda z \,.\, y)\, v)\, c$$

$$(\lambda z \,.\, y)\, v[v := c]$$

$$(\lambda z \,.\, y)\, c$$

$$y$$

Not all lambda expressions have a normal form, as is shown by the following example:

$$(\lambda x \,.\, x\, x)\, (\lambda x \,.\, x\, x)$$

This lambda expression does have a beta redex. Beta reduction can be applied as follows:

$$x\, x[x := \lambda x \,.\, x\, x] = (\lambda x \,.\, x\, x)\, (\lambda x \,.\, x\, x)$$

But no progress has been made. Applying beta reduction just yields the original lambda expression. Hence the expression has no normal form. Sometimes lambda expressions can get more "complicated" after applying beta reduction.

$$(\lambda x \,.\, xxx)\, (\lambda x \,.\, xxx)$$

$$(\lambda x \,.\, xxx)\, (\lambda x \,.\, xxx)\, (\lambda x \,.\, xxx)$$

Sometimes there is a choice in selecting the next beta redex to reduce.

$$(\lambda x \,.\, \lambda y \,.\, x)\, c\, ((\lambda z \,.\, f\, z)\, b)$$

$$\frac{(\lambda x \,.\, \lambda y \,.\, x)\, c\, ((\lambda z \,.\, f\, z)\, b)}{(\lambda y \,.\, c)\, ((\lambda z \,.\, f\, z)\, b)} \qquad \frac{(\lambda x \,.\, \lambda y \,.\, x)\, c\, ((\lambda z \,.\, f\, z)\, b)}{\dfrac{(\lambda x \,.\, \lambda y \,.\, x)\, c\, (f\, b)}{(\lambda y \,.\, c)\, (f\, b)}}$$

$$c \qquad\qquad c$$

One choice can even lead to a nonterminating computation. Take, for example, $f = z$ and $b = \lambda z \,.\, z\, z$ in the example above.

$$(\lambda x \,.\, \lambda y \,.\, x)\, c\, ((\lambda z \,.\, z\, z)\, (\lambda z \,.\, z\, z))$$

Such terms were considered meaningless by Church (in the original λ-**I**-calculus—the version we are using is sometimes called the λ-**K**-calculus), and he ruled out lambda abstractions, like $\lambda y \,.\, x$, that ignore their argument. But we permit such terms, and this raises the serious question about the uniqueness of results. Fortunately there is the Church-Rosser Theorem, which is the subject of the next section.

7.4   Church-Rosser Theorem

In this section we reach the important conclusion that no choice of which beta redex to reduce will result in a dead end. The proof requires introduction of a new binary relation on lambda expressions. This relation is closely related to beta reduction, but satisfies the following property.

Definition 10 A binary relation $\to$ on lambda expressions satisfies the *diamond property* if for all terms L, M_1, M_2 such that $L \to M_1$ and $L \to M_2$ there exists a term N such that $M_1 \to N$ and $M_2 \to N$.

Theorem 11 *If a relation satisfies the diamond property, so does the transitive closure.*

Proof. The proof of the theorem is suggested by the following diagram:

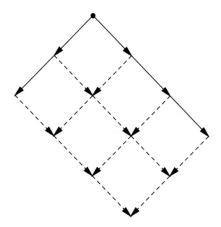

The diamond property of each step guarantees that, no matter how many "transitive" steps are taken, a common term can again be found.   ∎

The relation $\to_\beta$ does not have the diamond property as the following example shows.

$$(\lambda x . \, x \, x) \, ((\lambda x . \, x) \, b)$$

One beta reduction in the argument position requires two beta reductions if performed later in the body of an abstraction. This is suggested by the following diagram.

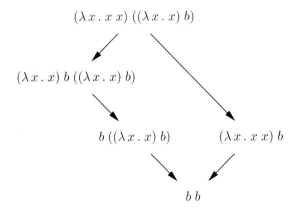

The ingenious part of proving that $\xrightarrow{*}_\beta$ has the diamond property is to invent a relation, whose transitive closure is equal to $\xrightarrow{*}_\beta$, which has the diamond property. The $\rightarrow_\diamond$ relation is this relation. The following four cases define the $\rightarrow_\diamond$ relation.

1. For all lambda expressions L, $L \rightarrow_\diamond L$.

2. If $L \rightarrow_\diamond M$, then $\lambda x . L \rightarrow_\diamond \lambda x . M$.

3. If $L \rightarrow_\diamond L'$ and $M \rightarrow_\diamond M'$, then $L M \rightarrow_\diamond L' M'$.

4. If $L \rightarrow_\diamond L'$ and $M \rightarrow_\diamond M'$, then $(\lambda V . L) M \rightarrow_\diamond L'[V := M']$.

Theorem 12 *The relation $\rightarrow_\diamond$ has the diamond property.*

So from this last theorem we conclude that the relation $\xrightarrow{*}_\beta$ satisfies the diamond property because the relation $\xrightarrow{*}_\beta$ is the transitive closure of $\rightarrow_\diamond$. With this fact it is possible to prove the important Church-Rosser Theorem.

Theorem 13 (Church-Rosser) *If $M \equiv_\beta N$, then there is a Z such that $M \xrightarrow{*}_\beta Z$ and $N \xrightarrow{*}_\beta Z$.*

Proof. The proof is by induction on the $\equiv_\beta$ relation.
Suppose $M \equiv_\beta N$ because $M \rightarrow_\beta N$. Take $Z = N$.
Suppose $M \equiv_\beta N$ because $M = N$. Take $Z = N = M$.
Suppose $M \equiv_\beta N$ because $N \equiv_\beta M$. By induction hypothesis there is a Z such that $N \xrightarrow{*}_\beta Z$ and $M \xrightarrow{*}_\beta Z$.
Suppose $M \equiv_\beta N$ because $M \equiv_\beta L$ and $L \equiv_\beta N$ for some L. By induction hypothesis there exist Z_1 and Z_2 such that $M \xrightarrow{*}_\beta Z_1$, $L \xrightarrow{*}_\beta Z_1$, and $L \xrightarrow{*}_\beta Z_2$,

$N \xrightarrow{*}_\beta Z_2$. By the diamond property there exists Z such that $Z_1 \xrightarrow{*}_\beta Z$ and $Z_2 \xrightarrow{*}_\beta Z$. This situation is illustrated in the figure below.

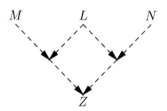

This ends the proof. ∎

If two sequences of beta reductions go their separate ways, all the expressions are beta equivalent. But can a branch be a dead end that cannot reduce to the "correct" branch? The next corollary of the Church-Rosser Theorem gives a negative answer.

Theorem 14 *If M is beta equivalent to a lambda expression N in normal form, then $M \xrightarrow{*}_\beta N$.*

Proof. Let $N \equiv_\beta M$ and let N be a beta normal form. By the Church-Rosser Theorem we have $M \xrightarrow{*}_\beta Z$ and $N \xrightarrow{*}_\beta Z$. So N is syntactically equal to Z. Hence $M \xrightarrow{*}_\beta N$. ∎

The most important corollary of the Church-Rosser Theorem is that normal forms are unique.

Theorem 15 *A lambda expression can have at most one beta normal form.*

Proof. Suppose N_1 and N_2 are both beta normal forms of L. By Theorem 14 $L \xrightarrow{*}_\beta N_1$ and $L \xrightarrow{*}_\beta N_2$. Then $N_1 \equiv_\beta N_2$. By the Church-Rosser Theorem $N_1 \xrightarrow{*}_\beta Z$ and $N_2 \xrightarrow{*}_\beta Z$ for some Z. Because N_1 and N_2 are normal forms, we must have $N_1 = Z$ and $N_2 = Z$. Therefore $N_1 = N_2$. ∎

These theorems as stated are not quite true. All the normal forms of L are not syntactically identical, but they are alpha-variants. Here again the names of the bound variables detract from the theory. The following is an example of a lambda expression that reduces to different normal forms (although they are alpha-variants):

$$\lambda y . (\lambda x . \lambda y . x\, y)\,((\lambda z . f)\, y)$$
$$\lambda y . \lambda u . (\lambda z . f)\, y\, u \qquad \lambda y . (\lambda x . \lambda y . x\, y)\, f$$
$$\lambda y . \lambda u . f\, u \qquad \qquad \lambda y . \lambda y . f\, y$$

The choice of the beta-redex in the left branch necessitates the introduction of a new variable in the course of the substitution. The right branch does not introduce a new variable. The end result is two lambda expressions that are alpha-equivalent, but not symbol for symbol the same. The correct statement of the theorems requires treating lambda expressions as representatives of alpha-equivalence classes.

7.5 Order of evaluation

From the Church-Rosser Theorem we know that no two orders of evaluation of a lambda expression can give different normal forms, although some may possibly fail to terminate even though there is a normal form. Is there an order of evaluation that is guaranteed to terminate whenever it is possible somehow to reduce a particular expression to normal form? Yes, there is such an order, known as *normal order*. Normal order reduces the leftmost redex at every stage. Normal order is also called call-by-name.

Another order which is of particular significance to programming languages is *applicative order* or call-by-value. This rule says evaluate the function and the argument of an application first. (This could be done in parallel.) If applicative order evaluation terminates, it terminates with the correct answer (by the Church-Rosser Theorem). But it may fail to terminate on some lambda expressions that are reducible to a normal form. When applicative order evaluation does terminate, it does so faster than normal order, as the next example illustrates.

$$(\lambda x \,.\, x + x + x + x)\, ((\lambda x \,.\, x)\, a)$$
$$(\lambda x \,.\, x)\, a + (\lambda x \,.\, x)\, a + (\lambda x \,.\, x)\, a + (\lambda x \,.\, x)\, a$$
$$a + (\lambda x \,.\, x)\, a + (\lambda x \,.\, x)\, a + (\lambda x \,.\, x)\, a$$
$$a + a + (\lambda x \,.\, x)\, a + (\lambda x \,.\, x)\, a$$
$$a + a + a + (\lambda x \,.\, x)\, a$$
$$a + a + a + a$$

In this example, normal order evaluation introduced four identical beta redexes that then had to be reduced individually. Applicative order evaluation would have reduced the redex once, before replicating it through the body of the abstraction.

7.6 Computation

Thus far it seems improbable that lambda expressions could be used to compute much of anything. In particular, how can one compute the factorial function with the lambda expressions? We will take this to be the primary goal of this section. There are three hurdles that appear to stand in the way of defining the factorial function.

1. How can a choice be made?

2. Where are numbers?

3. What about iteration or recursion?

The approach is to build lambda expressions of particular forms to represent the concepts we need. We will define "macros" for the concepts we introduce.

We first look at implementing the `if` statement. We define the three macros to stand for the two boolean values true and false, and the `if` statement. Here are definitions of the macros T and F:

$$T \overset{\text{df}}{=} \lambda x . \lambda y . x \qquad F \overset{\text{df}}{=} \lambda x . \lambda y . y$$

By the symbol $\overset{\text{df}}{=}$ we mean "defined to be." In all the equations below any occurrence of these macros is to be understood as being replaced by the appropriate definition. The macros are only an aid to the intuition and an effort to make complex lambda expressions more legible. The *If* macro has three arguments.

$$If[A, B, C] \overset{\text{df}}{=} A \; B \; C$$

An occurrence of the *If* macro (which will always appear with three lambda expressions as arguments) is to be understood as the lambda expression obtained by textually substituting the arguments for A, B, and C in the definition above.

The definitions for T, F, and *If* are appropriate if they fulfill the basic computational laws of the `if` statement. These laws are:

$$If[T, B, C] = B \quad \text{and} \quad If[F, B, C] = C$$

By the equals sign in these equations we mean computationally the same. As computation with lambda expressions has been defined in terms of beta reduction, these laws must be interpreted as claiming that the lambda expression on the left-hand side is *beta equivalent* to the lambda expression on the right-hand side. We verify the laws with the following two derivations:

$$
\begin{aligned}
If[T, B, C] \quad &\overset{\text{df}}{=} \quad T \; B \; C \\
&\overset{\text{df}}{=} \quad (\lambda x . \lambda y . x) \; B \; C \\
&\to_\beta \quad (\lambda y . B) \; C \\
&>_\beta \quad B
\end{aligned}
$$

$$
\begin{aligned}
If[F, B, C] \quad &\overset{\text{df}}{=} \quad F \; B \; C \\
&\overset{\text{df}}{=} \quad (\lambda x . \lambda y . y) \; B \; C \\
&\to_\beta \quad (\lambda y . y) \; C \\
&>_\beta \quad C
\end{aligned}
$$

Next we will use the same approach for defining numbers. Numbers are a little more complicated than boolean values. In fact, we first define lists and then define numbers in terms of lists. The data structure for lists can be built if we can find a pairing constructor, a head function, a tail function, a representation of the empty list, and a predicate to recognize the empty lists from nonempty lists. Here are the definitions for the macros *Pair*, *First* and *Rest*.

$$Pair[A, B] = \lambda x \,.\, If[x, A, B] = \lambda x \,.\, x \, A \, B$$

$$First[A] = A \, T$$

$$Rest[A] = A \, F$$

The laws of lists:

$$First[Pair[A, B]] = A \qquad Rest[Pair[A, B]] = B$$

hold, since

$$
\begin{aligned}
First[Pair[A, B]] \quad &= \quad Pair[A, B] \, T \\
&= \quad (\lambda x \,.\, If[x, A, B]) \, T \\
&>_\beta \quad If[T, A, B] \\
&\xrightarrow{*}_\beta \quad A
\end{aligned}
$$

and

$$
\begin{aligned}
Rest[Pair[A, B]] \quad &= \quad Pair[A, B] \, F \\
&= \quad (\lambda x \,.\, If[x, A, B]) \, F \\
&>_\beta \quad If[F, A, B] \\
&\xrightarrow{*}_\beta \quad B
\end{aligned}
$$

For the sake of completeness we include definitions for *Nil*, the empty list, and *Null*, the recognizer of the empty list. These macros are not needed for defining numbers.

$$Nil \stackrel{\mathrm{df}}{=} \lambda x \,.\, T \qquad Null[A] \stackrel{\mathrm{df}}{=} A \, (\lambda x \,.\, \lambda y \,.\, F)$$

These operations are correct because:

$$
\begin{aligned}
Null[Nil] \quad &= \quad Nil \, (\lambda x \,.\, \lambda y \,.\, F) \\
&= \quad (\lambda x \,.\, T) \, (\lambda x \,.\, \lambda y \,.\, F) \\
&>_\beta \quad T
\end{aligned}
$$

$$
\begin{aligned}
Null[Pair[X, Y]] \quad &= \quad Pair[X, Y] \, (\lambda x \,.\, \lambda y \,.\, F) \\
&= \quad (\lambda x \,.\, If[x, X, Y]) \, (\lambda x \,.\, \lambda y \,.\, F) \\
&>_\beta \quad If[\lambda x \,.\, \lambda y \,.\, F, X, Y] \\
&= \quad (\lambda x \,.\, \lambda y \,.\, F) \, X \, Y \\
&\rightarrow_\beta \quad (\lambda y \,.\, F) \, Y \\
&>_\beta \quad F
\end{aligned}
$$

We define numbers using the list data structure just developed. The number 0 is represented by the identity function.

$$Zero \overset{\text{df}}{=} I \overset{\text{df}}{=} \lambda x \,.\, x \qquad\qquad Succ[X] \overset{\text{df}}{=} Pair[F, X]$$

This provides us a representation of every natural number as a lambda expression. Furthermore, every such lambda expression is closed and in beta normal form. The operations we need on the lambda expression representation of numbers are a predicate to determine whether or not the number is zero and an operation to compute the predecessor.

$$IsZero[A] \overset{\text{df}}{=} First[A] \qquad\qquad Pred[A] \overset{\text{df}}{=} Rest[A]$$

These operations have the desired properties as indicated.

$$IsZero[0] = First[Zero] = First[I] = I \, T >_\beta T$$

$$IsZero[Succ[N]] = First[Succ[N]] = First[Pair[F, N]] \overset{*}{\to}_\beta F$$

$$Pred[Succ[N]] = Rest[Succ[N]] = Rest[Pair[F, N]] \overset{*}{\to}_\beta N$$

The definition of the predecessor at zero is not important. It turns out that $Pred[0]$ reduces to F. But what it reduces to, or even that it has a normal form, does not matter as we shall never make use of any property of $Pred[0]$.

Of course, addition, subtraction, multiplication can be defined for natural numbers represented this way. These definitions are complex and not illuminating when defined without using recursion.

7.6.1   Recursion

In this section we wish to make sense of a recursive function definition like that of

$$fact = \lambda n \,.\, \text{if } n = 0 \text{ then } 1 \text{ else } n \times fact(n - 1)$$

of the factorial function. Much of this equation we can already translate to a lambda expression. The conditional expression, the test for zero, and subtraction by one can all be translated using the macros of the previous section. In principle, we could find an appropriate macro definition for multiplication as well, leaving only the "recursive" part unresolved. The goal here, as in the last section, is to find lambda expressions that beta-reduce to the appropriate answers. In the case of the factorial function, we see a lambda expression that, when applied to a numeral, beta-reduces to the answer. The problem with the equation above is that it is not a definition, since it has *fact* on both sides of the equation. This is really a wish. We wish to find a lambda expression *fact* such that the equation is true. This is not unlike equations found in some parts of mathematics. For example,

$$x = x^2 - 6 \qquad f = \frac{1}{4}(Df)^2 + 3$$

The solutions to these equations can be considered fixedpoints of functions derived from these equations by abstracting over the variable we wish to solve for.

$$\lambda x \,.\, x^2 - 6 \qquad \lambda f \,.\, \frac{1}{4}(Df)^2 + 3$$

A solution to the equation $x = x^2 - 6$ is a fixedpoint of $\lambda x \,.\, x^2 - 6$. The number 3 is a fixedpoint as can easily be verified: $(\lambda x \,.\, x^2 - 6)\, 3 = 3^2 - 6 = 3$. A solution to the equation $f = \frac{1}{4}(Df)^2 + 3$ is a fixedpoint of $\lambda f \,.\, \frac{1}{4}(Df)^2 + 3$. The function $\lambda x \,.\, x^2 + 3$ is a fixedpoint, as we can verify:

$$
\begin{aligned}
(\lambda f \,.\, \frac{1}{4}(Df)^2 + 3)\,((\lambda x \,.\, x^2 + 3)) \;&=\; \frac{1}{4}(D(\lambda x \,.\, x^2 + 3))^2 + 3 \\
&=\; \frac{1}{4}(\lambda x \,.\, 2x)^2 + 3 \\
&=\; \lambda x \,.\, x^2 + 3
\end{aligned}
$$

Not all functions have fixedpoints however. For example, the equation

$$x = x + 1$$

has no fixedpoint, since no number can equal its successor. Some functions have more than one fixedpoint, for example,

$$x = x$$

has infinitely many fixedpoints, since every number is equal to itself. This suggests that we must be careful in devising a theory of fixedpoints.

We want to find a lambda expression that will find the fixedpoint of a function (if it exists). We will call this lambda expression **Y**. If we can find such a lambda expression, it has the property that $f\,(\mathbf{Y}\,f) = \mathbf{Y}\,f$.

Let F be the function associated with the recursive definition of *fact*, that is,

$$F = \lambda g \,.\, \lambda n \,.\, \text{if } n = 0 \text{ then } 1 \text{ else } n \times g(n-1)$$

Notice that the F is a lambda expression with no free variables and is not recursive. It is also a higher-order function, i.e., a function taking a function as an argument and returning a function. Roughly put, the type of F is that of a function from the domain *Nat* $\rightarrow$ *Nat* to the range *Nat* $\rightarrow$ *Nat*, where *Nat* $\rightarrow$ *Nat* is the type of functions from natural numbers to natural numbers.

The factorial function we seek is the fixedpoint of this function F. The type of the fixedpoint for F will be *Nat* $\rightarrow$ *Nat*, and this is appropriate for the factorial function. How can we compute the fixedpoint? Consider the sequence.

$$F_0 = F(\Omega) = \lambda n \,.\, \text{if } n = 0 \text{ then } 1 \text{ else } n \times \Omega(n-1)$$

$$F_1 = F(F_0) = \lambda n \,.\, \text{if } n = 0 \text{ then } 1 \text{ else } n \times F_0(n-1)$$

$$F_2 = F(F_1) = \lambda n \,.\, \text{if } n = 0 \text{ then } 1 \text{ else } n \times F_1(n-1)$$

$$F_i = F(F_{i-1}) = F^{i+1}(\Omega)$$

We don't care what the function Ω is; it can be anything at all, including a function that does not terminate. Whatever function Ω is, F_0 computes the factorial for $n = 0$, F_1 works for $n = 0$ and $n = 1$, F_2 works for $n = 0, 1, 2$, and so on. The fixedpoint is the limit of this sequence, call it F_ω. F_ω works for all natural numbers. We want enough copies of F produced in order to solve the problem. "Enough copies" means a potentially infinite number of them.

Consider the sequence of lambda expressions we introduced above.

$$\Omega \to F\,\Omega \to F\,(F\,\Omega) \to F\,(F\,(F\,\Omega)) \to \ldots$$

To compute 2! we just pick some F_i where $i \geq 3$ and evaluate

$$F_i(2)$$
$$(\lambda n \,.\, \text{if } n = 0 \text{ then } 1 \text{ else } n \times F_{i-1}(n-1))\,2$$
$$2 \times F_{i-1}(1)$$
$$2 \times (\lambda n \,.\, \text{if } n = 0 \text{ then } 1 \text{ else } n \times F_{i-2}(n-1))\,1$$
$$2 \times 1$$
$$2 \times 1 \times 1(\lambda n \,.\, \text{if } n = 0 \text{ then } 1 \text{ else } n \times F_{i-3}(n-1))\,0$$
$$2 \times 1 \times 1$$

So if we can just get enough copies of F we can compute the factorial of any number we choose.

What we want is some lambda expression that, for any function F, generates the previous sequence. We have already seen a lambda expression that can replicate itself.

$$X\,X \to X\,X \to X\,X \to X\,X \to \ldots$$

where $X = \lambda x \,.\, x\,x$. Perhaps it can help. What we really want is something like:

$$X\,X \to F\,(X\,X) \to F\,(F\,(X\,X)) \to F\,(F\,(F\,(X\,X))) \to \ldots$$

We can get that with the lambda expression $X_F = \lambda x \,.\, F\,(x\,x)$ as $X_F\,X_F \to F\,(X_F\,X_F)$. So $X_F\,X_F$ is a fixedpoint of F.

Abstracting over F we assert that the lambda expression

$$\lambda h \,.\, (\lambda x \,.\, h\,(x\,x))\,(\lambda x \,.\, h\,(x\,x))$$

is the fixedpoint operator we seek. We name this fixedpoint operator $\mathbf{Y}$.

The original goal was to find a lambda expression that computes the factorial function. This lambda expression is:

$$\mathbf{Y}\,(\lambda f \,.\, \lambda n \,.\, \text{if } n = 0 \text{ then } 1 \text{ else } n \times f(n-1))$$

For clarity, this lambda expression is written in a high-level notation.

We have actually seen this approach to computing a fixedpoint of a function before. Recall exercise 4. 22. In that problem we defined the recursive factorial function without recursion.

```
f (g,n)  = if n=0 then 1 else n * g(g,n-1);
fact (n) = f(f,n)
```

We can write these functions as lambda expressions:

$$f = \lambda g . \lambda n . \text{ if } n = 0 \text{ then } 1 \text{ else } n \times (g\,g)(n-1)$$
$$fact = f\,f$$

Now if we let b be a function that abstracts away the recursive call in the body of the factorial function:

$$b = \lambda r . \lambda n . \text{ if } n = 0 \text{ then } 1 \text{ else } n \times r\,(n-1)$$

then f can be rewritten:

$$f = \lambda g . b\,(g\,g)$$

In other words:

$$fact = (\lambda g . b\,(g\,g))\,(\lambda g . b\,(g\,g))$$

Finally, if we abstract over the function body we get:

$$\mathbf{Y} = \lambda h . (\lambda x . h\,(x\,x))\,(\lambda x . h\,(x\,x))$$

In Pascal and ML no type can be found for `f`. Likewise no type can be found for the fixedpoint operator $\mathbf{Y}$, because of the self-application. These languages require an extra mechanism in the language to introduce recursive function definitions. In Pascal, as most conventional languages, there is a mechanism for subprogram definition. This mechanism usually permits the name of the subprogram being defined to denote the subprogram even in the body of the subprogram itself.

7.6.2 Examples

An example of the evaluation of a recursive function is necessary to convince one that the $\mathbf{Y}$ combinator has the appropriate effect. We begin with a simple example and then the Fibonacci function.

Let f be the lambda expression $\lambda z . 6$. Then $\mathbf{Y}\,f$ reduces as follows

$$(\lambda h . (\lambda x . h\,(x\,x))\,(\lambda x . h\,(x\,x)))\,f$$

$$(\lambda x . h\,(x\,x))\,(\lambda x . h\,(x\,x))[h := f]$$

$$(\lambda x . f\,(x\,x))\,(\lambda x . f\,(x\,x))$$

$$f\ (x\ x)[x := \lambda x.\ f\ (x\ x)]$$
$$f\ ((\lambda x.\ f\ (x\ x))\ (\lambda x.\ f\ (x\ x)))$$
$$(\lambda z.\ 6)\ ((\lambda x.\ f\ (x\ x))\ (\lambda x.\ f\ (x\ x)))$$
$$6[z := (\lambda x.\ f\ (x\ x))\ (\lambda x.\ f\ (x\ x))]$$
$$6$$

Notice that we chose to reduce the outermost redex when there was a choice. The result is 6; exactly what we would expect the fixedpoint of the constant function f to be.

Let f be the function to compute the Fibonacci function.

$$\lambda n.\ \text{if}\ n < 3\ \text{then}\ 1\ \text{else}\ f(n-1) + f(n-2)$$

Let F be the functional associated with f, specifically:

$$F = \lambda g.\ \lambda n.\ \text{if}\ n < 3\ \text{then}\ 1\ \text{else}\ g(n-1) + g(n-2)$$

The Fibonacci function is the lambda expression $\mathbf{Y}\ F$. This is a closed lambda expression.

We next verify that $\mathbf{Y}\ F\ 3 = 2$; that is, $\mathbf{Y}\ F\ 3 \xrightarrow{*}_\beta 2$.

$$\mathbf{Y}\ F\ 3$$

$$(\lambda x.\ F\ (x\ x))\ (\lambda x.\ F\ (x\ x))\ 3$$

Now let $k = \lambda x.\ F\ (x\ x)$.

$$k\ k\ 3$$
$$(\lambda x.\ F\ (x\ x))\ k\ 3$$
$$F\ (k\ k)\ 3$$
$$(\lambda g.\ \lambda n.\ \text{if}\ n < 3\ \text{then}\ 1\ \text{else}\ g(n-1) + g(n-2))\ (k\ k)\ 3$$

Now we plug in the lambda expression we named F and reduce it.

$$(\lambda n.\ \text{if}\ n < 3\ \text{then}\ 1\ \text{else}\ k\ k\ (n-1) + k\ k\ (n-2))\ 3$$

$$k\ k\ 2 + k\ k\ 1$$

Now we follow the evaluation of $k\ k\ 2$.

$$k\ k\ 2$$

$$(\lambda x.\ F\ (x\ x))\ k\ 2$$

$$F\ (k\ k)\ 2$$

$$(\lambda g.\ \lambda n.\ \text{if}\ n < 3\ \text{then}\ 1\ \text{else}\ g(n-1) + g(n-2))\ (k\ k)\ 2$$

$$(\lambda n.\ \text{if}\ n < 3\ \text{then}\ 1\ \text{else}\ k\ k\ (n-1) + k\ k\ (n-2))\ 2$$

$$1$$

The evaluation of $k\ k\ 1$ is similar and likewise yields the identical result, namely, one. Hence the result of evaluating $\mathbf{Y}\ F\ 3 = 1 + 1 = 2$.

7.6.3 Least fixedpoint

In this section we consider in more detail the nature of the fixedpoints of recursive lambda expression equations computed by the process of (1) abstracting over the name of the recursive function, and (2) applying the **Y** combinator.

For example, consider the recursive equation:

$$f = \lambda n \,.\, f(n)$$

The fixedpoint solution to this equation is:

$$g(n) = \text{undefined}$$

In this case the fixedpoint is not a total function. There are even other fixedpoints to the equations.

Here is an intriguing recursive equation from [20]:

$$f = \lambda n \,.\, \text{if } n = 0 \text{ then } 1 \text{ else } 2 \times f(f(n-1))$$

Three fixedpoints, three functions, solve this equation. The function g defined above does. So does the function h:

$$h(n) = \begin{cases} 1, & \text{if } n = 0, \\ 0, & \text{if } n = 1, \\ 2, & \text{if } n = 2, \\ 4, & \text{if } n = 3, \\ \text{undefined}, & \text{otherwise.} \end{cases}$$

For we must have $h(1) = 2 \times h(h(0)) = 2 \times h(1)$, and this is satisfied by taking $h(1) = 0$. Similarly $h(2) = 2 \times h(h(1)) = 2$, and $h(3) = 2 \times h(h(2)) = 2 \times h(2) = 4$. A solution defined everywhere is possible for f:

$$j(n) = \begin{cases} 1, & \text{if } n = 0, \\ 0, & \text{if } n = 1 + 3i, & i = 0, 1, 2, \ldots, \\ 2, & \text{if } n = 2 + 3i, & i = 0, 1, 2, \ldots, \\ 4, & \text{if } n = 3 + 3i, & i = 0, 1, 2, \ldots. \end{cases}$$

All these possible fixedpoints raise an important question. Which fixedpoint does the **Y** combinator compute? The fixedpoint computed is always the one that is defined as little as possible. This is called the *least fixedpoint*. It is possible to develop a theory ordering functions $f_1 \sqsubseteq f_2$ if for all x we have $f_2(x) = f_1(x)$ or $f_1(x) = \text{undefined}$. In this ordering $g \sqsubseteq h \sqsubseteq j$.

Least fixedpoints of recursive programs are important for three main reasons:

- Any recursive program must have a unique least fixedpoint. Thus the least fixedpoint can be used to unambiguously define the "meaning" of recursive programs.

- The classical stack implementation of recursive programs computes the least fixedpoint of the program.

- There are powerful methods for proving properties of the least fixedpoint of recursive programs.

7.7 Combinators

The idea of eliminating variables goes back to Moses Schönfinkel, who in the early 1920s developed the *Funktionenkalkül* or *function calculus*. Haskell Curry developed the idea independently under the name of combinatory logic. The basic idea is that the use of variables is somewhat unnatural. For example, the tautology of propositional logic

$$P \Rightarrow (\neg P \Rightarrow Q)$$

is not a statement about the propositional symbols P and Q, but a statement about the logical connectives "$\Rightarrow$" and "$\neg$." We seek a development of the concepts that focuses on the different means of combination and does not require the artificial use of identifiers. As we have seen with substitution and the Church-Rosser Theorem, the names of variables can be a nuisance.

The only primitive operation in the combinatory calculus is application. We will denote f applied to a as $(f\,a)$. Parentheses are necessary, since application is not associative. But as in the lambda calculus we will make application left-associative so that some parentheses can be omitted.

There will be just two function symbols added to the combinatory calculus and no variables. To see how this works, we consider an example. Suppose we represent addition and multiplication in the combinatory calculus by two constants A and M such that

$$Axy = x + y \quad \text{and} \quad Mxy = x \cdot y$$

for all numbers x and y. Let F be a function such that

$$Fxyz = (x \cdot y) + (x \cdot z)$$

which by the definition of A and M above is the same as

$$Fxyz = A(Mxy)(Mxz).$$

The function F is defined in terms of A and M. The problem is how to define or construct F within the combinatory calculus (assuming that it contains A and M) without using the variables x, y, and z. Assume that we had a function Q in the calculus such that

$$Qxyzuv = x(yzu)(yzv)$$

for all x, y, z, u, and v. Then F could be constructed within the function calculus out of Q, A, and M by means of application only. We can take F to be QAM, and hence we have

$$Fxyz = QAMxyz = A(Mxy)(Mxz)$$

as required. Schönfinkel discovered that it is sufficient to introduce just two combining forms like Q to carry out every function definition. We prove this in the next section.

7.7.1 Combinator completeness

The combinatory calculus is constructed out of two combinators **S** and **K** such that

$$\begin{aligned} \mathbf{S}xyz &= xz(yz) \\ \mathbf{K}xy &= x \end{aligned}$$

S is Schönfinkel's "Verschmelzungsfunktion" or "fusion" combinator and **K** is his "Konstanzfunktion" or "constancy" combinator.

We will now show that every lambda expression can be expressed as a combination of these two combinators. In other words we want an algorithm that takes a lambda expression and returns a combinator with the same meaning.

Before we can understand what the meaning of a combinator is, we must give a precise definition of a combinator. In fact it is convenient to give the definition of the more general notion of a combinator term. A *combinator term* is a variable, a function symbol, one of **K**, **S**, or **I**, or an application. We include the combinator **I** just for convenience as it can be defined in terms of the other two.

$$\begin{aligned} V &\rightarrow x \mid y \mid z \mid v \mid \cdots \\ F &\rightarrow a \mid b \mid c \mid f \mid g \mid \cdots \\ L &\rightarrow V \mid F \mid \mathbf{I} \mid \mathbf{K} \mid \mathbf{S} \mid (L\,L) \end{aligned}$$

We have included function symbols as in the lambda calculus. The important difference is that we have no abstraction operator. In fact there is no operator that binds variables at all. So any variable that appears in a combinator term is free. As with lambda expressions we denote the set of free variables by $FV[X]$. A *combinator* is a combinator term with no variables.

There is an obvious mapping from combinator terms to lambda expressions, $\mathcal{M}[\![X]\!] = L$, which we give below:

$$\begin{aligned} \mathcal{M}[\![x]\!] &= x \\ \mathcal{M}[\![f]\!] &= f \\ \mathcal{M}[\![\mathbf{I}]\!] &= \lambda x \,.\, x \\ \mathcal{M}[\![\mathbf{K}]\!] &= \lambda x \,.\, \lambda y \,.\, x \\ \mathcal{M}[\![\mathbf{S}]\!] &= \lambda x \,.\, \lambda y \,.\, \lambda z \,.\, x\,z\,(y\,z) \end{aligned}$$

$$\mathcal{M}[\![FA]\!] \;=\; \mathcal{M}[\![F]\!]\,\mathcal{M}[\![A]\!]$$

The interesting question is, can we take any lambda expression and find an equivalent combinator term? The problem is how to translate an abstraction. More precisely, we want to take any combinator term X (possibly) containing a free variable v, and find an combinator term that does not contain v that is equivalent to abstracting v from X. We denote this combinator term $[v]X$, and call the operation *bracket abstraction*. We will give an algorithm for finding $[v]X$ that has the two properties expressed in the next two theorems.

Theorem 16 *(Lemma 5.2.1 in Stenlund [28, page 48]) For all combinator terms L:*

$$\mathcal{M}[\![[x]L]\!] \equiv \lambda x \,.\, \mathcal{M}[\![L]\!]$$

where the equivalence is alpha-beta equivalence.

Theorem 17 *For all combinator terms L we have $x \notin FV([x]L)$.*

The bracket abstraction algorithm is defined as follows:

$$
\begin{aligned}
[x]y &= \begin{cases} \mathbf{I} & \text{if } y = x \\ \mathbf{K}y & \text{otherwise} \end{cases} \\
[x]f &= \mathbf{K}f \\
[x]\mathbf{I} &= \mathbf{KI} \\
[x]\mathbf{K} &= \mathbf{KK} \\
[x]\mathbf{S} &= \mathbf{KS} \\
[x](FA) &= \mathbf{S}([x]F)([x]A)
\end{aligned}
$$

Theorem 16 is proved by induction on the structure of combinator terms. We examine the case of application, which is the only difficult case of the theorem. We want to prove that

$$\mathcal{M}[\]\!] \equiv \lambda x \,.\, \mathcal{M}[\![FA]\!]$$

assuming

$$\mathcal{M}[\![[x]F]\!] \equiv \lambda x \,.\, \mathcal{M}[\![F]\!] \quad \text{and} \quad \mathcal{M}[\![[x]A]\!] \equiv \lambda x \,.\, \mathcal{M}[\![A]\!]$$

We know that

$$\mathcal{M}[\]\!] = \mathcal{M}[\![\mathbf{S}([x]F)([x]A)]\!]$$

by the definition of the bracket abstraction algorithm. So

$$\mathcal{M}[\![\mathbf{S}([x]F)([x]A)]\!] = \mathcal{M}[\![\mathbf{S}]\!](\mathcal{M}[\![[x]F]\!])(\mathcal{M}[\![[x]A]\!])$$

follows from the definition of the $\mathcal{M}$ translation. Now the definition of S and the assumptions yield:

$$\mathcal{M}[\![S]\!](\mathcal{M}[\![x]F]\!])(\mathcal{M}[\![x]A]\!]) \equiv (\lambda x . \lambda y . \lambda z . x\, z\, (y\, z))\, (\lambda x . \mathcal{M}[\![F]\!])\, (\lambda x . \mathcal{M}[\![A]\!])$$

We can choose x, y, z such that they are not among the free variables of F and A. By beta reduction the following equivalence holds:

$$(\lambda x . \lambda y . \lambda z . x\, z\, (y\, z))\, (\lambda x . \mathcal{M}[\![F]\!])\, (\lambda x . \mathcal{M}[\![A]\!]) \equiv$$
$$\lambda z . (\lambda x . \mathcal{M}[\![F]\!])\, z\, ((\lambda x . \mathcal{M}[\![A]\!])\, z)$$

By further beta reductions we have

$$\lambda z . (\lambda x . \mathcal{M}[\![F]\!])\, z\, ((\lambda x . \mathcal{M}[\![A]\!])\, z) \equiv \lambda z . (\mathcal{M}[\![F]\!][x := z])\, (\mathcal{M}[\![A]\!][x := z])$$

By definition of substitution and the $\mathcal{M}$ translation we have

$$\lambda z . \mathcal{M}[\![F]\!][x := z]\, \mathcal{M}[\![A]\!][x := z] \equiv \lambda z . (\mathcal{M}[\![F\, A]\!][x := z])$$

Since we can ensure that $z \notin FV[\mathcal{M}[\![F\, A]\!]]$, an application of α equivalence yields:

$$\lambda z . \mathcal{M}[\![F\, A]\!][x := z] \equiv \lambda x . \mathcal{M}[\![F\, A]\!]$$

which is the desired result.

With the bracket abstraction algorithm defined above we can give an algorithm to convert any closed lambda expression to an equivalent combinator term in which no variables appear.

$$
\begin{aligned}
\mathcal{N}[\![x]\!] &= x \\
\mathcal{N}[\![f]\!] &= f \\
\mathcal{N}[\![FA]\!] &= \mathcal{N}[\![F]\!]\mathcal{N}[\![A]\!] \\
\mathcal{N}[\![\lambda x . b]\!] &= [x](\mathcal{N}[\![b]\!])
\end{aligned}
$$

Theorem 18 *(Lemma 5.2.3 in Stenlund [28, page 49].) For all lambda expressions L we have $\mathcal{M}[\![\mathcal{N}[\![L]\!]]\!] \equiv L$, where the equivalence is alpha-beta-eta equivalence.*

Proof. The proof is by induction on the structure of L. Theorem 16 is the difficult case. ∎

Here is an example of converting a simple lambda expression to a combinator. We assume that $+$ and 1 are function symbols.

$$
\begin{aligned}
&\mathcal{N}[\![\lambda x . + x\, 1]\!] \\
&[x](\mathcal{N}[\![+ x\, 1]\!]) \\
&[x](+ x\, 1) \\
&\mathbf{S}\, [x](+ x)\, [x]1 \\
&\mathbf{S}\, (\mathbf{S}\, [x]+\, [x]x)\, [x]1 \\
&\mathbf{S}\, (\mathbf{S}\, (\mathbf{K}\, +)\, \mathbf{I})\, (\mathbf{K}\, 1)
\end{aligned}
$$

$$\mathcal{N}[\![\lambda\,x\,.\,\lambda\,y\,.\,f\,x\,y]\!]$$

$$[x](\mathcal{N}[\![\lambda\,y\,.\,f\,x\,y]\!])$$

$$[x]([y](\mathcal{N}[\![f\,x\,y]\!]))$$

$$[x]([y](f\,x\,y))$$

$$[x](\mathbf{S}\,[y](f\,x)\,[y]y))$$

$$[x](\mathbf{S}\,(\mathbf{S}\,(\mathbf{K}\,f)\,(\mathbf{K}\,x))\,\mathbf{I})$$

$$\mathbf{S}\,[x](\mathbf{S}\,(\mathbf{S}\,(\mathbf{K}\,f)\,(\mathbf{K}\,x)))\,[x]\mathbf{I}$$

$$\mathbf{S}\,(\mathbf{S}\,[x]\mathbf{S}\,[x](\mathbf{S}\,(\mathbf{K}\,f)\,(\mathbf{K}\,x)))\,[x]\mathbf{I}$$

$$\mathbf{S}\,(\mathbf{S}\,(\mathbf{K}\,\mathbf{S})\,[x](\mathbf{S}\,(\mathbf{K}\,f)\,(\mathbf{K}\,x)))\,[x]\mathbf{I}$$

$$\mathbf{S}\,(\mathbf{S}\,(\mathbf{K}\,\mathbf{S})\,(\mathbf{S}\,[x](\mathbf{S}\,(\mathbf{K}\,f))\,[x](\mathbf{K}\,x)))\,[x]\mathbf{I}$$

$$\mathbf{S}\,(\mathbf{S}\,(\mathbf{K}\,\mathbf{S})\,(\mathbf{S}\,(\mathbf{S}\,[x]\mathbf{S}\,[x](\mathbf{K}\,f))\,[x](\mathbf{K}\,x)))\,[x]\mathbf{I}$$

$$\mathbf{S}\,(\mathbf{S}\,(\mathbf{K}\,\mathbf{S})\,(\mathbf{S}\,(\mathbf{S}\,(\mathbf{K}\,\mathbf{S})\,(\mathbf{S}\,[x]\mathbf{K}\,[x]f))\,(\mathbf{S}\,[x]\mathbf{K}\,[x]x)))\,(\mathbf{K}\,\mathbf{I})$$

$$\mathbf{S}\,(\mathbf{S}\,(\mathbf{K}\,\mathbf{S})\,(\mathbf{S}\,(\mathbf{S}\,(\mathbf{K}\,\mathbf{S})\,(\mathbf{S}\,(\mathbf{K}\,\mathbf{K})\,(\mathbf{K}\,f)))\,(\mathbf{S}\,(\mathbf{K}\,\mathbf{K})\,\mathbf{I})))\,(\mathbf{K}\,\mathbf{I})$$

Figure 7.1: Conversion of $\lambda x\,.\,\lambda y\,.\,fxy$ to a combinator

In the next example we convert the lambda expression $(\lambda\,x\,.\,x\,x)\,(\lambda\,x\,.\,x\,x)$ to a combinator.

$$\mathcal{N}[\![(\lambda\,x\,.\,x\,x)\,(\lambda\,x\,.\,x\,x)]\!]$$

$$\mathcal{N}[\![\lambda\,x\,.\,x\,x]\!]\,\mathcal{N}[\![\lambda\,x\,.\,x\,x]\!]$$

$$[x](x\,x)\,[x](x\,x)$$

$$\mathbf{S}\,[x]x\,[x]x\,(\mathbf{S}\,[x]x\,[x]x)$$

$$\mathbf{S}\,\mathbf{I}\,\mathbf{I}\,(\mathbf{S}\,\mathbf{I}\,\mathbf{I})$$

The lambda expression had a beta redex in it before we converted it. We expect, therefore, that some reductions are possible on the resulting combinator. In fact we have

$$\mathbf{S}\,\mathbf{I}\,\mathbf{I}\,(\mathbf{S}\,\mathbf{I}\,\mathbf{I}) \to \mathbf{I}\,(\mathbf{S}\,\mathbf{I}\,\mathbf{I})\,(\mathbf{I}\,(\mathbf{S}\,\mathbf{I}\,\mathbf{I})) \to \mathbf{S}\,\mathbf{I}\,\mathbf{I}\,(\mathbf{S}\,\mathbf{I}\,\mathbf{I})$$

an endless sequence of possible reductions.

A second example shows how tedious the conversion of even a simple lambda expression can get.

$$\mathcal{N}[\![\lambda\,x\,.\,\lambda\,y\,.\,f\,x\,y]\!]$$

We first express the combinator term in terms of the bracket abstraction algorithm.

$$[x](\mathcal{N}[\![\lambda y \,.\, f \, x \, y]\!])$$

$$[x]([y](\mathcal{N}[\![f \, x \, y]\!]))$$

Now applying the bracket abstraction algorithm yields an sequence of ever-growing combinator terms. The steps of the algorithm are shown in figure 7.1. The final result is a combinator (it has no variables), as the initial lambda expression was closed.

This last example demonstrates a problem with bracket abstraction. The resulting combinator term can be exponentially longer than the initial input term. It is possible to do better if we permit other combinators, for example, **B** and **C**. The new combinators **B** and **C** have the following meanings:

$$\mathbf{B} \, f \, g \, x \;=\; f \, (g \, x)$$
$$\mathbf{C} \, f \, g \, x \;=\; f \, x \, g$$

So we define another algorithm for bracket abstraction, the one that was originally proposed by Curry.

$$
\begin{aligned}
[x]y &= \begin{cases} \mathbf{I} & \text{if } y = x \\ \mathbf{K}y & \text{otherwise} \end{cases} \\
[x]f &= \mathbf{K}f \\
[x](Fx) &= F & x \notin FV[F] \\
[x](FA) &= \mathbf{K}(FA) & x \notin FV[F], FV[A] \\
[x](FA) &= \mathbf{C}([x]F)A & x \in FV[F], x \notin FV[A] \\
[x](FA) &= \mathbf{B}F([x]A) & x \notin FV[F], x \in FV[A] \\
[x](FA) &= \mathbf{S}([x]F)([x]A) & x \in FV[F], FV[A]
\end{aligned}
$$

The case for $[x](Fx)$ is not essential, but provides an extra optimization that is directly justifiable by eta conversion. This algorithm generates combinator terms whose lengths are at worst cubic in the length of the original lambda expressions.

Here is the new algorithm for bracket abstraction applied to the lambda expression of the last example.

$$
\begin{aligned}
&\mathcal{N}[\![\lambda x \,.\, \lambda y \,.\, f \, x \, y]\!] \\
&[x](\mathcal{N}[\![\lambda y \,.\, f \, x \, y]\!]) \\
&[x]([y](\mathcal{N}[\![f \, x \, y]\!])) \\
&[x]([y](f \, x \, y)) \\
&[x](f \, x) \\
&f
\end{aligned}
$$

One application of combinators is special machine architectures to do tree rewriting. Since all computation has been reduced to few special combinators, one

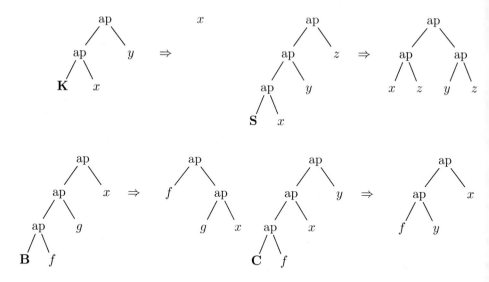

Figure 7.2: Graph reduction of **K**, **S**, **B**, and **S**

can conceive of a machine with these reduction rules as its only instruction set. The program is compiled into a combinator. This combinator is viewed as a graph and transformed according to the reduction rules for each combinator. Figure 7.2 shows reduction rules for the combinators **K**, **S**, **B**, and **S**. Each application of a combinator is represented by a node labeled "ap" in the figure. One appealing aspect of this approach is that each part of the tree can be rewritten independently, so parallel processing is possible [16].

7.7.2   Combinator families

There are yet other algorithms for bracket abstraction. We consider a good one from [7] that makes use of an infinite number of combinators. At first this may appear to be a disadvantage. After all, combinators seemed appealing because there were so few of them. Actually each family has very regular reduction rules, so this problem may be surmountable.

We require three families of combinators, roughly equivalent to the old **I**, **K**, and **S** combinators. One family of combinators generalizes the **K** combinator.

$$\mathbf{K}_1 xy = x$$
$$\mathbf{K}_{n+1} xy = \mathbf{K}_n x$$

In effect the combinator $\mathbf{K}_n$ is the constant function of n arguments $\mathbf{K}_n xy_1 \ldots y_n = x$.

Another family of combinators generalizes the $\mathbf{I}$ combinator.

$$\begin{aligned}
\mathbf{I}_1^1 x &= x \\
\mathbf{I}_1^{p+1} x &= \mathbf{K}_p x \\
\mathbf{I}_{i+1}^{p+1} x &= \mathbf{I}_i^p
\end{aligned}$$

In effect the combinator $\mathbf{I}_i^p$ is the i-th projection function of p arguments, in other words, $\mathbf{I}_i^p x_1 \ldots x_i \ldots x_p = x_i$.

The next family of combinators is not indexed by natural numbers, but by strings—strings over the four symbols #/\^. The symbols indicate the presence of an argument in an application. There are four possibilities: neither, left, right, or both.

$$\begin{aligned}
\mathbf{S}_{\#u} xyz &= \mathbf{S}_u xy \\
\mathbf{S}_{/u} xyz &= \mathbf{S}_u (xz)y \\
\mathbf{S}_{\backslash u} xyz &= \mathbf{S}_u x(yz) \\
\mathbf{S}_{\hat{\ } u} xyz &= \mathbf{S}_u (xz)(yz)
\end{aligned}$$

For notational convenience we consider $(xy) = \mathbf{S}_\epsilon xy$, i.e., the $\mathbf{S}$ family combinator indexed by the empty string is an abbreviation for application. This results in the following identities, which relate the $\mathbf{S}$ family to $\mathbf{B}$ and $\mathbf{C}$.

$$\begin{aligned}
\mathbf{S}_\# xyz &= \mathbf{K}(xy)z = xy \\
\mathbf{S}_/ xyz &= \mathbf{C}xyz = (xz)y \\
\mathbf{S}_\backslash xyz &= \mathbf{B}xyz = x(yz) \\
\mathbf{S}_{\hat{\ }} xyz &= \mathbf{S}xyz = (xz)(yz)
\end{aligned}$$

The bracket abstraction algorithm is as follows:

$$\begin{aligned}
[x]y &= \begin{cases} \mathbf{I}_1^1 & \text{if } y = x \\ \mathbf{K}_1 y & \text{otherwise} \end{cases} \\
[x]f &= \mathbf{K}_1 f \\
[x]\mathbf{I}_m^p &= \mathbf{I}_{m+1}^{p+1} \\
[x](\mathbf{K}_n x) &= \mathbf{K}_n \\
[x](\mathbf{K}_n A) &= \mathbf{K}_{n+1} A & x \notin FV[A] \\
[x](\mathbf{S}_u FA) &= \mathbf{S}_{\#u} FA & x \notin FV[F], FV[A] \\
[x](\mathbf{S}_u FA) &= \mathbf{S}_{/u}([x]F)A & x \in FV[F], x \notin FV[A] \\
[x](\mathbf{S}_u FA) &= \mathbf{S}_{\backslash u} F([x]A) & x \notin FV[F], x \in FV[A] \\
[x](\mathbf{S}_u FA) &= \mathbf{S}_{\hat{\ } u}([x]F)([x]A) & x \in FV[F], FV[A]
\end{aligned}$$

We wish to consider the lambda expression

$$N = (\lambda x.\,(\lambda z.\,z\,x)\,y)\,((\lambda t.\,t)\,z) \to yz$$

We have $[z](zx) = \mathbf{S}_{/}\mathbf{I}_1^1 x$ and

$$
\begin{aligned}
[x](\mathbf{S}_{/}\mathbf{I}_1^1 xy) &= \mathbf{S}_{/}([x](\mathbf{S}_{/}\mathbf{I}_1^1 x))y \\
&= \mathbf{S}_{/}(\mathbf{S}_{\backslash}\mathbf{I}_1^1\mathbf{I}_1^1)y
\end{aligned}
$$

The lambda expression N is converted to

$$\mathbf{S}_{/}(\mathbf{S}_{\backslash}\mathbf{I}_1^1\mathbf{I}_1^1)y(\mathbf{I}_1^1 z)$$

Now we apply the reduction rules on the resulting expression.

$$
\begin{aligned}
\mathbf{S}_{/}(\mathbf{S}_{\backslash}\mathbf{I}_1^1\mathbf{I}_1^1)y(\mathbf{I}_1^1 z) &\to \mathbf{S}_{\backslash}\mathbf{I}_1^1\mathbf{I}_1^1(\mathbf{I}_1^1 z)y \\
&\to \mathbf{S}_{/}\mathbf{I}_1^1(\mathbf{I}_1^1(\mathbf{I}_1^1 z))y \\
&\to \mathbf{S}_{/}\mathbf{I}_1^1(\mathbf{I}_1^1 z)y \\
&\to \mathbf{S}_{/}\mathbf{I}_1^1 zy \\
&\to \mathbf{I}_1^1 yz \\
&\to yz
\end{aligned}
$$

7.8   Compiling functional languages

Functional languages can be compiled to the native code of machines with conventional architectures just as imperative languages can. Unlike imperative languages, which translate into imperative assembly languages, functional languages
require the right mental bridge between the functional paradigm and the imperative
paradigm. This bridge is an abstract-machine model. In this section we look at
the original model for evaluating lambda expressions, the SECD machine [19]. We
give a simple compiler of the SECD machine written in the programming language
ML. Finally, we use the SECD machine to suggest how an efficient implementation
of functional languages can be made using continuation passing style.

7.8.1   SECD machine

Now we want to define an abstract machine that evaluates lambda expressions for
us. This machine is called the SECD machine and was originally proposed by
Landin. The SECD machine manipulates four stacks:

S the stack of intermediate answers,

E the environment,

C the control stack, and

D the dump to hold the state for recursive calls.

Pushing information on and off the stacks of the SECD machine is controlled by five instructions:

- LDV i: load the value of the variable at static depth i.

- LDC a: load the constant a directly.

- LDF l: load the function represented by the list of instructions l.

- APP: apply a function to its arguments.

- RTN: return from subroutine call.

We will define these instructions by giving an ML program that does the appropriate action for each instruction. We will require a data type in ML for the instruction set. Later we will write a compiler in ML from lambda expressions to these instructions.

```
type Location = int;       (* Static distance of variable *)

datatype Command =
    ldv of Location      |   (* Load variable from location *)
    ldc of FuncSymbol    |   (* Load constant *)
    ldf of Command list  |   (* Load function *)
    app                  |   (* Application     *)
    rtn                  ;   (* Return          *)
```

Notice that the definition of the type `Command` must be recursive, since the load function command requires the list of the commands comprising the function as an argument.

The basic actions cannot be fully understood without seeing the SECD machine in more detail. The basic idea is to evaluate a lambda expression by pushing the results into the S stack until the application instruction is encountered. This causes the top of the stack (which had better be a function) to be applied to its argument, which is found under it in the stack. The evaluation of this function requires that the state of the SECD machine be saved (by pushing it in the dump) and the evaluation be continued after the function body has been evaluated. The only difficulty is that the evaluation of the function body must be carried out in the environment in which the function was defined. This prompts the definition of a closure. A *closure* for the SECD machine is a pair consisting of the code for the function body and the environment. The environment for the SECD machine will consist of a stack of values. (One might have expected that the environment would consist of pairs of variables and their values. The variable names themselves are unnecessary, since the compiler can easily compute the location in the environment where the value will be found.) The values of variables are, of course, lambda expressions, but so too are closures. Closures are values too, because the result of evaluating a lambda expression might well be a closure. This leads to the following ML definition:

```
datatype Result =
  Closure of (Command list * Result list) |
  Result of LambdaExp                       ;
```

All the stacks of the SECD machine are more conveniently represented as lists, since lists are a built-in data structure in ML and stacks are not. In the definition of the program `exec` a nonempty list is represented `first::rest`. The stack S and the environment E will be a list of results, and the stack C will be a list of commands. The stack D must save the state of the machine. It will be a stack of triples, one for each of S, E, and C.

The machine is simple enough that we can describe it in essentially five lines of ML code. The five lines correspond to the five basic actions that the machine can take.

```
fun
  exec (s, e,  ldv(l)::c, d) = (    (nth (e,l))::s, e, c, d)   |
  exec (s, e,  ldf(c')::c, d) = (Closure (c',e)::s, e, c, d)   |
  exec (s, e,  ldc(f)::c, d) = ( Result(Fun f)::s, e, c, d)   |
  exec (Closure (c',e')::a::s, e, ap::c, d) =
    ([], a::e', c', (s,e,c)::d)                                 |
  exec ([a], e', [rtn], (s,e,c)::d) = (a::s, e, c, d)         ;
```

Before we describe the execution of each instruction, we define the overall action of the SECD machine. The function `machine` takes four arguments corresponding to the four stacks S, E, C, and D, and recursively transforms the stacks until the resultant value is found.

```
fun machine (s,e,c,d) =
  let val (s',e',c',d') = exec (s,e,c,d)
  in
    if null (c') then hd (s') else machine (s',e',c',d')
  end;
```

When the E, C, and D stacks are empty, the remaining value (there should be only one) on top of the S stack is the value sought. This is the final action of the SECD machine.

If the control stack is not empty, then the execution of the SECD machine proceeds according to the type of the expression found on the top of the control stack. The first case we consider is when a LDV i instruction is at the top of the control stack.

```
exec (s, e, ldv(1)::c, d) = ((nth (e,1))::s, e, c, d)
```

The location stored in the load instruction was computed by the compiler to be used at this point in determining which value to load from the environment. The location is how far down in the environment stack we must go to find the value. The function call `nth(e,1)` picks out the 1th member of the list.

In the case where the LDF *l* is the instruction on the top of the control stack, a closure is formed and pushed into the stack.

```
exec (s, e, ldf(c')::c, d) = (Closure (c',e)::s, e, c, d)
```

The closure consists of the instructions of the function and the current environment.

The load constant instruction pushes the function symbol immediately into the stack.

```
exec (s, e, ldc(f)::c, d) = (Result(Fun f)::s, e, c, d)
```

The case of application in the definition of the SECD machine is the most complex. The SECD machine assumes that the closure of the function and its argument are on the top of the stack when an application instruction is executed. In effect a subroutine call is executed. This subroutine is the body of the function (found in the closure) executed in the environment that was saved in the closure. The current state of the SECD machine is saved in the dump to be recovered later, after the body of the function has been executed.

```
exec (Closure (c',e')::a::s, e, ap::c, d) = ([],a::e',c',(s,e,c)::d)
```

The stack has been replaced with the empty list `[]`. The code in the closure `c'` is ready to be executed. Presumably the last instruction will be a `rtn`.

```
exec ([a], e', [rtn], (s,e,c)::d) = (a::s, e, c, d)
```

If there is something in the dump, execution proceeds by recovering the state stored previously in the dump. The value returned is found (by itself) on the top of the stack. This value is pushed into the old stack before continuing execution.

We show the execution of the SECD machine on the following list of instructions:

LDC *b*, LDC *a*, LDF (LDF (LDV 0, RTN), RTN), APP, APP

This particular set of instructions was obtained by compiling the lambda expression $(\lambda x . \lambda y . y) \, a \, b$. We will explain compiling later; here is the execution of the SECD machine on these instructions.

S	E	C	D
		LDC b, LDC a, LDF (...), APP, APP	
b		LDC a, LDF (...), APP, APP	
a, b		LDF (...), APP, APP	
$\mathcal{CL}$(LDF (...); ϵ), a, b		APP, APP	
	a	LDF (LDV 0, RTN), RTN	$(b; \epsilon; \text{APP})$
$\mathcal{CL}$(LDV 0, RTN; a)	a	RTN	$(b; \epsilon; \text{APP})$
$\mathcal{CL}$(LDV 0, RTN; a), b		APP	
	b, a	LDV 0, RTN	$(\epsilon; \epsilon; \epsilon)$
b	b, a	RTN	$(\epsilon; \epsilon; \epsilon)$
b			

7.8.2 A simple compiler

The compiler is defined below. It compiles a lambda expression into instructions for the SECD machine. It computes the static distance of each variable by keeping a list of the enclosing bound variables. Since only one variable is bound at a time, each variable represents one level of static nesting. Free variables cause an error.

```
fun Position (v, env) =    (* Compute static distance *)
   if v = hd (env) then 0 else 1+Position (v, tl env);
```

```
fun
  Compile (Var v, env) = [ldv (Position (v, env))]           |
  Compile (Fun f, env) = [ldc (f)]                           |
  Compile (Abs (v,b), env) =
    let val bdy = Compile (b, v::env) in [ldf (bdy@[rtn])] end  |
  Compile (App(f,a), env) = Compile(a,env) @ Compile(f,env) @ [app];
```

Here, for example, is how the lambda expression $(\lambda x . \lambda y . y) \, a \, b$ is compiled starting with the empty environment []:

$$\text{Compile} ((\lambda x . \lambda y . y) \, a \, b, \, [])$$
$$\text{LDC } b, \text{Compile} ((\lambda x . \lambda y . y) \, a, \, []), \text{APP}$$
$$\text{LDC } b, \text{LDC } a, \text{Compile} (\lambda x . \lambda y . y, \, []), \text{APP, APP}$$
$$\text{LDC } b, \text{LDC } a, \text{LDF } F, \text{APP, APP}$$

Here F is the code for the "subroutine" $\lambda x . \lambda y . y$:

$$\text{Compile} (\lambda y . y, \, [x]), \text{RTN}$$
$$\text{LDF (Compile} (y, \, [y, \, x])), \text{RTN}$$
$$\text{LDF (LDV 0, RTN), RTN}$$

Now consider another simple example. What happens when we compile the lambda expression $f \, a$, where f and a are function symbols? The code produced by the compiler is:

$$\text{LDC } a, \text{ LDC } f, \text{ APP}$$

But the SECD machine will arrive at a state where it is executing an application and the top of the stack is not a closure. The SECD machine is unable to progress further. More interesting is the case where we have *interpreted* function symbols. Here we know what the function is supposed to do. Take, for example, the binary addition function. The compiler can generate an add instruction when it finds the function symbol "+" applied to two arguments.

```
fun
    ...
    Compile (App (App (Fun (FuncSymbol "+"), a), b), env) =
        Compile (a, env) @ Compile (f, env) @ [add]
    ...
```

The SECD machine would have to be modified to recognize the add instruction.

```
fun
    ...
    exec (a::b::s, e, add::c, d) = (Add(a,b)::s, e, c, d)
    ...
```

where Add is the function that performs the operation required on lambda-expression arguments.

The execution of the modified machine will look like this:

S	E	C	D
		LDC 3, LDC 2, ADD	
3		LDC 2, ADD	
3,2		ADD	
5			

Another property of the SECD machine is that it does not always find the normal form of a lambda expression even if it does exist. The lambda expression, call it L,

$$(\lambda z . \lambda y . (\lambda x . x) z) \, a$$

has normal form $\lambda y . a$. The compiler generates the following code for L:

$$\text{LDC } a, \text{ LDF (LDF } (cd), \text{ RTN), APP}$$

where *cd* is the list of commands

$$\text{LDV 1, LDF (LDV 0, RTN), APP, RTN}$$

The execution of the SECD machine is as follows:

S	E	C	D
		LDC a, LDF (LDF (cd), RTN), APP	
a		LDF (LDF (cd), RTN), APP	
$\mathcal{CL}$(LDF (cd), RTN; ϵ), a		APP	
	a	LDF (cd), RTN	$(\epsilon; \epsilon; \epsilon)$
$\mathcal{CL}(cd; a)$	a	RTN	$(\epsilon; \epsilon; \epsilon)$
$\mathcal{CL}(cd; a)$			

Thus the answer the SECD machine finds is not a lambda expression at all. It is a closure. Even if we perform the substitution of a for z as indicated by the information in the environment of the closure, we obtain the lambda expression $\lambda y.\,(\lambda x.\,x)\,a$, which is not in normal form. The SECD machine does not bother to reduce beta redexes found in the body of an abstraction. And what is the point? A closure is some value of a procedure; the form it takes is of no consequence as long as it able to perform the computation when asked.

An important property of the SECD machine is its call-by-value semantics. This can by seen by tracing the execution of the machine on the *If* macro. Observe that both branches of the conditional statement are evaluated. This may not be the behavior we want, if we want the machine to find beta normal forms. The solution is to make the conditional statement a primitive construct in the language, so we may treat it specially. By adding a new instruction to the command language of the SECD machine, we can obtain the semantics we require.

```
fun
    ...
    Compile (cond(b,t,e), env) =
      Compile (b, env) @ [sel (Compile (t,env), Compile (e,env))]
    ...
```

```
fun
   ...
   exec (Result (Fun (FuncSymbol  "true"))::s, e, sel(c1,c2)::c, d) =
      (s, e, c1@c, d)                                             |
   exec (Result (Fun (FuncSymbol "false"))::s, e, sel(c1,c2)::c, d) =
      (s, e, c2@c, d)
   ...
```

The call-by-value semantics also causes a problem with the **Y** combinator. This is especially important if recursive functions are compiled into a lambda expression containing the **Y** combinator. The SECD machine will loop infinitely on any such lambda expression. As with the conditional statement, the solution is to treat recursion specially. The modifications require circular data structures, and so we do not give a solution here, but rather leave it as an exercise (exercise 7.28).

7.8.3   Continuation passing style

We have remarked that certain optimizations to the SECD machine, like tail recursion, bypass the "dump" entirely. It is promising to pursue source-to-source
transformations of lambda expressions that, while preserving the semantics of the
functions, are compiled into abstract machine code that never requires the state
of the machine to be saved in the dump. This is achieved by *continuation passing
style* lambda expressions in which every function implicitly takes the remainder of
the program as an argument. This enables the function to always continue forward
in its execution and never "return" to some previous state.

We will describe an algorithm to convert any lambda expressions to one in
continuation passing style. We do this by giving an ML function `Convert`, which
transforms the ML data structures for lambda expressions given earlier. We suppose
that we have some ML function

```
NewVar : unit -> LambdaExpr
```

which generated new variables. The function `Convert` is quite simple and is shown
in figure 7.3. A special case is needed for a function symbol in the function position
of an application. We assume that this function symbol is known to the compiler,
which will generate code to directly compute the proper value given the argument
on the top of the stack. We cannot arbitrarily change the meaning of these functions
to expect a continuation as an argument.

The remaining cases guarantee that the pattern

```
App (f, App (g, x))
```

does not appear in the resulting expressions. Consider what happens when we
compile the code with the compiler for the SECD machine. All applications will
appear at the end of the compiled code. Thus we no longer need the "dump."

This may not seem like much progress, but we are on the verge of designing a
new abstract machine that suggests a model of code generation of practical importance. Although the SECD machine could easily be realized in a simple imperative
language, it would not be very efficient. Often the machine requires copying the
environment and copying segments of the code. In general, it is difficult to eliminate
copying the environment, and this is the goal of much current research. But copying
segments of the code is most unnatural, and should, if at all possible, be eliminated
in favor of simple jumps in control flow. The next abstract machine is designed
to reveal how the code can be executed without copying code segments—indeed,
using nothing more than goto statements.

The commands are similar to the commands of the SECD machine.

```
datatype Command =
  ldv of Location              |
  ldf of Command list          |
  ldc of FuncSymbol            |
```

```
fun
  Convert (App (Fun f, a), k) =
    let
      val v = NewVar ();
    in
      Convert (a, Abs (v, App (k, App (Fun f, Var v))))
    end |

  Convert (App (f,a), k) =
    let
      val w = NewVar ();
      val u = NewVar ();
    in
      Convert (f,
        Abs (w, Convert(a,Abs(u,App(App(Var w,k),Var u)))))
    end |

  Convert (Abs (v,b), k) =
    let
      val w = NewVar ();
    in
      App (k, Abs (w, Abs (v, Convert (b, Var w))))
    end |

  Convert (Cond (b,t,e), k) =
    let
      val u = NewVar ();
    in
      Convert (b,
        Abs (u, Cond (Var u, Convert(t,k), Convert(e,k))))
    end |

  Convert (exp, k) = App (k, exp);
```

Figure 7.3: CPS conversion

```
fun
  exec (s, e, (ldv l)::c,  d)        = (   (nth (e,l))::s,e,c,d)|
  exec (s, e,(ldf c')::c,  d)        = (Closure (c',e)::s,e,c,d)|
  exec (s, e, (ldc f)::c,  d)        = ( Result(Fun f)::s,e,c,d)|
  exec (Closure(c',e')::a::s, _, tlr::nil,d)= (   s, a::e', c', d)|
  exec (s, e, rmr(c')::c, d)         = (    s, e, c, c'::d)|
  exec (s, e, rtn::nil,    c::d)     = (    s, e, c,     d)|
  exec (Result(Fun "true")::s,e,sel(c1,c2)::nil,d)=   (s, e, c1, d)|
  exec (Result(Fun"false")::s,e,sel(c1,c2)::nil,d)=   (s, e, c2, d);



fun
  Compile (Var v, env, cont)   = ldv (Position (v, env))::cont    |
  Compile (Fun f, env, cont)   = (ldc f)::cont                    |
  Compile (Abs (v,b), env, cont)=ldf(Compile(b,v::env,[rtn]))::cont|
  Compile (App (f,a), env, rtn::nil) =
    Compile (a, env, Compile (f, env, [tlr]))                     |
  Compile (App (f,a), env, tlr::nil) =
    Compile (a, env, (rmr [tlr])::Compile (f, env, [tlr]))        |
  Compile (Cond (b,t,e), env, rtn::nil) =
    Compile(b,env,[sel(Compile(t,env,[rtn]),Compile(e,env,[rtn]))])|
  Compile (Cond (b,t,e), env, cont) =
    Compile (b, env,
       (rmr cont)::[sel(Compile(t,env,[rtn]),Compile(e,env,[rtn]))]);
```

Figure 7.4: Abstract machine and compiler for CPS expressions

```
tlr                                 |(* tail application       *)
rmr of Command list                 |(* execute this code later*)
rtn                                 |
sel of (Command list) * (Command list);(* conditional construct  *)
```

There is no general application command, as all applications are at the end of a function. These applications require no state to be saved.

We now describe the new machine, which we call the CPS machine. The CPS machine has four stacks just like the SECD machine. Like the SECD machine, there is the "S" stack for function arguments, return values, and temporary values; the "E" stack for nonlocal variables; and the "C" stack, which represents the stream of execution. The "D" stack of the SECD machine is gone, but a new stack is used to hold instruction sequences that need to be executed later.

The abstract machine and its compiler are shown in figure 7.4. The new dump has a simpler interpretation than the old one. It is a stack of entry points. The rem command pushes an entry point on the stack. The return instruction means that control should jump to the entry point at the top of the stack (and pop the stack). The tail command does not affect the dump; it causes control to jump to the entry point found in the closure.

7.9 Exercises

7.1 The formal definition of lambda expressions is not actually a grammar because of the use of "$\cdots$". Yet it is essential that there are an infinite number of variables. (The number of function symbols is a matter of choice.) Replace the productions for V with new productions that are legal, yet generate an infinite number of variables. *Hint.* This is easy, but the customary concrete syntax of variables will have to be sacrificed.

7.2 The following lambda expressions are written in the formal notation. Rewrite these expressions using our conventional notation.

(a) $(\lambda x . x (y z))$

(b) $(\lambda x . (x y) \lambda z . z)$

(c) $\lambda x . \lambda y . (x y)$

(d) $\lambda x . (\lambda y . (r y) (s t))$

(e) $(\lambda x . (x (x x)) \lambda x . (x (x x)))$

7.3 Reduce each lambda expression in the previous exercise to (beta) normal form, if it has one.

7.4 Explain why the restriction about variable names is required in the eta-contraction rule

$$\lambda V . L V >_\eta L$$

Explain where your "meaning" of lambda expressions comes from.

7.5 Find two lambda expressions A and B (not function symbols) such that $A \twoheadrightarrow_\eta B$, but it is not the case that $A \twoheadrightarrow_{\alpha\beta} B$.

7.6 Consider the (completely pointless) *gamma* contraction defined by the following:

$$(\lambda V . L) M >_\gamma L$$

where V stands for any variable, and L and M for any lambda expressions.

For each of the following ordered pairs, state if the pair is in the $>_\gamma$, the $\rightarrow_\gamma$, the $\twoheadrightarrow_\gamma$, and the $\equiv_\gamma$ relations.

$$
\begin{array}{lll}
\text{(a)} & (\lambda x \,.\, x)\, a & a \\
\text{(b)} & (\lambda x \,.\, x)\, b & x \\
\text{(c)} & b & (\lambda y \,.\, b)\, c \\
\text{(d)} & \lambda x \,.\, a & \lambda x \,.\, a \\
\text{(e)} & (\lambda x \,.\, x)\,(\lambda y \,.\, y)\,(\lambda z \,.\, z) & (\lambda y \,.\, y)\,(\lambda z \,.\, z) \\
\text{(f)} & (\lambda x \,.\, x)\,(\lambda y \,.\, y)\,(\lambda z \,.\, z) & x\,(\lambda z \,.\, z) \\
\text{(g)} & (\lambda x \,.\, (\lambda y \,.\, a)\, b)\, c & a \\
\text{(h)} & (\lambda x \,.\, (\lambda y \,.\, a)\, b)\, c & \lambda y \,.\, a \\
\end{array}
$$

7.7   Let R be any set of pairs of lambda expressions. Show that the reflexive, transitive closure of R is an inductive definition of a set.

7.8   For any contraction prove that the relation $\equiv$ is closed under the formation of lambda expressions.

7.9   Answer the following two questions:

(a) What does it mean for a combinator to be a fixedpoint operator?

(b) For convenience we adopt the notation

$$
\lambda\, abc \ldots z \,.\, L \;=\; \lambda\, a \,.\, \lambda\, b \,.\, \lambda\, c \,.\, \ldots \lambda\, z \,.\, L
$$

Given the following two definitions:

$$
A = \lambda\, abcdefghijklmnopqrstuvwxyzr \,.\, r\ (thisisafixedpointcombinator)
$$
$$
X = AAAAAAAAAAAAAAAAAAAAAAAAAAA
$$

show that X is a fixedpoint operator.

7.10 Prove Lemma 7 in the text: For all lambda expressions L, M, and A, and all variables V, if $L \equiv_\alpha M$, then $L[V := A] \equiv_\alpha M[V := A]$. *Hint:* The proof is on the inductive definition of $\equiv_\alpha$.

7.11 Prove Lemma 8 in the text: For all lambda expressions L, A, and B, and all variables V, if $A \equiv_\alpha B$, then $L[V := A] \equiv_\alpha M[V := B]$.

7.12 Show that $\mathbf{Y}$ is a fixedpoint operator by showing that $\mathbf{Y}F \overset{*}{\to} F(\mathbf{F})$ for all lambda expressions F.

7.13 Give a lambda expression that, when applied to the numerals representing the natural numbers n and m, reduces to the representation of $n + m$. You may use the $\mathbf{Y}$ combinator and you may use the "macros" of section 7.6. (*Hint:* Recall that addition can be defined recursively using the successor function.)

7.14 An explanation using the $\mathbf{Y}$ combinator has been given for recursive definitions in section 7.6.1. Extend this approach to mutually recursive definitions such as the following one written in the programming language ML.

```
fun
  f (x) = if x=0 then 0 else g(x-1)+1
and
  g (x) = if x=0 then 1 else f(x-1)+1
```

Hint: Use the macro $Pair[X, Y]$.

7.15 Find three distinct fixedpoints of:

$$f = \lambda n . \text{ if } n = 0 \text{ then } 1 \text{ else } f(n + 1)$$

What is the least fixedpoint?

7.16 Write a nonrecursive function in the programming language ML to compute the factorial function that takes advantage of recursive data types.

7.17 Convert the following lambda expressions to the combinators **I**, **K**, and **S** using the first abstraction algorithm, `abstract`.

(a) $\lambda x . y$

(b) $\lambda x . f (g\, x)$

(c) $\lambda x . x\, a$

7.18 The language FP [2] has a wide selection of combinators. Some familiar ones are written differently; for example, **I** is written id, **K**x is written $\bar{x}$, and the composition combinator **B**fg is infix $f \circ g$. FP has primitive data structures for integers, pairs, which are written with parentheses, and lists, which are written with angle brackets. One combinator in FP is written $[f, g]$ and is defined by

$$[f, g]x = (fx, gx)$$

In other words, it applies f and g each to x and forms the pair. Conditionals are written

$$x \to y; z$$

in FP. FP has the usual functions for integers; for example, 0 and 1 stand for the obvious constants, $\times$ and $-$ are binary functions for the operations of multiplication and subtraction, and the function eq tests for the equality of two integers.

(a) Below is the definition of an FP function X. What does X compute? Explain the purpose of Z and Y.

$$
\begin{aligned}
Z &\equiv eq \circ [id, \bar{0}] \\
Y &\equiv - \circ [id, \bar{1}] \\
X &\equiv Z \to \bar{1}; \times \circ [id, X \circ Y]
\end{aligned}
$$

    (b) Write a recursive FP program to compute $f(x) = \sum_{i=0}^{x} i^2$.

7.19 (a) Write the combinators **I**, **K**, and **B** in ML.

    (b) Write the FP combinator $[f, g]$ of the previous exercise as an ML function D.

    (c) Using the ML combinators of the previous two parts, write the combinators Z, Y, X defined in the previous exercise.

    (d) The combinators Z and Y can be written with ML **val** bindings, but X cannot. Write Z and Y in ML using **val** bindings and not **fun** bindings (or the **fn** construct). Explain why X cannot be written this way.

    (e) Is it possible to write a combinator corresponding to the conditional construct? Explain why or why not.

7.20 Prove the following identities about the combinators $\mathbf{K}xy = x$, $\mathbf{S}xyz = xy(xz)$, $\mathbf{I}x = x$, $\mathbf{B}xyz = x(yz)$, $\mathbf{C}xyz = xzy$.

    (a) $\mathbf{S\,K} \equiv_{\alpha\beta} \mathbf{K\,I}$

    (b) $\mathbf{S\,(K\,I)} \equiv_{\alpha\beta} \mathbf{B\,I}$

    (c) $\mathbf{S\,I\,(K\,K)} \equiv_{\alpha\beta} \mathbf{C\,I\,K}$

7.21 Express the following lambda expressions as combinations of the combinators **K**, **B**, and **C**.

    (a) $\lambda x . a\ (b\ x)$

    (b) $a\ (b\ c)\ d\ e$

7.22 Given a pairing combinator $\mathbf{P}\,x\,y = (x, y)$ write the FP combinator $[f, g]$ of exercise 7.18 using the combinator system **K**, **S**, **B**, **C**. In other words, define **D** such that $\mathbf{D}fgx = \mathbf{P}(fx)(gx)$.

7.23 Programming in the language J a descendent of APL, has similarities to programming with combinators. Arrays are important data structures in J and lists are viewed as one-dimensional arrays. In J there is a function **#**, which computes the number of elements in a list. The expression `+/` in J computes the sum of the elements in a list. Here is a little program to compute the mean of the list.

```
sum  =. +/
mean =. sum % #
```

The infix function % is overloaded; on numbers it means division. On functional arguments, like sum and #, it means a combination of its arguments sum and # called a fork. The expression sum % # applied to a list x is equal to sum of x divided by length of x. Using the combinator system **K**, **S**, **B**, **C**, define the fork combinator **F** such that $\mathbf{F}hfgx = h(fx)(gx)$.

7.24 The programming language SASL is a functional programming language much like ML. But unlike ML, SASL forbids side effects and all the lists are "lazy"; i.e., the elements of a list are only computed when they are actually required. This permits the definition of (potentially) infinite lists. Also SASL differs from ML in the choice of the mechanism for parameter passing. ML uses call-by-value.

Please answer the following questions:

(a) Why are side effects forbidden in SASL?

(b) What parameter-passing mechanism does SASL use?

(c) Is there some reason why SASL cannot use call-by-value? If so, give the reason. If not, explain why SASL does not use call-by-value.

(d) What advantage does SASL gain in parameter passing by forbidding side effects?

7.25 The definition of COMMON LISP requires that tuples are evaluated in left-to-right order. For example, in

```
(fn (PLUS 2 3) (TIMES 4 5))
```

the expressions (PLUS 2 3) must be evaluated before (TIMES 4 5).

Sometimes a definition for a language is given by an interpreter for the language. The functions Eval and Apply are often used to define a LISP dialect. Let us look closely at the order of evaluation defined by the following LISP interpreter written in ML-like syntax:

```
fun Eval (exp, env) =
  ...
  else if IsFuncAndArgs (exp)
    then Apply (Func (exp), EvalList (ArgList (exp), env), env)
  ...

fun EvalList (exps, env) =
  if Null (exps)
    then Nil
    else Concat (Eval(First exps,env), EvalList(Rest exps,env))
```

(a) What difference does the order of evaluation make?

(b) Under what conditions does the definition of EvalList given above ensure left-to-right order?

(c) Suppose we may only assume that interpreter is evaluated by a call-by-value machine. Rewrite EvalList to guarantee left-to-right order. Explain.

7.26 Suppose the length of a lambda expression is measured by the number of abstractions plus the number of applications plus one. Suppose the length of a combinator term is measured by the number of applications plus one. Show that converting lambda expressions to combinator terms using algorithm `Abstract` can increase the length exponentially. *Hint:* Consider n abstractions on a term without any variables.

7.27 Compile the following lambda expression

$$(\lambda x . \lambda y . y \, x) \, a \, (\lambda z . b)$$

for the SECD machine in section 7.8.1. Trace the execution of the SECD machine on the code.

7.28 Modify the SECD machine of section 7.8.1 to handle recursion.

7.29 The SECD machine of section 7.8.1 implements applicative-order evaluation. Modify the machine to implement normal-order evaluation. (As before, abstractions should return closures that may not be fully evaluated.) The lazy SECD machine requires "suspending" the argument and delaying its evaluation until it is actually needed (if ever). Add a new instruction to the machine; also a new `Result` type is needed:

```
datatype Command = ... | sup of Command list | ...
datatype Result =
    ... | Suspend of (Command list * Result list) | ...
```

(a) Show the changes to the compiler and to the SECD machine to implement these ideas. *Hint:* The commands `ldf`, `ldc`, and `rtn` of the machine act exactly as before.

(b) Compile the following lambda expression and trace the execution of the lazy SECD machine on the code.

$$(\lambda x . \lambda y . x \, y) \, (\lambda x . a) \, ((\lambda x . x \, x) \, (\lambda x . x \, x))$$

(c) Show the execution of the SECD machine on the **Y** combinator applied to an arbitrary function f. Let F denote the list of commands compiled for the function f.

7.10 Bibliography

[1] Abdali, S. Kamal. "An abstraction algorithm for combinator logic." *Journal of Symbolic Logic*, volume 41, number 1, March 1976, pages 222–224.

[2] Backus, John. "Can programming be liberated from the von Neumann style? A functional style and its algebra of programs." *Communications of the ACM*, volume 21, number 8, 1978, pages 613–641. Reprinted in *Programming Languages: A Grand Tour*, edited by Ellis Horowitz, 1987, pages 174–202.

[3] Barendregt, Hendrik Pieter. *The Lambda Calculus: Its Syntax and Semantics*. Revised edition. Studies in Logic and the Foundations of Mathematics, volume 103. North-Holland, Amsterdam, 1984.

[4] Church, Alonzo. *The Calculi of Lambda-Conversion*. Annals of Mathematical Studies, number 6. Princeton University Press, Princeton, New Jersey, 1941.

[5] Church, Alonzo and J. Barkley Rosser. "Some properties of conversion." *Transactions of the American Mathematical Society*, volume 39, 1936, pages 472–482.

[6] Cousineau, Guy, Pierre-Louis Curien, and M. Mauny. "The categorical abstract machine." In *Functional Programming Languages and Computer Architecture*, edited by Jean-Pierre Jouannaud, Springer-Verlag, Berlin, 1985, pages 50–64.

[7] Curien, Pierre-Louis. *Categorical Combinators, Sequential Algorithms and Functional Programming*. Research notes in theoretical computer science. Pitman, London, 1986.

[8] Curry, Haskell Brooks, and Robert Feys. *Combinatory Logic*. Studies in Logic and the Foundations of Mathematics. North-Holland, Amsterdam, 1958.

[9] Darlington, John, Peter Henderson, and David A. Turner, editors. *Functional Programming and Its Applications: An Advanced Course* Cambridge University Press, Cambridge, 1982.

[10] Dijkstra, Edsger Wybe. "On the cruelty of really teaching computing science." *Communications of the ACM*, volume 32, number 12, December 1989, pages 1398–1404.

[11] Downey, Peter J., and Ravi Sethi. "Correct computation rules for recursive languages." *SIAM Journal on Computing*, volume 5, number 3, September 1976.

[12] Eisenbach, Susan, editor. *Functional Programming: Languages, Tools and Architectures*. Ellis Horwood series in computers and their applications. Ellis Horwood, Chichester, England, 1987.

[13] Field, Anthony J., and Peter G. Harrison. *Functional Programming*. International computer science series. Addison Wesley, Wokingham, England, 1988.

[14] Henderson, Peter. *Functional Programming: Application and Implementation*. Prentice Hall International series in computer science. Prentice Hall International, Englewood Cliffs, New Jersey, 1980.

[15] Hillis, W. Daniel, and Guy L. Steele, Jr. "Data parallel algorithms." *Communications of the ACM*, volume 29, number 12, December 1986, pages 1170–1183.

[16] Hudak, Paul, and Benjamin Goldberg. "Experiments in diffused combinator reduction." In *Proceedings of the 1984 ACM Conference on LISP and Functional Programming*, ACM, 1984, pages 167–176.

[17] Huet, Gérard P. "Confluent reductions: Abstract properties and applications to term rewriting systems." *Journal of the ACM*, volume 27, number 4, October 1980, pages 797–821.

[18] Huet, Gérard P., and Derek C. Oppen. "Equations and Rewrite Rules." In *Formal Languages: Perspectives and Open Problems*, edited by Ronald V. Book, Academic Press, New York, 1980.

[19] Landin, Peter J. "A lambda-calculus approach." In *Advances in Programming and Non-Numerical Computation*, edited by L. Fox, Pergamon Press, Oxford, 1966, pages 97–141.

[20] Manna, Zohar, and Adi Shamir. "A new approach to recursive programs." In *Perspectives on Computer Science*, edited by Anita K. Jones, Academic Press, New York, 1977, pages 103–124.

[21] O'Donnell, Michael J. *Equational Logic As a Programming Language.* Foundations of Computing Series. MIT Press, Cambridge, Massachusetts, 1985.

[22] Rosen, Barry K. "Tree manipulation systems and Church-Rosser theorems." *Journal of the ACM*, volume 20, number 1, January 1973, pages 160-187.

[23] Schönfinkel, Moses. "On the building blocks of mathematical logic." In *From Frege to Gödel*, edited by Jean van Heijenoort, Harvard University Press, Cambridge, Massachusetts, 1977.

[24] Scott, Dana S. "Outline of a mathematical theory of computation." In *Proceedings of the 4th Annual Princeton Conference on Information Sciences & Systems*, Princeton, 1970, pages 169–176.

[25] Scott, Dana S. "Lattice theory, data types and formal semantics." In *Formal Semantics of Programming Languages*, edited by Randall Rustin, Prentice Hall, Englewood Cliffs, New Jersey, 1972, pages 65–106.

[26] Scott, Dana S. "Logic and programming languages." *Communications of the ACM*, volume 20, number 9, September 1977, pages 634–641.

[27] Smullyan, Raymond M. *To Mock a Mockingbird.* Knopf, New York, 1985.

[28] Stenlund, Sören. *Combinators, λ-terms, and Proof Theory.* D. Reidel Publishing Company, Dordrecht, Holland, 1972.

[29] Turner, David A. "A new implementation technique for applicative languages." *Software—Practice and Experience*, volume 9, number 1, 1979, pages 31–49.

[30] Vuillemin, Jean. "Correct and optimal implementations of recursion in a simple programming language." *Journal of Computer and System Science*, volume 9, number 3, December 1974, pages 332–354.

Chapter 8

Denotational semantics

The primary purpose of this chapter is to describe one approach to the formal semantics of programming languages. But first we give an overview of formal semantics in general.

8.1 Formal semantics

The study of language distinguishes between syntax and semantics. Thus far we have been fairly informal about semantics. We can get by in this way, but it is not always appropriate. For example, we may have been surprised at the subtlety of aliasing, parameter passing, etc. How can we be sure that we have not overlooked anything?

We want the meaning of languages to be complete, consistent, precise, unambiguous, concise, understandable, and useful (cf. [11]). This much is clear. What is sometimes debated is, to what extent do formal methods accomplish these goals?

There have been two controversial articles that argue against formal methods, in particular, against proofs of program correctness, a primary application of formal methods. In [2] the authors argue against formal proofs as being too unwieldy to be convincing. A scathing and unilluminating reply can be found in [3]. Certainly, formal proofs of "useful" software have been infrequent, and it remains a challenge to apply formal methods to the routine development of software. Programming is sufficiently difficult that one may despair of ever applying program verification.

More recently, James Fetzer in [4] argues that program verification is inherently impossible because there are no reasons to believe that formal methods model reality. A thoughtful reply by Jon Barwise can be found in [1]. Despite the lack of guarantees, formal methods seem to be reasonably useful. This point has been made often in various contexts in the philosophy of science, for instance, by Richard Hamming, a past president of the ACM and Turing Award recipient, in his article [8] entitled "The unreasonable effectiveness of mathematics."

In any case, the formal semantics of programming languages hold much potential. We list some of the possible uses of formal semantics.

Standardization of programming languages. Much effort is spent on standardizing languages such as FORTRAN, COBOL, and PL/I, which were defined by informal means. A definitive semantics would at least make the debate over standards clearer, if not shorter.

Reference for users. Programmers need a definitive document. It should not be the case that users have to run experiments to find out what programs do.

Proof of program correctness. Mathematical reasoning about what programs do is impossible without formal semantics.

Reference for implementors. A formal semantics, even if accessible to only the implementors, would prevent ill-defined and incompatible dialects spawned by different implementations of the "same" language.

Automatic implementation. Tools that automate creating language translators that go beyond parsing are possible only if the semantics of the language is formalized. Some interesting work on these so-called *compiler compilers* has been done in this area [12].

Better understanding of language design. If the semantics of a construct is complex to describe formally, then the construct may well be difficult for the programmer to use. This can be a guide to language design. One example of this is the ALGOL 60 `for` statement that was so baroque it was difficult to understand. Another example is the `goto` statement. All the general arguments for and against it are put in perspective by the formal semantics (section 8.12) of the construct.

This last reason is the most important from the point of view of the average programmer. First, understanding language design contributes to using existing languages better. Understanding programs in minute detail helps programmers appreciate the program development process better. And many programming applications themselves involve "language" design. Any sort of user interface is a challenge of natural expressiveness not unlike programming language design.

There is no one right approach to the formal semantics to programming languages. Rather, there are a number of techniques with different strengths and weaknesses. We briefly enumerate the primary ones.

1. *Operational semantics.* In this approach we define an abstract machine with primitive instructions, not necessarily realistic, but so simple that no misunderstanding can arise. The semantic description of the programming language specifies a translation into this code. The SECD machine in chapter 7 is a good example of this.

2. *Denotational semantics.* In this approach to semantics we give functions that map computer programs to the abstract mathematical values they denote (numbers, truth values, functions etc.).

3. *Axiomatic semantics.* In this approach we define the action of a program construct by the logical properties that hold of the state of the computer before and after the execution of the construct. We discuss this in chapter 9.

4. *Algebraic semantics.* In this approach we consider the objects of computation to be terms in multi-sorted algebras. Programs implement functions that can be expressed by equations between terms [6].

5. *Structured operational semantics* or *natural semantics.* As in natural deduction in logic, programs are given meaning by derivation rules that describe the evaluation of the constructs in the language (see exercise 4.15).

Finally we quote a passage from *Through the Looking Glass* by Lewis Carroll that is a favorite of semanticists.

> "I don't know what you mean by 'glory,'" Alice said.
> Humpty Dumpty smiled contemptuously. "Of course you don't—till I tell you. I meant 'there's a nice knock-down argument for you!'"
> "But 'glory' doesn't mean 'a nice knock-down argument,'" Alice objected.
> "When *I* use a word," Humpty Dumpty said, in rather a scornful tone, "it means just what I choose it to mean—neither more nor less."
> "The question is," said Alice, "whether you *can* make words mean so many different things."
> "The question is," said Humpty Dumpty, "which is to be master—that's all." ...
> "When I make a word do a lot of work like that," said Humpty Dumpty, "I always pay it extra."

8.2 Denotational semantics

In the rest of this chapter we are interested in the practical aspects of reading and giving a denotational description of the semantics of a programming language. We start with a few simple languages to gain practice with the approach. Then we develop ever more complex definitions to cope with more and more features of languages, in particular, imperative ones.

The denotational approach associates mathematical denotations to syntactical parts of the language. We will always proceed in the following four steps:

(a) Give the syntactic categories.

(b) Define the (abstract) syntax of the language.

(c) Give the value domains.

(d) Define functions that map each syntactic object to some semantic value.

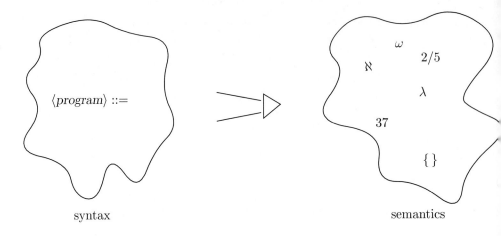

Figure 8.1: The mapping of programs to mathematical objects

In steps (a) and (b) we set down the syntax of the, presumably unfamiliar, language under consideration. In step (c) we give the, presumably familiar, mathematical objects that serve as the target of the definition. The last step, the definition, is the substance of the semantic definition of the language and conveys the "meaning" of the language. This definition is done inductively on the structure of the syntactic objects. The situation is suggested in figure 8.1.

8.3   Language of decimal numerals

The first example of the denotational approach is that of decimal numbers. The language of decimal numerals has two syntactic categories that are listed in the following table:

syntactic categories

$D \in$ **Digits**	the decimal digits
$N \in$ **Num**	decimal numerals

The syntax of decimal numerals is given by the following BNF grammar.

$$D \quad ::= \quad 0 \mid 1 \mid 2 \mid 3 \mid 4 \mid 5 \mid 6 \mid 7 \mid 8 \mid 9$$
$$N \quad ::= \quad D \mid N\,D$$

The mathematical denotations of decimal numerals come from the set of natural numbers. Hence the only value domain required is the set of natural numbers.

value domains

Nat $= \{0, 1, 2, \ldots\}$	natural numbers

We require two semantic functions to give the meaning to decimal numerals, one for each syntactic category. Each function is a mapping from elements of the syntactic category to their denotations. Both digits and numerals are denoted by natural numbers.

semantic functions
$\mathcal{D} : \textbf{Digits} \rightarrow \textbf{Nat}$
$\mathcal{M} : \textbf{Num} \rightarrow \textbf{Nat}$

We use script letters to name semantic functions. We enclose the arguments to these functions, which are pieces of syntax, in double brackets.

The following equations define the two semantic functions inductively:

$$
\begin{aligned}
\mathcal{D}[\![0]\!] &= 0 \\
\mathcal{D}[\![1]\!] &= 1 \\
&\;\;\vdots \\
\mathcal{D}[\![9]\!] &= 9 \\
\mathcal{M}[\![D]\!] &= \mathcal{D}[\![D]\!] \\
\mathcal{M}[\![ND]\!] &= 10 \times \mathcal{M}[\![N]\!] + \mathcal{M}[\![D]\!]
\end{aligned}
$$

We have a case of the definition for each production of the grammar. Presumably the operations of $\times$ (multiplication) and $+$ are familiar to the reader of the denotation definition, and so the definition conveys the formal meaning of decimal numbers.

For example, the numeral 021 denotes the number $\mathcal{M}[\![021]\!] = 10 \times \mathcal{M}[\![02]\!] + \mathcal{M}[\![1]\!] = 21$.

8.4 Language of regular expressions

The next example concerns regular expressions. Once again we pick a familiar example to exhibit the form of denotational definitions, and not actually to convey the meaning of regular expressions, which is already familiar to many.

We require two syntactic categories.

syntactic categories	
$A \in \textbf{Alpha}$	the alphabet
$R \in \textbf{RE}$	regular expressions

The abstract syntax of regular expressions is given below:

$$
R \quad ::= \quad A \mid \emptyset \mid (R + R) \mid (R \cdot R) \mid R^*
$$

We imagine the alphabet to be some set of atomic symbols. The exact nature of the alphabet is not important for the purposes of this example, and so we omit it.

The meaning of a regular expression is a formal language, i.e., a set of strings over the alphabet. Therefore, we pick sets of strings as the one value domain.

value domains
Lang	formal languages (sets of strings over **Alpha**)

Corresponding to each syntactic category we have two semantic functions of the following types:

semantic functions

$\mathcal{A} : \textbf{Alpha} \to \textbf{Lang}$
$\mathcal{D} : \textbf{RE} \to \textbf{Lang}$

The definition of the semantic functions are given below.

$$
\begin{aligned}
\mathcal{A}[\![A]\!] &= \{A\} \\
\mathcal{D}[\![A]\!] &= \mathcal{A}[\![A]\!] \\
\mathcal{D}[\![\emptyset]\!] &= \{\} \\
\mathcal{D}[\![(R_1 + R_2)]\!] &= \mathcal{D}[\![R_1]\!] \cup \mathcal{D}[\![R_2]\!] \\
\mathcal{D}[\![(R_1 \cdot R_2)]\!] &= \{x \cdot y \mid x \in \mathcal{D}[\![R_1]\!] \ \& \ y \in \mathcal{D}[\![R_2]\!]\} \\
\mathcal{D}[\![R^*]\!] &= \bigcup_i (\mathcal{D}[\![R]\!])^i
\end{aligned}
$$

If, for example, the alphabet contains the symbols a and b, then $\mathcal{D}[\![(\emptyset + a)]\!] = \mathcal{D}[\![\emptyset]\!] \cup \mathcal{D}[\![a]\!] = \{a\}$ and $\mathcal{D}[\![a \cdot \emptyset]\!] = \{\}$.

8.5   Language of propositional logic

The next example is the syntax and semantics of propositional logic. Propositional logic is the language of assertions. In the language we have some collection of fundamental propositions from which we make formulas.

syntactic categories
$P \in \textbf{Prop}$	propositions
$F \in \textbf{Form}$	formulas

We define formulas as follows:

$$
F \quad ::= \quad P \mid \neg F \mid F \Rightarrow F
$$

The syntax of propositions P is immaterial.

Notice that this BNF grammar is ambiguous as there are two ways to parse the formula $F \Rightarrow F \Rightarrow F$. We do not wish to consider problems of parsing in this chapter. We view this grammar as the abstract syntax of formulas. Any time we write $F \Rightarrow F$ we presume that it has already been parsed correctly, and that $\Rightarrow$ is the principle operator. (See exercise 2.25.) This is the best of both worlds. We will write ambiguous grammars, and consider the semantic function definitions well defined.

Now we come to the meaning of propositional formulas. We consider a proposition to be true or false, and likewise a formula can be true or false. It is no surprise, therefore, that we pick boolean values as a value domain. But the truth of a formula cannot be determined without knowing the truth of all the constituent propositions. Thus we are forced to introduce an additional semantic entity called an assignment.

$$
\begin{array}{ll}
\hline
\multicolumn{2}{c}{\text{value domains}} \\
\hline
\mathbf{Bool} = \{\textit{True}, \textit{False}\} & \text{boolean values} \\
\rho \in \mathbf{Assign} = \mathbf{P} \rightarrow \mathbf{Bool} & \text{assignments} \\
\hline
\end{array}
$$

An assignment is an oracle that reveals if a proposition is true or not.

Now the choice of denotations for formulas can be made. The semantic function $\mathcal{M}$ maps the formulas to functions—functions from assignments to boolean values.

$$
\begin{array}{c}
\hline
\text{semantic functions} \\
\hline
\mathcal{M} : \mathbf{Form} \rightarrow \mathbf{Assign} \rightarrow \mathbf{Bool} \\
\hline
\end{array}
$$

The definition of $\mathcal{M}$ is given by the following three cases:

$$
\begin{aligned}
\mathcal{M}[\![P]\!]\,\rho &= \rho(P) \\
\mathcal{M}[\![\neg\, F]\!]\,\rho &= \neg\,\mathcal{M}[\![F]\!]\,\rho \\
\mathcal{M}[\![F_1 \Rightarrow F_2]\!]\,\rho &= \neg\,\mathcal{M}[\![F_1]\!]\,\rho \vee \mathcal{M}[\![F_2]\!]\,\rho
\end{aligned}
$$

We write the definition of $\mathcal{M}$ in the customary manner of function returning functions. This explains why the formal parameter ρ appears on the left of the equals sign. Using lambda expressions as a notation for functions, we could be more explicit and write: $\mathcal{M}[\![P]\!] = \lambda\rho\,.\,\rho(P)$ and so on, but this is less concise.

Using this denotation definition for formulas, the formula $\mathcal{M}[\![P \Rightarrow Q]\!]$ denotes a function that given an assignment ρ returns the boolean value $\neg\rho(P)\vee\rho(Q)$. The meaning of some formulas are constant functions, e.g., the formula $P \Rightarrow P$. Consider any assignment ρ. If $\rho(P)$ is false, then $\mathcal{M}[\![P \Rightarrow P]\!] = \neg\,\rho(P) \vee \rho(P)$ is true. Likewise for the case where $\rho(P)$ is true. No other value for ρ effects the result of $\mathcal{M}[\![P \Rightarrow P]\!]$. Such formulas are called *tautologies*.

8.6   Language of simple expressions

In this section we give the denotational semantics of a simple expression language. The syntactic categories of this language are given below:

syntactic categories

$I \in$ **Ident**	identifiers
$E \in$ **Exp**	expressions

Here is the BNF description of the language. (The micro syntax of identifiers is omitted because it is not important here.)

$$E \quad ::= \quad 0 \mid 1 \mid I \mid (E_1 + E_2) \mid (E_1 - E_2) \mid \textbf{let } I = E_1 \textbf{ in } E_2 \textbf{ end}$$

The **let** construct binds an identifier I to the value of some expression E_1 throughout the expression E_2. The exact meaning for this construct and the rest of the language will be made clear in the following few paragraphs.

We view all expressions as denoting numbers, so we take the set of integers as one of the value domains. But there is a problem with the expression I. What integer does an identifier denote? Without context it is impossible to say. Thus we add context, the bindings of all visible identifiers, and call it an environment.

value domains

Int $= \{\dots, -2, -1, 0, 1, 2, \dots\}$	integers
$\rho \in$ **Env** $=$ **Ident** $\rightarrow$ **Int**	environments

An environment must be a total function. All functions discussed in this chapter are assumed to be total.

The meaning of an expression will be given by the function $\mathcal{E}$.

semantic functions

$\mathcal{E} :$ **Exp** $\rightarrow$ **Env** $\rightarrow$ **Int**

This function is defined by the following cases and the case for the **let** construct, which is given in the next paragraph.

$$\begin{aligned}
\mathcal{E}[\![0]\!]\rho &= 0 \\
\mathcal{E}[\![1]\!]\rho &= 1 \\
\mathcal{E}[\![I]\!]\rho &= \rho(I) \\
\mathcal{E}[\![E_1 + E_2]\!]\rho &= \mathcal{E}[\![E_1]\!]\rho + \mathcal{E}[\![E_2]\!]\rho \\
\mathcal{E}[\![E_1 - E_2]\!]\rho &= \mathcal{E}[\![E_1]\!]\rho - \mathcal{E}[\![E_2]\!]\rho
\end{aligned}$$

Notice the two different uses of the plus sign and minus sign. On the right-hand side, the plus sign is a syntactic construct for an operation of the programming language. On the left-hand side, the plus sign denotes the mathematical operation of addition between integers.

The let construct modifies the environment. Its definition is as follows:

$$\mathcal{E}[\![\text{let } I = E_1 \text{ in } E_2 \text{ end}]\!]\rho \;\; = \;\; \mathcal{E}[\![E_2]\!](\rho[I \mapsto \mathcal{E}[\![E_1]\!]\rho])$$

The notation $f[x \mapsto y]$ means that the function f is modified so that $f(x) = y$. Written in ML, this function is defined by:

```
fun Update (f,x,y) (x0) = if x0=x then y else f(x0);
```

This is a good place to consider the choice of the meta-language for communicating the denotational definitions to the reader. The meta-language must be meaningful to the reader and as unambiguous as possible. Thus far we have used arithmetic expressions, boolean expressions, and set expressions in the meta-language. These simple ideas are nearly universally accessible because of the common mathematical education that links the scientific community. Also the examples are mostly self-evident. But more and more the definitions will become foreign and the language of mathematics will be less adequate, primarily because of a lack of standard notation for functions. We will use an ML-like meta-language for several reasons.

- ML emphasizes the constructive nature of the definitions. The definitions are actually interpreters of the language.

- The language is ideally suited for unambiguous descriptions of higher-order functions.

- ML has a reasonable and natural syntax likely to be understood by many.

There is yet another significant link between ML and denotational definitions. The abstract syntax of languages corresponds exactly to ML recursive type definitions. The following ML type definition represents the abstract syntax of the simple expression language defined in this section.

```
datatype Expression =
     Zero | One | Ident of string          |
     Plus of Expression * Expression        |
     Minus of Expression * Expression       |
     Let of string * Expression * Expression ;
```

Notice that the problem of ambiguous grammars goes completely away, as any ML expression of type Expression is already "parsed" into its proper constituent components. Given the previous data type definition, the function $\mathcal{E}$ can be written as follows:

```
fun
     E (Zero)        rho = 0                    |
     E (One)         rho = 1                    |
```

```
E (Plus  (e1,e2)) rho = (E e1 rho) + (E e2 rho) |
E (Minus (e1,e2)) rho = (E e1 rho) - (E e2 rho) |
E (Let (i,e1,e2)) rho =
      let val n = E e1 rho in E e2 (Update (rho,i,n)) end;
```

Compare this with the interpreter for this **let** language written in PROLOG for exercise 6.8. For more examples of using ML as the meta-language for denotational definitions of programming languages see [16].

8.7   Language with error values

In this section we extend the semantics of the simple **let** language to include error elements. These error elements make the definition of the language more realistic by accounting for programs with semantics errors, like type errors, and run-time errors, like dividing by zero. Fully defining all the abnormal situations is tedious and makes the definitions more difficult to comprehend, so after this section we will not handle all such cases.

syntactic categories	
$I \in$ **Ident**	identifiers
$E \in$ **Exp**	expressions
$P \in$ **Prog**	programs

We add the operation of division in order to look at the problem caused by dividing by zero.

$$E \quad ::= \quad 0 \mid 1 \mid I \mid (E_1 + E_2) \mid (E_1/E_2) \mid \textbf{if } E_1 \textbf{ then } E_2 \textbf{ else } E_3 \mid$$
$$\textbf{let } I = E_1 \textbf{ in } E_2 \textbf{ end}$$

$$P \quad ::= \quad \textbf{program } (I); \ E \textbf{ end.}$$

We also add the **program** construct and the conditional expression to make the language look somewhat more realistic. We often think of programs as computing a function from the input to the output. Programs in the simple language will closely approximate integer functions as indicated by the type of the semantics function $\mathcal{P}$ in the table below.

The value domains are nearly the same as before.

value domains	
Int $= \{\ldots, -2, -1, 0, 1, 2, \ldots\}$	integers
$\rho \in$ **Env** $=$ **Ident** $\rightarrow$ (**Int**+*undefined*)	environments

However, the range of environments is not just integers anymore, but either an integer or a special element named *undefined*. By (**Int** + *undefined*) we mean the

$\mathcal{E}[\![I]\!]\,\rho =$
   `let`
      $n = \rho(I)$
   `in`
      `if` $IsInt(n)$ `then` n `else` $error$
   `end`

$\mathcal{E}[\![E_1 + E_2]\!]\,\rho =$
   `let`
      $n = \mathcal{E}[\![E_1]\!]\,\rho; \qquad n' = \mathcal{E}[\![E_2]\!]\,\rho$
   `in`
      `if` $IsInt(n)$ `andalso` $IsInt(n')$ `then` $n + n'$ `else` $error$
   `end`

$\mathcal{E}[\![E_1/E_2]\!]\,\rho =$
   `let`
      $n = \mathcal{E}[\![E_1]\!]\,\rho; \qquad n' = \mathcal{E}[\![E_2]\!]\,\rho$
   `in`
      `if` $IsInt(n)$ `andalso` $IsInt(n')$ `andalso` $n' \neq 0$ `then` n/n' `else` $error$
   `end`

$\mathcal{E}[\![\textbf{if } E_1 \textbf{ then } E_2 \textbf{ else } E_3]\!]\,\rho =$
   `let`
      $n = \mathcal{E}[\![E_1]\!]\,\rho$
   `in`
      `if` $IsInt(n)$ `then if` $n = 0$ `then` $\mathcal{E}[\![E_2]\!]\,\rho$ `else` $\mathcal{E}[\![E_3]\!]\,\rho$ `else` $error$
   `end`

$\mathcal{E}[\![\textbf{let } I = E_1 \textbf{ in } E_2 \textbf{ end}]\!]\,\rho =$
   `let`
      $n = \mathcal{E}[\![E_1]\!]\,\rho$
   `in`
      `if` $IsInt(n)$ `then` $\mathcal{E}[\![E_2]\!]\rho[I \mapsto n]$ `else` $error$
   `end`

$\mathcal{P}[\![\textbf{program } (I); E \textbf{ end.}]\!]\,n =$
   `let`
      `fun` $\rho(J) = undefined$
   `in`
      $\mathcal{E}[\![E]\!]\rho[I \mapsto n]$
   `end`

Figure 8.2: Semantic function for a language with error values

disjoint union of sets **Int** and {*undefined*}. We assume we have a function *IsInt* that can discriminate between the different kinds of elements in the disjoint union.

Expressions no longer will denote just integers. This is reflected in the type of the semantic function $\mathcal{E}$. The function returns either an integer or a special element named *error*. Likewise the entire program may denote an ordinary integer function or a function that fails to compute an integer. The types of the semantics functions $\mathcal{E}$ and $\mathcal{P}$ appear in the following table:

semantic functions
$\mathcal{E} : \mathbf{Exp} \to \mathbf{Env} \to (\mathbf{Int}{+}error)$
$\mathcal{P} : \mathbf{Prog} \to \mathbf{Int} \to (\mathbf{Int}{+}error)$

The definitions of $\mathcal{E}$ and $\mathcal{P}$ appear in figure 8.2. The definitions make heavy use of the `let` statement in the meta-language. This is used make the definitions easier to read by introducing names for certain expressions in the meta-language. The function $\mathcal{P}$ is required for the new **program** construct. The construct does very little. It introduces a name for the input value. It also sets up the initial environment, namely, the one that is everywhere undefined except for the input value.

8.8   Language with state

The languages thus for have been functional; i.e., the syntactic expressions denote values (we have been using integers primarily) fairly directly. Imperative languages do not work this way. The presence of actions with side effects in imperative languages requires introducing state into the denotational description. Commands in imperative languages denote operations on the state of the computer memory. In this section we provide a brief overview of states without considering all the details. In the next section we fill in some of the details.

We add a syntactic category for commands to the already used syntactic categories for identifiers, expressions, and programs.

syntactic categories	
$I \in \mathbf{Ident}$	identifiers
$E \in \mathbf{Exp}$	expressions
$C \in \mathbf{Com}$	commands
$P \in \mathbf{Prog}$	programs

For the language in this section we consider three commands: the `if` statement, the `while` statement, and the sequencing of statements.

$$C \quad ::= \quad C_1; C_2 \mid \mathbf{if}\ E\ \mathbf{then}\ C_1\ \mathbf{else}\ C_2 \mid \mathbf{while}\ E\ \mathbf{do}\ C \mid \ \ldots$$

$$P \quad ::= \quad \mathbf{program}\ (I);\ C\ \mathbf{end}.$$

We add a new value domain for states. Just what a state is will not matter until the next section. The absence of the assignment statement permits the structure of states to be ignored.

value domains	
$n \in \mathbf{Int} = \{\ldots, -2, -1, 0, 1, 2, \ldots\}$	integers
$\sigma \in \mathbf{States}$	states

We choose that the denotation of commands will be state transformations, i.e., functions from states to states.

semantic functions
$\mathcal{C} : \mathbf{Com} \rightarrow \mathbf{States} \rightarrow \mathbf{States}$
$\mathcal{P} : \mathbf{Prog} \rightarrow \mathbf{Int} \rightarrow \mathbf{Int}$

All the commands of the language must be mapped to the appropriate functions from states to states.

The effect of the if statement is the same as one of its branches. Which branch is determined by the expression E.

$\mathcal{C}[\![\textbf{if } E \textbf{ then } C_1 \textbf{ else } C_2]\!]\, \sigma =$
    if $IsTrue(\mathcal{E}[\![E]\!]\, \sigma)$ then $\mathcal{C}[\![C_1]\!]\, \sigma$ else $\mathcal{C}[\![C_2]\!]\, \sigma$

Presumably $\mathcal{E}$ can evaluate an expression given a state. Also, we assume that the function $IsTrue$ determines if the value represents "truth" or not. These details will be addressed in the next section.

The execution of one command after another has the accumulated effect of executing each command. This is exactly what one would expect. (After all, we are defining the semantics of this simple imperative language to be in agreement with general expectations.)

$\mathcal{C}[\![C_1; C_2]\!]\, \sigma = \texttt{let } \sigma' = \mathcal{C}[\![C_1]\!]\, \sigma \texttt{ in } \mathcal{C}[\![C_2]\!]\, \sigma' \texttt{ end}$

The definition above is really just composition of state transformers, and we could have written it: $\mathcal{C}[\![C_1; C_2]\!] = \mathcal{C}[\![C_1]\!] \circ \mathcal{C}[\![C_2]\!]$.

The final case in the definition of $\mathcal{C}$ is for the **while** statement.

$\mathcal{C}[\![\textbf{while } E \textbf{ do } C]\!]\, \sigma =$
    let
        fun $p\,(\sigma') = $ if $IsTrue(\mathcal{E}[\![E]\!]\, \sigma)$ then $p\,(\mathcal{C}[\![C]\!]\, \sigma')$ else σ'
    in
        $p\,(\sigma)$
    end

The function p is a function from states to states, and is defined recursively. Here we come up against a significant problem in the naive approach to denotational semantics. For any denotational definition to be an adequate explanation of the semantics of a language, the mathematical object being produced as the denotation must be clearly specified. Are we sure what function p is? We must not appeal to some intuitive semantics for the meta-language, say, a translator for the ML programming language, as in "whatever function some ML implementation computes." For this would beg the question, and we would then have to ask what is the semantics of ML. Fortunately, in chapter 7 we have developed an explanation of recursion in terms of lambda expressions and the **Y** combinator. These are elements primitive enough to be satisfying, yet beta reduction (although simple and mechanical) is an operational explanation of functions, and so lambda terms may not be a satisfactory definition of a function. Furthermore, since p may not terminate we have a new outcome (besides simply an integer) for the meaning of a program, namely, one in which the program fails to compute any integer and loops forever. These problems are overcome if we have a denotational semantics for lambda expressions themselves. There is one [7, 13, 14] that uses domains structured by partial orders. If we continue to use well-mannered value domains and functions defined using lambda expressions, the theory will cover the definitions, so we continue with the fiction the value domains are ordinary sets.

Finally, to complete the denotational definition of the simple imperative language we define the semantic function $\mathcal{P}$. It defines the overall meaning of a program to be an integer function.

$\mathcal{P}[\![\mathbf{program}\ (I);\ C\ \mathbf{end.}]\!]\,n =$
   $\mathtt{let}\ \sigma_f = \mathcal{C}[\![C]\!]\,\sigma_i\ \mathtt{in}\ Contents(\sigma_f, \alpha)\ \mathtt{end}$

We let σ_i be the initial state, whatever that may be. We assume the contents of initial state σ_i at address α is n. The program returns the contents of address α in the final state.

8.9   Language with commands

In this section we extend the language of the previous section by introducing the assignment statement. We also must introduce variables; this requires adding locations and filling in the details about state omitted in the previous section.

The syntactic categories we need are listed in the following table:

syntactic categories

$I \in \mathbf{Ident}$	identifiers
$L \in \mathbf{Lexp}$	l-expressions or references
$E \in \mathbf{Exp}$	expressions
$C \in \mathbf{Com}$	commands
$P \in \mathbf{Prog}$	programs

Here is the BNF description of the language.

$L\quad ::=\quad I$

$$E \quad ::= \quad 0 \mid 1 \mid I \mid !L \mid (E_1 + E_2) \mid \text{if } E_1 \text{ then } E_2 \text{ else } E_3 \mid$$
$$\text{let } I = E_1 \text{ in } E_2 \text{ end}$$

$$C \quad ::= \quad C_1; C_2 \mid \text{if } E \text{ then } C_1 \text{ else } C_2 \mid L := E \mid \text{new } I := E \text{ in } C \text{ end}$$

$$P \quad ::= \quad \textbf{program } (I); C \textbf{ end.}$$

The assignment statement has been added as well as a construct to declare variables. The **new** construct has a design that is parallel to that of the **let** construct. In particular, both constructs have a body (the scope) in which the identifier is defined. We have omitted the **while** construct whose semantics is an easy generalization of that of the previous language to focus on the new constructs.

We introduced a syntactic category for references (l-expressions) even though we have allowed only identifiers as references. We could have dispensed with the syntactic category of references altogether, but we have chosen to emphasize this feature of the language that in real languages may be quite complex. We require some set of locations to be the denotations of references. The structure of the set, which we call **Loc**, is not important in this section, so we leave it unspecified.

value domains	
$n \in \textbf{Int} = \{\ldots, -2, -1, 0, 1, 2, \ldots\}$	integers
$\alpha \in \textbf{Loc}$	locations
$\sigma \in \textbf{States} = \textbf{Loc} \rightarrow (\textbf{Int} + \textit{unused})$	states
$\rho \in \textbf{Env} = \textbf{Ident} \rightarrow (\textbf{Int} + \textbf{Loc} + \textit{undefined})$	environments

The range of **States** are the storable values (things that can be stored in memory). The range of **Env** are the denotable values (objects that identifiers can denote). Here we have made a choice that an identifier can denote either an integer or a location, but not both. An identifier introduced in the **let** construct denotes an integer and can be thought of as a constant. An identifier introduced in the **new** construct denotes a location and can be thought of as a variable. In some languages the same identifier can denote different objects in different contexts. (This has nothing to do with the scope of the identifier.) For example, in LISP an atom can denote both an s-expression and a function. This would lead to a different choice for the value domain of environments (see exercise 8.12).

Corresponding to the four syntactic categories we must define four semantic functions.

semantic functions
$\mathcal{L} : \textbf{Lexp} \rightarrow \textbf{Env} \rightarrow \textbf{States} \rightarrow \textbf{Loc}$
$\mathcal{E} : \textbf{Exp} \rightarrow \textbf{Env} \rightarrow \textbf{States} \rightarrow \textbf{Int}$
$\mathcal{C} : \textbf{Com} \rightarrow \textbf{Env} \rightarrow \textbf{States} \rightarrow \textbf{States}$
$\mathcal{P} : \textbf{Prog} \rightarrow \textbf{Int} \rightarrow \textbf{Int}$

We clearly see the distinction between expressions and commands. Commands modify states and expressions return (integer) values. Unfortunately this orderly distinction is too simplistic for programming languages, which allow expressions with side effects, but it will serve here. The choice of the range of L, namely, **Env** $\rightarrow$ **States** $\rightarrow$ **Loc**, is also simplistic, as it preludes modeling l-valued expressions that change the state. Of course, in many real programming languages this is possible. For example, in C one can write `A[i++]`.

The only case of the semantic function $\mathcal{L}$ is for an identifier I.

$$\mathcal{L}[\![I]\!]\,\rho\,\sigma = \rho\,(I)$$

The state σ is ignored—in a more sophisticated language it might get used—and the identifier is looked up in the environment. Presumably, the result is a location, an l-value is suppose to denote a location, but this definition does not ensure that this is the case, since an environment may return an integer or the special symbol *undefined* as well.

Most of the cases of the function $\mathcal{E}$ are unremarkable.

$$\mathcal{E}[\![0]\!]\,\rho\,\sigma = 0$$
$$\mathcal{E}[\![1]\!]\,\rho\,\sigma = 1$$
$$\mathcal{E}[\![I]\!]\,\rho\,\sigma = \rho(I)$$
$$\mathcal{E}[\![E_1 + E_2]\!]\,\rho\,\sigma = \mathcal{E}[\![E_1]\!]\rho\,\sigma + \mathcal{E}[\![E_2]\!]\rho\,\sigma$$
$$\mathcal{E}[\![\textbf{let } I = E_1 \textbf{ in } E_2 \textbf{ end}]\!]\,\rho\,\sigma = \mathcal{E}[\![E_2]\!]\rho[I \mapsto \mathcal{E}[\![E_1]\!]\rho]\sigma$$

The definition of the **if** construct is not surprising either. However, we are now forced to make a definition of when an expression represents "truth." In order to avoid introducing boolean value to the semantic domains, we adopt the ridiculous definition that the integer zero is true.

$$\mathcal{E}[\![\textbf{if } E_1 \textbf{ then } E_2 \textbf{ else } E_3]\!]\,\rho\,\sigma =$$
$$\texttt{if } (\mathcal{E}[\![E_1]\!]\,\rho\,\sigma) = 0 \texttt{ then } \mathcal{E}[\![E_2]\!]\,\rho\,\sigma \texttt{ else } \mathcal{E}[\![E_3]\!]\,\rho\,\sigma$$

Because we have variables in the language, and not just constants, we have added a construct to explicitly obtain the contents of a location.

$$\mathcal{E}[\![!L]\!]\,\rho\,\sigma = \texttt{let } \alpha = \mathcal{L}[\![L]\!]\rho\,\sigma \texttt{ in } \sigma(\alpha) \texttt{ end}$$

In this case the value at location α, the location denoted by L, is returned. Since the state σ is modeled as a function, applying it to a location yields the value of the state at that location. This completes the definition of $\mathcal{E}$.

The function $\mathcal{C}$ is analogous to the one in the previous section. We omit the cases for **while** and **if** statements. The case for $C_1; C_2$ is also analogous, but we give it just for reference.

$$\mathcal{C}[\![C_1; C_2]\!]\,\rho\,\sigma = \texttt{let } \sigma' = \mathcal{C}[\![C_1]\!]\,\rho\,\sigma \texttt{ in } \mathcal{C}[\![C_2]\!]\,\rho\,\sigma' \texttt{ end}$$

Notice that the environment in which the second command is executed is the same as the environment in which the first command was executed. If the first command were to make some modifications to the environment, these modifications would be lost.

The main point of this section and models of imperative languages altogether is the assignment statement. States are snapshots of memory and assignment statements are the atomic actions that change the state. The definition of $\mathcal{C}$ for the assignment statement finds the location denoted by the left-hand side and updates the state accordingly.

$\mathcal{C}[\![L := E]\!] \rho \sigma =$
    `let`
        $\alpha = \mathcal{L}[\![L]\!] \rho \sigma; \qquad n = \mathcal{E}[\![E]\!] \rho \sigma$
    `in`
        $\sigma[\alpha \mapsto n]$
    `end`

The environment, the meaning of the identifiers, remains unchanged. The contents of only one location is affected. This models what we called storage semantics in chapter 3.

For assignment and deferencing to work we require variables in the language. Variables are introduced with the **new** construct, which is similar to the **let** construct.

$\mathcal{C}[\![\textbf{new } I := E \textbf{ in } C \textbf{ end}]\!] \rho \sigma =$
    `let`
        α be some Loc such that $\sigma(\alpha) = unused$
        $n = \mathcal{E}[\![E]\!] \rho \sigma$
    `in`
        $\mathcal{C}[\![C]\!] \rho[I \mapsto \alpha] \sigma[\alpha \mapsto n]$
    `end`

The environment in which the body C is evaluated is changed so that I refers to a new location. This location is initialized with the value of E. We have not given sufficient detail of the structure of locations and states to be able to define the allocation of new memory locations. This is left as an exercise (exercise 8.13).

In the definition of the semantics for the **program** construct we must create the initial environment (all undefined) and the initial state (all unused). The input variable I is associated with some location in the state and initialized to the given integer.

$\mathcal{P}[\![\textbf{program } (I); C \textbf{ end.}]\!] n =$
    `let`
        `fun` $\rho(J) = undefined$
        `fun` $\sigma(\alpha') = unused$
        α be some Loc such that $\sigma(\alpha) = unused$
        $\sigma_f = \mathcal{C}[\![C]\!] \rho[I \mapsto \alpha] \sigma[\alpha \mapsto n]$
    `in`
        $\sigma_f(\alpha)$
    `end`

The result is the value (presumably an integer) left in the state after the effects of the program have been applied. The input variable is not a constant. Thus a program can use I on the left-hand side of an assignment.

The following is a sample program P:

program (x); **new** $y := !x$ **in** $x := $ **let** $z = !y$ **in** z **end end end.**

Unwinding the semantic definition reveals that the program P denotes the identity function:

$$\mathcal{P}[\![P]\!] \quad = \quad \lambda n . \sigma_f(\alpha_0)$$

where α_0 is the location chosen for the input variable x, and

$$
\begin{aligned}
\sigma_f &= \mathcal{C}[\![\textbf{new } y := !x \textbf{ in } \cdots \textbf{ end}]\!]\, \rho_1\, \sigma_1 & \rho_1 &= \rho_0[x \mapsto \alpha_0] \quad \sigma_1 = \sigma_0[\alpha_0 \mapsto n] \\
&= \mathcal{C}[\![x := \textbf{let } z = !y \textbf{ in } z \textbf{ end}]\!]\, \rho_2\, \sigma_2 & \rho_2 &= \rho_1[y \mapsto \alpha_1] \\
& & \sigma_2 &= \sigma_1[\alpha_1 \mapsto \mathcal{E}[\![!x]\!]\rho_1\sigma_1] \\
&= \mathcal{C}[\![x := \textbf{let } z = !y \textbf{ in } z \textbf{ end}]\!]\, \rho_2\, \sigma_2 & \sigma_2 &= \sigma_1[\alpha_1 \mapsto \sigma_1(\rho_1(x))] \\
&= \mathcal{C}[\![x := \textbf{let } z = !y \textbf{ in } z \textbf{ end}]\!]\, \rho_2\, \sigma_2 & \sigma_2 &= \sigma_1[\alpha_1 \mapsto n] \\
&= \sigma[\mathcal{L}[\![x]\!]\rho_2\sigma_2 \mapsto m] & m &= \mathcal{E}[\![\textbf{let } z = !y \textbf{ in } z \textbf{ end}]\!]\, \rho_2\, \sigma_2 \\
&= \sigma[\rho_2(x) \mapsto m] \\
&= \sigma[\alpha_0 \mapsto m]
\end{aligned}
$$

So $\sigma_f(\alpha_0) = m$ where m is given by:

$$
\begin{aligned}
m &= \mathcal{E}[\![\textbf{let } z = !y \textbf{ in } z \textbf{ end}]\!]\, \rho_2\, \sigma_2 \\
&= \mathcal{E}[\![z]\!]\, \rho_3\, \sigma_2 & \rho_3 &= \rho_2[z \mapsto \mathcal{E}[\![!y]\!]\rho_2\sigma_2] \\
&= \mathcal{E}[\![z]\!]\, \rho_3\, \sigma_2 & \rho_3 &= \rho_2[z \mapsto \sigma_2(\rho_2(y))] \\
&= \mathcal{E}[\![z]\!]\, \rho_3\, \sigma_2 & \rho_3 &= \rho_2[z \mapsto n] \\
&= \rho_3\,(z) \\
&= n
\end{aligned}
$$

Thus $\mathcal{P}[\![P]\!] = \lambda n . n$. The program denotes the identity function.

8.10 Language combining expressions and commands

In this section we combine expressions and commands into one syntactic category. This is appropriate if we wish to model expression languages in which every command has both a potential value and a potential effect on the state. This language thus illustrates some of the techniques for modeling constructs with both purposes mixed together. This language also serves as preparation for the language of the next section that has subprocedures.

We merge the syntactic category of commands into the category of expressions and so we now have four categories.

$$\underline{\text{syntactic categories}}$$

$I \in$ **Ident**	identifiers
$L \in$ **Lexp**	l-expressions or references
$E \in$ **Exp**	expressions and commands
$P \in$ **Prog**	programs

Here is the BNF description of the language. All the constructs are familiar.

$L \quad ::= \quad I$

$E \quad ::= \quad 0 \mid 1 \mid I \mid {!}L \mid (E_1 + E_2) \mid \text{let } I = E_1 \text{ in } E_2 \text{ end} \mid E_1; E_2 \mid$
$\qquad\qquad \text{if } E_1 \text{ then } E_2 \text{ else } E_3 \mid L := E \mid \text{new } I := E_1 \text{ in } E_2 \text{ end}$

$P \quad ::= \quad \textbf{program } (I); E \textbf{ end.}$

One consequence of merging expressions and commands is that we need only one **if** construct.

Although the value domains **Int**, **Loc**, **Env**, and **States** remain the same as in the previous section, they are used slightly differently.

$$\underline{\text{semantic functions}}$$

$\mathcal{L} : \textbf{Lexp} \to \textbf{Env} \to \textbf{States} \to \textbf{Loc}$
$\mathcal{M} : \textbf{Exp} \to \textbf{Env} \to \textbf{States} \to \textbf{Int} \times \textbf{States}$
$\mathcal{P} : \textbf{Prog} \to \textbf{Int} \to \textbf{Int}$

We call the semantic function for expressions and commands $\mathcal{M}$. Its range contains the cartesian product **Int** × **States** to account for the value and state change of every **Exp**.

The definition of the function $\mathcal{M}$ is shown in figure 8.3. The evaluation of the expressions 0, 1, I, and $!L$ do not change the state, and so their definitions are of the form $\mathcal{M}[\![E]\!]\rho\sigma = \langle n, \sigma \rangle$. Each case returns a pair consisting of the appropriate integer value and the unchanged state σ.

Notice that in the definition of $\mathcal{M}$ for $E_1 + E_2$, the second expression is evaluated in the state obtained by evaluating E_1. Also, in the case of the sequential expression $E_1; E_2$ we throw away the value of E_1.

The definition for $\mathcal{P}$ can be essentially the same as in the last section. Other plausible meanings can be given to programs in this language. Instead of returning the value stored in the input variable at the end of the program $\sigma_f(\alpha)$, we could return the value of the program body E, i.e., the first element of the pair $\mathcal{M}[\![E]\!]\rho[I \mapsto \alpha]\sigma[\alpha \mapsto n]$. These two values could well be different. As we are giving a definition for the semantics of the language, we are free to make whatever choice we like.

$\mathcal{M}[\![0]\!] \, \rho \, \sigma = \langle 0, \sigma \rangle$
$\mathcal{M}[\![1]\!] \, \rho \, \sigma = \langle 1, \sigma \rangle$
$\mathcal{M}[\![I]\!] \, \rho \, \sigma = \langle \rho(I), \sigma \rangle$
$\mathcal{M}[\![!L]\!] \, \rho \, \sigma = \texttt{let} \;\; \alpha = \mathcal{L}[\![L]\!] \, \rho \, \sigma \;\; \texttt{in} \;\; \langle \sigma(\alpha), \sigma \rangle \;\; \texttt{end}$

$\mathcal{M}[\![E_1 + E_2]\!] \, \rho \, \sigma =$
   `let`
        $\langle n, \sigma' \rangle = \mathcal{M}[\![E_1]\!] \, \rho \, \sigma; \qquad \langle m, \sigma'' \rangle = \mathcal{M}[\![E_2]\!] \, \rho \, \sigma'$
   `in`
        $\langle n + m, \sigma'' \rangle$
   `end`

$\mathcal{M}[\![\textbf{if } E_1 \textbf{ then } E_2 \textbf{ else } E_3]\!] \, \rho \, \sigma =$
   `let` $\langle n, \sigma' \rangle = \mathcal{M}[\![E_1]\!] \, \rho \, \sigma$ `in if` $n = 0$ `then` $\mathcal{E}[\![E_2]\!] \, \rho \, \sigma'$ `else` $\mathcal{E}[\![E_3]\!] \, \rho \, \sigma'$ `end`

$\mathcal{M}[\![\textbf{let } I = E_1 \textbf{ in } E_2 \textbf{ end}]\!] \, \rho \, \sigma =$
   `let`
        $\langle n, \sigma' \rangle = \mathcal{M}[\![E_1]\!] \, \rho \, \sigma; \qquad \rho' = \rho[I \mapsto n]$
   `in`
        $\mathcal{M}[\![E_2]\!] \, \rho' \, \sigma'$
   `end`

$\mathcal{M}[\![E_1; \, E_2]\!] \, \rho \, \sigma = \texttt{let} \;\; \langle n, \sigma' \rangle = \mathcal{M}[\![E_1]\!] \, \rho \, \sigma \;\; \texttt{in} \;\; \mathcal{M}[\![E_2]\!] \, \rho \, \sigma' \;\; \texttt{end}$

$\mathcal{M}[\![L := E]\!] \, \rho \, \sigma =$
   `let`
        $\alpha = \mathcal{L}[\![L]\!] \, \rho \, \sigma$
        $\langle n, \sigma' \rangle = \mathcal{M}[\![E_1]\!] \, \rho \, \sigma$
   `in`
        $\langle n, \sigma'[\alpha \mapsto n] \rangle$
   `end`

$\mathcal{M}[\![\textbf{new } I := E_1 \textbf{ in } E_2 \textbf{ end}]\!] \, \rho \, \sigma =$
   `let`
        $\langle n, \sigma' \rangle = \mathcal{M}[\![E_1]\!] \, \rho \, \sigma$
        α be some Loc such that $\sigma'(\alpha) = unused$
   `in`
        $\mathcal{M}[\![E_2]\!] \rho[I \mapsto \alpha] \sigma'[\alpha \mapsto n]$
   `end`

Figure 8.3: A language with expressions and commands combined

8.11   Language with function calls

We extend the previous language to include subprocedures of one parameter. By combining commands and expressions in the previous section we avoid the complication of a **return** statement for subprocedures, yet we still represent the two aspects of subprocedures: side effects and return values.

   The syntactic categories are as in the previous language. The constructs of the language are extended to include two new ones: a function definition and a function call.

$$L \quad ::= \quad I$$

$$E \quad ::= \quad 0 \mid 1 \mid I \mid !L \mid (E_1 + E_2) \mid \textbf{let } I = E_1 \textbf{ in } E_2 \textbf{ end} \mid E_1; E_2 \mid$$
$$\textbf{if } E_1 \textbf{ then } E_2 \textbf{ else } E_3 \mid L := E \mid \textbf{new } I := E_1 \textbf{ in } E_2 \textbf{ end} \mid$$
$$\textbf{function } I_1(I_2) = E_1 \textbf{ in } E_2 \textbf{ end} \mid \textbf{call } I(E)$$

$$P \quad ::= \quad \textbf{program } (I); E \textbf{ end}.$$

The function definition construct is analogous to **new** and **let**. It introduces an identifier. The construct is similar in one other way also. The entire scope of the identifier is between the **in** and the **end**. Real programming languages with static scoping usually have a general block construct with a declarations sections. All the various declarations, constants, variables, subprocedures, types, exceptions, and so on, have scopes related to the block. Such an approach is certainly possible (see exercise 8.16), but is slightly more complex.

   The value domains for a language with subprocedures are more complicated because we need to denote functions.

value domains

$n \in \textbf{Int} = \{\dots, -2, -1, 0, 1, 2, \dots\}$	integers
$\alpha \in \textbf{Loc}$	locations
$\sigma \in \textbf{States} = \textbf{Loc} \to (\textbf{Int} + \textit{unused})$	states
$f \in \textbf{Func} = \textbf{States} \to \textbf{Int} \to \textbf{Int} \times \textbf{States}$	
$\quad \textbf{Denote} = \textbf{Int} + \textbf{Loc} + \textbf{Func}$	denotable values
$\rho \in \textbf{Env} = \textbf{Ident} \to (\textbf{Denote} + \textit{undefined})$	environments

The denotation of a subprocedure is a higher-order function taking as arguments **States** for context, and **Int** for the value of the actual argument to the function, and returning the value and the state after execution of the subprocedure. The choice in denotations for subprocedures already reveals important clues about the semantics of the language. The absence of **Env** as an argument suggests that the meaning of all identifiers are resolved where the function is defined and not dynamically when the function is called. Also, the argument **Int** not only suggests functions with just one argument, but also that the parameter passing is be done by value. These hints are borne out by the definition in figure 8.4.

   The semantic functions have the same form as the previous language.

$\mathcal{M}[\![\textbf{function } I_1(I_2) = E_1 \textbf{ in } E_2 \textbf{ end}]\!]\,\rho\,\sigma =$
```
  let
```
$\qquad f\,\sigma'\,n = \mathcal{M}[\![E_1]\!]\,\rho[I_2 \mapsto n]\,\sigma'$
```
  in
```
$\qquad \mathcal{M}[\![E_2]\!]\,\rho[I_1 \mapsto f]\,\sigma$
```
  end
```

$\mathcal{M}[\![\textbf{call } I(E)]\!]\,\rho\,\sigma =$
```
  let
```
$\qquad \langle n, \sigma' \rangle = \mathcal{M}[\![E]\!]\,\rho\,\sigma$
$\qquad f = \rho(I)$
```
  in
```
$\qquad f\,\sigma'\,n$
```
  end
```

Figure 8.4: Semantics of a language with subprocedures

semantic functions

$$\mathcal{L} : \textbf{Lexp} \rightarrow \textbf{Env} \rightarrow \textbf{States} \rightarrow \textbf{Loc}$$
$$\mathcal{M} : \textbf{Exp} \rightarrow \textbf{Env} \rightarrow \textbf{States} \rightarrow \textbf{Int} \times \textbf{States}$$
$$\mathcal{P} : \textbf{Prog} \rightarrow \textbf{Int} \rightarrow \textbf{Int}$$

Figure 8.4 shows the cases of the semantic functions for the new constructs in the language, namely, function definition and function call. As this language is strictly an extension of the previous one, the other cases of $\mathcal{M}$ and, indeed, the function $\mathcal{L}$ and $\mathcal{P}$ remain the same.

Some important checking has (as usual) been omitted. The following program fragment is presumably illegal because z is an integer variable, not a function.

$$\textbf{new } z := \textbf{function } g(x) = x + 1 \textbf{ in call } g(0) \textbf{ end in call } z(1) \textbf{ end}$$

A more thorough definition would resolve this. The definition we gave is satisfactory for "ordinary" expressions like E:

$$\textbf{function } g(x) = x + 1 \textbf{ in call } g(0); \textbf{ call } g(1 + 1) \textbf{ end}$$

Using the definition of $\mathcal{M}$ yields:

$$\mathcal{M}[\![E]\!]\,\rho\,\sigma \quad = \quad \mathcal{M}[\![\textbf{call } g(0); \textbf{ call } g(1 + 1)]\!]\,\rho[g \mapsto f]\,\sigma$$

where $f\sigma'n = \mathcal{M}[\![x+1]\!]\,\rho[x \mapsto n]\,\sigma'$.

$$
\begin{aligned}
\mathcal{M}[\![E]\!]\,\rho\,\sigma &= \mathcal{M}[\![\mathbf{call}\ g(0);\ \mathbf{call}\ g(1+1)]\!]\,\rho[g \mapsto f]\,\sigma \qquad f\sigma'n = \langle n+1, \sigma'\rangle \\
&= \mathcal{M}[\![\mathbf{call}\ g(1+1)]\!]\,\rho[g \mapsto f]\,\sigma \\
&= f\,\sigma\,(\mathcal{M}[\![1+1]\!]\,\rho[g \mapsto f]\,\sigma) \\
&= f\,\sigma\,2 \\
&= \langle 3, \sigma\rangle
\end{aligned}
$$

Thus the meaning of E is a function returning the integer 3 and leaving the given state alone. The call $g(0)$ has no effect.

8.12 Language with goto

The final language we examine in this chapter is a language with a goto statement. We add this construction in the simple setting where commands are completely separate from expressions. Thus we can focus on commands again and ignore expressions.

The new technique used to model the goto statement is called a *continuation*. A continuation encapsulates the entire rest of the computation. Since we have been viewing programs as functions from integers to integers **Prog** $\rightarrow$ **Int** $\rightarrow$ **Int**, the "rest of the computation" is a function returning an integer.

We use the same syntactic categories as in section 8.9.

syntactic categories

$I \in \mathbf{Ident}$	identifiers
$L \in \mathbf{Lexp}$	l-expressions or references
$E \in \mathbf{Exp}$	expressions
$C \in \mathbf{Com}$	commands
$P \in \mathbf{Prog}$	programs

The BNF description of the language contains three new command constructs including **goto** I.

$$
\begin{aligned}
L \ &::= \ I \\
E \ &::= \ 0 \mid 1 \mid I \mid !L \mid (E_1 + E_2) \mid \mathbf{if}\ E_1\ \mathbf{then}\ E_2\ \mathbf{else}\ E_3 \mid \\
&\qquad \mathbf{let}\ I = E_1\ \mathbf{in}\ E_2\ \mathbf{end} \\
C \ &::= \ C_1;\ C_2 \mid \mathbf{if}\ E\ \mathbf{then}\ C_1\ \mathbf{else}\ C_2 \mid L := E \mid \mathbf{new}\ I := E\ \mathbf{in}\ C\ \mathbf{end} \mid \\
&\qquad \mathbf{skip} \mid \mathbf{goto}\ I \mid I : C \\
M \ &::= \ \mathbf{program}\ (I);\ C\ \mathbf{end}.
\end{aligned}
$$

The meaning of these new constructs will be given by the definition of $\mathcal{C}$ to follow.

To handle the unstructured jumping we required some new value domains. The most prominent of these is command continuations **CC**. A label I in the program will denote the rest of the computation from that point forward to the end of the program—a command continuation. So **CC** is added to the range of environments. An identifier can denote an integer, a location, or a continuation.

value domains

$n \in$ **Int** $= \{\dots, -2, -1, 0, 1, 2, \dots\}$	integers
$\alpha \in$ **Loc**	locations
$\sigma \in$ **States** $=$ **Loc** $\to$ (**Int** $+$ *unused*)	states
$\theta \in$ **CC** $=$ **States** $\to$ **Int**	command continuations
$\rho \in$ **Env** $=$ **Ident** $\to$ (**Int**+**Loc**+**CC**+*undefined*)	environments

A command is no longer denoted by a simple state transformation, but rather a function that gives the whole rest of the computation.

semantic functions

$$\mathcal{L} : \textbf{Lexp} \to \textbf{Env} \to \textbf{States} \to \textbf{Loc}$$
$$\mathcal{E} : \textbf{Exp} \to \textbf{Env} \to \textbf{States} \to \textbf{Int}$$
$$\mathcal{C} : \textbf{Com} \to \textbf{Env} \to \textbf{CC} \to \textbf{States} \to \textbf{Int}$$
$$\mathcal{P} : \textbf{Prog} \to \textbf{Int} \to \textbf{Int}$$

Having each command denote the whole rest of the computation has its drawbacks. Gone is the property that each command denotes its own local effect in the total chain of state transformation. This is the motivation for calling denotational semantics without continuations *direct*.

The semantics of expressions stay the same as in section 8.9. If desired, it is possible to introduce expression continuations in much that same way as we are now introducing command continuations.

To get the feel for continuations we start by looking at the skip statement—a command that does nothing.

$$\mathcal{C}[\![\text{skip}]\!] \, \rho \, \theta \, \sigma = \theta(\sigma)$$

The continuation θ encapsulates what to do after the command is finished. Since the command does nothing we use θ to compute the final result.

All the "normal" commands act similarly. They compute their effect on the state and apply the given continuation to compute the final result. For example, the assignment statement updates the state in the familiar manner and applies the continuation to it.

$$\mathcal{C}[\![L := E]\!] \, \rho \, \theta \, \sigma =$$
```
let
      α = 𝓛⟦L⟧ ρ σ;     n = 𝓔⟦E⟧ ρ σ
   in
      θ(σ[α ↦ n])
end
```

The **if** statement chooses which branch gets the current continuation.

$\mathcal{C}[\![\textbf{if } E \textbf{ then } C_1 \textbf{ else } C_2]\!]\, \rho\, \theta\, \sigma =$
   if $(\mathcal{E}[\![E]\!]\, \rho\, \sigma = 0)$ then $\mathcal{C}[\![C_1]\!]\, \rho\, \theta\, \sigma$ else $\mathcal{C}[\![C_2]\!]\, \rho\, \theta\, \sigma$

The sequencing construct requires the addition of C_2 to the continuation θ and then giving the resulting continuation to C_1.

$\mathcal{C}[\![C_1;\ C_2]\!]\, \rho\, \theta\, \sigma =$
   let
       fun $\theta'(\sigma') = \mathcal{C}[\![C_2]\!]\, \rho\, \theta\, \sigma'$
   in
      $\mathcal{C}[\![C_1]\!]\, \rho\, \theta'\, \sigma$
   end

Here is the case for the **new** construct:

$\mathcal{C}[\![\textbf{new } I := E \textbf{ in } C \textbf{ end}]\!]\, \rho\, \theta\, \sigma =$
   let
      α be some Loc such that $\sigma(\alpha) = unused$
      $n = \mathcal{E}[\![E]\!]\, \rho\, \sigma$
   in
      $\mathcal{C}[\![C]\!]\, \rho[I \mapsto \alpha]\, \theta\, \sigma[\alpha \mapsto n]$
   end

     The key case in the definition is for $I : C$. The label I is associated with the command C. This means that any **goto** I appearing within C (remember C could be a sequence of commands) causes a jump to the beginning of C. The scope of the label I is entirely inside C. This is actually a severe restriction when considering the way the goto statement is generally used. But it is necessary here to gain some locality of structure. Less severe restrictions can be modeled, but the definitions become correspondingly more complex. To realize a continuation representing I requires that the continuation for $I : C$ be the same as the continuation for any command **goto** I within C. This is accomplished with a recursive function definition.

$\mathcal{C}[\![I : C]\!]\, \rho\, \theta\, \sigma =$
   let fun $\theta'(\sigma') = \mathcal{C}[\![C]\!]\rho[I \mapsto \theta']\, \theta\, \sigma'$ in $\theta'(\sigma)$ end

We would expect that recursion would play a role somehow because any form of interation could be implemented with the goto construct.

     The definition of **goto** I is simple. We ignore the current continuation θ and go to the continuation denoted by I instead.

$\mathcal{C}[\![\textbf{goto } I]\!]\, \rho\, \theta\, \sigma = (\rho\, I)\, \sigma$

As usual we are making assumptions. In this case we assume that $(\rho\, I)$ is a continuation as opposed to an integer, a location, or *undefined*.

In this language we can write a nonterminating program quite easily. Consider, for example, the statement I : **goto** I. What is its meaning in the formal semantics just given?

$$\mathcal{C}[\![I : \textbf{goto } I]\!]\, \rho\, \theta\, \sigma = \theta'(\sigma)$$

where the function θ' is given by:

$$
\begin{aligned}
\theta'(\sigma) &= \mathcal{C}[\![\textbf{goto } I]\!](\rho[I \mapsto \theta'])\, \theta\, (\sigma) \\
&= \rho[I \mapsto \theta']\, I\, \sigma \\
&= \theta'(\sigma)
\end{aligned}
$$

The conclusion is that θ' represents a continuation that does not terminate.

The semantics of the program construct is given by $\mathcal{P}$. As usual it provides the initial environment and state, but here it must also provide the top-level continuation. This continuation merely returns the contents of the location α associated with the input variable I.

$\mathcal{P}[\![\textbf{program } (I);\, C \textbf{ end.}]\!]\, n =$
    let
        fun $\rho(J) = undefined$
        fun $\sigma(\alpha) = unused$
        α be some Loc such that $\sigma(\alpha) = unused$
        fun $\theta(\sigma) = \sigma(\alpha)$
    in
        $\mathcal{C}[\![C]\!]\rho[I \mapsto \alpha]\, \theta\, \sigma[\alpha \mapsto n]$
    end

8.13   Exercises

8.1   Consider the language of regular expressions given in section 8.4. What does $\emptyset^*$ denote?

8.2   Consider the language of regular expressions given in section 8.4. Let the alphabet be the set $\{a, b\}$. Prove that the language denoted by the regular expression $(b^* + (a \cdot b^*))$ is the same language as the one denoted by $((\emptyset^* + a) \cdot b^*)$.

8.3   Consider the language of propositional formulas given in section 8.5. Prove that the following formulas are tautologies by showing that their denotations are constant functions returning $True$.

    (a) $(\neg P \Rightarrow P) \Rightarrow P$
    (b) $P \Rightarrow (Q \Rightarrow P)$

(c) $(P \Rightarrow (Q \Rightarrow R)) \Rightarrow ((P \Rightarrow Q) \Rightarrow (P \Rightarrow R))$

(d) $P \Rightarrow (\neg P \Rightarrow Q)$

(e) $(P \Rightarrow Q) \Rightarrow ((Q \Rightarrow R) \Rightarrow (P \Rightarrow R))$

8.4 Extend the language of propositional formulas (section 8.5) to the language of first-order predicate logic with equality:

$$
\begin{aligned}
E &\;::=\; 0 \mid 1 \mid I \mid (E + E)\\
F &\;::=\; E = E \mid \neg F \mid F \Rightarrow F \mid \forall I\,.\,F \mid \exists I\,.\,F
\end{aligned}
$$

Give the usual formal semantics for this language.

8.5 Using the approach of denotational semantics give a meaning function $\mathcal{M}$ to the language in the attribute grammar presented in exercise 2.15. Define $\mathcal{M}$ such that $\mathcal{M}[\![S]\!] = S.m$ where S is the start symbol of the attribute grammar and m is the real-value attribute of S.

8.6 Consider the simple **let** language of section 8.6. Given the definition of $\mathcal{E}$ in that section what functions do the following programs denote?

(a) x

(b) $x - y$

(c) **let** $x = 1$ **in** x **end**

(d) $x +$ **let** $x = 1$ **in** x **end**

8.7 Consider the simple **let** language of section 8.6. Prove that $\mathcal{E}[\![E]\!]$ is a constant function if E has no free variables.

8.8 Consider the simple **let** language of section 8.6. Answer the following questions.

(a) What does the program **let** $x = (x + 1)$ **in** x **end** denote?

(b) Give the denotational semantics of a *recursive* **let** construct of the form **let rec** $I = E_1$ **in** E_2 **end**. In this construct any occurrence I in E_1 is not undefined, but is to have the same value that is given to E_1 as a whole.

(c) What does the program **let rec** $x = (x + 1)$ **in** 0 **end** denote?

(d) What does the program **let rec** $x = (x + 1)$ **in** x **end** denote?

8.9 Consider the simple **let** language with error values. Given the definition of $\mathcal{E}$ and $\mathcal{P}$ in figure 8.2, what functions do the following expressions and programs denote?

(a) x

    (b) $x/1$

    (c) **program** (x); x **end.**

    (d) **program** (x); y **end.**

8.10 In the simple language of commands (section 8.9) extend the syntax of references to also include arrays. Make the necessary modifications to the semantic functions.

8.11 In the simple language of commands (section 8.9) extend the syntax of references to also include conditionals as in (if x>2 then i else j) := 3. Make the necessary modifications to the semantic functions.

8.12 In the simple language of commands (section 8.9) what modifications to the value domain of environments are necessary to accommodate a language in which an identifier can denote *both* values and locations?

8.13 Make the modifications necessary to be able to define a location allocating function for the language of section 8.9.

8.14 Make the modifications necessary to accommodate side effects in the evaluation of l-values in the language of section 8.10.

8.15 Consider a simple expression language with exception handling based roughly on ML.

$$E \quad ::= \quad 0 \mid 1 \mid I \mid (E_1 + E_2) \mid \textbf{let } I = E_1 \textbf{ in } E_2 \textbf{ end} \mid$$
$$\textbf{exception } I \textbf{ in } E \textbf{ end} \mid \textbf{raise } I \mid E_1 \textbf{ handle } I \texttt{ => } E_2$$

Give a complete denotational semantics for this language.

8.16 Give a denotational semantics for a language that has a syntactic category for declarations with the following syntax.

$$D \quad ::= \quad \textbf{const } I = E \mid \textbf{var } I := E \mid \textbf{fun } I_1 \, (\, I_2 \,) = E$$

The **let** and **new** construct are no longer needed. Instead we add a general block construct with a declarations section.

$$C \quad ::= \quad \dots \mid \textbf{decl } D \textbf{ in } C$$

8.17 Rewrite the following Ada-like program into the language of section 8.11. What function does it denote?

```
program Main (in out n) is
    function f (x) is
    begin
        return (x+1);
    end f;
begin
    n := f (1);
end
```

8.18 Suppose we extend the language with functions of section 8.11 in the obvious way to include multiplication and subtraction. Consider the following program written in this language:

program (n);
    function $f(x) = $ **if** n **then** 1 **else** $n \times$**call** $f(x-1)$ **in** $n := $**call** $f(!x)$ **end**
end.

(a) Why doesn't this program compute the factorial function? Be very specific; refer to the relevant cases of the semantic functions.

(b) Fix the problem by modifying the definitions of the semantic functions necessary to extend the programming language to deal with this case.

8.19 Rewrite the following Ada-like program into the language of section 8.11. What function does it denote in the semantics of the previous exercise?

```
program Main (in out n) is
    function f (x) is
        function g (y) is begin return x; end g;
    begin
        if x=0 then
            return (g (0));
        else
            return (f (x-1));
        end;
    end f;
begin
    n := f (2);
end
```

8.20 Consider a simple command language with variable references.

$$L \quad ::= \quad I$$
$$E \quad ::= \quad 0 \mid 1 \mid I \mid !L$$

$$C \quad ::= \quad C_1; C_2 \mid L := E \mid \textbf{new } I := E \textbf{ in } C \textbf{ end}$$
$$M \quad ::= \quad \textbf{program } (I); C \textbf{ end}.$$

Give a complete denotational semantics for this language similar to the semantics given in section 8.9, but define precisely a scheme for the allocation of locations. This scheme should attempt to capture the usual stack allocation of local variables.

What is the meaning of the following program in your semantics:

> **program** (z); **new** $x := 0$ **in** C **end**; **new** $y := 1$ **in** $z := !x$ **end end**.

8.21 Please study the following definition of a PROLOG-like language, PPP (Purdue Propositional PROLOG). Then answer the questions.

There are four syntactic categories in PPP.

syntactic categories

$I \in \textbf{Ident}$	identifiers
$D \in \textbf{Decl}$	assertions
$C \in \textbf{Clause}$	clauses
$P \in \textbf{Prog}$	programs

The abstract syntax of PPP is given by the following BNF grammar. Parentheses will be used wherever necessary to clarify how programs are to be parsed.

$$C \quad ::= \quad I \mid \textbf{succ} \mid \textbf{fail} \mid \textbf{cut} \mid C, C \mid C \textbf{ or } C$$
$$D \quad ::= \quad I :\text{-} C \ . \mid DD$$
$$P \quad ::= \quad DC?$$

The semantics of PPP requires the following value domains.

value domains

$a \in \textbf{Ans} = \{Yes, No\}$	answers
$fc \in \textbf{FailCont} = \textbf{Ans}$	fail continuations
$sc \in \textbf{SuccCont} = \textbf{FailCont} \rightarrow \textbf{Ans}$	success continuations
$\sigma \in \textbf{Strat} = \textbf{SuccCont} \rightarrow \textbf{FailCont} \rightarrow \textbf{Ans}$	strategies
$\rho \in \textbf{Env} = \textbf{Ident} \rightarrow \textbf{Strat}$	environments

We now define the three semantic functions $\mathcal{C}$, $\mathcal{D}$, and $\mathcal{P}$. Their types are as follows:

$$\underline{\text{semantic functions}}$$

$$\mathcal{C} : \textbf{Clause} \to \textbf{Env} \to \textbf{Strat}$$
$$\mathcal{D} : \textbf{Decl} \to \textbf{Env} \to \textbf{Env}$$
$$\mathcal{P} : \textbf{Prog} \to \textbf{Ans}$$

The definition of the three semantics functions is by cases.

$$\mathcal{C}[\![I]\!]\rho \;=\; (\rho\,I)$$
$$\mathcal{C}[\![\textbf{succ}]\!]\rho\,sc\,fc \;=\; sc\,fc$$
$$\mathcal{C}[\![\textbf{cut}]\!]\rho\,sc\,fc \;=\; sc\,No$$
$$\mathcal{C}[\![\textbf{fail}]\!]\rho\,sc\,fc \;=\; fc$$
$$\mathcal{C}[\![C_1,C_2]\!]\rho\,sc \;=\; (\mathcal{C}[\![C_1]\!]\rho)\,(\mathcal{C}[\![C_2]\!]\rho\,sc)$$
$$\mathcal{C}[\![C_1 \textbf{ or } C_2]\!]\rho\,sc\,fc \;=\; (\mathcal{C}[\![C_1]\!]\rho)\,sc\,(\mathcal{C}[\![C_2]\!]\rho\,sc\,fc)$$

Declarations are functions from **Env** to **Env**.

$$\mathcal{D}[\![I\text{:-}C]\!]\rho \;=\; \rho[I \mapsto \mathcal{C}[\![C]\!]\rho]$$
$$\mathcal{D}[\![D_1 D_2]\!]\rho \;=\; (\mathcal{D}[\![D_2]\!])(\mathcal{D}[\![D_1]\!]\rho)$$

where $\rho[I \mapsto \sigma]$ denotes the updated environment formed by modifying ρ at I to have the strategy σ.

$$\mathcal{P}[\![DC?]\!] = (\mathcal{C}[\![C]\!])(\mathcal{D}[\![D]\!]\rho_0)(\lambda fc.\,Yes)No$$

where the initial environment ρ_0 is $\lambda\,J\,.\,\lambda\,sc\,.\,\lambda\,fc\,.\,fc$.

(a) What does the PPP program *A:-B. B:-**succ**. A?* denote? What does the PPP program *B:-**succ**. A:-B. A?* denote?

(b) How would you rewrite the following simple PROLOG program in PPP?

```
A.    /*  Assert nullary predicate A is true.   */
A?    /*  Query if nullary predicate A is true. */
```

How would you rewrite the following simple PROLOG program in PPP?

```
A :- B.   /* Nullary predicate A is true, if B is true. */
A :- C.
A?
```

(c) What do the following PPP programs do? Explain.

$$C\text{:-}\textbf{fail}.\ B\text{:-}\textbf{succ}.\ A\text{:-}C, \textbf{cut}, B.\ A?$$
$$Z\text{:-}\textbf{fail}.\ (\textbf{cut}, \textbf{fail}) \textbf{ or succ}?$$
$$Z\text{:-}\textbf{fail}.\ (\textbf{fail}, \textbf{cut}) \textbf{ or succ}?$$

(d) What does the program A:-**succ.** A:-**fail.** A? do? Explain.

(e) What does the program A:-A. A? do? How does this compare to PRO-LOG?

8.22 Give a denotational semantics to the following language.

$$D \quad ::= \quad \textbf{let } I = E \mid \textbf{function } I_1(I_2) = E \mid D_1; D_2$$

$$E \quad ::= \quad 0 \mid 1 \mid I \mid (E_1 + E_2) \mid \textbf{call } I(E) \mid D; E$$

The keyword **function** introduces a (nonrecursive) function definition.

8.23 Extend the language given in the previous part of this question to include the following constructs:

$$D \quad ::= \quad \textbf{class } I(D)$$

$$E \quad ::= \quad E\texttt{<-}I$$

where the **class** construct defines an object as in Smalltalk or C++. The other construct sends the "message" I to an object. Extend the denotational definition you gave in the previous part to include the new construct.

8.14   Bibliography

[1] Barwise, Jon. "Mathematical proofs of computer system correctness." *Notices of the American Mathematical Society*, September 1989, pages 844–851.

[2] DeMillo, Richard A., Richard J. Lipton, and Alan J. Perlis. "Social processes and proofs of theorems and programs." *Communications of the ACM*, volume 22, number 5, May 1979, pages 271–280.

[3] Dijkstra, Edsger Wybe. "On a political pamphlet from the middle ages (Commentary on a paper by DeMillo, Lipton, and Perlis)." *Software Engineering Notes*, volume 3, number 2, April 1978, pages 14–17.

[4] Fetzer, James H. "Program verification: The very idea." *Communications of the ACM*, volume 31, number 9, September 1988, pages 1048–1063.

[5] Gehani, Narain, and Andrew D. McGettrick, editors. *Software Specification Techniques*. International Computer Science Series. Addison-Wesley, Wokingham, England, 1986.

[6] Goguen, Joseph A., J. W. Thatcher, and E. G. Wagner. "An initial algebra approach to the specification, correctness, and implementation of abstract data types." In *Data Structuring*, edited by Raymond Tzuu Yeh, Prentice Hall, Englewood Cliffs, New Jersey, 1978, pages 80–149.

[7] Gunter, Carl A. *Semantics of Programming Languages: Structures and Techniques.* MIT Press, Cambridge, Massachusetts, 1992.

[8] Hamming, Richard W. "The unreasonable effectiveness of mathematics." *American Mathematical Monthly*, February 1980, pages 81–90.

[9] Marcotty, Michael, Henry F. Ledgard, and Gregor V. Bochmann. "A sampler of formal definitions." *Computing Surveys*, volume 8, number 2, June 1976, pages 191–276.

[10] Hennessy, Matthew. *The Semantics of Programming Languages: An Elementary Introduction Using Structural Operational Semantics.* Wiley, Chichester, 1990.

[11] Pagan, Frank G. *Formal Specification of Programming Languages: A Panoramic Primer.* Prentice Hall, Englewood Cliffs, New Jersey, 1981.

[12] Paulson, Lawrence C. "Compiler generation from denotational semantics." In *Methods and Tools for Compiler Construction*, edited by Bernard Lorho, Cambridge University Press, Cambridge, 1984, pages 219–250.

[13] Schmidt, David A. *Denotational Semantics: A Methodology for Language Development.* Allyn and Bacon, Boston, 1986.

[14] Stoy, Joseph E. *Denotational Semantics: The Scott-Strachey Approach to Programming Language Theory.* MIT Press, Cambridge, Massachusetts, 1977.

[15] Thomas, Peter G., Hugh Robinson, and Judy Emms. *Abstract Data Types.* Oxford applied mathematics and computing science series. Oxford University Press, Oxford, 1988.

[16] Watt, David Anthony. "Executable semantic descriptions." *Software–Practice and Experience*, volume 16, number 1, January 1986, pages 13–43.

Chapter 9

Axiomatic approach of Hoare

Imperative programs are difficult to understand and to reason about. Further insights into the nature of imperative programs and programming can be won by formalizing the mathematical properties of programs. In the denotational method we approach this problem obliquely by viewing programs as denoting formal, mathematical objects. Presumably, we can reason about these objects using the usual mathematical machinery. In this chapter we approach the problem of proving that programs do something desired or useful more directly. We give a Post system for deriving programs that meet a specification. The rules of the Post system are the axioms of the language; i.e., they are the fundamental facts defining the language, and no other properties about the language can be assumed except those derivable from these rules.

9.1 State

The axiomatic approach defines each language construct in terms of a statement about what the construct accomplishes when executed. Accomplishment will be gauged by describing the state of the computation before and after the execution of the construct. A simple notion of a state will suffice for our purposes. We will view the memory of the computer as a collection of cells, each uniquely labeled. The contents of the labeled cells is the *state*. We can view the state as a function from names to values. We will consider only integer values. This is the same view of state that we adopted in the denotational approach to commands in section 8.8.

9.1.1   Logic as a specification language

To describe sets of states we need a specification language. An ingenious way of specifying states takes advantage of the fact that an assignment in logic is just like a snapshot of memory: they are both functions from labels to values.

We begin by constructing the language of first-order predicate logic with equality in the usual way. We include a few simple function symbols and predicate symbols for convenience in expressing the usual sort of arithmetic calculations. The language consists of terms denoting integers and formulas. The following clauses outline the basic syntax we will use.

- Terms.

    1. If x is a variable, then x is a term.

    2. If n is an integer constant, then n is a term.

    3. If t_1 and t_2 are terms, then $t_1 + t_2$ and $t_1 * t_2$ are terms.

- Formulas.

    1. *True* and *False* are formulas.

    2. If t_1 and t_2 are terms, then $t_1 = t_2$ and $t_1 < t_2$ are formulas.

    3. If ϕ and ψ are formulas, then $\phi \,\&\, \psi$, $\phi \vee \psi$, $\neg\phi$, and $\phi \Rightarrow \psi$ are formulas.

    4. If $\phi(x)$ is a formula possibly containing the variable x free, then $\forall x.\phi(x)$ and $\exists x.\phi(x)$ are formulas.

We freely add other function symbols and relational symbols to the specification language as long as the meaning is clear. Also, we use the usual conventions about precedence and parentheses. All these things are more trouble to completely formalize than it is worth.

If a formula is constructed without using the fourth clause above, it is said to be *quantifier-free*.

9.1.2   Characterization of states

A formula of first-order predicate logic can be used to characterize a set of states. We will make this characterization precise shortly, but the notion is intuitively quite compelling. For example, the formula $x = 3$ characterizes all those states in which the value of memory cell x is three. The values of the other cells are immaterial. Figure 9.1 depicts the situation. The set of all states Σ is represented as a large rectangle. The states characterized by $x = 3$ are depicted by the shaded oval. For example, the set in which the cell y has the value 2, cell x has the value 3, and the rest of the cells have value 0, is in the shaded oval. In figure 9.2 the shaded region corresponds to the set of states characterized by the formula $(x = 3 \Rightarrow y = 4)$. This formula is logically equivalent to $(x \neq 3 \vee y = 4)$. The region contains, for

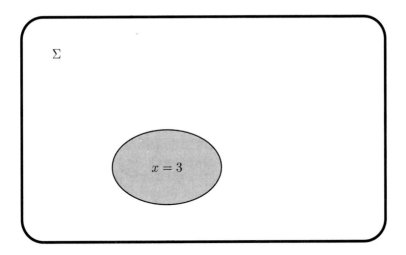

Figure 9.1: States characterized by the formula $x = 3$

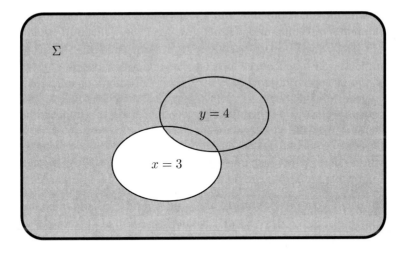

Figure 9.2: States characterized by the formula $(x = 3 \Rightarrow y = 4)$

example, the state in which the cell x has value 3, the cell y has value 4, and the rest of the cells have value 0. It also contains $x = 5$, $y = 6$ regardless of the rest of the contents. It does not contain $x = 3$, $y = 6$ regardless of the rest of the contents.

In using formulas to characterize states there is a vast difference between free and bound variables. Formulas with free variables, like the formula $x = 3$, have an intuitive reading, like

the states in which the cell x has the contents 3.

But formulas with bound variables, like the formula $\exists x.x = 3$, can be misleading. The names of bound variables are not relevant. The formula $\exists x.x = 3$ is the same as $\exists y.y = 3$. Thus the name of a bound variable is not significant and does not have any relation to the "labels" for the cells in memory. The formula $\exists z.z = 3$ does *not* mean that some cell has contents 3. Rather it asserts that some *value* is equal to 3. Quantification ranges over the set of possible values, not labels. Hence $\exists z.z = 3$ is equivalent to $3 = 3$, or any other true formula. As such, it characterizes all states. More generally, formulas without free variables are either true or false, and hence characterize all the states or none of the states.

More formally, we define the set of states characterized by the formula ϕ to be the set $\{\sigma \in \Sigma \mid \sigma \models \phi\}$, where "$\models$" is the relation that the state σ satisfies the formula ϕ. This relation is the basic semantic definition of first-order predicate logic. The definition of the relation goes as follows. We define the *value of a term* in state σ, denoted t^σ, to be $\sigma(x)$, if t is the variable x, and $n^\sigma = n$ for integer constants. The state σ is said to satisfy the formula $t_1 = t_2$, if $t_1{}^\sigma = t_2{}^\sigma$. The state σ is said to satisfy the formula $\phi \,\&\, \psi$, if $\sigma \models \phi$ and $\sigma \models \psi$. The definition for the other logical connectives is similar. For the universal quantifier we define:

$$\sigma \models \forall x.\phi(x) \quad \text{iff} \quad \sigma[x \mapsto n] \models \phi(n) \quad \text{for every integer } n$$

The definition of $\sigma \models \exists x.\phi(x)$ is similar.

9.2   Partial correctness

Ordinary programming languages and the language of first-order predicate logic share some common parts. This overlap makes it possible to connect the execution of the programming language constructs with a specification expressed in logic. Statements and expressions of programming languages contain terms, formulas, and variables. For example, the test in a conditional statement is a formula. And the assignment statement assigns the value of a term to a variable. In this section we introduce a new construct, the Hoare triple, for a particular, simple imperative language.

The execution of a construct S in a programming language can be described by the state obtained by executing a program segment starting in some other state. This suggests that we consider triples $\{P\}\, S\, \{Q\}$, where P and Q are formulas and S is a piece of code. Constructs of this form are called Hoare triples. A Hoare triple is an assertion of fact. As assertions, Hoare triples can be true or false. We say the triple $\{P\}\, S\, \{Q\}$ is *valid* if execution of the program segment S is begun in any state satisfying P, and if S terminates, then it terminates in a state satisfying Q.

Some examples of valid Hoare triples are:

$$\{\, 2 = 2 \,\}\; x\; :=\; 2\; \{\, x = 2 \,\}$$

$$\{\, \textit{True} \,\}\; \texttt{if}\; B\; \texttt{then}\; x\texttt{:=2}\; \texttt{else}\; x\texttt{:=1}\; \{\, x = 1 \lor x = 2 \,\}$$

In the first of these, the knowledge of the usual semantics for assignment assures that after executing $x\texttt{:=2}$ the resulting state satisfies $x = 2$. In the second, regardless of the boolean condition B, both of the assignments establish the postcondition. Some examples of invalid Hoare triples are:

$$\{\, 2 = 2 \,\}\; x\; :=\; 2\; \{\, y = 1 \,\}$$

$$\{\, \textit{True} \,\}\; \texttt{if}\; B\; \texttt{then}\; x\texttt{:=2}\; \texttt{else}\; x\texttt{:=1}\; \{\, x = 1 \;\&\; x = 2 \,\}$$

In the first case, if the execution of the program begins in a state in which y is not equal to one, then the resulting state will also fail to satisfy $y = 1$. In the second example, no program can establish *both* $x = 1$ and $x = 2$ for the same state.

Hoare triples are especially useful in proving programs correct because proof systems exist for deriving valid Hoare triples. (We give one in the next section.) A "correct" program is one that meets its specification. Sometimes, instead of saying the Hoare triple $\{\,P\,\}\; S\; \{\,Q\,\}$ is valid, we say that the program segment S is *partially correct* with respect to the precondition P and the postcondition Q. We say *partially* correct because we assume that the program terminates. Knowing that a Hoare triple is valid guarantees that the postcondition is established, *if* the program terminates. No assurances are given that the program does indeed terminate. This is not wholly satisfactory and leads to some counterintuitive behavior. A total-correctness semantics, where termination is assured instead of assumed, is possible. But a total correctness logic is more complex.

Partial correctness is a useful description of the behavior of a program. Suppose that we know that the following Hoare triple is valid:

$$\{\, 0 \le a \;\&\; 0 \le b \,\}\; S\; \{\, z = a * b \,\}$$

This means that if we execute the program segment S beginning in a state such that $0 \le a$ and $0 \le b$, and if the program terminates, then the program segment S establishes that $z = a * b$. We know that S causes z to be equal to the product of a times b, even when this was not the case beforehand. The program is in some sense correct. (If, indeed, we intended S to set z equal to the product.) But formal correctness can be subtle. If the program segment S is $\texttt{z:=0; a:=0}$, we can prove the formal correctness of S with respect to the assertion $z = a * b$, but S does not perform any multiplication!

There are no theoretical limits to the axiomatic approach for formally verifying software. The specification and program segment of a Hoare triple could be of great complexity. An axiomatic definition exists for the programming language Pascal [8]. One could imagine using it to specify the correctness of a compiler:

{ *Legal-input(p)* } *Compiler* { *Assembly-code(q)* & *Semantically-equivalent(p, q)* }

But, in practice, proofs tend to be of small programs, due to the complexity of proofs and since axiomatizations tend to be for small "toy" languages.

We consider one such simple language, the language of `while` programs described by the following BNF definition:

$$
\begin{aligned}
W &\ ::=\ V\ :=\ T \\
W &\ ::=\ \texttt{if}\ B\ \texttt{then}\ W\ \texttt{else}\ W \\
W &\ ::=\ \texttt{while}\ B\ \texttt{do}\ W\ \texttt{end} \\
W &\ ::=\ W\ ;\ W
\end{aligned}
$$

It is important that this language has some parts in common with the specification language. The nonterminal V stands for any of the variables in the specification language. The expressions of this `while` language, T, are any terms from the language of first-order predicate logic. And we take B to be from the set of quantifier-free formulas of the specification language, since these formulas most closely resemble conditional expressions in programming languages.

9.3   Proof system

In this section we give a Post system for deriving true Hoare triples about `while` programs. Each construct of the language has a rule. The rule constitutes the definition of the construct.

The first rule is for the assignment statement. This rule is an axiom, or, more precisely, an axiom scheme. The rule can be applied without any previous proof steps.

$$\overline{\ \{\,Q[V := T\,]\,\}\ V\ :=\ T\ \{\,Q\,\}\ } \qquad \text{(assignment rule)}$$

This rule contains three meta-variables,[1] which must be instantiated to obtain an instance of the rule. These meta-variables are Q, which stands for any formula, T, which stands for any term, and V, which stands for any variable (of the `while` language). This rule also uses the notation $Q[V := T]$ to mean the formula obtained by substituting T for V in Q. We use substitution freely on expressions and formulas trusting that definition is clear as it is analogous to the one given in section 7.1.2.

---

[1] In the context of Post systems as defined earlier, section 2.4.1, we called these parts of a Post rule variables. But in this context we call them meta-variables to distinguish them from the variables of the object language.

We now look at a couple of uses of the assignment rule. If we take Q to be $x = 2$, T to be 2, and V to be x, we get the following instance of the assignment rule:

$$\overline{\{\, 2 = 2 \,\} \; x \; := \; 2 \; \{\, x = 2 \,\}}$$

since $x = 2[x := 2]$ is just another way of writing $2 = 2$. The Hoare triple beneath the horizontal line is valid. Now consider the case where T is $x + 1$. Then the following valid Hoare triple is derivable from the assignment axiom: $\{\, x + 1 = 2 \,\} \; x \; := \; x + 1 \; \{\, x = 2 \,\}$.

At first glance the rule for assignment appears to be backward. There is no correct direction in a Hoare triple: it is valid or it is not; there is no direction involved. The mechanics of the rule imply that one picks the postcondition Q and from this choice the precondition is determined, namely, $Q[x := e]$. This "flow" from postcondition to precondition has been formalized by Dijkstra [4] and Gries [6] into a weakest precondition calculus. The weakest or most useful precondition of the assignment $V := T$ and the arbitrary postcondition Q (written $WP(V := T, Q)$ is the condition $Q[V := T]$. It is possible to describe the most useful or strongest postcondition in terms of the precondition for the assignment statement, but this is harder. (See exercise 9.12.) This flow from precondition to postcondition is formalized in the strongest postcondition calculus.

The remaining three constructs of the `while` language each have a rule.

$$\frac{\{\, B \,\&\, P \,\} \, S_1 \, \{\, Q \,\} \quad \{\, \neg B \,\&\, P \,\} \, S_2 \, \{\, Q \,\}}{\{\, P \,\} \, \texttt{if} \; B \; \texttt{then} \; S_1 \; \texttt{else} \; S_2 \, \{\, Q \,\}} \qquad \text{(conditional rule)}$$

$$\frac{\{\, B \,\&\, I \,\} \, S \, \{\, I \,\}}{\{\, I \,\} \, \texttt{while} \; B \; \texttt{do} \; S \; \texttt{end} \, \{\, \neg B \,\&\, I \,\}} \qquad \text{(while rule)}$$

$$\frac{\{\, P \,\} \, S_1 \, \{\, Q \,\} \quad \{\, Q \,\} \, S_2 \, \{\, R \,\}}{\{\, P \,\} \, S_1; \; S_2 \, \{\, R \,\}} \qquad \text{(composition rule)}$$

The previous rules, one for each construct of the `while` language, define the meaning of the language constructs. The final rule, the rule of consequence, has a different character.

$$\frac{P' \Rightarrow P \quad \{\, P \,\} \, S \, \{\, Q \,\} \quad Q \Rightarrow Q'}{\{\, P' \,\} \, S \, \{\, Q' \,\}} \qquad \text{(rule of consequence)}$$

This rule injects information from outside Hoare logic. The judgments above the line are not all Hoare triples; two of them are formulas. This is an abuse of the Post system for deriving Hoare triples as it appears the rule is useless since we cannot derive formulas, but only Hoare triples. What we mean by the formulas above the line in the rule of consequence is that the rule is applicable *only if* the two formulas are tautologies. Notice that if P is syntactically equal to P' and Q is equal to Q', the formulas $P \Rightarrow P'$ and $Q \Rightarrow Q'$ are tautologies and the rule has no purport. In this case the rules says: if you can derive $\{P\} S \{Q\}$, then you can derive $\{P\} S \{Q\}$. The significance of the rule of consequence is that it permits less precise (but more focused) formulas as preconditions and postconditions. In addition, the rule can be used for arithmetic simplification as in $y = 1+1 \Rightarrow y = 2$.

We look at some theorems we can derive about proofs in this proof system.

Theorem 19 *All Hoare triples of the form $\{P\} S \{True\}$ are derivable.*

Proof. One can prove by induction on the structure of S that Hoare triples of the form $\{True\} S \{True\}$ are derivable. Then using the rule of consequence one derives immediately $\{P\} S \{True\}$. There are four cases in the induction.

- Assignment. Since $True[x := e]$ is syntactically equivalent to $True$, the Hoare triple $\{True\} x := e \{True\}$ is an instance of the assignment axiom.

- While. From the induction hypothesis we assume that $\{True\} S \{True\}$ is derivable. Then the following derivation is the one we want.

$$\frac{\dfrac{(B \& True) \Rightarrow True \quad \{True\} S \{True\}}{\{B \& True\} S \{True\}}}{\{True\} \text{ while } B \text{ do } S \text{ end} \{\neg B \& True\}} \quad (\neg B \& True) \Rightarrow True}{\{True\} \text{ while } B \text{ do } S \text{ end} \{True\}}$$

- Conditional. From the induction hypothesis we assume that the Hoare triples $\{True\} S_1 \{True\}$ and $\{True\} S_2 \{True\}$ are derivable. Then the following derivation is the one we want (where T stands for $True$).

$$\frac{\dfrac{(B \& T) \Rightarrow T \quad \{T\} S_1 \{T\}}{\{B \& T\} S_1 \{T\}} \quad \dfrac{(\neg B \& T) \Rightarrow T \quad \{T\} S_2 \{T\}}{\{\neg B \& T\} S_2 \{T\}}}{\{T\} \text{ if } B \text{ then } S_1 \text{ else } S_2 \{T\}}$$

- Composition. This case follows immediately from the induction hypothesis.

∎

So all the Hoare triples of the form $\{P\} S \{True\}$ are valid. This means that if you execute a program and it terminates, then it terminates. This is clearly tautologous, so the theorem is not surprising.

From $\{True\} S \{True\}$ one can derive:

$$\frac{\dfrac{(True \& True) \Rightarrow True \quad \{True\} S \{True\}}{\{True \& True\} S \{True\}}}{\{True\} \text{ while } True \text{ do } S \text{ end} \{\neg True \& True\}} \quad (\neg True \& True) \Rightarrow False}{\{True\} \text{ while } True \text{ do } S \{False\}}$$

By the rule of consequence, we can get:

$$\{P\} \texttt{ while } \textit{True} \texttt{ do } S \texttt{ end } \{Q\}$$

for any assertions P and Q. If the program does not terminate, then one can prove anything about the program whatsoever. This is a consequence of the fact that termination is in the antecedent of the implication that we took as the meaning of Hoare triples. This is not a particularly welcome consequence. We name this approach partial correctness because we ignore the issue of whether the program terminates at all. We could remove this hypothesis and formulate the notion of total correctness, but we will not pursue this further.

Furthermore, one can prove by induction that all Hoare triples of the form $\{$ *False* $\}$ S $\{$ *False* $\}$ are valid. Therefore, by the rule of consequence, the Hoare triple $\{$ *False* $\}$ S $\{Q\}$ holds for any assertion Q. (See exercise 9.16.)

Using denotational semantics to describe the state-transforming action of a statement in the language, it is possible to define partial correctness formally. We say that the Hoare triple $\{P\}$ S $\{Q\}$ is valid (or that the program segment S is partially correct with respect to precondition P and postcondition Q), if the following holds:

$$\sigma \models P \text{ and } S \text{ terminates} \quad \Rightarrow \quad M_S(\sigma) \models Q$$

for all states σ and where M_S is the state transformer for the program segment S.

With this formal definition it is possible to prove the following important fact about the Hoare calculus: only true Hoare triples can be derived and all true Hoare triples can be derived.

Theorem 20 (Cook) *The proof system for the* while *language is sound and complete.*

Proof. The original proof can be found in [3] or in other expositions [2, 10]. ∎

9.4 Example proof of correctness

An important use of Hoare logic is in proving the correctness of programs. In this section we prove a Hoare triple is derivable from the proof rules. The goal is to prove that the program

$$z := 0; \ n := y; \ \texttt{while } n > 0 \texttt{ do } z := z + x; \ n := n - 1 \texttt{ end}$$

computes the produce of x and y by repeated addition. This program works only if y is not negative, so we take $y \geq 0$ as the precondition.

We want to prove that the following Hoare triple is valid.

$\{y \geq 0\}$
$z := 0;\ \ n:=y;\ \texttt{while}\ n > 0\ \texttt{do}\ z:=z + x;\ \ n:=n - 1\ \texttt{end}$
$\{z = x * y\}$

The proof requires four applications of the assignment axiom, three applications of the composition rule, one application of the rule for `while` loops, three tautologies of arithmetic, and three applications of the rule of consequence. The key insight in the proof is the choice for the invariant in the `while` rule (Hoare triple 9.11). Once this choice is made, the application of all the other rules is mechanical. The structure of the whole proof can be depicted in the following tree:

$$
\cfrac{4 \quad \cfrac{1 \quad 2}{3}}{\cfrac{5 \qquad\qquad\qquad \cfrac{9 \quad \cfrac{\dfrac{6 \quad 7}{8}}{\cfrac{10}{11}} \quad 12}{13}}{14}}
$$

Each number refers to the correspondingly numbered Hoare triple of the following proof. We present the proof working systematically from the leaves to the conclusion.

We begin by using the axiom of assignment to prove the following two Hoare triples:

$$\{\, z = x * (y - y)\ \&\ y \geq 0\,\}\ n:=y\ \{\, z = x * (y - n)\ \&\ n \geq 0\,\} \tag{9.1}$$

$$\{\, 0 = x * (y - y)\ \&\ y \geq 0\,\}\ z:=0\ \{\, z = x * (y - y)\ \&\ y \geq 0\,\} \tag{9.2}$$

By the composition rule using valid Hoare triples 9.1 and 9.2 above, we obtain the following Hoare triple:

$$\{\, 0 = x * (y - y)\ \&\ y \geq 0\,\}\ z:=0;\ \ n:=y\ \{\, z = x * (y - n)\ \&\ n \geq 0\,\} \tag{9.3}$$

The following fact of arithmetic is needed to derive Hoare triple 9.5 below.

$$y \geq 0 \ \Rightarrow\ 0 = x * (y - y)\ \&\ y \geq 0 \tag{9.4}$$

$$\{\, y \geq 0\,\}\ z:=0;\ \ n:=y\ \{\, z = x * (y - n)\ \&\ n \geq 0\,\} \tag{9.5}$$

We now leave Hoare triple 9.5 for the moment and work on another branch of the tree. The assignment axiom yields the following two Hoare triples:

$$
\begin{aligned}
&\{(z + x) = x * (y - (n - 1))\ \&\ (n - 1) \geq 0\} \\
&z := z + x \\
&\{z = x * (y - (n - 1))\ \&\ (n - 1) \geq 0\}
\end{aligned} \tag{9.6}
$$

$$\{z = x * (y - (n - 1)) \ \& \ (n - 1) \geq 0\}$$
$$n := n - 1 \tag{9.7}$$
$$\{z = x * (y - n) \ \& \ n \geq 0\}$$

Applying the rule of composition to Hoare triples 9.6 and 9.7 yields:

$$\{(z + x) = x * (y - (n - 1)) \ \& \ (n - 1) \geq 0\}$$
$$z := z + x; n := n - 1 \tag{9.8}$$
$$\{z = x * (y - n) \ \& \ n \geq 0\}$$

The following formula is a tautology:

$$z = x * (y - n) \ \& \ n \geq 0 \ \& \ n > 0 \ \Rightarrow \ (z + x) = x * (y - (n - 1)) \ \& \ (n - 1) \geq 0 \tag{9.9}$$

The law of consequence applied to Hoare triple 9.8 and the tautology 9.9 yields the following Hoare triple:

$$\{z = x * (y - n) \ \& \ n \geq 0 \ \& \ n > 0\}$$
$$z := z + x; \ n := n - 1 \tag{9.10}$$
$$\{z = x * (y - n) \ \& \ n \geq 0\}$$

Appling the rule for `while` statements with Hoare triple 9.10 yields the following Hoare triple:

$$\{z = x * (y - n) \ \& \ n \geq 0\}$$
$$\texttt{while } n > 0 \texttt{ do } z := z + x; \ n := n - 1 \texttt{ end} \tag{9.11}$$
$$\{z = x * (y - n) \ \& \ n \geq 0 \ \& \ \neg (n > 0)\}$$

The loop invariant I is $z = x * (y - n) \ \& \ n \geq 0$.

$$z = x * (y - n) \ \& \ n \geq 0 \ \& \ \neg (n > 0) \ \Rightarrow \ z = x * y \tag{9.12}$$

$$\{z = x * (y - n) \ \& \ n \geq 0\}$$
$$\texttt{while } n > 0 \texttt{ do } z := z + x; \ n := n - 1 \texttt{ end} \tag{9.13}$$
$$\{z = x * y\}$$

Using Hoare triples 9.5 and 9.13, and by applying the rule of composition we obtain the Hoare triple that we were seeking:

$$\{y \geq 0\}$$
$$z := 0; \ n := y; \texttt{ while } n > 0 \texttt{ do } z := z + x; \ n := n - 1 \tag{9.14}$$
$$\{z = x * y\}$$

The whole proof is very large. It can be summarized compactly by annotating the program with the conditions that hold between every statement.

$\{y \geq 0\}$
$\{0 = x * (y - y) \,\&\, y \geq 0\}$
$z \,:=\, 0; \;\; n \,:=\, y;$
$\{z = x * (y - n) \,\&\, n \geq 0\}$
while $n > 0$ **do**
$\quad\quad \{z = x * (y - n) \,\&\, n \geq 0 \,\&\, n > 0\}$
$\quad\quad \{z + x = x * (y - (n - 1)) \,\&\, (n - 1) \geq 0\}$
$\quad\quad z \,:=\, z + x; \;\; n \,:=\, n - 1$
end
$\{z = x * (y - n) \,\&\, n \geq 0 \,\&\, \neg\,(n > 0)\}$
$\{z = x * y\}$

Many of the steps of the proof are purely mechanical, and so it is possible to express the proof even more succinctly:

$\{y \geq 0\}$
$z \,:=\, 0; \;\; n \,:=\, y;$
$\{z = x * (y - n) \,\&\, n \geq 0\}$
while $n > 0$ **do**
$\quad\quad z \,:=\, z + x; \;\; n \,:=\, n - 1$
end
$\{z = x * y\}$

Notice that the invariant of the **while** is the key part of the proof.

We give an example of another proof. This time the proof is of an algorithm to compute the quotient and remainder of x divided by y.

$\{x \geq 0 \,\&\, y > 0\}$
$q \,:=\, 0; \;\; r \,:=\, x;$
$\{x \geq 0 \,\&\, y > 0 \,\&\, r = x \,\&\, q = 0\}$
$\{(x = q * y + r) \,\&\, 0 \leq r\}$
while $(r \geq y)$ **do**
$\quad r \,:=\, r - y; \;\; q \,:=\, q + 1$
end
$\{(x = q * y + r) \,\&\, 0 \leq r \,\&\, r < y\}$

The loop invariant is $(x = q * y + r) \,\&\, 0 \leq r$. This is easily established by the first two assignment statements under the assumption that $x \geq 0 \,\&\, y > 0$. The two assignment statements in the body of the loop maintain this invariant as long as $r \geq y$. When this condition no longer holds, then this fact together with the loop invariant imply the correctness of the program: $(x = q * y + r) \,\&\, 0 \leq r \,\&\, r < y$.

9.5 Proof rules for procedures

Proof rules can be developed for other programming constructs. The book by de Bakker [2] has many of the details worked out. Of great practical interest are rules for procedures. In this section we examine one of these proof rules.

We look at one rule developed by Alain Martin [11]. This rule assumes that parameter passing is either call-by-value, copy-in/copy-out, or copy-out. Somewhat as in Ada, the programmer specifies which parameter-passing mechanism is used with the keywords `in`, `inout`, and `out`, respectively. For simplicity we consider the case of procedures with three formal parameters, one of each kind, and no global variables. A procedure definition will be written `proc` p `(in` x, `inout` y, `out` x`);` S where p is the name of the procedure and S is the body of the procedure.

We need to augment the language to permit procedure definitions and procedure calls (for which we use the keyword `call`). For convenience, we also need to add the simultaneous assignment statement `x,y:=`e_1`,`e_2 (see exercise 9.21).

The proof rule for the procedure call `call` $p(a,b,c)$ is

$$\frac{Q \,\&\, A \;\Rightarrow\; R[b,c := y,z]}{\{\,P[x,y := a,b]\,\&\,A[x := a]\,\} \;\texttt{call}\; p(a,b,c)\;\{\,R\,\}}$$

with the following restrictions

1. the Hoare triple $\{\,P\,\}\,S\,\{\,Q\,\}$ holds,

2. the procedure body S does not change x,

3. the postcondition Q has only the variables x, y, and z free,

4. the actual `inout` arguments b and the `out` arguments c are variables, and

5. the predicate A does not have the variables y and z free.

9.5.1 Development of the procedure rule

The development of the procedure rule is quite straightforward. The key idea is that a procedure call `call` p (a,b,c) can be replaced by the program segment

$$x,y:=a,b; \quad S; \quad b,c:=y,z \tag{9.15}$$

where S is the body of procedure p. The formal arguments x, y, and z are treated like local variables. The `in` parameter x is initialized with the value of the actual argument a. The `out` parameter z is not initialized by the value left in z is copied back to the actual argument c (so c must be a variable and not an expression). The `inout` parameter y is both initialized and copied back.

The goal is to achieve the postcondition R after executing the program segment `call` p (a,b,c). Working right to left on the sequence of statements 9.15 we have:

$$\{\,R[b,c := y,z]\,\}\; b,c \;:=\; y,z \;\{\,R\,\}$$

from the axiom of assignment. Since $Q \& A \Rightarrow R[b, c := y, z]$ we can use the rule of consequence to derive:

$$\{Q \& A\} \, b,c \; := \; y,z \, \{R\}$$

We know that S, the body of the subprocedure, has the property: $\{P\} \, S \, \{Q\}$. Since S does not change x and A does not mention x or y, we can strengthen this to:

$$\{P \& A\} \, S \, \{Q \& A\}$$

Therefore, by the rule of composition:

$$\{P \& A\} \, S; \;\; b,c \; := \; y,z \, \{R\}$$

Finally, using composition and assignment again we get

$$\{\, P[x, y := a, b] \, \& \, A[x := a] \,\} \, x,y \; := \; a,b; \;\; S; \;\; b,c \; := \; y,z \, \{R\}$$

And so using the assumption that $Q \& A \Rightarrow R[b, c := y, z]$ we have derived

$$\{\, P[x, y := a, b] \, \& \, A[x := a] \,\} \, \texttt{call} \;\; p \;\; (a,b,c) \, \{R\}$$

which is the basic content of the procedure call rule.

9.5.2   Some examples

We now use the proof rule for procedures in a couple of cases. In the first example, we write a program `inc` that increments its `out` parameter z by one plus the `in` parameter x. The subprocedure looks like this:

```
proc inc (in x, out z)
```
$P \;=\; \{True\}$
```
z := x + 1
```
$Q \;=\; \{z \;=\; x \;+\; 1\}$

We pick the precondition P to be *True* and the postcondition Q to be $z = x + 1$. Clearly the Hoare triple $\{P\} \; z:=x+1 \; \{Q\}$ is valid, so the subprocedure is verified. We consider what conclusions we can draw about the procedure call `call inc (a,a)` in which the actual arguments are the same variable. Let R be the formula $(a = a_0 + 1)$. Then the procedure call rule for this case simplifies to:

$$\frac{(z = x + 1) \, \& \, A \Rightarrow (z = a_0 + 1)}{\{\, True \, \& \, A[x := a] \,\} \, \texttt{call inc} \; (a,a) \, \{a = a_0 + 1\}}$$

If we take A to be $x = a_0$, then the hypothesis of the rule is a tautology, and we conclude that $\{a = a_0\} \, \texttt{call inc} \; (a,a) \, \{a = a_0 + 1\}$. In other words, the result of the call is the initial value of the actual argument a plus one. Consider the following program:

```
proc p (out z)
P  =  {True}
z := 1;
Q  =  {z  =  1 ∨ z = 2}
```

This program assigns its output variable z to the value 1. If we take P to be *True* and Q to be $(z = 1 \lor z = 2)$, we can certainly prove the following Hoare triple:

$$\{\,\textit{True}\,\}\; z \;:=\; 1\;\{\,z = 1 \lor z = 2\,\}$$

Suppose we wish to examine in which circumstances this specification of the procedure will establish the postcondition $c = 2$ for the call `call p(c)`. Considering the definition of procedure `p` this outcome should not be possible.

We have yet to choose A, but all the conditions for applying Martin's rule have been met so far:

1. the subprocedure specification is valid,

2. $z := 1$ does not change the `in` parameters (there are none),

3. the postcondition Q contains only the parameters (the one variable z, in this case) as free variables, and

4. all actual `inout` and `out` arguments are variables.

Now we come to the choice of the predicate A. Incorporating all the decisions we have made thus far into procedure rule yields (R is $c = 2$):

$$\frac{((z = 1 \lor z = 2)\ \&\ A)\ \Rightarrow\ (z = 2)}{\{\,\textit{True}\ \&\ A\,\}\ \texttt{call p}(c)\ \{\,c = 2\,\}}$$

Is it possible to find an A to make the hypothesis true? Choosing A to be $z = 2$ or $z \neq 1$ would make the hypothesis a tautology, but the final provision in Martin's rule prohibits a choice of A containing the `out` parameters. No choice respecting this restriction can make the hypothesis a tautology. We conclude that the ill-advised choice for the specification did not cause any harm and that the restriction on the use of variables in the assertion A is necessary.

9.6   Exercises

9.1 What set of states does the formula $\forall x.\, x = 3$ characterize? What set of states does the formula $\forall x.\, x = x$ characterize?

9.2 Is it possible to find a formula that characterizes the states in which all locations have the value 0?

9.3 Give the definition for what it means for the state σ to satisfy the formula $\phi \Rightarrow \psi$.

9.4 What would be the consequences to the `while` language of permitting boolean conditions to contain quantifiers?

9.5 Which of the following Hoare triples are valid:

(a) $\{\, True \,\}\; x \;:=\; 2 \,\{\, True \,\}$
(b) $\{\, True \,\}\; x \;:=\; x \,\{\, False \,\}$
(c) $\{\, False \,\}\; x \;:=\; 2 \,\{\, True \,\}$
(d) $\{\, False \,\}\; x \;:=\; 2 \,\{\, False \,\}$
(e) $\{\, True \,\}\; \texttt{while}\; True\; \texttt{do}\; x \;:=\; 2\; \texttt{od}\; \{\, False \,\}$
(f) $\{\, True \,\}\; x \;:=\; x + 1 \,\{\, x = x + 1 \,\}$
(g) $\{\, x = y \,\}\; t \;:=\; x;\; x \;:=\; y;\; y \;:=\; t \,\{\, x = y \,\}$
(h) $\{\, x \geq 0 \,\}\; x \;:=\; y \,\{\, y \geq 0 \,\}$

9.6 Which of the following Hoare triples are valid:

(a) $\{\, False \,\}\; x \;:=\; 3 \,\{\, y = 4 \,\}$
(b) $\{\, x = 5 \,\}\; x \;:=\; x + y;\; y := x - y \,\{\, y = 5 \,\}$
(c) $\{\, y = 6 \,\}\; x \;:=\; x + y;\; y := x - y \,\{\, y = 5 \,\}$
(d) $\{\, x = 7 \,\}\; \texttt{while}\; False\; \texttt{do}\; x := 2\; \texttt{od}\; \{\, x = 7 \,\}$
(e) $\{\, x = 7 \,\}\; \texttt{while}\; False\; \texttt{do}\; x := 2\; \texttt{od}\; \{\, True \,\}$

9.7 (E. Pershits.) Find the precondition that makes the following Hoare triple valid:

$$\{\,?\,\}\; \textbf{if}\; x > 0\; \textbf{then}\; x := 5\; \textbf{else}\; x := -1\; \{\, x < 0 \,\}$$

9.8 Give a good (i.e., sound and complete) rule for the `if` construct without an `else` branch. In other words, fill in what goes above the line in the following proof rule.

$$\frac{?}{\{\,P\,\}\; \textbf{if}\; B\; \textbf{then}\; S\; \textbf{fi}\; \{\,Q\,\}}$$

9.9 Show that the axiom of assignment is *not* sound, if distinct identifiers may refer to the same location.

9.10 Find a counterexample in the simple `while` language to the following axiom proposed for the assignment statement:

$$\{\, True \,\}\; V \;:=\; T \,\{\, V = T \,\}$$

9.11 What is wrong with the following axiom proposed for the assignment statement:

$$\{\,P\,\}\; V \;:=\; T \,\{\, P[T := V] \,\}$$

9.12 Give a good (i.e., sound and complete) rule for the assignment statement where the postcondition is determined by the precondition. In other words, fill in the question mark in the following proof rule.

$$\overline{\{P\}\, V \;:= \; T\, \{?\}}$$

9.13 Prove the rule found for exercise 9.12 is as good as the usual assignment rule by proving that every proof using one rule can be replaced by a proof using the other and vice versa.

9.14 Find a counterexample to the following proposed rule of inference for the while loop:

$$\frac{\{P \,\&\, B\}\, S\, \{Q\}}{\{P\}\, \texttt{while } B \texttt{ do } S \texttt{ end}\, \{\neg B \,\&\, Q\}}$$

9.15 Give a rule to add to the calculus of Hoare triples for the following (simplified) loop construct from Ada:

$$\textbf{loop } S_1 \textbf{ exit when } B; \ S_2 \textbf{ end loop}$$

where S_1, S_2 are statements and B is a quantifier-free formula of predicate logic.

9.16 Prove that the Hoare triple $\{\,False\,\}\, S\, \{Q\}$ is true for all program segments S and formulas Q.

9.17 Prove that the `while` program below correctly computes the factorial function by showing the following Hoare triple can be derived:

$$\{n \geq 0\}$$
$$y\texttt{:=}1; \ f\texttt{:=}1;$$
$$\texttt{while } y \leq n \texttt{ do } f\texttt{:=}f + y; \ y\texttt{:=}y = 1 \texttt{ end}$$
$$\{f = n!\}$$

9.18 Consider the following program S, which computes the greatest common divisor of two integers.

```
a := x;  b := y;
while (a < b) do
   b := b − a;
   while (b < a) do a := a − b end
end
```

Answer the following questions.

(a) Let the greatest common divisor of integers i and j be denoted by $GCD(i, j)$. What is the relationship between $GCD(i, j)$ and $GCD(j, i)$? What is the relationship between $GCD(i, j)$ and $GCD(i, i - j)$?

(b) What property of the greatest common divisor is used by the program to ensure that the *greatest*, and not just some, common divisor is computed? Explain.

(c) What is a reasonable postcondition Q expressing the correctness of the program S above?

(d) What is a reasonable precondition P for which $\{P\} S \{Q\}$ is valid?

(e) Given the choice of postcondition Q in part (c) above, what is the loop invariant for each of the two loops?

(f) Prove the correctness of the program by showing $\{P\} S \{Q\}$ is valid.

9.19 Consider the following well-known puzzle.

> Four people are stranded on a tropical island. They gather a large pile of coconuts before going to sleep. During the night each person gets up and reduces the pile of coconuts. Each time, the person divides the pile into four equal shares and finds one coconut left over. This coconut is given to a monkey. The person takes one of the shares and pushes the rest of the coconuts together. In the morning the people divide the pile into four equal shares and again one coconut is left over. How many coconuts were gathered to begin with?

(a) Let n be the number of coconuts. Write a `while` program to compute the number of coconuts found in the morning.

(b) What postcondition concerning n expresses the condition that four equal shares plus one coconut are left over?

(c) Prove the program correct with respect to some reasonable precondition depending on n. *Hint:* You may need the following fact:

$$a^n - b^n = (a - b)(a^{(n-1)} + a^{(n-2)} * b + \cdots + b^{(n-1)})$$

(d) Use the precondition of the program to find how many coconuts there were initially.

9.20 Consider adding a `for` loop to the simple `while` language:

$$W \quad ::= \quad \text{for } x := e_1 \text{ to } e_2 \text{ do } W$$

The semantics of the `for` construct is quite tricky. We give its semantics informally as follows: The expressions e_1 and e_2 are evaluated once. If $e_1 \leq e_2$ the `for` construct is equivalent to

$$x := e_1; \ W; \ x := e_1 + 1; \ W; \ \ldots; \ x := e_2; \ W$$

Which of the following `for` rules are sound? For all unsound rules give an example showing that it is unsound. In all rules we require that x and any variable occurring in e_1 and e_2 are not modified by S.

(a)

$$\frac{\{\,P\,\}\,S\,\{\,P[x:=x+1]\,\}}{\{\,P[x:=e_1]\,\}\,\texttt{for}\ x\texttt{:=}e_1\ \texttt{to}\ e_2\ \texttt{do}\ S\,\{\,P[x:=e_2+1]\,\}}$$

(b)

$$\frac{\{\,P\,\}\,S\,\{\,P[x:=x+1]\,\}}{\{\,P[x:=e_1]\,\&\,e_1\le e_2\,\}\,\texttt{for}\ x\texttt{:=}e_1\ \texttt{to}\ e_2\ \texttt{do}\ S\,\{\,P[x:=e_2+1]\,\}}$$

(c)

$$\frac{\{\,P\,\&\,e_1\le x\,\&\,x\le e_2\,\}\,S\,\{\,P[x:=x+1]\,\}}{\{\,P[x:=e_1]\,\&\,e_1\le e_2\,\}\,\texttt{for}\ x\texttt{:=}e_1\ \texttt{to}\ e_2\ \texttt{do}\ S\,\{\,P[x:=e_2+1]\,\}}$$

9.21 Consider the multiple assignment statement of the form $x,y\ :=\ e_1,e_2$.

(a) Devise a proof rule for the multiple assignment statement that preserves validity. Your rule must be able to derive the Hoare triple:

$$\{\,x=2\,\&\,y=3\,\}\,x,y\ :=\ y,x\,\{\,x=3\,\&\,y=2\,\}$$

(b) Consider the case in which x and y are the same identifier. Is the Hoare triple

$$\{\,\textit{True}\,\}\,x,x\ :=\ 0,1\,\{\,x=0\,\}$$

derivable or not from your rule? Explain.

9.22 Consider augmenting the simple `while` language of this chapter to handle `goto` statements.

$$
\begin{aligned}
W &\ ::=\ & x\ :=\ e\\
W &\ ::=\ & \texttt{if}\ B\ \texttt{then}\ W\ \texttt{else}\ W\\
W &\ ::=\ & \texttt{while}\ B\ \texttt{do}\ W\\
W &\ ::=\ & \texttt{goto}\ l\\
W &\ ::=\ & l\texttt{: null}\\
W &\ ::=\ & W\ \texttt{;}\ W
\end{aligned}
$$

The `goto` statement has the effect of transferring control to the appropriately labeled statement. To the proof system we add the following two axioms:

$$\overline{\{\,\textit{True}\,\}\,\texttt{goto}\ l\,\{\,\textit{False}\,\}}$$

$$\overline{\{\,P\,\}\,l\texttt{: null}\,\{\,P\,\}}$$

    (a) Prove that the two axioms are sound.

    (b) Derive a false Hoare triple in the augmented proof system.

    (c) Explain how the previous two parts are both possible.

9.23 Prove that Martin's rule is not complete by exhibiting a true Hoare triple invoking a procedure that is not derivable.

9.7 Bibliography

[1] Apt, Krzysztof R. "Ten years of Hoare's logic: A survey—part I." *ACM Transactions on Programming Languages and Systems*, volume 3, number 4, October 1981, pages 431–483.

[2] de Bakker, Jacobus Willem. *Mathematical Theory of Program Correctness*. Prentice Hall International series in computer science. Prentice Hall International, London, 1980.

[3] Cook, Steven A. "Soundness and completeness of an axiom system for program verification." *SIAM Journal on Computing*, volume 7, number 1, February 1978, pages 70–90.

[4] Dijkstra, Edsger Wybe. *A Discipline of Programming*. Prentice Hall, Englewood Cliffs, New Jersey, 1976.

[5] Gordon, Michael J. C. *Programming Language Theory and Its Implementation: Applicative and Imperative Paradigms*. Prentice Hall international series in computer science. Prentice Hall, Englewood Cliffs, New York, 1988.

[6] Gries, David. *The Science of Programming*. Texts and monographs in computer science. Springer-Verlag, New York, 1981.

[7] Hoare, Charles Antony Richard. "An axiomatic basis for computer programming." *Communications of the ACM*, volume 12, number 10, October 1969, pages 576–580, 583. Reprinted in *Tutorial, Programming Language Design*, edited by Anthony I. Wasserman, 1980, pages 500–505.

[8] Hoare, Charles Antony Richard, and Niklaus Emil Wirth. "An axiomatic definition of the programming language Pascal." *Acta Informatica*, volume 2, 1973, pages 335–355. Reprinted in *Tutorial, Programming Language Design*, edited by Anthony I. Wasserman, 1980, pages 506–526.

[9] Hoare, Charles Antony Richard and J. C. Shepherdson, editors. *Mathematical Logic and Programming Languages*. Prentice Hall International series in computer science. Prentice Hall International, Englewood Cliffs, New Jersey, 1985.

[10] Loeckx, Jacques J. C., Kurt Sieber, and Ryan D. Stansifer. *The Foundations of Program Verification*, second edition. Wiley-Teubner series in computer science. Teubner, Stuttgart, 1987.

[11] Martin, Alain J. "A general proof rule for procedures in predicate transformer semantics." *Acta Informatica*, volume 20, 1983, pages 301–313.

[12] O'Donnell, Michael J. "A critique of the foundations of Hoare style programming logics." *Communications of the ACM*, volume 25, number 12, December 1982, pages 927–935.

Index

Symbols

! cut in PROLOG, 198
() unit element in ML, 95
:- turnstile in PROLOG, 191
[] empty list in ML, 95
[] empty list in PROLOG, 95, 202
_ anonymous variables in PROLOG, 192

A

abstract syntax, 68
Achilles, 66
activation record, 150
actual parameters, 155
ad hoc polymorphism, 123
Ada
    access types, *see* Ada pointers
    aggregates, 109
    arrays, 107, 110
    comments, 42
    default parameters, 155
    derived types, 120
    exception handling, 164
    generics, 125, 167
    identifiers, 45
    initialization, 183 (Ex. 5.13)
    integer literals, 95
    iteration, 83
    loop statements, 83
    modules, *see* Ada packages
    origins, 23, 32
    overloading, 136 (Ex. 4.2), 137
        (Ex. 4.3), 147
    packages, 169

parameter passing, 164
passing procedures, 153
pointers, 107
RANGE attribute, 82
records, 107, 109
scope rules, 101 (Ex. 3.4), 101
    (Ex. 3.6), 146
strings, 108
subtypes, 120
syntax of block, 49
tables, 184 (Ex. 5.15)
TPK program, 33
type definitions, 107
variant record example, 114
Ada 9X
    origins, 23, 34
aggregates
    in Ada, 109
al-Khorezmi, 4
Algebraic Interpreter, 12
algebraic semantics, 271
ALGOL
    origins, 14, 23
ALGOL 60
    origins, 23
    TPK program, 15
ALGOL 68
    origins, 16, 23
    records, 107
    recursive types, 141 (Ex. 4.22)
ALGOL W
    and PROLOG, 28
    origins, 16
    parameter passing, 159